DOUBLE IMPACT

DOUBLE IMPACT

France and Africa
in the
Age of Imperialism

EDITED BY
G. WESLEY JOHNSON

Contributions in Comparative Colonial Studies, Number 16

Greenwood Press
Westport, Connecticut • London, England

Library of Congress Cataloging in Publication Data

Main entry under title:

Double impact.

(Contributions in comparative colonial studies,
ISSN 0163-3813 ; no. 16)
  Bibliography: p.
  Includes index.
    1. Africa, West—Civilization—French influences—
Addresses, essays, lectures. 2. France—Civilization—
West African influences—Addresses, essays, lectures.
I. Johnson, G. Wesley. II. Series.
DT474.D68   1985   966'.0097541   84-9005
ISBN 0-313-23386-1 (lib. bdg.)

Library of Congress Catalog Card Number: 84-9005
ISBN: 0-313-23386-1
ISSN: 0163-3813

First published in 1985

Greenwood Press
A division of Congressional Information Service, Inc.
88 Post Road West
Westport, Connecticut 06881

Printed in the United States of America

10 9 8 7 6 5 4 3 2 1

Contents

Illustrations

Maps

Series Foreword

In recent years historians have turned increasingly to what G. Wesley Johnson calls "the double impact"—to the study of the mutual interaction between societies in an imperial setting. The easy, and potentially racist, assumption that the indigenous society was invariably the victim of the imperial power, as though native cultures lacked the capacity to respond, has long been disproven. Clearly we understand now that "imperialism" is not largely, or even mainly, about mechanisms of control. The development of collaborator studies, of resistance theory, of concepts concerning "social engineering," and the use of indigenous languages side-by-side with the written documentation of the traditional historian have demonstrated that both sides to an uneven equation, despite being uneven, must be studied. Each party had an impact on the other, whether in the transmission of ideas and the diffusion of knowledge, or in changing tastes in clothing or food and drink, or in military organization. It is to this double impact that the writers assembled here by Professor Johnson address themselves.

Of course, there were not simply two sides, two parties, to an imperial transaction. Indigenous cultures contained simultaneously those who collaborated and those who resisted; the encroaching imperial society contained simultaneously those who were proud to be called imperialists and those who doubted, for one reason or another, that expansion into other continents and across other seas was wise. These essays recognize these divisions within societies and thus serve to help us think again about the nature of the imperial exchange, so that we do not continue to think of it in the simplistic terms of side against side. The collective result is an important contribution to the substantial literature on "impact theory," already rich and fruitful with respect to the British Empire and for white settler-Native American interaction in North America. This gathering of talent, which comes from the best American-based scholars now at work on the former French Empire, is a welcome addition to this series of volumes in comparative history.

Robin W. Winks

Acknowledgments

The completion of a large volume of original essays necessitates thanking many persons who helped make such a project feasible. First I would like to thank Professor Boniface Obichere of UCLA's African Studies Center, who made it possible for some participants in this volume to give papers at a UCLA colloquia series on French-speaking Africa under my direction. Second I need to thank Dr. Peter Duignan of the Hoover Institution who provided both moral and financial support for the early phase of the project. Third I am indebted to the Community and Organization Research Institute of the University of California, Santa Barbara, and to the Center for Family and Community History of Brigham Young University for assistance in the final phase of the project. I would also like to thank staff members of UCSB, BYU, and Arizona State University for their assistance in preparing this volume. More specifically, I want to thank Judith Parker, Meredith Snapp, Barbara Hagen and Mari Lou Conner. A word of thanks to Antoinette Padgett of the UC-Santa Barbara Cartographic Laboratory for the maps. I owe a debt of gratitude to my graduate students, all doctoral candidates in African history, who have spent countless hours helping to bring this manuscript to completion: James Matthews, Ranford Hopkins, Emmanuel Chiabi, and François Manchuelle. I also need to thank Charles Vogel, my editorial assistant, for untiring help in copyediting and in preparation of the index, and Lynn Sedlak Flint of Greenwood Press for editorial direction. Their suggestions and insights have been much appreciated, and their enthusiasm for this project has helped make it possible. I would also like to thank the authors of the individual chapters who have shown patience and skill in revising, answering queries, and participating in this cooperative endeavor. If there are any errors, they should be attributed to me as the editor.

Various chapters were read by colleagues in the United States, France, and several countries of French-speaking Africa. I appreciate their criticisms and suggestions. I also need to thank the general editor for this series, Professor Robin Winks, for his valuable insights. It is my hope that this volume will suggest the depth of interest and scholarship that now characterizes American specialists on *Afrique Noire*. Not all but most of our contributors are Americans who went through area studies programs on Africa and later did original field work in Black Africa. Most American Africanists have been attracted to other parts of Africa, but scholars interested in francophone Africa have usually also manifested strong interest in French society and history. The participants in this volume were chosen because most of them had prior experience in both *Afrique Noire* and France. If this volume makes a small contribution towards a better understanding of the histories of French-speaking Africa and France, then our labors will be richly rewarded.

G. Wesley Johnson
University of California,
Santa Barbara

DOUBLE IMPACT

1

Introduction: Reciprocal Influences between French and Africans in the Age of Imperialism

When independence came to most Black African nations in the late 1950s and early 1960s, ornate statues of illustrious colonial proconsuls were usually sacked, destroyed, or put in storage. One exception was the statue of General Louis Faidherbe, which stood directly opposite the presidential palace in Dakar. For almost a quarter of a century after independence it resisted change. I asked a venerable African friend why this was so and he replied "Why sack Faidherbe? He was the real founder of modern Senegal." He went on to extoll Faidherbe as a great man, more African than the Africans, a man of great stature who deserved to be remembered despite his colonial era connections. Faidherbe dominated the plaza opposite the palace until recently, his career a symbol of the dualism and ambiguity that characterized the French and African colonial relationship. On the one hand, he made a great impact on Black Africa as perhaps the greatest governor of Senegal, a colony used as a model for the creation of France's other West African dominions; on the other hand, he was among the first of the *vieux africain* generals and administrators who learned African languages, studied African culture and mores, took African wives, and pioneered modern African history and ethnography. Faidherbe exercised great influence on West Africa, but in return, he was profoundly influenced by his African sojourn.

The colonial experience for an African was a far different matter—or was it? The African was in a prejudiced position, to be sure, as a subject in a colonial empire. And yet some subjects gained a position to make an impact upon the colonial ruler. Consider the instance of the country boy who later became the first African inhabitant of the French baroque palace in Dakar, across from the statue of Faidherbe: Léopold Senghor. Born into an ancient Manding and Serere family, young Léopold was a brilliant local student who won a scholarship to attend the prestigious *lycée* Louis le Grand in Paris. Senghor later took his *agrégation* in grammar, helped found a school of African philosophy and literature (*négritude*), and was chosen by the French to serve as grammarian during the writing of the constitution of the Fourth Republic. Senghor and his colleagues created an African style that won the affection of post-war French intellectuals much as the vogue for *négrophilie* had swept over France after World War I. Senghor, child of the bush, brought by colonialism to Paris, elected a living literary tradition that brought African culture to France and prepared the way for thousands of African students to study there after the war. It surprised no one that Senghor was elected to become an *immortel* in 1983, a member of France's most prestigious intellectual institution, the Académie Française.

The careers of Faidherbe and Senghor are suggestive of the title of this volume, *Double Impact*, for both were creations of the colonial period, and both were influenced by the meeting of French and African culture, whether in Paris or Dakar. Reciprocal influence is another way of putting it: for example, the impact of the French colonial administration on the Africans is well documented and described in the literature on imperial rule in Black Africa: words such as "new imperialism," "conquest," "pacification," "white man's burden," and "civilizing mission" all connote the monopoly of power held by the French and other Europeans. But was there a reverse side to the colonial impact? Did Europeans colonizing south of the Sahara come under the influence of Africa? Did African society make an impact upon the manners and mores of the colonizer? Did African peoples influence resident Europeans? Did African culture (art, music, literature, architecture) have an impact on Europeans? In sum, was there a significant reciprocal influence in the colonial equation?

We are not suggesting that double impact or reciprocal influence was equal on both sides. For the first several centuries of contact between France and West Africa, for instance, the Africans held the upper hand.[1] African military power was in most instances feared and avoided by small trading or slaving expeditions until the technological developments of the nineteenth century changed the parameters of contact. For four centuries European traders operated on the coast of Senegal or on its river banks at the pleasure of the local Wolof sovereigns. Only with the advent of Faidherbe and a sustained French military effort in the 1850s did this balance change. Within the next half century, the lion's share of West African territory was conquered by the French, to add to their new dominions in Equatorial Africa and North Africa. An immense sub-continent, from Bingerville to Gabon, from Saint-Louis to Chad, came under domination of the Third Republic, dedicated to fostering the republican ideals of 1789. This seeming omnipotence of the *tricolore* was misleading, however, since France did not hold its subject peoples under absolute control. Although paramount chiefs were undermined or pensioned off in many areas, local chiefs continued to maintain authority, often far from the suzerainty of the *commandant de cercle*.[2]

Afrique Noire was far from metropolitan France, and to provide enough manpower for the scattered garrisons in West and Equatorial Africa was impossible. France, like other European colonial powers, had to rule with much bluff and calculated show of force. A careful reading of the archival materials in Paris and Dakar suggests that French colonial officers, whether governors or simple administrators, maintained a healthy respect for the potential of uprisings and rebellions. (There is good evidence that if World War I had continued much longer, France might have lost control of parts of the Soudan to local African forces.)[3] France ruled with a firm hand, and the legal codes promulgated in the colonies put Africans to a terrible disadvantage: they were classified (with few exceptions) as *sujets*, without right of trial or right of appeal in most instances. It was a regime of summary administrative justice. The business of colonialism was indeed exploitation, but France managed to conceive an intellectualized rationale for its activities. The quest for national prestige was linked to *la mission civilisatrice* to justify the expense and complexity of maintaining the world's second largest overseas empire at a time when the ruling country was steadily declining in resources, population, and productivity.[4]

Europe in the nineteenth century benefited from the Industrial Revolution, surpassing the rest of the world, especially traditional societies such as those found in Africa south of the Sahara, in manufacturing, steam navigation, military technology, and commercial organization. Whereas original encounters between French and African culture did not find such great differences (mores, manners, and language to be sure), by mid-century one could speak of a "gap" from a European perspective.[5] The French (and other Europeans) confused the bounteous harvest of the technological revolution with moral superiority and concluded that France possessed a culture and history that were innately superior to those of the conquered peoples. The seeds of racism, as aptly demonstrated by William Cohen in this volume and elsewhere, had been sown much earlier and now bore fruit (as shown by Edmund Burke's essay herein).[6] France was prepared psychologically for the political rationale proposed by the disillusioned leaders after the Prussian victory of 1871: seek glory in colonial achievements, far from the banks of the Rhine. For those who doubted this course of action, there was the splendid example of Britain across the channel, a nation grown rich and powerful from a gluttonous appetite for colonies. French ambition, whether among politicians with a colonial bent, commercial leaders, or the military, became increasingly unbridled and dictated that France should procure as much of Africa as possible. The original "mission impossible" when the French sent Marchand to Fashoda was launched to secure even more African land.

France made the transition from conquest to administration around 1900; the norms and form which governed the colonial empire were set for the next sixty years. In retrospect, it is possible to divide those decades into three major compartments: 1900–1920, the "classical" era of empire, when institutions were created and heroes (according to colonial rhetoric) walked the land; 1920–1940, the inter-war years, a period of consolidation and adjustment to war losses and the realities of depression; and 1940–1960, the period of decolonization, when France, defeated by Germany, managed to hold its African colonies and unsuccessfully maneuvered to retain them in the face of independence movements.[7]

We have used the word "compartment" to describe these periods because in many ways they were separate one from the other. This is important when considering the concept of double impact, because the relationship between the French and Africans, between master and subject, changed during each period. At the outset, this linkage resembled that of noble and commoner, with Africans possessing few rights. The second period, although few legal changes took place, saw most Africans released from forced labor, Africans trained as auxiliaries, and Africans viewed as human beings—almost. During the third period, France attempted to convince its subjects, now citizens of the French Union, that they should stay in the empire. It was a time of disintegration, an era when some French tried to sell the idea of equal partnership, "L'Eurafrique." But placing Europe first in that hybrid word doomed an idea championed by such luminaries as Robert Delavignette.[8]

The point is that the equation delineating double impact has changed during the colonial period. At the outset, France was so powerful that there was little room for reciprocal influence from the Africans, but as the colonial era progressed after 1900, this was modified. There was not necessarily a linear progression, since impact fluctuated from decade to decade. On the whole, African influence on the colonizer grew steadily. A good example of this impact was in the cultural sphere: as Gerard Le Coat points out in his essay on the arts, initial African impact on the post-impressionists in Paris took place by chance because African art objects were filtering into Paris. By contrast, impact on French literature had to wait until an African elite was educated, fluent in French, and prepared to write novels later awarded French literary prizes.[9]

Our contention is that the study of the idea of colonial impact was limited for many years, especially during these three colonial periods, to the process of European influence upon Africans. Only with the rise of an independent conceptualization of African history, as distinct from imperial history, was the climate ready for a changed notion of the colonial relationship. As A. G. Hopkins had observed, "The political and ideological assumptions which underlay the work of an earlier generation of imperial historians appear all too controvertible today."[10] Colonial era historians rarely admitted that the subject peoples (or their culture) might have had an impact upon the colonizer, whether in the field or in the home country. A turning point came in the 1960s when Jacob Ajayi wrote that "although the Europeans were generally masters of the colonial situation and had political sovereignty and cultural and economic dominance, they did not possess a monopoly of initiative during the colonial period."[11] While this stand was designed to allow the entrance of the new scholarship on African resistance movements, it primarily measured African reaction to events set in motion by Europeans. We are suggesting in this volume that in fact the colonial situation was a two-way street, with impact flowing from France to Africa, to be sure, as our imperial historians have told us for years. But the newer scholarship strongly suggests that impact also flowed in the other direction, from African society, people and institutions to the colonizing power's agents, institutions, and cultural life.[12]

Now that we have moved a quarter of a century beyond independence, new perspectives for interpreting the colonial history of the first six decades of the twentieth century are needed. This is further suggested if we examine the same three "compartmental" periods from a different perspective, that of the Africans. The first, 1900–1920, can be viewed as the period of heaviest foreign domination, when the yoke of forced labor and forced military service in the French Army in World War I became a reality for countless Africans. The second, 1920–1940, was the period of growing resistance, when returning veterans and brash traditional authorities challenged colonial rule, despite the economic disaster of the depression for African products. The third, 1940–1960, was the period of nationalism, when most Africans began to understand that it was becoming possible, with or without violence, to terminate European rule.[13]

This course of history was just as real as the sixty-year period described earlier from a colonial perspective, and in many aspects, was just as segmented. The status of Africans under colonialism was never static: colonial rule evolved amidst constant change, and the reciprocal African influence became more manifest as the century progressed. Take for example Ernest Roume, a governor-general who created the framework of French West Africa. His conception of his powers and mandate was quite different from a pro-African Joost Van Vollenhoven, a governor with a conscience who did not want to send Africans into battle, or a Socialist governor such as Marcel de Coppet, who was responsible for promulgating *Front Populaire* social reforms from the metropole in West Africa. Or take the example of local politics in Senegal where in 1910 Africans could elect a deputy but not aspire to office; by 1930, Africans were serving as deputy and mayors of cities; by 1950, African voters (male and female) could vote for deputies, mayors, and councils all over West and Equatorial Africa. Such examples suggest the progress made by Africans under French rule as the fundamental colonial power equation was constantly in a state of alteration.[14]

Or take the example furnished by the colonial press. In the pre-World War I period, few publications were allowed; during the inter-war period, there was a rapid increase in newspapers, bulletins, and ephemeral publications; and during World War II and afterwards, independent newspapers, political action sheets, and clandestine bulletins multiplied. In fact, it is fair to say that by the end of the colonial period, *Afrique Noire* enjoyed a situation of comparative freedom of the press unknown in a post-independence world of state-controlled or one-party presses.[15]

The growth of African input, whether described as power resistance, or influence, becomes more clearly discernible when we look at the impact of Africa upon the colonial ruler. Increasingly the idea of single impact, or European influence on Africa, stands out as an inadequate monocausal conceptualization.

Yet if the pluralism of African impact seems to be suggested by the emerging data, it is not easy to demonstrate, since France at all times held the upper hand in the colonial relationship. The colonial period was geared for French reports, articles, and books focused on the impact of France upon Africa. We are talking about a phenomenon for which much evidence exists, but more particularly in Africa itself, rather than in archives and libraries in Europe or the United States, although some evidence for areas of reverse impact exists in France itself as demonstrated in this volume by Le Coat and Vaillant.

The scholars who are represented in *Double Impact* were chosen because all of them have lived or worked in France or French-speaking Africa for long periods of time and possess the sensitivity and perspective needed for a reassessment of colonialism. It should be stressed, however, that no one was asked to fit his or her research into any pre-existing hypothesis or framework, save that of looking for evidence (or lack of it) of reciprocal influences. The only notion agreed upon was that each person would start with the premise that reverse (Afro-European) impact was a possibility during the colonial period under examination in addition to single (Euro-African) impact. Implicit was the desire to see if this theme were useful as a mode of analysis for gaining a deeper understanding of the colonial experience. The results, in the essays that follow, should be read as individual efforts of scholars who worked with a variety of source materials and who arrived at independent conclusions, but who have been unified thematically. This brings us to questions of methodology for studying double impact.[16]

First, how does one measure impact? David Gardinier in his essay on French impact on education in Africa tells of hundreds of thousands of African students enrolled in French-sponsored schools on the eve of independence. This is a quantitative measure, verifiable in enrollment statistics. But how does one measure African impact on French economic life? Robert Griffeth's essay suggests that French merchants and government officials were constrained by the realities of African trading patterns and groups (the Djula) in order to make their trading system functional in the western Sudan. His evidence differs from Gardinier; yet the conclusions seem just as sound. To this extent, we are relying upon comparative types of evidence to sustain the general argument of this volume. We have not gone as far as Dewey and Hopkins did in their volume comparing imperial impact in Africa and India, where two subcontinents were put to general comparison; rather, the contributors here have tried to compare the two facets of impact from a thematic perspective.[17]

Second, the inequities of power are still with us despite a quarter century of independence. Economic, diplomatic, financial, and cultural dependence still characterize many African nations, and cultural, financial, and economic imperialism, not to mention military advantage, still preoccupy former colonial powers—especially France. France is a strong, unified nation, still struggling to retain its status as a world power. Its former African colonies (excepting perhaps Ivory Coast) are still balkanized, weak, and subordinate. True independence, despite the bold rhetoric of politicians such as Sekou Touré, may well belong to the future. Such imbalances make it difficult to proceed with a measured analysis, since in some ways, the colonial regime is still with us and neo-colonial considerations make it more difficult to perceive the era of full colonial rule.[18]

Third, interested researchers were obliged to proceed with caution because of the dearth of materials that historians ordinarily use. For example, the French in Dakar kept magnificent archives on the West African colonial regime. The colonial presence, until the 1940s and eventually to the late 1950s, when the archives were opened, can be minutely studied and documented. But are there African archives, and most specifically records of African impact upon the colonial regime? The problem of the imbalance in source materials is well known to the African historian. Where were the African counterparts of the European anthropologists who came to Africa in the 1920s, 1930s, 1940s, and 1950s to study traditional life and (later) social change? Who represented Africans in studying social change ("impact of European urbanization," "impact of European railways," "impact of European education," and so on)? Did anyone study the impact on the colonial psyche and mores that living among the Africans brought about? Few studies of this variety were commissioned during colonialism because there was no need or official rationale for them. Only in the area of literature do we find some French interest in this subject, such as Robert Arnaud's brilliant novel on Governor-General William Ponty, *Le Chef des porte-plumes*. It satirically points out how even a powerful authority figure was heavily influenced by things African during his quarter century in West Africa.[19]

Perhaps the major reason for indifference in looking at areas of reverse impact was the fundamental French assumption that France was the bearer of civilization to other parts of the world, especially Black Africa. France never pursued assimilation to its logical end because the doctrine held out that one might aspire to become assimilated to French culture, if one wanted to become an *homme de culture*. To be sure, one had to agree to live under and recognize French codes, become educated in the French school, but the heart of the assimilation doctrine was the presumption that France possessed a brilliant culture and that a receiving nation had little or nothing to offer in return.[20] This is why Alioune Diop and the founders of *Présence Africaine* enjoyed such prestige in post-World War II France. The war had shaken French belief in many areas, and in the vacuum that characterized a Sartre-esque Paris after the war, it now became possible for intellectuals to entertain the idea that former subject peoples might have claims to cultural and historical achievements. This curiosity about overseas peoples under French tutelage (which had earlier existed primarily at the level of exotic travel books) was now transformed to provide a sensitive intellectual and political climate in which the seeds of decolonization took root. *La mission civilisatrice* was gradually abandoned after World War II as Frenchmen began to realize that other peoples, other cultures had a right to exist within their own cultural tradition. This turning point is portrayed in the Jean Rouch film, *Petit à Petit*, in which Africans go to Paris to study the folkways and mores of the French.

Having the spotlight put on one's own civilization can be terribly uncomfortable; the plea for cultural relevance is unmistakable. The colonial presumption that Africans were incapable of making any impact on the home country was now put in question.[21]

A third major consideration on assessing impact is to study topics which warrant study. Examining the possible impact of African ideas on physics would probably be unproductive. On the other hand, African notions of healing and traditional pharmacy have been lauded in Paris and prizes have been given to African medical researchers. In this collection of essays, we investigate ten basic subject areas that promise to provide insight into both aspects of double impact: French influence on the Africans and the reverse influence of Africa and Africans on the French. Our choice was tempered by practical matters such as the availability of qualified researchers: some participants are Europeanists with an African interest; others are Africanists with French experience. Some participants were able to respond more directly to the problem of double impact because of their own research agendas and the availability of relevant source materials. Some authors have emphasized French impact, some African impact, others both. Some found few reciprocal influences to explore. Omissions, such as African music, are readily acknowledged. Our purpose here is to stimulate further studies, to ask questions in order to open inquiry rather than to pronounce the last word.

Ultimately, the question of cultural contact is at the heart of these essays. In the most basic terms, that is what occurred during the three-hundred-year French presence in Senegal and the seventy-five-year presence in West and Equatorial Africa. To this extent, we have not investigated the obvious: France, as a European power, did bring the telegraph, telephone, paved roads, railways, dredged harbors and deepwater ports, and high-rise urban construction to Africa. But these were aspects of Western industrial culture that were spreading throughout the world anyway. Rather we have chosen certain thematic areas in which there was the possibility of cultural contact—economic life, service in the military, electoral politics, growth of elites, race relations, education, and cultural expression as shown in architecture, art, and literature.

An introduction is provided to each part covering these subjects, and we conclude with two chapters which examine the possibility of double impact in British and Portuguese colonial dominions. Finally, in the editor's conclusion, we look at the utility of double impact as a concept for understanding France, French colonial society, Africa, African colonial society, and the colonial period which enmeshed two cultures.

NOTES

1. The works of the explorers and observers of the West African coast, whether Portuguese, Dutch, French, or English, made clear that local political power was concentrated on the mainland and that European interests were focused on islands such as

Gorée or strongholds such as El Mina on the Gold Coast; this dominance of African military and political suzerainty was not seriously violated in West Africa until the nineteenth century. As John Barbot noted in the late seventeenth century, French trading privileges on the Senegal River were available, but only after payment of "certain customs, duties, and fees to those Black princes and their officers." See Barbot, "A Description of the Coasts of North and South Guinea," in A. and J. Churchill, *A Collection of Voyages and Travels*, 3rd ed., vol. 5 (London, 1746), pp. 18–22, 43–48, as cited in John D. Hargreaves, *France and West Africa* (London, 1969), pp. 34–40.

2. *Commandant de cercle* is best translated in English as a district commissioner. In my opinion, the role and power of chiefs during the French colonial regime has been underestimated; the view put forth by such a shrewd observer of the French dominions as Michael Crowder (*West Africa Under Colonial Rule* [Evanston, Ill., 1968], pp. 187–194) is colored by proximity to events of the 1930s and immediate post-war days. The impressions gained by careful reading of reports in the Rue Oudinot and Dakar archives suggest a meaningful role for chiefs continued in many areas well after World War I and until the 1940s, especially during the two world wars. Until more studies are done on a regional and local basis, we shall not know for certain the depth of French suzerainty among the bulk of African peoples.

3. Archival materials for French Soudan for the period 1915–1918 in Dakar are especially suggestive. Reports from commandants and annual reports of governor of the Soudan (at times sanitized) make it clear the French presence hung by a thread, particularly when there were few Frenchmen available for colonial service. See also discussion on the "grande revolte" (November 1915 to July 1916) in Western Volta region in Marc Michel, *L'Appel a l'Afrique* (Paris, 1982), pp. 100–116.

4. Paul Leroy-Beaulieu went so far as to suggest that "la fusion de l'element indigène avec l'element européen. . .C'est la seule harmonie qui soit indispensable." This basic lack of respect for African cultures was later to help create the climate for the emergence of *négritude*. Quoted in Hubert Deschamps, *Méthodes et Doctrines Coloniales de la France* (Paris, 1953), p. 128.

5. One major reason for a changed relationship was the decline of the slave trade, which ironically had kept relations between Africans and Europeans on a level of parity. With the demise of the slave trade, Europeans were constrained to push inland (the French on the Senegal and the British on the Niger) by the 1850s and 1860s in search of new trading products and markets. See John D. Hargreaves, *West Africa: The Former French States* (New York, 1967), pp. 78–96.

6. As Gabriel Angoulvant, governor of the Ivory Coast, put it, "To make ourselves understood we must totally change the Negro mentality. . . .our subjects must be led to progress despite themselves, as some children are educated despite their reluctance to work." Quoted in Hargreaves, *France and West Africa*, p. 202.

7. On decolonization, the final period of French presence, see the interpretation of Edward Mortimer, *France and the Africans, 1944–1960* (New York, 1969).

8. Despite a certain bias, the works of Jean Surêt-Canale are helpful to establish an alternate perspective to Delavignette, especially Canale, *Afrique Noire: l'Ere Coloniale, 1900–1945* (Paris, 1964).

9. On the formation of such an elite, see G. Wesley Johnson, "The Senegalese Urban Elite, 1900–1945," in Philip D. Curtin, ed., *Africa and the West: Intellectual Responses to European Culture* (Madison, Wisc., 1972), pp 139–187.

10. A. G. Hopkins, "Imperial Connections," in Clive Dewey and A. G. Hopkins,

eds., *The Imperial Impact: Studies in the Economic History of Africa and India* (London, 1978), p. 2.

11. J.F.A. Ajayi, "Colonialism: An Episode in African History," in L. H. Gann and Peter Duignan, eds., *Colonialism in Africa, 1870–1960*, Vol. 1: *The History and Politics of Colonialism, 1870–1914* (Cambridge, England, 1969), p. 505.

12. See my essay on the career of Governor-General William Ponty, who like Faidherbe before him was heavily influenced by his African experiences: Johnson, "William Ponty and Republican Paternalism in French West Africa," in L. H. Gann and Peter Duignan, eds., *African Proconsuls: European Governors in Africa*, New York, 1978, pp. 127–156.

13. See Mortimer, *France and the Africans*, esp. pp. 100–105, for a succinct description of the *prise de conscience* that took place among Africans who had been called to Paris under the prestige of de Gaulle. Also see Guy de Lusignan, *French-Speaking Africa Since Independence* (New York, 1969), pp. 3–83, and chapters of francophone Africa in Prosser Gifford and William Roger Louis, eds., *The Transfer of Power: Decolonization, 1940–1960* (New Haven, Conn., 1982).

14. See Michael Crowder, *Senegal: A Study in French Assimilation Policy*, rev. ed. (London, 1967), pp. 63–80, for the later period; for the earlier period, see G. Wesley Johnson, *Emergence of Black Politics in Senegal* (Stanford, Calif., 1971), especially chapters 4, 9, and 11.

15. The accuracy of this statement may be tested by comparing the number of publications extant in French West Africa during the 1930s, 1940s, and 1950s with the number present in the 1980s, and by comparing content for critical insights expressed about governmental policies and rule. While French colonialism did not allow freedom of the press as defined in the United States or the United Kingdom, the ability of various groups to organize publications, to disseminate them, and to bring critical insights to bear upon the government was not generally impaired, as compared to the present, where government groups opposing or criticizing the ruling regime are allowed to publish and disseminate regular publications. This does not become an apology for French colonial rule, but a sad commentary on the reality of post-colonial rule.

16. It should be noted that some of these essays were given during a colloquium series at UCLA's African Studies Center, in which the major theme was "Double Impact." Other essays in the volume were researched and written at a later date.

17. Hopkins chose the "comparative method" for assessing colonial impact in the volume he and Dewey edited on Africa and India. We are not comparing French Africa and France straight across the board, but rather are assessing impact in selected topical areas. The Hopkins volume looks at two entities (British Africa and British India) which were on the receiving end of British imperial policy, whereas in this volume we are looking at different phenomena. While I am the first to recognize the merits of a well-planned comparative history, it does not strike me that this approach was warranted in the quest for double impact. See Hopkins, "Imperial Connections," *The Imperial Impact*, pp. 1–9.

18. A history detailing French neo-colonial policy since 1960 has yet to be written; such a volume would be particularly useful if emphasis were put upon both cultural and economic policy. Compared to Britain, France has (with a few exceptions) proved to be singularly successful in maintaining a presence in Black Africa, especially when one confronts the reality that more French people live in Africa now than on the eve of independence.

19. See my discussion of Ponty as portrayed by Robert Arnaud in *Le Chef des porte-*

plumes in Johnson, "William Ponty and Republican Paternalism in French West Africa," in Gann and Duignan, *African Proconsuls*, pp. 152–154. Unfortunately, the guarantee of French privacy for papers of long-dead public officials is such that we may never have access to the range and quantity of colonial era documents and memoirs assembled by the British. For this reason a novel such as Arnaud's becomes important for shedding light on the French colonial psyche.

20. See the critique of assimilation by Robert Delavignette in his *Freedom and Authority in French West Africa* (London, 1968), pp. 49–54. Delavignette closes his argument with this statement: "The rule of action of native policy, applicable to every country, is to organize and give life to public authority over the natives by recognizing that they have rights and by caring for their interests" (page 54, *supra*). See also a British critic, Michael Crowder, in his *Senegal: A Study of French Assimilation Policy*, pp. 9–34. The ambiguity of French policy, now favoring assimilation, now favoring association, has yet to be studied in historical depth with reference to case studies during the operational years of French West and Equatorial Africa.

21. Robert Delavignette had the intuitive grasp to understand the changing colonial milieu and changing Franco-African relationships: "The new African world is aiming at making Europe revise its ideas about Africa." Perhaps the post-war novelists such as Ousmane Sembene, Camara Laye, and others were the most successful purveyors of this new attitude which stood in stark contrast to the accommodation of the 1920s and 1930s. Delavignette, *Freedom and Authority*, p. 141.

I

THE ECONOMICS OF IMPERIALISM

West and Equatorial Africa had several centuries of economic contact with France before the imposition of formal colonial rule in the nineteenth century. When the aggressive imperialism of the Third Republic caused French military commanders to annex vast areas, many Africans were already familiar with Europeans as trading partners. The new regime changed the association from one that was often marked by mutual respect to one characterized by fear and resentment in the face of loaded weapons. Economic activity was increased by colonial rule, but the terms were different: now the African produced and worked for the European company, railroad, or office.

An important casualty by 1900 was the middleman, who had traditionally played an important role between African producer or farmer and French merchants. With the arrival of big French commerce and the multinational corporations such as Unilever and Nestlé, African traders, family businesses, and especially enterprises owned by old mulatto families were pushed to the wall. A favorite tactic was to extend credit to an African firm, help it expand, and then call in the loan when repayment was impossible. While it is true that Africans could theoretically join the French-dominated chambers of commerce that sprang up in the French colonies, a careful reading of those membership rosters suggests that only a few Africans qualified for membership or were placed in a nonvoting category. By 1940 and the decade of nationalist awakenings, Africans had been almost systematically eliminated from larger business sectors by French wholesalers and chain merchants and the expanding Lebanese and Syrian traders, who had profited from French diversion during World War I to establish a tenacious hold on *Afrique Noire*'s mid-level economy.

It would be a mistake to think that Africans no longer maintained any commercial activity or influence in the business arena. Robert Griffeth's essay looks at the fundamentals of economic change during these years to measure subtleties of the African impact upon French economic colonial policy. He suggests that to compete in the West African market, the French were forced to adapt and borrow from African merchandising and trading models. Griffeth, who has carried out extensive field research in Upper Volta, is concerned with the realities of economic activity during a time when official rhetoric had all but eliminated the African. The same is true of Paul Pheffer's essay; Pheffer is primarily interested in how the French built railroads in Africa and how they operated—French impact upon the economic life of Africa. But in the process of doing painstaking archival and oral history research in Senegal, he found that the parameters of French railroad operations were framed by African needs, African personnel, and the African landscape. The Africans came to have the ability to affect the precarious state of finances which characterized rail activities in later years; they succeeded therefore in having some degree of influence over the determination of railroad financial policy.

2

Economic Change in Colonial French West Africa, 1900–1940: The African Impact on French Colonial Economic Policy and Practice

The central question posed by the theme of this collection rests upon two basic assumptions. The first is that French colonialism in Africa profoundly transformed both the content and the structures of traditional African life. The second assumption is that Africans made noticeable—although less important—marks on French culture. Together, these two assumptions suggest that a "dual impact" of unequal weights describes what happened.

This brief essay will address itself to this stated theme and the two main assumptions which inform it. First, it will assess the validity and usefulness of analytically separating the component parts (African and French) of a process which I think is better described as "mutual cultural borrowing." Second, I propose to examine very briefly one dimension of that mutual borrowing process—economic change. Three key areas of economic activity will be stressed: changes in the modes of production, the creation of marketable surpluses, and access to foreign markets.[1] I shall argue that one way of understanding the African "impact" on the French colonizer lies along the road of describing and analyzing processes of economic change *within* West Africa.[2] The period to be examined is 1900–1940, the central decades of formal French empire.

Whether it is regarded as something generally beneficial or as a dreadful, self-perpetuating evil, France's "successful" colonialism in West Africa is frequently portrayed as the process of transformation and ultimate replacement of African cultures by the culture of the colonizer. That which is to be transformed is usually characterized as "traditional" and is unable to withstand the challenges which confront it owing to inherent structural weakness. That which is to provide the ultimate replacement is termed "modern" and derives its power to transform from its inherent structural strengths. The study of economic change is often considered the best way to test this proposition, since the all-important question of "influence" can actually be measured. The formula employed for measurement speaks of movement from a state of economic "underdevelopment" to various stages along a scale of "development." The distinction between traditional and modern is necessarily blurred, since the information required to make precise measurements is often sadly inadequate (lack of statistical data, for example); but that such a distinction surely exists is taken as axiomatic.

More is involved here than the crude justifications employed by the French colonizers to rationalize their physical conquest of West Africa. The critics of colonialism also tend to agree about how the process of economic change occurred: that is, by the forcible transformation of traditional West African economic life by alien—and usually detrimental—French economic policy and practice.[3] Therefore, disagreements between the apologists of French colonialism and its vociferous critics center not on whether the character of economic change is correctly described, but on whether the kinds of change that took place were largely beneficial and deserve support in the interests of accelerating economic development or were mainly detrimental and should be attacked and greatly modified.[4]

Neither the descriptive nor the analytical features presented by the two sides in this debate over "development" stress one other central feature of the process: that is, mutual cultural borrowing, a process which, by its very nature, is difficult to discern in a development model that posits the radical transformation and replacement of African traditional cultures by modern French culture.[5] What may shed some light on the mutual borrowing aspect of this process of economic change is the following question: To what extent were the economic structures of French West Africa in the period 1900–1940 the products of French adaptation to (or borrowings from) existing and dynamic African economic modes, as well as the reverse—African responses to French colonial policy and practice? It is the first half of this formulation—French adaptation to West African economic modes—which I will address in the balance of this essay.

Recent studies in West African economic history have been quite positive in the assertion that African "traditional" economic institutions formed the bedrock of the colonial and economic systems. According to A. G. Hopkins, in what he characterizes as the "completion of the open market"[6] in West Africa, "It was Africans who grasped the new opportunities [created by colonial rule], made the key entrepreneurial decisions, and introduced fundamental changes in the vital agricultural sector."[7] Furthermore, Africans accomplished these ends by "utilizing established and allegedly antiquated economic and social institutions."[8] The expatriate role in this process, Hopkins states, was mainly that of providing greater West African access to international markets.[9] The colonizer's role was not, as many earlier analysts had assumed,[10] the creation of a "modern" economic sector—at least as far as the system of production of surplus for foreign exchange was concerned.[11]

Clearly, the assessments of Hopkins and of most other recent students of West Africa's colonial history[12] have taken us a long way toward a more sophisticated understanding of just what the Africans' "contribution" was to their own economic development in the twentieth century. In that sense they have all said much that badly needed saying about the "allegedly antiquated economic institutions" from which the colonial system was in fact built. But what is lacking in their studies is the element which I have designated as the process of "mutual cultural borrowing." Put differently, what was involved in the process whereby Europeans came to terms with the durability and the vitality of traditional West African economies? What did the colonizers borrow from them? Why?

The central ideas which inspired French colonialism in West Africa throughout the nineteenth century and well into the first decades of the twentieth certainly envisaged the transformation and ultimate replacement of traditional Africa by "civilizing" French culture.[13] Equally clearly, the French drastically scaled down their grandiose notions of "assimilating" their colonial subjects to French institutions and ways of life. From the French point of view, practical circumstances (mainly the resilience of African institutions and the constant threat of resistance to forced change) dictated that the process of assimilation must give way to the more gradual stages of "accommodation." Although accommodation was to take place on a broad front, economic considerations lay at the heart of the problem.[14]

Three reasons are often advanced to explain this modification of French economic policy in West Africa from the stated ideal of forced modernization to accommodation. The first of these reasons involved the lack of sufficient colonial development capital.[15] The lengthy conquest (from the mid-1870s until the first decade of the present century) had cost the French treasury a great deal. Despite significant investment in creating the beginnings of a modern transportation network of rail and road (an investment directed as often by military exigencies as by coherent economic planning), the hoped for rapid expansion of a French-controlled market-export economic sector did not materialize.[16] Colonial administrative costs—particularly in the face of continuing African resistance—remained consistently high. Given the then-prevailing theory that costs of administration should be carried by revenues generated within the colonies themselves, such funds as could be raised through import-export duties and direct taxation of colonial subjects were immediately channeled to supporting an expatriate class of rulers.[17] Development capital from the outside private sector occasionally sought, but rarely found, ripe opportunities for short-term profit taking.[18]

The second reason advanced to explain the accommodation of French colonial economic policy to the existing African systems concerns the lack of an adequate indigenous labor force. French policy at various times and places throughout the nineteenth century had encouraged the establishment within French controlled territories of plantation agricultural production. This policy was occasionally urged at other times in the high colonial period, too.[19] But the record of such efforts was largely one of dismal failure. Among the reasons most often given were both the small size of the potential labor force to work plantations and the incompetence of those who could be found to perform the labor services which were required. Added to this, once again, was African hostility expressed as open resistance to any efforts made to conscript them as plantation workers on French-owned estates. This particular line of argument contains more than a little unfounded cultural bias; for, as will be demonstrated later, African systems of "peasant" production for export used migrant workers and have had a pretty fair record of success.[20]

The third reason, which has only recently been given prominence in the literature,[21] is the one which stands as the basis for the argument in this essay. The argument is that the "traditional" African systems of production and exchange as they had developed over the course of the nineteenth century were economically competitive with those proposed and attempted by the French during the first decades of formal empire. They therefore survived well into the colonial period to be "borrowed" by the French when the more grandiose schemes of modern colonial economic development failed to become established. Accommodation, in other words, can be explained in part by the persistent economic vitality of certain groups of African producers and traders and French willingness to adjust to that fact.

Support for this argument may be found in at least three areas: African modes of production that developed in the precolonial era and survived on into the period of colonial rule; expansion of surplus productive capacity to meet increased external market demand; and effective reorientation of trade to new external markets through the efforts of "traditional" African entrepreneurs.

What was to be incorporated as the vast territorial bloc centrally administered as *Afrique occidentale française (AOF)* experienced two dramatic upheavals in the nineteenth century. Both had a profound impact on African modes of production.

The formal abolition of the trans-Atlantic slave trade beginning in the 1820s presented many African producers as well as middlemen with the challenging problem of how to develop new commodities that would satisfy European merchants' demands. Whereas the suppression of the external slave trade cut off a major source of income for those Africans who had directly participated in supplying slaves to the old markets at the coast, suppression did not extend to the internal slave trade until more than a century later. But the absence of the old external market outlet, coupled as it was with the continuation of the slave trade *within* important areas of West Africa, sometimes had the effect of creating a new class of landless workers. The problem that African producers faced was to match this labor potential to the task of producing commodities for sale on international markets serviced by the European merchant community.[22]

Dahomey is probably the best known example of a West African kingdom which successfully adjusted to these new demands of European "legitimate commerce."[23] The Dahomean kings and their designated officials who had managed the slave trade economic sector throughout the eighteenth century redirected their energies to employing slaves as agricultural laborers producing palm oil, the tropical raw material which felt the heaviest demand on the international market. Although this system of production did not survive intact in the colonial period (the monarchy which controlled it was dismantled by French conquest in the 1890s), many variations of a less dramatic kind on the same theme occurred elsewhere in the regions of the *AOF*. The case of Gūbu in the Nioro du Sahel (Mali) examined by Meillassoux may serve to illustrate the situation.[24] Gūbu's wealth had always depended primarily on its agricultural productivity (including cotton and textile manufactures) coupled to its strategic market location on the southern fringe of the Sahara where it could service both the Saharan trade itself and the trade in slaves to the coast. As this later market was closed to slaving, the noble and trading classes of Gūbu increasingly turned their attention to the slave trade as a means of recruiting agricultural workers. This means of production was by no measure a new one, but its scale increased very substantially throughout the nineteenth century and well into the colonial period.[25] The French, upon encountering the results of this system both during conquest and in the initial period of colonial settling in, at first attempted to dismember it and subsequently accommodated to it as the only way in which the economic vitality of the region could be sustained. The legal status of slaves was changed through orders directing manumission; but a class of landless laborers remained to be employed in pretty much the same fashion as before.[26] In these circumstances, a new class of African producers—direct descendants of the old noble landholder and slave laborer groups—emerged.

In the savannah grasslands region of *AOF*, those who became the new controllers of productive enterprise were the heirs of the second major transformation of West African life to occur in the nineteenth century: the leaders of the reforming Islamic *jihad* movements who had risen to power on a wave of military success in the first half of the century.[27] Until the establishment of locally effective French administration (which, in some important areas, did not occur until after World War I) the *marabouts*[28] who had largely replaced traditional chiefs as the key controllers of land and labor in the zones of successful *jihad* activity continued to perfect the mode of production that used increased unfree labor. But of even greater significance were developments in areas where slave status was removed early by the imposition of French authority. Here the *marabouts* remained as the central figures in directing economic enterprise along lines already set out, but under the circumstances as the key regulating component in "peasant" agricultural economies. Since economies of this kind came to represent by far the largest sector in which production for external exchange developed in French colonial West Africa,[29] a detailed example of one of them deserves mention.

Senegal, the original base of French colonial operations in West Africa, had early and forceful experience of both major upheavals discussed here. Abolition of the slave trade that serviced external markets and continuous agitation from *jihadic* leaders had thrown the economic systems of its three major peoples, the Peul, Wolof, and Serer, into chaos. At first the French hoped to reconstitute economic order in Senegal under their tutelage both through establishment of a plantation agriculture[30] and dominance over the commerce in "legitimate" articles of trade in the Senegal River valley.[31] French efforts in both areas proved unsuccessful. The political disruptions caused by French interference ultimately proved to be less significant in establishing the bases of new forms of economic development than did the unsuccessful efforts by the Muslim *marabouts* to establish themselves as the paramount local authorities. Once established, the *marabouts* then turned their attention toward creating agricultural export economies with the cultivation of the peanut as its base. The best example of this form of development may be seen in the case of the Mouride brotherhood which, from the 1880s under the direction of its founder, Ahmadou Bamba, virtually refounded the political and social as well as the economic bases of life for the Wolof peoples.[32] At the heart of the Mouride movement was the idea that hard physical labor (mainly directed to peanut production) in this life was a guarantee of spiritual salvation in the afterlife. Quiet acceptance of political authority was a corollary of this work ethic promulgated by Ahmadou Bamba and his successors. Initially, the French resisted and tried to suppress Mouridisme; by the second decade of French rule, the policy of official hostility gave way to one of enthusiastic toleration. The reasons for this change of heart are not difficult to understand: peanut exports from the *marabout*-dominated "peasant" production sector had come to represent the largest single element in French economic dealings with colonial subjects.[33] They remain so in the modern economy of Senegal today. For purposes of illustrating the argument presented in this essay, the "borrowing" of the mode of production introduced and perfected by the Mourides to form the heart of French economic policy in Senegal is sufficient. The theme could be extended to other areas of *AOF* with equal force.[34]

The second major question to be addressed in this assessment of African impact on French colonial policy and practice is a logical extension of the first. That is the question of efficiency. Whereas the French may well have needed to compromise the grander schemes of expanding a "modern" economic sector by accommodating to groups such as the Mourides in the short run, it remains to be asked how successful were these new African-controlled modes of production in creating marketable surpluses? The answer appears to be that for most of the colonial period the "peasant" economies were not only competitive with French efforts to "modernize" economic life, but grew in scale and efficiently used labor resources in a fashion that caused French official policy to accommodate to and actually assist traditional enterprise in its growth. That is to say, the efficiency of African modes of production in creating marketable surpluses was such as to influence and set what became official French colonial economic policy.[35]

Since expansion of economic activity designed to service a market based on tropical agricultural exports was the central issue, measures taken to increase productivity in that sector obviously speak to the question of efficiency. As has been noted previously, the French frequently sought to increase efficiency by founding or encouraging plantation agricultural developments. These experiments were not successful in *AOF*. But the mere transformation of the modes of production by Africans along lines suggested by the Mouride, Gūbu, or Dahomean examples would not have been sufficient for inspiring rapid growth of surplus agricultural production either. The techniques employed in production of crops like peanuts experienced no dramatic technological advances (at least during the main decades of colonial rule), and yet productive capacity did expand rapidly to meet market demand.[36] This efficiency also had to come on top of maintenance of the subsistence agricultural sector upon which the feeding of the colonial subject populations depended. The only way in which productivity could be expanded under such circumstances was for the African worker to expand individual output. With the commercialization of agriculture, this involved two things: gaining access to land where both cash and subsistence crops could be grown and access to markets capable of absorbing the surplus production. Those who rose to become controllers of important agricultural lands in the nineteenth century proved themselves better able than enterprising French colonialists to provide such access.

A major migrant labor force, often seasonally employed, was developed to cultivate the cash crops. The improvement of transportation networks by the French obviously stimulated and assisted the capacity of workers to move long distances to secure seasonal employment. On the other hand, one of the major new systems that incorporated seasonal migrant workers on a large scale came into existence before the colonial transport networks had been built. This occurred in Senegal where the reorganization of land tenure under the control of *marabouts* meant that these new local rulers determined access to land. Through their own intelligence networks with fellow Muslims the word spread to a very wide region of dispersed subsistence farmers of opportunities to enter the cash crop production sector on a seasonal basis. Without abandoning their own farms and becoming wholly subservient tenant farmers on the *maraboutic* lands, such workers could make a notable—and to them largely non-disruptive impact—on agricultural efficiency.[37] The supposed efficiency of European-owned and operated planta-tions might in theory have been competitive with seasonal migration patterns described here; but in the event, they proved not to be.

The establishment and development of African-owned plantations in Ivory Coast (where they were in direct competition with the one major French effort in *AOF* to establish that mode of production) appears to be adequate proof of the greater efficiency which African control of migrant labor could bring about.[38] In this case the crop that developed initially to meet a new export market demand was cocoa. Unlike peanuts, cocoa cultivation required a much higher labor input, and the time needed to realize a profit from it had to be measured over the number of years it took the cocoa trees to mature. Even so, the attraction of what was in the early years of cocoa development in Ivory Coast a seasonal migrant labor force laid the basis for added efficiency in export production, which is the issue being addressed. The particular circumstances under which this development came about differed from the Senegalese example where the migrant worker only very slowly came to seek permanent residence on *maraboutic* lands. In the Ivory Coast the process soon came to involve the granting of usufructuary rights to land by the local title holders to the migrants. In the case of cocoa this meant ownership of the cocoa plants themselves as well as to the subsistence crops raised to feed the workers who resided on the landlord's estate.[39] The European-owned plantations provided no personal security of this sort and, therefore, were not attractive to a prospective group of migrant workers. As in the case of French policy in Senegal toward the peanut production system developed under *maraboutic* control, so too in Ivory Coast, French colonial policy ultimately adjusted to the obviously greater efficiency in production which the African-controlled lands had brought about.[40]

These two reasonably successful developments of the African commercialization of agriculture in Senegal and Ivory Coast were not necessarily repeated elsewhere in *AOF*. The great distance to market for bulk agricultural commodities meant that added transport costs would render large-scale agriculture non-competitive throughout much of the western Sudan. But the reason the Senegalese and Ivorien cases are crucial to an understanding of African influence upon French colonial economic policy and practice is that, together, these two areas came to generate more than three-quarters of *AOF*'s production for foreign exchange.[41] While the landlocked regions that made up the bulk of France's West African territories represented a growing drain on colonial revenues, Senegal and Ivory Coast contributed to the growth of colonial earnings—just as the original theory of imperialism said it should be. And so, French policy "borrowed from" what was demonstrably successful: indigenous landholding and modes of production that had evolved on those lands.

Access to foreign markets represents the third area to be discussed with regard to French borrowing from the economic systems of West Africa. If one were to single out a central element from the whole history of West Africa's economic development for highlighting, surely it would be the connection between West African merchants and producers with external markets.[42] Indeed, the commerce sustained across the Saharan caravan routes and the western Sudanic market centers where the exchange of goods took place is often posited as *the* history of West Africa up to the era of the slave trade. And then, for the coastal areas and their hinterlands which became embroiled in it, the slave trade itself is superimposed over the entire area as if that alone could account for every aspect of economic change. More recently, increased attention has been paid to the internal trade and market systems of West Africa, especially to how they operated in the nineteenth century; and in these studies, too, the relationship between the internal and the foreign market has formed a central concern.[43] What seems to be indicated from this emphasis is that a fully installed system of colonial rule in the twentieth century must in some fashion have either altered dramatically or accommodated itself to the developed and very old networks of West African commerce.

The evidence suggests that both things occurred: the construction of modern transport systems (although in the French case these were never fully integrated) altered once and presumably for all time the orientation of commerce toward the coast and consequently through the port cities that were established as colonial administrative centers. For most of the product to be moved in trade, the railroad at first and then heavy trucking over all-weather roads replaced the classic head-porterage system which had sustained pre-colonial commercial movement of goods. The Saharan caravan routes, which had remained active right up to the twentieth century, ceased to possess any real significance to West African producers as an opening to major foreign markets.[44] For the majority of landlocked peoples living in *AOF*, gradual inland expansion of modern transport systems clearly redirected their attention—as colonial policy intended it to do—toward the colonial capitals. It would appear that very little in the way of cultural borrowing resulted from this European-directed and dominated economic enterprise. And yet a minor case can be made for at least one aspect of substantial African influence on French economic policy and practice in all this.

That case involves the actual emplacement of the modern transport network to both service and expand as well as to alter and redirect the commercial arteries that had formed much of *AOF*'s pre-colonial trade patterns. Those groups best equipped to provide the French with the information which they needed to begin construction of roads and railroads were, naturally enough, West Africa's specialized long-distance merchants. In some instances these merchants stood to benefit handsomely if improved communications were built in a fashion that knit together their dispersed market centers. In other situations, these same long-distance traders were better prepared to establish new commercial activities in areas where they had not previously ventured.[45]

The adjustment of the Dyula, the principal long-distance trade specialists of the western half of *AOF*, to both these opportunities does reflect some measure of their influence upon how and where the French pushed the new transport network into the interior of that region. Once again the case of the Ivory Coast and its hinterland regions of Upper Guinea, southern Mali, and Upper Volta can serve as an example. During the time of the pre-colonial trade, this region was clearly oriented to the north. The produce of its forest margins in Ivory Coast was exchanged for imported goods from the savannah zone. This reasonably prosperous trade was exclusively organized and operated by Dyula traders. The area was also the last to be incorporated under the French colonial administration. Its peoples were primarily dispersed in a small-scale settlement pattern over a huge area, and the main link between them was that forged by the Dyula trading network.[46]

When the French, after 1900, had managed to establish themselves on the Ivory Coast at the water's edge, the problem of how and where to link up with the interior became vitally important. As indicated, the older interior connections were to the north—to the Niger River and its market cities. The French had already pushed a railroad from the colonial capital in Senegal to the Niger and had hoped thereby to funnel the "rich" commerce of the Sudan out through the opening in Dakar where the rail line terminated. But the Dyula of this Voltaic region were at the same time pushing south, toward the French establishments on the Ivory Coast.[47] This was a much shorter route to a place where foreign articles of trade could be purchased and then taken to the interior than was the very extended line to the Niger and, by rail, to Dakar. Therefore, the interests of the Dyula who lived and traded in the Ivorien hinterland were definitely keyed to making this route permanently usable. To the degree that these interests actually took the form of influencing the French to begin a rail line to the interior from what is now Abidjan, a case could be made that the Dyula had an important impact on colonial economic policy.[48] But the greater importance of determining what happened after the rail line was built lies in the role which the Dyula played as agents of economic change generally in this region. While they first moved toward the coast to expand the realm of their commercial activities, they soon began to seek places to establish themselves in new roles. They were among the first groups to begin small-scale agricultural production for export (the cocoa growers discussed briefly above); they moved equally quickly to found the secondary system of transport that ran from the railway line to the dispersed farms and rural market centers that they had mostly founded; and using their very wide commercial contacts far into the hinterland, they became recruiters of other Voltaic peoples to come as migrant workers for them on their plantations.[49] In this fashion the Dyula not only participated as one group among others who responded to and profoundly influenced the character of a commercialized agricultural export sector in the colonial economy; they also had a decided impact on how the product thus generated found its access to external markets.

The features of the French colonial economy in West Africa that have been discussed here were naturally selected for the bearing which they have on the theme of this book on "dual impact." It would appear, at the very minimum, that the economic system cannot be understood without very careful consideration of the African influence on French colonial economic policy and practice, even if that understanding must be confined to one sector of economic activity: cash crop cultivation. Since, however, that was the most important sector of the colonial economy (it has since 1900 been responsible for more than two-thirds of export earnings), the crucial character of what the French "borrowed" from African practice is self-evident.

NOTES

1. With the exception of some of the materials relating to Dyula enterprise in Ivory Coast handled in the latter part of this essay, I have relied on secondary literature to present the brief case examples used to illustrate the main argument stated here.

2. All students of West African history owe a debt of gratitude to A. G. Hopkins whose *Economic History of West Africa* (New York, 1973) has so clearly and completely laid out the major themes of the subject. This is especially true of his treatments of African economic behavior, a subject that has usually been consigned to peripheral status

outside the main area of concern: European economic developments in colonial Africa. Chapters 4–6 of Hopkins's work are particularly informative and thought-provoking on the matters to be examined in this essay.

3. The classic justification of European colonialism using arguments about economic benefits is A. McPhee, *The Economic Revolution in British West Africa* (London, 1926). While not wholly uncritical of French economic practice, V. Thompson and R. Adloff's chapter on "French Economic Policy in Tropical Africa," in P. Duignan and L. Gann, eds., *The Economics of Colonialism*, 4 vols. (London, 1975), Vol. 4: *Colonialism in Africa, 1870–1960*, pp. 127–164, generally stresses French contributions to a presumably archaic African economic setting. The critics are best represented by J. Surêt-Canale, *L'Afrique Noire: L'Ere Coloniale, 1900–1945* (Paris, 1964), and the very stimulating writings of the Senegalese economic theorist Samir Amin whose *L'Afrique de L'Ouest Bloquée, L'Economie Politique de la Colonisation, 1880–1970* (Paris, 1971), is the specific text among his writings that is most directly related to this essay.

4. See especially Amin, *L'Afrique de L'Ouest*, and the fully developed case he presents on Third World "underdevelopment" generally in *Accumulation on a World Scale: A Critique of the Theory of Underdevelopment*, trans. B. Pearce, 2 vols. (New York, 1974).

5. This, of course, is the policy usually referred to in a precise sense as "French Assimilation Policy," which was explicitly touted as the means to transform and replace traditional African cultures by the complete substitution of French institutions, language, and so on. In attacking the policy, the critics have not very carefully examined the borrowing and modification elements which are part of the story.

6. Hopkins, *Economic History of West Africa*, p. 235. Hopkins carefully explains his use of economic models labeled "open" and "closed" economies in Chapter 5, pp. 167–172. The main characteristics of "open economies" are (1) producers export a limited range of agricultural or mineral raw materials in exchange for manufactured goods; (2) expatriate interests dominate one or more economic sectors (foreign but not internal trade in West Africa); (3) expatriate policy is aimed at keeping the flow of goods open (low tariffs levied, for example); and (4) the colonial power attempts to minimize its fiscal obligations in administering the colony.

7. Ibid., p. 235.

8. Ibid.

9. Ibid., pp. 188–209 discusses the main contributions of the expatriate role to the development of the colonial economies of West Africa.

10. The standard by which earlier analyses can be measured in this respect is S. H. Frankel's *Capital Investment in Africa* (Oxford, 1938).

11. Michael Crowder's excellent treatment of the politics of European colonialism in West Africa barely touches the subject of agricultural production (and then only to enumerate the negative impact of European policies), despite the fact that this sector formed the basis of the colonial economic system. See *West Africa Under Colonial Rule* (Evanston, Ill., 1968), pp. 271–292, 345–350.

12. The list of articles in scholarly journals and monographs on specialized economic subjects has grown very long over the last twenty years. Hopkins, *Economic History of West Africa*, provides an enormously useful guide to this literature up to 1973 in the bibliographies which accompany each chapter of the book.

13. The best summary of these ideas described by the label "Assimilation Policy" is M. Crowder, *Senegal: A Study of French Assimilation Policy* (London, 1962).

14. That which became the semi-official proclamation of this change of policy from Assimilation to Accommodation was A. Sarraut's *La Mise en Valeur des Colonies Françaises* (Paris, 1923), which, as its title indicates, was clearly an effort to examine French colonial economic policy and practice.

15. The burden of Frankel's *Capital Investment in Africa* was to demonstrate what a tiny fraction of Europe's development capital for all purposes had actually been directed to Africa.

16. B. E. Thomas, "Railways and Ports in French West Africa," *Economic Geography* (Jan., 1957): pp. 1–15.

17. Hopkins, *Economic History of West Africa*, pp. 188–192.

18. The most obvious reason for this was the absence of major exploitable mineral deposits in West Africa such as those which existed elsewhere on the continent. Gold, tin, diamonds, and coal were mined in the British colonies and did attract important capital investment upon occasion. But mining in the French-controlled areas (Guinean bauxite and iron ore, Senegalese and Togolese phosphate deposits, rare earths in the Saharan regions, and others) came later and a good deal more slowly.

19. On the nineteenth-century efforts see G. Hardy, *La Mise en Valeur du Sénégal de 1817 à 1854* (Paris, 1921); on the colonial period see H. Frechou, "Les Plantations Européenes en Côte d'Ivoire," *Cahiers d'Outre-Mer* 8 (1955): 56–83.

20. M. Dupire, "Planteurs Autochtones et Etrangers en Basse Côte D'Ivoire Orientale," *Etudes Eburnéennes* 8 (1960); and A. Köbben, "Le Planteur Noir," *Etudes Eburnéennes* 5 (1956).

21. Hopkins, *Economic History of West Africa*, pp. 209–231, develops the argument that follows for a different purpose than that of demonstrating the competitive advantage enjoyed by the African agricultural producer in the colonial period. His purpose is to state the African "contribution" to completing the "open economy." What he does provide for my purpose is an excellent review of the recent special studies which speak to the issue of African modes of production.

22. A number of contributions to the volume edited by C. Meillassoux, *The Development of Indigenous Trade and Markets in West Africa* (London, 1971) discuss this problem and are cited in Notes 23 through 26 below.

23. C. Coquery-Vidrovitch, "De la Traité des Esclaves à L'Exportation de L'Huile de Palme et des Palmistes au Dahomey: XIXe Siècle," in Meillassoux, ed., *The Development of Indigenous Trade*, pp. 107–123.

24. C. Meillassoux, "Le Commerce Pré-Coloniale et le Développement de L'Esclavage à Gũbu de Sahel [Mali]," in Meillassoux, ed., *The Development of Indigenous Trade*, pp. 182–198.

25. Meillassoux, "Le Commerce Pré-Coloniale," pp. 193–194.

26. Even the French themselves made an unsuccessful effort to settle the former slaves whom they had manumitted by colonial decree into agricultural "villages of liberty." See D. Bouche, *Les Villages de Liberté en Afrique Noire* (Paris, 1968).

27. A good summary of this critically important chapter in nineteenth-century West African history may be found in M. Last, "Reform in West Africa: The Jihad Movements of the Nineteenth Century," in J. Ajayi and M. Crowder, eds., *History of West Africa*, vol. 2 (New York, 1973), pp. 1–29.

28. This term, which is universally employed in francophone West Africa (in Nigeria the comparable term is the Hausa word *mallam*), indicates a prestigious member of the Islamic intelligentsia. Its etymology is a bit obscure, but can most generally be rendered

as "teacher." The *marabouts* became, during the *jihads*, important political officials in the new Islamic governments. Thus, the following discussion reflects this new and powerful position they had achieved in Senegal.

29. Hopkins, *Economic History of West Africa*, pp. 172–186, presents a statistical demonstration of this for the period 1925–1955.

30. Hardy, *Le Mise en Valeur du Sénégal*.

31. A very detailed study of a key period in this enterprise is L. Barrows, "General Faidherbe, the Maurel and Prom Company and French Expansion in Senegal" (Ph.D. dissertation, University of California at Los Angeles, 1974).

32. On the Mourides generally, see D. B. O'Brien, *The Mourides of Senegal* (Oxford, 1970). On the Mouride work ethic, see A. Wade, "La Doctrine Economique du Mouridisme," *Annales Africaines* (1967): 175–206.

33. A general treatment of the major cases can be found in Abdoulaye Wade, *Economie de L'Ouest Africain* (Paris, 1952).

34. Wade, *Economie de L'Ouest*.

35. This was the burden of Saurraut's argument in *La Mise en Valeur des Colonies Françaises*. Since there was no rigidly formal policy established, the change indicated here and in Saurraut's plan was to make such a formal declaration.

36. Thompson and Adloff, "French Economic Policy," Table 19, p. 146.

37. The season migratory workers throughout the Senegambian region are referred to by the French name *navatanes*. See, M. Keita, *Evolution de la Population et de la Production Agricole du Sénégal* (Dakar, 1970).

38. Köbben, "Le Planteur Noir," pp. 4–13.

39. Ibid.; Hopkins, *Economic History of West Africa*, p. 218.

40. Thompson and Adloff, "French Economic Policy," pp. 139–143.

41. Ibid., Table 18, p. 143.

42. R. Mauny, *Tableau Géographique de L'Ouest Africain au Moyen Age* (Dakar, 1961).

43. Meillassoux, ed., *The Development of Indigenous Trade*, clearly reflects this.

44. The surprising vitality of the trans-Saharan trade right up to the colonial period is discussed in Hopkins, *Economic History of West Africa*, pp. 78–123.

45. B. Lewis, "The Dioula Diaspora in the Ivorien South," (unpublished paper presented to the Conference on Manding Studies, School of Oriental and African Studies, University of London, July 1972).

46. R. Griffeth, "The Dyula Impact on the Peoples of the West Volta Region," in L. Hodge, ed., *Papers on the Manding* (Bloomington, Ind., 1971), pp. 167–182.

47. Lewis, "The Dioula Diaspora."

48. Ibid.

49. Dupire, "Planteurs Autochtones et Etrangers," pp. 212–223.

PAUL E. PHEFFER

3

African Influence on French Colonial Railroads in Senegal

One of the more potent tools available to the European powers that divided West Africa in the nineteenth century, railroads were employed forcefully by those powers in their efforts to consolidate colonial rule and organize colonial development in that region. By reducing freight haulage along lengthy, narrow corridors, railroads altered the nature of West African trade and reordered its structures along new geographical lines, thus enabling colonial authorities to enhance the volume and importance of the export trade and to extend its reach much farther inland. New patterns of trade based on railroads helped the colonial authorities to attract populations, and hence scarce labor resources, into those areas favored by the new colonial dispensation, creating thereby new urban centers while selectively draining or expanding older centers. And, at the same time, railroads also helped the authorities to reallocate African labor resources sectorally within the economy, first of all by releasing needed African workers from the drudgery of overland porterage and secondly by training sizable contingents of Africans to be railway workers accustomed to toiling as part of an industrial work force.[1]

Railroads, to be sure, also certainly benefited Africans directly and indirectly in a number of ways, some of them not clearly anticipated or necessarily desired by the railroad designers. Railroads made cash cropping more profitable for African farmers, reduced the prices of imports for African consumers, and facilitated travel for Africans—with easier travel obviously increasing and intensifying social and economic interactions among Africans over wide regions as well as between Africans and Europeans. Nevertheless, the railroads, clearly designed by Europeans to serve European interests in an African environment and only secondarily to serve Africans, hardly seems a means whereby Africans might exercise some sort of influence over Europeans. Rather the contrary is more obviously the case.

The railroad was, in fact, a particularly outstanding example of an array of devices whose technological superiority enabled Europeans to master West Africa and to manipulate West Africans. Just as the power and attractiveness of a superior European weaponry had, for instance, often apparently fostered at least a partial African dependence upon Europeans since the earliest European contacts with West Africa, so too colonial railroads, where the technical disparity was all the greater, generated similar, obviously less surmountable patterns of African subordination and tutelage. Railroads, after all, unlike firearms, could neither be purchased nor fabricated by nineteenth-century West Africans.[2] Europeans, clearly monopolizing technological and managerial control over the West African railroads, operated them in accordance with metropolitan views of the national interest in the colonial arena, whereas Africans for their part were obliged to comply with European wishes while obtaining the requisite technical training and equipment from European sources.

Yet, even if Africans were unable to match railroads as technical devices, and if European policy makers, moreover, often tended to overlook or downgrade the needs of Africans, one should be wary of assuming that railroading in West Africa was simply a matter of Europeans acting on Africans without any reverse influence of Africans in the process. Technical devices can make a significant impact within a given society only insofar as they are employed by an effectively functioning enterprise (individual or collective) operating in some manner within that society. As enterprises, colonial railroads were required to measure up to high standards of operational performance, labor utilization, and control—matters which forced Europeans to rely upon Africans. It was these ties of European dependence on African support, made all the more critical by the financial weaknesses of West African railroads as enterprises, that opened the way, potentially at least, for Africans to exercise a measure of "influence," albeit limited and perhaps only local, over colonial policies.

It became pertinent, therefore, to ask just how much Africans were actually able to influence European colonial railroad policy in West Africa. The point in pursuing such an inquiry would be less to document African activity in a subsidiary role than to obtain a more incisive insight into the dynamics of the colonial process; that is, more specifically, to analyze the adaptation of a European colonial enterprise to its West African environment, of which the Africans were so prominent a part. Apparently, evidence of just such an adaptation can be obtained for the case of French colonial railroads in Senegal.

COLONIAL RAILROADS IN SENEGAL

Detecting any significant African ability to sway colonial railroad policy would be particularly rewarding for the case of colonial railroads in Senegal given the abiding, pivotal importance of these railroads for long-range French policies in West Africa. Railroads were considered for Senegal as far back as the 1850s and were actually undertaken in the 1880s as part of a grandiose scheme to conquer a vast territorial empire in the heart of the Sudan by tracing a twelve-hundred-kilometer railroad from the coast of Senegal to the Niger River (See Map 1). The 264-kilometer Dakar–Saint-Louis railroad (DSL), built from 1882 to 1885, was one result of the scheme, as was also the 552-kilometer Kayes-Niger railroad, which, though largely built from 1898 to 1904, had been undertaken as part of the scheme in 1881. The French carried out the intended territorial conquest during the 1880s and 1890s, but the overall Senegal-Sudan rail scheme itself remained largely unfulfilled until the construction, from 1907 to 1923, of the 667-kilometer Thiès-Kayes railroad (TK), which finally bound together the various sections of what now forms the Dakar-Niger railroad. The Dakar-Niger rail axis itself came in turn to form part of a much more ambitious French plan of 1902 for consolidating the unity of the newly formed colonial federation of French West Africa by means of a vast grid network of interconnecting railroads covering the federation's territory—a plan that ultimately was never fulfilled (See Map 2).[3]

Economic concerns were naturally of prime importance for all of these railroads. The fancied wealth of the Sudan had been a major argument, for instance, in originally helping to convince French metropolitan authorities to allow work to begin on portions of the Senegal-Sudan rail link. The DSL line became famous for generating an important peanut traffic in Senegal, and the Thiès-Kayes in particular was designed to unlock new economic opportunities in the hinterland of Senegal.

Nevertheless, it should be emphasized that economic considerations were not decisive for their sake alone in determining French colonial railroad policy. Other researchers may find that economic objectives were of primary importance in formulating British colonial policy for West Africa. However, for French policy makers, political goals taken in their widest sense were far more fundamental, with railroads and the economic opportunities they offered considered essentially as prime means for advancing toward more basic political goals.

To conquer and develop the Niger Bend region with an east-west rail link from the coast of Senegal, to cripple foreign colonial enclaves economically by hemming them in with railroads designed to siphon off trade from the interior, to concentrate and centralize colonial administrative and economic activities in the port of Dakar—these were the main goals mapped out in the original Senegal-Sudan scheme of 1879 and pursued assiduously thereafter by French authorities throughout the colonial period. And French authorities were clearly willing to sacrifice those economic opportunities not fully consonant with these goals, one clear example being the juggling of regional rail freight rates, despite the overall financial loss, to encourage an east-west flow of goods through Dakar—an arrangement costly to other French colonial ports and wasteful of the potential commerce that otherwise might have developed along north-south lines.[4]

This French willingness to de-emphasize economic matters in order to pursue political goals of course would diminish the likelihood that Africans would be able to exert an influence over rail policy. Nevertheless, Africans were still able

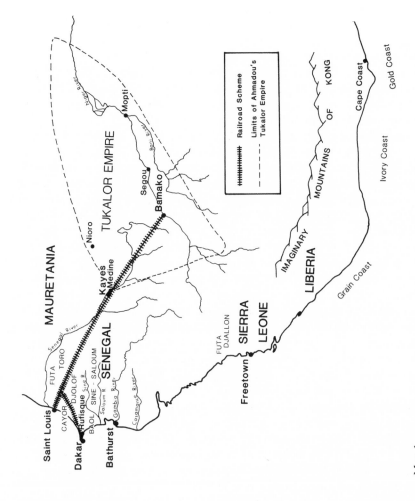

Map 1
The Senegal-Sudan Scheme of 1879

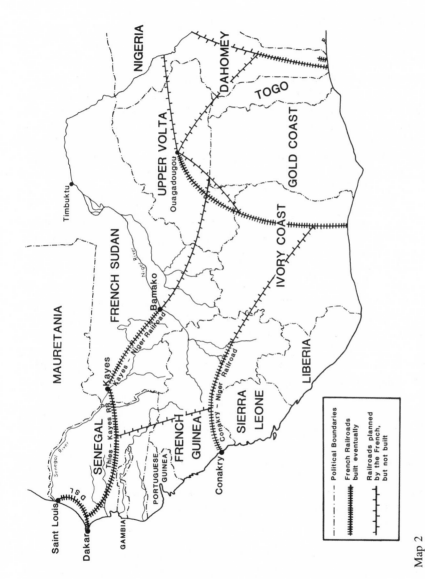

Map 2
Actual and Planned Railroads of French West Africa

to exert some leverage over policy in this case. The best approach, perhaps, is to begin by considering the dependence of the rail enterprise upon African labor resources.

AFRICANS CONSIDERED FOR LABOR RESOURCES

The application of human skills and labor to the tasks at hand is obviously an essential part of any functioning enterprise. Imperialist ventures were particularly dependent on extracting labor and services from the colonized, who often formed the muscles and nerves, bones and sinews of the colonial enterprise in action. This was certainly true for European colonial enterprises in tropical West Africa, where the tiny number of Europeans actually on hand relied heavily on the local labor supply to carry out most of the work for all phases of colonial economic and political activities, whether for growing crops, building roads and railroads, filling out the ranks of the colonial military forces, or executing even the simplest commands of the few imperial proconsuls and merchants on the scene.

French dependence on African labor in the West African colonies could be particularly worrisome given the small available labor pool and chronic labor shortages that were the natural result of the region's relatively low population density. From a French colonial standpoint, railroads might have been excellent instruments for harnessing the scarce labor reserves of the African interior, but then of course railroads were also subject to the same regional labor shortages.

Much like other West African enterprises, railroad operations in Senegal relied heavily on unskilled labor to perform the more backbreaking tasks of loading and unloading, of repairing and reconstructing railroad tracks, and of hauling heavy materiel and parts. Higher administrative and technical posts on the railroad might generally be occupied by expatriate Frenchmen, but skilled African workers and clerks were still needed to fill the lower administrative echelons on the railroad, to carry out most of the skilled fabrication and repairs in its workshops, and above all to run the locomotives, which Europeans were unable to drive for very long under the tropical sun.[5]

Proving that Africans were indispensable for running the railroads in Senegal is therefore easy enough. What is difficult is to relate that dependence to any purported African influence. Mutual dependence does not necessarily translate into mutual acceptance, nor equitably shared benefits, nor openhearted collaboration. In real life, unfortunately, the contrary is very often, perhaps most often, true.

In fact, African railwayworkers, as might be expected, had little discernible influence on general railroad policy despite their obvious indispensability. Notions of ultimate indispensability would count less in practice than workers' perceptions of their own interests, making it unlikely that African railwayworkers would attempt to assume any role in influencing general rail policy. It is instructive to note by way of comparison that African traders, by dint of their key positions as middlemen in the colonial trade, did indeed try to exert some influence over general commercial policies in the colony and even succeeded at times; but then the economic fate of these traders was closely bound up with those commercial policies. As wage earners, African railwayworkers would naturally consider their well-being to be tied more narrowly to wages and working conditions, and these issues occupied worker attention.

Even within this limited, more pertinent sphere of labor relations, moreover, African workers were able to win scant recognition of their grievances before the 1920s. There is little trace of any concerted African attempts to voice labor grievances before 1919, and during the strikes in 1919–1920 African workers were initially both hesitant and apologetic in their approaches to rail management. Significantly, the strikes of 1919 began, and perhaps only took place, because African and European strikers had closely cooperated at first.

The apparent docility of African labor in the pre-1920 period can perhaps be largely attributed to chronic worker transiency, which robbed the African work force both of a necessary, minimal cohesiveness and of the potential leadership of the more capable malcontents. However, some of the blame, one suspects, probably should be pinned squarely on a naively optimistic sense of well-being among African workers, in spite of whatever latent tensions may have existed between employer and employee. In West Africa, after all, skilled African railwayworkers were a privileged, salaried elite to whom management in its role as paymaster could be perceived, at least at first, less as an exploiter than as a bearer of unusual opportunities. It was only with the formation of a more stable work force and the spread of French trade union doctrines that more militant African worker attitudes were to crystallize in the 1920s.[6]

There was never any question, in any case, of allowing untutored rail employees to recommend changes in general railroad policy, which was always left strictly to the discretion of rail management and the colonial authorities. Nor is it easy to question the reasonableness of this arrangement. It was not simply that rail management monopolized the requisite know-how for running a railroad; but, perhaps more importantly, that only management together with the colonial administration possessed a coherent vision of the railroad's purpose. Even later on, the ideologies advanced by trade union or anti-colonial doctrines hardly questioned the basic tenets of this vision. Basically the patterns and routines for formulating rail policy after African independence were those that had been established earlier by the colonizers.[7]

Management retained a firm controlling grip over the railroad enterprise partly because of its technical nature, which required a sophisticated mastery of technical procedures and permitted ongoing rail operations to be carried out for a short time at least by machines and a small elite of workers. Control ultimately was also assured, at any rate, by rail management's inherent ability to call upon the coercive power of the colonial authorities. And yet, since punitive measures would in practice hardly be suitable for running a railroad, effective operations and control also required some consideration for African sensibilities and needs.

Force, or the threat to use it, might serve to suppress any overt opposition and to check occasional disorders, but a display of force could easily miscarry by inducing experienced workers to seek employment elsewhere and lowering the productivity of those resentful workers who stayed. Work discipline on the railroad may have been stern, but it could not be oppressive.[8] Perhaps contented African rail workers might not be indispensable, strictly speaking. However, the alternative methods for running a railroad—by compulsion or by substituting large numbers of imported European workers for Africans—would have been too costly over the long run.[9]

The available financial resources, therefore—a measure of the availability of material resources—imposed limits on the reach of the various colonial railroad administrations and bade them take the welfare of their African labor forces seriously, at least to some extent. By inference, it is clear that the state of rail finances and the ability to affect those finances potentially gave Africans some degree of influence over general issues of colonial railroad policy. It is indeed by following the thread of colonial rail financing that the nature of the relations between Africans and European colonial enterprise can be more clearly understood.

BUDGETS AND AFRICAN WELL-BEING

Railroads, especially railroads of great length, were economically risky ventures in French West Africa, a relatively underpopulated region offering few rail passengers and little marketable freight of modest bulk and high value. As a consequence, all of these railroads, even the privately owned DSL, had to be built either with funds raised through government guarantees or by outright public subsidies. Operating railroad budgets, especially fragile because of the imperfections of the French colonial rail net (its construction difficulties and structural defects, the excessive lengths of the rail lines necessary to reach exploitable areas inland, and its juggled freight rates, which channeled long-haul traffic at a loss along an east-west axis) were also a source of grave concern.

Such concerns had been of less consequence during the era of military expansion, when the irresolution, inattentiveness, or outright collusion of various French parliamentary factions had permitted the French colonial enthusiasts to divert a rich flow of metropolitan government funds into the colonies to cover the costs of conquest. That, and alleged military and strategic needs, had enabled an unprofitable, incomplete and scarcely usable Kayes-Niger Railroad to consume vast sums of money over a long period with little to show for it economically. The relatively generous funding of the era had also granted the DSL company long-term government assurances to cover operating deficits and guarantee a minimum dividend on invested capital, thereby permitting DSL management to be relatively complacent about internal developments in Senegal. To be sure, railroad operations in Senegal—especially the annual statistics for traffic and receipts that figured so prominently in calculating government subsidies—had to be a prime concern for DSL management. Nevertheless, the Paris-based company was apt to concentrate more on wringing the maximum profits out of government contracts regulating DSL operations than to trouble itself too much about local opportunities in Senegal.

An end to metropolitan prodigality was heralded by a law of April 13, 1900. It threw responsibility for colonial budgets on the individual colonies themselves, dictated greater fiscal prudence for future rail construction and operations, and stimulated more interest in the kind of vigorous colonial development that would generate the needed funds locally. An increased interest in the financial profitability of rail operations would in turn direct greater attention to the additional revenues that African patronage might generate for the railroads, and thereby prompt greater interest in the welfare of those Africans.

A sizable African population settled in the vicinity of the rail lines would generate revenues for the railroad's treasury not only by increasing the tonnage of export traffic hauled over the railroad, but also by swelling rail ridership. Third- and fourth-class passengers, it should be noted, comprised one of the most lucrative elements of rail traffic in Senegal, and the profits accrued from these passengers permitted significant rate and fare reductions for other, more favored elements of traffic, such as certain long-haul runs, selected export products and the relatively privileged higher-class passengers (mainly European and official). African ridership had indeed been a profitable source of revenue for the DSL from its earliest operations, but at the inception colonial authorities, having designed the DSL basically for strategic purposes, seem to have been genuinely surprised by the rapid development of local traffic and African ridership.[10]

A more thoughtful appreciation of the importance of African population distribution for railroad design becomes more apparent by 1903. This is evident in the decision taken by the presiding governor-general of French West Africa to abandon earlier plans for connecting the DSL and Kayes-Niger Railroads via a relatively short railroad from the vicinity of Saint-Louis eastwards across the Ferlo Desert, and to substitute for it instead a new line traced over a longer, more southerly course through Baol and Sine—fertile areas, already well populated, and capable of immediately generating a substantial and profitable local traffic (See Map 3).[11] The same interest in the potential African economic contribution is demonstrated perhaps even more obviously in the same era by the regional campaigns of well drilling undertaken by the colonial government of Senegal. Many of the new well sites were installed near the DSL line and the projected Thiès-Kayes railroad with the obvious intention of attracting permanent African settlers to these sites with newly abundant and reliable water sources.[12]

If anything, an appreciation for Africans as economic resources became even keener after World War I, especially after completion in 1923 of a unified Thiès-Niger rail network, whose financial difficulties naturally intensified French official interest in attracting more Africans to the vicinity of the railroads comprising

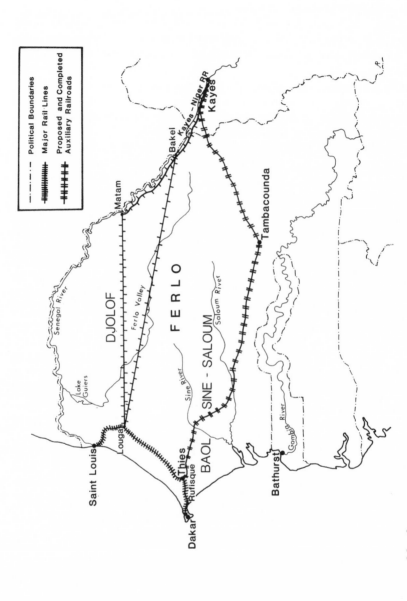

Map 3
Alternate Traces for Linking the DSL Railroad with the Kayes-Niger

this net. And indeed by the 1930s active government effort to encourage African settlers and migratory sharecroppers to move to the vicinity of the rail lines became a more prominent feature of official policy.[13]

European official interest in African welfare, it should be noted, nonetheless, apparently went further than a merely narrow concern for the potential economic contribution of Africans to the colonial fisc and to the railroads—as if the colonized were a sort of species of economic resource. For, in fact, such concerns did shade off into a genuine solicitude for a long-term economic and social well-being of the Africans involved, and the idealistic imagery associated with railroads certainly played a part in developing such attitudes.

RAILROADS AND THE "CIVILIZING MISSION"

Colonial railroads, along with other colonial public works, also served as tangible proofs to the French colonizers of the value of the colonial enterprise and of their own heroic roles as pioneering builders on an alien frontier. Various comments made by French observers about colonial railroads convey all too often an unmistakable note of pride that in transcending the expediency of the moment, it was not simply a matter of reassuring the metropolitan public about the worthiness of the colonial effort, but also of justifying one's own participation in it.

A desire to benefit Africans, to liberate them from the shackles imposed by a demanding nature, formed an important part of this sentiment. The difficulty lies in gauging exactly what role a desire for moral vindication or a finer humanitarian concern for African well-being played in formulating French railroad policy. A thick curtain of colonialist rhetoric clothes and obscures all too well the welter of diverse personal opinions, cynical and idealistic, that colonial policy makers held. The sentimental imagery associated with railroads could, moreover, cut just as easily for or against African welfare because many rail enthusiasts unfortunately relished far more the thought of overcoming physical obstacles with railroads or the thought of designing well-run economic enterprises than the thought of bestowing economic blessings upon African recipients. In fact, a narrow obsession with the technical or economic aspects of railroading could lead some colonial enthusiasts to exploit Africans all the more brutally.

To be sure, lofty phrases about the building of colonial railroads to enrich Africans and to "uplift" African societies had been stock features of French colonialist literature going back even to the earliest railroad projects. Much of this rhetoric, however, needs to be discounted, since it was designed, after all, more to create a favorable impression on metropolitan opinion than to transmit an accurate picture of colonial realities or to clarify the intentions of the colonizers.[14]

The truth was that the earliest rail projects were drawn up with little regard for the wishes or for the economic and social needs of West African societies, of which French authorities were largely ignorant in any case. The superficiality of French intentions in this regard is indeed underscored by the marked tardiness of the colonial government in undertaking thorough, systematic studies of the diverse African societies under its control.[15] And the early French colonial rail planners generally seemed to assume, even when it came to the planning of the Thiès-Kayes (TK) Railroad, that the Africans themselves would assume the necessary social and economic adjustments in order to grasp the new opportunities offered.

One should, nevertheless, refrain from being too skeptical about the sincerity of French idealism in this regard, thereby losing sight of the influence such sentiments certainly had in shaping French policy, even if their impact is difficult to trace and gauge. That they could play a serious role at the highest levels of the colonial administration is perhaps illustrated in a negative sense in 1917 by the firm official rejection of a proposal to resettle Sudanese farmers forcibly on lands adjoining sections of the TK in Senegal—a project discarded less perhaps because of any presumed financial dangers than because of the thorny moral issues that such an action could raise.[16] Moreover, at first glance, the apparently liberal policies followed by French officials in undertaking to construct local auxiliary railroads in Senegal in the 1920s seem to offer more conclusive evidence of the sincerity of such concerns. It is these policies that seem at least to indicate some ability on the part of Africans to exercise a degree of influence over railroad planning and operations.

COLONIAL RAILROADS AND AFRICAN COLLABORATION

Thus, if African welfare had been a lesser concern for French colonial railroad policy before World War I, a modified, more liberal railroad policy during the post-war period, until at least 1931, apparently gave this issue much higher priority. And this development can in large measure be attributed to a magnified importance of financial matters and perhaps sentiment within French calculations during the post-war period.

The economic burdens of the war and the economic uncertainties afterwards had, on the one hand, tightened metropolitan budgets, curbing post-war outlays for the colonies and thereby curtailing pre-war plans for strategic railroads in West Africa. By the same token, nevertheless, the war also prompted a keener appreciation among government officials and the French public for the resources and economic strength lent by the colonies to the metropole and, not incidentally, for the wartime contributions of a colonial labor force.[17] Enlightened metropolitan self-interest, perhaps commingled with sentiments of pride and gratitude, therefore encouraged greater interest in building the kind of railroads that would foster long-term economic and social development in the colonies, that is, railroads aimed not simply at strategic ends or at short-term profits, but also at a steady, long-term growth beneficial to Africans as well as to their colonial masters.

Certainly these preoccupations were evident in plans devised for the Louga-Linguère Railroad, an auxiliary line built from 1926 to 1929 as a spur from the DSL line. This 134-kilometer railroad, though obviously designed to produce more export business for French commercial interests, also explicitly aimed, at the behest of local African notables, at bringing new prosperity to Africans settled in an area hitherto too remote to benefit directly from the export trade; to revive in effect the ancient prosperity of what had been the precolonial inland kingdom of Djolof (See Map 4).[18] The Upper Casamance Railroad, another auxiliary railroad project of the 1920s, was designed with similar intentions. Local merchants in the Casamance certainly hoped to generate a greater export trade by means of a railroad penetrating into those territories lying beyond the economic reach of the Casamance River; but like the Louga-Linguère scheme, the Casamance project was also explicitly intended to serve Africans hitherto isolated in a remote area.[19]

To some, of course, it may seem ludicrous to use as evidence these particular projects, both of which were notable fiascos. Mounting operating deficits on the Louga-Linguère, for instance, forced a partial shutdown of this line after 1934, a weekly service being maintained thereafter only to avoid the political embarrassment of shutting the line down entirely. The Casamance project was botched so badly that it never even advanced beyond the planning stage. Nevertheless, both serve as clear indications of decidedly liberal official attitudes in that era, since both had targeted African prosperity as a primary concern, essential for the success of the undertaking, in contrast to the earlier strategic railroad projects for which African well-being had been only a secondary, if desirable by-product.[20]

Both projects, furthermore, clearly testify to the visible, if modest role of African political figures in influencing the direction of railroad policy. In the case of the Louga-Linguère project, the rail line was finally built partly as a result of the efforts of the influential *bourba* (paramount chief) of Djolof, Bouna N'Diaye, among others, who had been campaigning on its behalf for years (and who perhaps had hoped to profit from a railroad passing through his ancestral domains). Similarly, the Casamance project only made the headway it did because of the dogged support for this project from local politicians representing the region on the colony's *Conseil Colonial* and from the local chamber of commerce, which once threatened to resign if the project were not undertaken.[21]

Economic policy is, of course, always a function of politics at some level, and the close interconnections in the 1920s between railroad policy, an expanded governmental interest in economic development, and local political affairs in Senegal are also reflected in the increasingly favorable official attitudes toward the religious Mouride brotherhood of Senegal during the latter part of this period. These new attitudes and their political and economic underpinnings are indicated, for one thing, by the construction from 1929 to 1933 of the forty-six kilometer Diourbel-Touba auxiliary rail spur, which was obviously designed, despite its subsequent commercial success, largely to win for the administration the gratitude of the Mouride faithful by facilitating religious pilgrimages to the holy city of Touba.[22] Of even greater significance in the long run was the reversal from around 1928 of an earlier, deep-seated official hostility toward the wide-ranging Mouride efforts to plant new peanut-growing settlements throughout sparsely

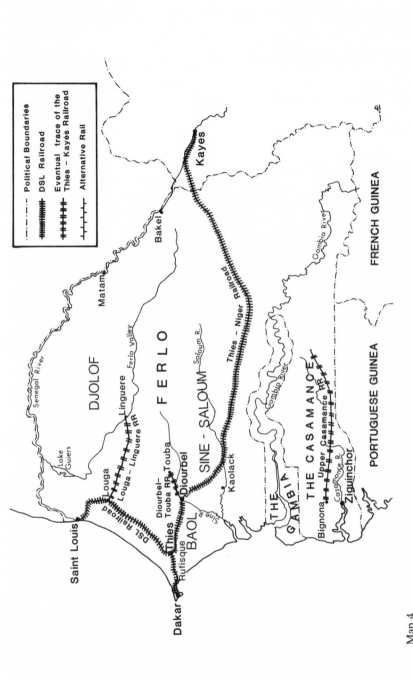

Map 4
Auxiliary Railroads in Senegal

occupied portions of the hinterland, especially near sections of the financially ailing Thiès-Niger Railroad in Senegal—a signal tribute to the potency of rail finances in shaping French policy toward its African subjects.[23]

Taken together these various developments offer convincing evidence both of a decidedly liberal turn in French railroad policy and, perhaps much more significantly, of a corresponding African ability to make use of the opportunities presented. French policy during this era aimed less at moving Africans to service railroads than at building railroads to serve Africans. It now responded more favorably to African economic initiatives and even admitted African opinion, at least to a limited extent, into the decision-making process. A relative French liberality, coupled to African initiative, amounted in short to a policy of mutual, partial collaboration.

It would perhaps be tempting, therefore, to see in the apparently rising curve of French generosity—as railroad policy passed from mere lip service about African well-being in the 1880s to a more active concern by the 1900s, and then to the partial collaboration of the 1920s—a gradual, natural flowering of ties of mutual respect and accommodation between Europeans and Africans, or perhaps a widening liberality of the official colonial mind were it not, however, for the many contrary indications of harsher French attitudes during the same period in such diverse fields as political representation, commerce, and property rights. In reality, there were decided limitations to this one-sided apparent collaboration, which was strictly confined, in fact, to those pursuits congenial with the broad policy objectives of the colonial power; for example, those activities tending to expand the volume of export trade or to swell traffic on the colonial railroads. In the case of transportation policy itself, for instance, the repressive measures taken against Senegalese motor vehicle traffic in the early 1930s expose all too clearly the underlying fragility of this official "liberality."

Thus, if French authorities were originally eager to introduce automobiles into West Africa, with the expectation that motorized road traffic would swell both trade exports and railroad traffic, the spectacular mushrooming of road vehicle traffic in the middle and late 1920s must have been keenly disappointing to these officials as truckers, many of them carrying produce from farmer to port, diverted business from the railroads and from French-owned trade centers along the railroads, while autos and buses were also simultaneously stealing much of the railroads' profitable ridership. Disenchanted French officials, though reluctant at first to do more than badger road traffic with petty restrictions, letting the railroads compete as best they could, finally undertook more drastic measures with the coming of the Great Depression.[24]

In order to preserve the railroads and rail trade centers, official policy acted in effect to eliminate all serious commercial motorized road traffic in the interior of Senegal, and it did so at the expense of African (and Lebanese) entrepreneurs in the carrying trade and at the cost of a promising commercial network of domestic and export trade that died in birth. By acting in this manner, French authorities, while clearly demarcating the tightly limited bounds within which

African economic growth would be permitted, certainly gave the lie to their earlier apparent "liberality." But perhaps this "liberality" of the 1920s had not been entirely a lie.

Perhaps instead these "liberal" attitudes had really arisen in good measure out of naive French assumptions that colonial modernization and economic growth necessarily led to mutually complementary advantages for both Europeans and Africans. If that was so, then perhaps the relatively sterner French policies of the 1930s—which witnessed forced migrations of Serere farmers to the vicinity of the TK rail line, the official regimentation of the seasonal sharecropper migrations into Senegal, and compulsory African colonization of lands devoted to an official Niger River development scheme—betoken in effect a French loss of faith in an earlier optimistic dream.[25]

CONCLUSION

The apparently inconsistent variations of French policy toward Africans in West Africa during the colonial era become more understandable if it is recognized that French officials were simply responding tactically to altered circumstances, both external and internal, while actually adhering to policy objectives that remained markedly fixed both for West Africa in general and for colonial railroads in particular from the 1880s down through the 1930s.

In pursuing colonial domination in West Africa, French policy makers were basically playing a game of international competition against other colonial powers in which conquest and control and the justification of that control were the essential stakes and signposts of success.[26] And French railroads, as well as colonial economic policies, were specifically designed as instruments for pursuing this strategic and political game. Though of lesser priority as objectives, economic matters, especially fiscal matters, were of the utmost importance within the overall picture because they supplied the wherewithal without which the game, after all, could not be played.

For colonial railroads and for the French colonial bureaucracy, colonial finances, whether funded by sums doled out from the metropolitan fisc or by revenues raised locally, was of critical importance—a major regulator that guided and shaped, and alternately quickened and restrained, the thrust and vitality of the policies being carried out by harried colonial officials. Despite occasional breaches of budgetary prudence, it was the transfer of colonial funding from the metropole to the colonies themselves, and the dictates of various phases of fiscal prudence and retrenchment, that inexorably thrust the colonial administration upon local, homegrown resources in the colonies, and thereby into a greater reliance upon its colonial subjects.

It was thus true that finances together with sentiment had accorded Africans some degree of influence over French railroad policies. But this was only partly true.

Budgetary limitations and humanitarian sentiments could indeed be beneficial to Africans in a negative, passive sense by limiting the reach of the colonial apparatus and curbing the violence of colonial agents. These factors could likewise be beneficial in a more active sense by promoting among colonial officials a genuine interest in improving the well-being of Africans as a vital part of the overall growth of the colony. Yet, both finances and sentiment could cut just as easily in the other direction—toward greater official coercion and brutality—whenever the colonial administration, thrust upon local resources, was unable to find them easily. If that was apparent in the official actions taken against Senegalese motorized road traffic in the early 1930s, it was all the more vividly manifest in the same era in such human tragedies as the recruitment and employment of laborers in French Equatorial Africa for the construction of the Congo-Océan Railroad.

The critical factor, therefore, that had accorded Africans in Senegal more consideration, and even a measure of influence, within the pattern of French official action, especially in the 1920s, was the magnitude of the internal economic and social development of African societies in Senegal under African initiative, while the conscious African efforts to take full advantage of their own usefulness also should be stressed. To be sure, there was a degree of French control and selectivity in the process as official policy sought to favor certain promising developments within African societies and to discourage others. That this domestic African development was nevertheless autonomous, following an internal logic of its own, is indicated by the increasing divergence between African and French needs, even during the era of apparent collaboration in the 1920s.

Recognition both of these basic divergencies and of the slenderness of available resources was to lead French decision makers in the 1930s to aim at a more rigidly controlled and monitored growth in the colonies. For Africans, these increased divergences and the subsequent rigidities of official policy were to be sources of disillusionment that boded ill for the future of French hegemony.

It should be remembered—as indicated earlier in the discussion on railroad labor—that French rule depended ultimately on a modicum of passive African willingness to run the colonial machinery, and this depended to a large extent on a complacently sanguine African appraisal of the benefits to be derived from the colonial connection. African disappointments in this regard and new African perceptions of the truly reciprocal nature of mutual dependence in a colonial situation were in the future to shake French domination both on the railroads and throughout the colonies.

NOTES

1. See, for example, A. G. Hopkins, *Economic History of West Africa* (London, 1973), pp. 192–198.

2. The purchase of firearms was widespread in West Africa and was one factor in promoting the pre-colonial Atlantic slave trade. The fabrication of copies of European

rifles, or at least replacement parts, by African craftsmen is mentioned in Yves Person, "Guinea-Samori," in Michael Crowder, ed., *West African Resistance* (London, 1971), pp. 122–123.

3. The history of Senegalese railroads is taken up in Paul Pheffer, "Railroads and Aspects of Social Change in Senegal, 1878-1933," (Ph.D. dissertation, University of Pennsylvania, 1975).

4. These points were covered in Paul Pheffer, "Political and Economic Strategies for French Colonial Railroads in West Africa: The Senegal-Sudan Rail Axis," *Proceedings, French Colonial Historical Society* 2 (1977): 60–69.

5. The railroad's dependence on African locomotive engineers was a seemingly crucial weakness, but in fact troubled railroad management on only a few occasions. For African railroad labor in Senegal, see for example, Pheffer, "Railroads and Social Change," pp. 295-358.

6. Pheffer, "Railroads and Social Change," pp. 330-333. The attitudes of the small elite of independently minded skilled workers was perhaps more akin to those of the independent European craftworkers of an earlier age than to those of industrial workers in mass industry. According to Peter Stearns, *Revolutionary Syndicalism and French Labor* (New Brunswick, N.J., 1971), pp. 35–72, such attitudes were common among French workers in the metropole before World War I.

7. The given pattern of organization fits conventionally accepted criteria for economic and technical efficiency. It also fits the political needs of both the colonial and postcolonial eras, but one may wonder just how inevitable that pattern really was.

8. This seems to be confirmed by some personal interviews with retired Senegalese railwaymen in the spring and summer of 1972.

9. In a perceptive analysis of the dynamics of colonial rule, Donal Cruise O'Brien, *Saints and Politicians* (New York, 1975), pp. 87-94, indicates the limits of colonial power and authority under regular conditions of governance, but perhaps does not stress enough the constant preoccupation of colonial officials with financial matters nor the ability of changes in the state of finances to alter the basic tone or even the overall direction of a given administration. The problem is that financial matters tend all too often to lurk half unseen in the background of policy formulation.

10. France, National Archives, Section France Outre-mer (FOM), *Bideau Report*, 23 September 1886, Sénégal XII, 66. An idea of the importance of passenger traffic for railroads can be obtained from FOM, *Provost Report*, 25 June 1935, unclassified records, esp. 70.

11. Senegal, National Archives (ARS), Governor-General to Colonel Rougier, Chief of the Exploratory Mission, 9 January 1903, 062. There seem to be earlier signs of an appreciation of African economic potential during the reconnaissance in 1893 of a possible railroad in Baol, at a time, incidentally, when colonial expenses were drawing sharp parliamentary criticism. See FOM, *Marmier Report*, 5 June 1893, Sénégal XII, 81.

12. Some useful documents relating to the well-drilling campaign are: ARS, *The Friry Report*, 16 January 1907, P37; ARS, Administrator Sine-Soloum to Governor of Senegal, 23 December 1910, unclassified records, with accompanying maps; and ARS, List of Drilling Sites by the Director of the TK Railroad, 7 June 1913, O87.

13. These concerns are noted in ARS, *Economic Report—1932*, 2G32-40; ARS, *Economic Report—1933*, 2G33-4; ARS, *Economic Report—1935*, 2G35-36; ARS, *Economic Report—1936*, 2G36-3; ARS, *Political Report—1937*, 2G37-17.

14. A case in point was the misleading use by Paul Bourde, "La France au Soudan.

Le Chemin de fer du Sénégal au Niger," *Revue des Deux Mondes* 6 (1 December 1879): 659–688, of a treaty signed by the *damel* (paramount chief) of Cayor supposedly showing that this sovereign was eager to have a railroad running through his domains.

15. Really beginning with Maurice Delafosse's three-volume work on the Sudan, appearing under the auspices of Governor Clozel, *Haut-Sénégal-Niger*, 5 vols. (Paris, 1912). The many previously published studies by various French officials going back to the time of Faidherbe are of the nature more of reconnaissances aimed at political mastery. Thorough studies aiming at a more enlightened governance of subject peoples were lacking for the most part.

16. ARS, Governor-General Joost Van Vollenhoven to Governor of Senegal, 10 September 1917, unclassified records.

17. See Albert Sarraut, *La Mise en Valeur des Colonies Françaises* (Paris, 1923), especially pp. 37–61.

18. This is indicated in FOM, Note for Provost, 26 June 1935, unclassified records; FOM, *Coste Report*, 4 June 1938.

19. On the Casamance project, see, e.g., FOM, *The Monguillot Report*, 10 February 1938, unclassified records.

20. It is significant that, despite the interest of private French firms in undertaking several auxiliary rail lines in Senegal, an especially strong interest in the 1920s, the colonial government eventually reserved construction of all these lines for itself. One may see, for example, the ARS, Note on 60 cm Railroads in Senegal, 22 February 1928, 6P46-36.

21. See, for example, ARS, Friry to IGTP, 6 October 1908, 065; ARS, Bouna N'Diaye to Governor-General, 26 December 1920, 17G 239-108; ARS, Governor of Senegal to Governor-General, 3 March 1923, 088; FOM, *Müller Report*, 1 January 1928, unclassified records.

22. Touba assumed a much greater significance after the death of the founder of the Mouride brotherhood and his subsequent burial there in 1927. Only one of a number of rail spurs considered for the Baol region in the 1920s, the Diourbel-Touba line was definitely *not* the line favored by prominent French merchants, especially those whose operations in Diourbel would be bypassed by this branch line. This can be seen in the minutes of the special session of the presidents of the Senegalese commercial assemblies, ARS, 23 April 1927, 6P46-36; ARS, *Minutes of the Syndicate for the Defense of Senegalese Interests*, 18 January 1929, unclassified records; ARS, President of the Chamber of Commerce of Dakar to the President of the Syndicate for the Defense of the Senegalese Interests, 28 March 1929.

23. On Mouride settlements, see Paul Pélissier, *Les Paysans du Sénégal* (Saint-Yrieix, France, 1966), pp. 302-310. As ARS, Letter from the Governor of Senegal to the Administrator of Louga, 4 February 1928, unclassified records, indicates, the administration was highly suspicious of Mouride colonization efforts as late as 1928.

24. Much of the story is in FOM, *Dossier* AP 545(5); see also Pheffer, "Political and Economic Strategies."

25. Coercive aspects of Serere settlement near the railroad is mentioned in Pélissier, *Les Paysans*, pp. 308-310; on the coercive aspects of the Niger Valley development scheme, see Jean Surêt-Canale, *Afrique Noire. L'Ere Coloniale (1900-1945)* (Paris, 1964), pp. 354–360.

26. Other colonial powers, it should be noted, were not necessarily playing exactly the same game.

II

THE ROLE OF THE MILITARY

French military contacts with Africa appear in the historical record almost as early as the economic exchanges; the scale remains restrained and almost insignificant until the time of General Louis Faidherbe, who inaugurated an aggressive and acquisitive new foreign policy for France in Black Africa. Earlier, military activity was reconnaissance, barter, occasional punitive expeditions, but basically a small-scale support activity for merchants and traders, who needed a modicum of protection.

A century before Faidherbe recruited heavily from the Senegalese for his military missions, Africans were already serving the French military. The dependence of France on African military men does not date from the great efforts of the *Armée Noire* of World War I, but from colonial needs of France in the eighteenth and nineteenth centuries. In fact, France never mounted a major military effort in Black Africa with French troops; the profile would always be African troops surrounded by French cadres and officers. It does not take an overly subtle mind to argue that from the beginning, the French military was influenced by Africans, because in fact the majority of the French army were always Africans.

In the essay that follows, Leland Barrows examines the impact of the imperial experience abroad on the French armed forces from 1830 to the immediate post–World War I period. Barrows, who has written the definitive biographical history of the life and times of Louis Faidherbe in Africa, based upon exhaustive archival research in Paris and Dakar, has also carried out detailed inquiry into the French army's overseas activities. Barrows believes that French army leadership styles were influenced by the way French commanders had to relate personally to their men, to make a personal appeal and develop an *esprit de corps* to carry the day in battle. It also may have bred an indifferent attitude towards the expendability of the infantry—after all, in the colonial situation, if one charged an enemy and lost heavily, there were always more African recruits to fill the ranks. And in the final analysis, France's chief strategist who believed that World War I would be a long, sustained conflict (unlike his superiors) was General Charles Mangin, veteran of African campaigns and father of the *Armée Noire* of 1914–1918.

Charles Balesi also looks at the French army, but from a somewhat different perspective. Balesi, who completed a major study of West African involvement with the military of France from 1885 to 1918, *From Adversary to Comrades-in-Arms*, focuses in this essay on the impact West Africans had on the French army on the eve of and during World War I. He explodes the idea that African troops were ineffective and had a high attrition rate. France's use of Black Africans was without parallel in the annals of European history since the time of the Roman legions. It was also without parallel in the history of European dominion in Black Africa—colonial subjects requisitioned to leave home and family to defend the colonial master.

LELAND BARROWS[1]

4

The Impact of Empire on the French Armed Forces, 1830-1920

When General Bourmont's expeditionary force took Algiers on July 5, 1830, few imagined that France was beginning the conquest of its second colonial empire. Not only would the French move into neighboring Tunisia and Morocco, but the Algerian experience would have an impact on all of France's later conquests in tropical Africa, Indochina, and Madagascar.

The military were the primary builders and almost always the first administrators of each segment of this new empire.[2] Because French rule was for the most part established militarily and maintained by force, French officers and men from one or another of the French armed forces saw action almost continuously on the colonial frontier from 1830 until well into the twentieth century. Although usually of small scale, this activity contrasted with long periods of peace which characterized France during this period so far as Europe was concerned. Constant colonial activity during the period under study influenced the French army in a number of ways even after 1871 when French public opinion and a number of officers held the so-called Algerian school responsible for France's defeat.

This essay analyzes this influence and serves as an introduction to further research on what is a very neglected subject. In particular it will discuss (1) the development and performance of several types of African troops attached to the regular French army and the colonial, as well as the development of predominantly French formations with African names; and (2) the impact of the colonial experience on discipline, decorum, and innovation.

Although at its inception the Algerian venture was not strictly speaking a colonial conquest, it rapidly took on the characteristics of one. Even before the July Monarchy resolved to retain Algeria, the Army of Africa (the French expeditionary and the permanent French occupation forces) began to develop forms of colonial warfare adapted to the Algerian environment and administrative organs for the conquered indigenous Algerians as well as for the European settlers. The French learned slowly in both cases and made many errors and false starts. But by the resignation of Marshal Bugeaud, French Algeria's greatest governor-general, in 1847, and the surrender of Abd el-Kader, his greatest adversary, the Army of Africa had evolved a workable if authoritarian system of military colonialism for Algeria. It would strongly influence all of France's later colonial activities even in those areas where responsibility for conquest and embryonic administration went primarily to the navy.

Three characteristics of the French involvement in Algeria combined to make the conquest particularly violent. The first was the decision to settle French and other European colonists on the land. It was the idea of the second French commander-in-chief, Marshal Clauzel, who had been inspired by his earlier service in the United States and Saint-Domingue.[3] Colonization would be sustained and furthered by future commanders and governors and the French government. The struggle with the indigenous Algerians consequently became one not only for political control—as would be the case in France's other possessions—but one for the ownership and use of land. The second characteristic, one which drew upon the first one and France's centralizing heritage, was an eschewal of any true sharing of power with indigenous authorities. When attempted, such sharing was only to be a temporary (if in some cases a long-term) expedient. The third was the guerrilla nature of the Algerian resistance. To come to terms with it, the Army of Africa would engage in counter-insurgency tactics best summarized as "war of extermination."[4]

The reality of the Algerian situation forced the early commanders of the Army of Africa, for the most part veterans of the Napoleonic wars, to break with much of their earlier training and habits: their tactics of "mass maneuver," and their practice of "sending heavy columns with powerful artillery deep into the country."[5] They also scrapped the strategies of static defense which by 1840 had led to the proliferation of military posts that ended up controlling little territory beyond the range of their guns. The Algerian warriors, virtually all of whom were mounted, were able to avoid contact with the French heavy columns, slip behind them, cut their supply lines, and decimate their rears.[6] They also avoided the French posts, swooping down on French farms, killing the farmers, and making off with livestock and grain supplies. One governor-general, Marshal Valée, sought to bring security to the Mitidja Plain around Algiers by having a one-hundred-kilometer-long wall and moat constructed around it to be defended by two hundred blockhouses at five-hundred-meter intervals.[7] Construction of this "predecessor of the Morice Line" was halted by General Bugeaud when he acceded to the governor-generalship of Algeria in 1841.

Marshal Robert Thomas Bugeaud more than anyone else adapted the Army of Africa to the realities of Algerian colonial warfare. True to his first criticisms of his predecessors, he drastically reduced the number of French posts. He retained only a few large ones strategically located at interior points and connected by road with coastal points.[8] The garrisons of these posts were to coordinate with one another and to move rapidly around the countryside wreaking destruction on the persons and property of recalcitrant Algerians.

Bugeaud made his columns small enough to be mobile and as rapid as the Algerian raiders themselves but large enough to repulse any possible attacks. His formula for size was that six to eight thousand well-disciplined troops of the Army of Africa could always be counted upon to beat twenty thousand to thirty thousand less well-disciplined Algerians. However, he also realized that six to eight thousand Algerians could always defeat six to eight hundred troops of the Army of Africa. Moreover, Bugeaud insisted that sections of columns on the march never be separated by such a distance as to prevent them from acting in unison when threatened.[9] Bugeaud lightened the columns by reducing their supplies to a bare minimum and by having these transported by pack animals rather than by wagon. He thus did away with the necessity of constructing anything more than a very basic road system. He developed ways of coordinating the objectives of several columns from several bases with the use of *spahi* couriers, semaphores, and solar telegraphs. When the topography permitted, Bugeaud's columns marched in square formation protected on the fringes by French and indigenous cavalry. Bugeaud would eventually develop methods for operating his columns in heavily mountainous areas,[10] but generally his system did not work as well in the mountains as in the plains. The cavalry played such a major role in the pacification of Algeria, that one historian has observed that France during that era really had two cavalries, "that of France intended for parades, that of Algeria intended for action."[11]

In the final analysis, however, Bugeaud's system depended on two factors. One was that he was allowed a much larger army than had been the case with his predecessors. By 1846 the French effectives of the Army of Africa numbered 108,000, fully one-third of the regular French army, one French soldier for each twenty-five to thirty indigenous inhabitants of Algeria.[12]

The second factor was that to a great extent a degree of violence that would have been considered unacceptably barbaric in Europe became the rule in Algeria. Bugeaud himself justified what he called the domination of the Algerians' "only seizable interest. . . , their resources in crops, and livestock to bring them to bay."[13] Unable for the most part to engage the Algerians in formal European-style battles, Bugeaud's columns systematically seized or destroyed crops and livestock.[14] The Algerians would submit or die of starvation. Increasingly the Army of Africa massacred the Algerians themselves.

The art of the sudden attack by mounted raiders, the *razzia* on Algerian encampments, was perfected by General Juchaut de La Moricière, commandant of Oran province after 1840. He simply adopted a tactic that had been part of Algerian intertribal warfare. Since this general was not very strong in logistics, his men increasingly relied on *razzias*, in fact initiated them, to reprovision themselves. An observer and sometime practitioner of the *razzia* system, Colonel

Montagnac of Sidi-Brahim fame, gave credit to La Moricière for having "solved the major problem which had defied so many minds, that of permitting. . .soldiers to live in Africa without needing periodically to be supplied by heavy columns."[15]

Bugeaud added a particular refinement to his columns by providing them with portable mills. These the men used to grind the wheat which they found in the silos which they seized to make bread for the troops, hence increasing the range of their actions.

The Algerian conquest became a veritable "chasse à l'homme."[16] Occasionally, particularly brutal actions created a stir in France, an example being the *affaire des grottes* in which Colonel Pélissier, a future marshal of France and governor-general of Algeria, caused the death by suffocation of members of the Ouled-Riah tribe in a cave in the Dahra Mountains. Marshal Bugeaud publicly defended and exonerated him.

The legitimation of ruthlessness and brutality was the most significant of the various contributions of the Algerian conquest to France's more recent colonial campaigns. However, with increasing experience and sophistication in such matters, later French proconsuls learned to be selective in their use of violence and to win submission by diplomacy with only the threat of violence. Less violence was needed to conquer France's other colonies because they were not settler colonies. Although some colonization occurred in Tunisia and Morocco, it was strictly regulated, for both nations became protectorates in which the indigenous authorities were retained. Hence the indigenous peoples and their leaders were less threatened in their vital interests than had been the case with the Algerians and could more easily reach compromises with the French invaders. But even relatively enlightened colonialists like Galliéni and Lyautey adhered to the view formulated in Algeria that one could legitimately apply a separate standard of military morality to the "less civilized" people of the world who were being brought under colonial rule—a practical application of the White supremacist doctrines that were a major component of the intellectual outlook of the West during the era of imperialism.

When Louis Faidherbe was named to the governorship of Senegal in 1854 (he had been a major in the engineer corps), he brought some of the tactics of Algerian warfare to Senegal, successfully adapting them to a very different environment. Here, rather than conquest, Faidherbe's object was to pacify a vast commercial catchment area consisting of the navigable portions of the Senegal basin, the Atlantic coast south of Saint-Louis, and other smaller river basins, those of the Saloum and the Casamance. Initially Faidherbe wished only to intimidate certain recalcitrant Senegambian polities, but he ended up having to conquer a few of them and to remove their traditional rulers and ruling lineages from power in order to break their resistance.

Using the colony's fleet of steam gunboats and vessels of the local merchants, Faidherbe and his officers launched numerous waterborne *razzias* directed against the riverine societies of the Senegal. Not only did the boats shell and burn hostile villages, but they also landed mounted raiders to hit settlements several miles inland. They seized livestock and grain supplies, which they either took back to Saint-Louis or destroyed. During the dry season, the French boats prevented the populations of hostile polities from watering their livestock in the Senegal River.

One of Faidherbe's major African opponents was El-Hadj Omar Tal, a Muslim theocratic stateholder who, beginning in 1852, had attempted to knit the Mandé-speaking peoples of the upper Senegal, the Toucouleurs (Fulani) of his homeland, Fouta-Toro, on the lower Senegal, and the Bambara kingdoms of Kaarta and Ségou to the east in the Sahel and along the middle basin of the Niger River, into one hegemony. Having prevented Omar from realizing his ambitions in the west, Faidherbe was prepared to leave him alone in the east and then after 1863 to propose to collaborate peacefully with him to open an overland training route to link Médine, the easternmost French post on the Senegal River, to Bamako on the Niger. The route would be lightly garrisoned with three posts. From its terminus at Bamako, French steamboats would sail to Timbuktu and beyond.

Faidherbe did not realize this ambition, and when his successors initiated French expansion to the Niger in 1879, it was anything but peaceful. But Faidherbe's plan influenced the direction in which the French penetration of tropical Africa would move.[17]

Faidherbe's period of activity represents a transitional period between the era of trade and more or less informal empire and the era of serious conquest. Indeed, after the death of Faidherbe's successor, Pinet-Laprade, in 1861, French authority waned in Senegal. Only after 1879 when a new generation of proconsuls began the outright conquest of the West African interior was Senegal definitely conquered. The French then fought such formidable adversaries as Ahmadou, El-Hadj Omar's son and successor, Samory, Mahmadou-Lamine, and Béhanzin. Although French forces in West Africa were spread out over a vast area and consisted of a much larger proportion of indigenous troops than had been the case with the Army of Africa in Algeria, the naval troops came to resemble the old Army of Africa in spirit and even to some extent in tactics.[18]

What the Senegalese experience added to the art of colonial warfare was the intensive use of steam gunboats for ferrying troops, for patrolling, and for conducting amphibious operations along navigable rivers, in deltas, and in coastal areas. Experience gained in Senegal would be put to profit in other parts of West Africa, Indochina, Equatorial Africa, and Madagascar.

Even while fighting, the French commanders, first in Algeria and then in the other French possessions, began the elaboration of systems of indigenous administration. Although practices varied from colony to colony, the later conquests borrowing from the earlier ones, one can detect a progression in methods of colonial rule from crude non-rule backed by intermittent force to the elaboration of sophisticated systems of direct rule which paralleled to military effort from intimidation to conquest, to consolidation, and finally from military to civilian rule.

The two parallel problems which the French authorities had to face when they captured Algiers were the administration of the Muslims of the towns who came directly under French sway and the development of some kind of system for ruling the hinterland peoples. After several attempts at administering the peoples of the towns through local notables like the merchant and landowner Si Hamdan ben Othman Khodja of Algiers, the French simply subjected them to the rule of their own military and civilian municipal authorities.

The case of the hinterland was more complicated and changing. During the period of *occupation restreinte*, which closed in 1840, successive French governors attempted varieties of vassalage and protectorate schemes. During his first governorship, Marshal Clauzel tried to coax the beys of Constantine and Oran into becoming French vassals. Later he considered setting a relative of the Bey of Tunis on a French-protected throne at Oran. In some quarters even Abd el-Kader was thought to have agreed to becoming a French vassal when he signed the Treaty of Tafna by which France recognized him as the independent ruler of most of western Algeria. That Abd el-Kader disagreed with this interpretation was certainly one of the reasons why he drifted into war with France in 1839. The French recognized lesser feudatories and gave them, initially at least, considerable authority. Mustapha Ben Ismaïl, leader of the Douair and Sméla tribes of the environs of Oran, is a good example of this type of cooperating indigenous leader. Later, even after the destruction of Abd el-Kader's hegemony and the French conquest of the tribes which had formally been loyal to him, Bugeaud attempted to entrust large blocks of territory (which housed numbers of tribes) to appointed members of the local aristocracy. According to Julien, Bugeaud reasoned, "If the Arab, like the worker in France, was to be left to his condition and [required] to obey without discussion, one had to rally the aristocracy, the opposition of which could be as dangerous as its prestige profitable."[19]

As time went on, however, the French authorities fractioned these indigenous commands and reduced the powers of their holders, who became little more than minor indigenous functionaries. For the truth is that the French were never able either to share power with indigenous authorities in Algeria or in any of their other colonies except in the cases of chieftaincies in very remote areas that were never totally subjected to the full force of French control. France's centralizing, Jacobin, and military traditions almost guaranteed that this would be so. In fact, the Algerian experience would give rise to the belief held by many colonial proconsuls, Faidherbe in particular, that a given subject polity should be defeated militarily at least once before it could be trusted to comply with even minimal French demands. Hence many cooperative and even pro-French polities were unjustly punished.

A characteristic of the Algerian conquest and of Faidherbe's period of rule in Senegal was that the use of force, often called chastisement (*châtiment*), was not followed by any immediate creation of institutions for colonial rule. Moreover, having been raided once, the indigenous rulers were warned that their polities would be raided again if they did not conform scrupulously to French wishes.

When a strong governor was in command, this method could give good results, at least temporarily. In 1847 after nearly six years of what he called *occupation agissante* Bugeaud wrote, "the Arabs have never been so supple; I can make them obey 140 leagues from the coast. They police the roads and the whole country themselves. I dominate nothing directly, but I dominate everything by the moral power which our system of war, albeit vicious. . ., has given us."[20]

Such crude intimidation could not produce lasting peace. The supposedly pacified tribes of western Algeria revolted in 1845 while Bugeaud was paying a visit to his estates in Dordogne. His invasions of the Kabylie Mountains in 1845 and 1847 and Saint-Arnaud's in 1851 did much damage but had to be redone between 1852 and 1857 before the area could be brought under any kind of permanent French control. The treaty system which Faidherbe elaborated in the Senegal Valley between 1854 and 1861 broke down during the governorship of Jauréguiberry, his interim successor in 1862 and 1863, and broke down again after 1865.

What was needed, given the demands which the French were in the habit of making on even "independent" indigenous societies, was a more sophisticated system of indigenous administration. This the French had begun to elaborate quietly in Algeria after 1831. After much trial and error, the final product, the *Bureaux Arabes*, were given final form in 1844. These, headed in Algiers by a director of Arab affairs who reported to the governor-general, were responsible for administering the subjected indigenous Algerians into the formally annexed territories of Algeria, for supervising the "protected" rulers on the fringes of these territories, and for conducting diplomatic relations with the independent tribes beyond.

The director of the *Bureaux Arabes* was usually a ranking general. He headed a hierarchical but decentralized organization of provincial bureaus which corresponded to the three provinces of French Algeria. A director for each province, more under the control of the divisional general commanding the province than under that of the titular head of the bureaus in Algiers, headed the provincial bureaus. Each subdivisional headquarters, like Bône or Batna in Constantine province, was the site of a first-class bureau. Each of the *cercles* of which the subdivisions were composed was the site of a second-class bureau.

A hierarchy of indigenous authorities was created in each *cercle*. The basic unit was the *douar* or group of families or tents each headed by a *cheikh*. Several *douars* constituted a *ferka*, several *ferkas*, a tribe, and several tribes, an *agahlik* or *caïdat*. A *cercle* grouped together several *agahliks* under the administrative rule of a French commandant who, advised by the *Bureau Arabe* chief, appointed the indigenous officials at each level. In *cercles* consisting entirely of military territory the *cercle* commandant might be the *Bureau Arabe* chief.

The chiefs of local second-class bureaus, lieutenants or captains, were the most important links between the masses of rural indigenous Algerians and the French regime. The staffs of the *Bureaux Arabes* as a whole never constituted a separate corps but drew upon officers who were detached temporarily from almost all the units of the French army. *Bureaux Arabes* officers generally knew

Arabic and had a particular interest in the indigenous people. They reigned supreme in their jurisdictions, protecting, they believed, "their" Arabs from *colon* rapacity. They were authoritarian, paternalistic, but often efficient and fair. Many believed in uncompromising assimilation. "[We must] make the Algerians into men before we can make them into brothers," exclaimed one *Bureau Arabe* chief.[21] Some of them viewed themselves not only as rulers but also as teachers, doctors, and builders. Although abuses sometimes crept into the *Bureaux Arabes*, a consequence of the often unlimited local authority given to the young and often inexperienced officers who staffed the local levels, the majority of them were conscientious and took seriously the interests of their Algerian charges. Most of the *Bureaux Arabes* were abolished in 1870 when Algeria went under civilian rule. The bureaus had protected their indigenous charges from the *colons* all too well.

The *Bureaux Arabes* and the various questions of indigenous administration in Algeria influenced the establishment of an embryonic administration of indigenous affairs in Senegal, which in turn influenced the elaboration of similar institutions in the rest of French West and Equatorial Africa, Indochina, and Madagascar. The naval captain, Bouët-Willaumez, created the first Directorate of Exterior Affairs in Saint-Louis in 1844. Faidherbe strengthened it and introduced a skeletal system of indigenous administration for the hinterland replete with Algerian terminology of more form than substance. Later this system would acquire substance and strength as the French expanded their military and political control. Later still this system of military administration would become the basis of civil administration.

An important difference between the Algerian method and that which evolved in the tropical colonies was an increasing attempt to have the officers who took part in the conquest of a given region remain as its first peacetime administrators.[22] When this occurred in Algeria, it required that the officers concerned transfer from their fighting units to the *Bureaux Arabes* and run the risk of being promoted at a slower rate. In the tropical colonies where the naval units were smaller, poorer, and necessarily more eclectic, officers and men regularly performed varieties of functions not the least of which was service as *commandants de poste*. Writing in 1900 Lyautey considered that this versatility—this ability of the colonial soldier to fight, administer, and build—to be the hallmark of an excellent colonial army. He urged that the legislation proposed in France, to transform the naval troops into a formal colonial army, bear in mind these requirements and provide for proper rewards particularly for administrative service.[23]

The difficulty faced by Lyautey and other officers who thought the way he did was that the French armed forces were geared to award promotions primarily on the basis of military action and seniority. Favoritism also played an important role.

The beginning of the French conquest of Algeria corresponded with the adoption of the Soult Law of 1832 regarding promotions which amended the earlier

Gouvion-Saint-Cyr Law of 1818. The latter had based promotion almost exclusively on seniority and had required long waiting periods in each rank. The
former speeded things up considerably.

A lieutenant could now become a captain in four instead of eight years; a
captain could become a major in eight instead of twelve years; a major could
become a lieutenant-colonel in eleven instead of sixteen years; a lieutenant-
colonel could become a colonel in thirteen instead of twenty years; and a colonel
could become a brigadier general in three instead of four years. For the ranks
above, major promotions were based completely on merit. In wartime, half the
openings for lieutenants and captains were opened exclusively on the basis of
merit. Finally and most importantly for the *algériens*, the law made very ample
provision for exceptional promotions for *actions d'éclat* in battle. Moreover, for
a period of time, in Algeria young officers who volunteered to serve in the special
corps—*zouaves*, Foreign Legion, and the like—were offered double seniority.[24]
So Algeria attracted ambitious young men, promoted them rapidly, and by the
1850s had given France much of its high command.

The naval troops were not so privileged, at least not until after 1870. They
tended to attract the lowest-ranking graduates of the French service academies
who joined them because they had no other options or because they wished to
make up for past mistakes.[25] By the end of the nineteenth century, naval/colonial
officers, too, had become avid for the *course aux galons* that had characterized
the Army of Africa in the 1840s and 1850s.

By 1848 almost all the top French generals owed their ranks and positions to
Algerian exploits. Younger men like Changarnier, Bedeau, and La Moricière
had acquired all or most of their military experience and had reached the highest
ranks in Algeria. Even an older officer like Bugeaud, a veteran of the empire,
a man already distinguished by 1830, reached the pinnacle of his career in
Algeria. Here he earned his marshal's *bâton* and the title duke of Isly.

In addition to being a boon to graduates of France's service academies, Saint-
Cyr and the *Ecole Polytechnique*, Algeria was also a place where ordinary soldiers
could rise through the ranks to distinguished positions even when in some cases
they had begun quite humbly, even irregularly. General Cousin-Montauban as
a young man had enlisted illegally in his father's regiment. General Du Barail
had enlisted initially in an indigenous *spahi* unit. General Margueritte had begun
his military career in a short-lived *spahi* unit of *gendarmes maures*. The three
of them quickly achieved regular officer's status.[26]

With the crisis of 1848 and the rise to power in France of Louis Napoleon,
political reliability now became much more a major factor in the selection of
the holders of major commands. Following the events of December 1851, La
Moricière, Bedeau, Changarnier, and Cavaignac were forced into retirement or
exile, but their places were for the most part taken by a new crop of *algériens*.
One of these, Saint-Arnaud, minister of war in December 1851, deliberately
hand picked for the post by Fleury and Louis Napoleon, had been encouraged
while commandant of Constantine province in 1850 and 1851 to lead a large

expedition into the Kabylie. A spectacular action here would facilitate his promotion to the rank of lieutenant-general enhancing his suitability for appointment to the War Ministry. In this key position he would play the determining role in the coup of 2 December 1851.[27] Saint-Arnaud would go on to serve as the first French commander-in-chief in Crimea. He would be followed by Canrobert and Pélissier, both *algériens*.

The principal divisional commands in Crimea also went to Algerian veterans: Bosquet, Forey, and MacMahon. Of the top officers, only Prince Napoleon had had no previous combat experience in Algeria or anywhere else. But his was a blatantly political appointment.

The ranking generals in Italy, MacMahon and Canrobert, received their commands in this war because of prior service in Algeria and in the Crimea. *Algériens* led the smaller Syrian and Chinese expeditions of 1860. General Hautpoul commanded the former; General Cousin-Montauban commanded the latter. The ranking general in the Mexican War, Bazaine, had risen through the ranks in the Foreign Legion and the *Bureaux Arabes* in Algeria.

Unfortunately for the respective reputations of the Army of Africa and the pedagogical value of colonial war, the top French commanders in the Franco-Prussian War, Marshals Bazaine, Canrobert, and MacMahon were *algériens*. MacMahon indeed came into his wartime post from the governor-generalship of Algeria. Other ranking generals—Margueritte, Ducrot, Gallifet, Bourbaki, and Trochu, to mention a few—were veterans of Algeria. However, the commanders of Gambetta's armies of national defense were also Algerian and colonial veterans, some of whom like Chanzy, Faidherbe, and Admiral Jauréguiberry, the latter two having served as governors of Senegal, fought well and helped to salvage at least a portion of France's reputation.

Even after this war and the discrediting of the Army of Africa which ensued, veterans of Algeria like Changarnier, MacMahon, Vinoy, Ducrot, Gallifet, and Billot played crucial roles in the creation of France's post-war army. They took part in parliamentary commissions which passed on the validity of promotions made by the Government of National Defense and reformed various aspects of France's military institutions. But when they were done, their new army resembled the old to a very great extent.[28]

In the years following the Franco-Prussian War the number of officers with colonial experience who reached high and influential positions in France's regular army dropped off. With the completion of the conquest and pacification of Algeria and its transferral to civilian rule, the purely colonial role of the Army of Africa dwindled. The conquest of Tunisia in 1881 by the army was a minor affair. Indeed the regular French army did not become actively involved in colonial conquests on a large scale until the Moroccan venture began in 1906. The ranking officers in the naval troops, the corps which would bear the main burdens of the colonial conquests of the Third Republic, rarely acceded to positions of major importance in the French metropolitan military hierarchy, which was primarily concerned with France's European defense posture.

The most influential French officers came increasingly to be those who were associated as teachers or as graduates with the new *Ecole Supérieure de Guerre*. It had been founded in 1878 in imitation of the Prussian staff college in an effort to give the art of war in France an intellectual foundation. It paid almost no attention to France's colonial wars but concentrated on the Prussians, Clausewitz, and the campaigns of Napoleon.[29] In theory at least the commanding generals of France's future armies were to be graduates, *brevetés*, of this school or at least officers who had passed its qualifying examinations even if they had not actually attended the school. But even in this intellectual sanctum the influence of Algeria and the colonies would still, however slightly, be felt. The school's real founder, Colonel Lewel, had served extensively in Algeria.[30] Periodically a colonial officer would pass through the school or at least earn the *brevet* through independent study. Galliéni attended the school and won the *brevet* with honors in between Sudanese and Tonkinese assignments. Mangin passed the *brevet* examinations through independent study after his return from Fashoda.[31]

Although colonial officers would never dominate the upper echelons of the military hierarchy of the Third Republic the way Army of Africa officers had dominated the higher military ranks of the Second Empire, their importance would grow as the army-nation entente that had been forged in 1871 broke down in the wake of the Dreyfus affair. Some politicians came to view colonial officers who had spent their careers far away from metropolitan France and France's recurring political feuds as better political risks for sensitive appointments than metropolitan officers.

One war minister with strong colonial antecedents who turned out to be po- litically unreliable was General Jean-Marie Boulanger. During his period in office in 1886 and 1887 he promoted various liberal reforms which would improve living and working conditions in the army for conscripts and non-commissioned officers. He was instrumental in having the Lebel rifle introduced. But he was a man on horseback who before he committed suicide on his mistress's grave posed a real threat to the Third Republic.

General Joseph Simon Galliéni is a better example of a colonial officer who reached high rank and gave reliable service in metropolitan France. After he quit the governor-generalship of Madagascar in 1905, he commanded first the Thirteenth Corps in Clermont-Ferrand and then the Fourteenth Corps in Lyon. In 1909 he was appointed to the *Conseil Supérieur de Guerre*. Here in 1911 he played a role of some importance in having General Joffre appointed to the vice presidency of the *Conseil Supérieur de Guerre*, hence generalissimo in time of war.[32] And Joffre, who until December 1916 would command the French armies in World War I, was also considered a colonial.[33]

The first French disasters of the Great War and Joffre's resulting *limogeage* of 147 generals cleared the way for a number of colonials to reach top positions among them Mangin, Gouraud, Brulard, Guillaumat, Humbert, Degoutte, and Franchet d'Esperey. Galliéni, who had retired in 1914, was recalled to active duty at the outbreak of the war to serve as a technical advisor to the minister of war, Messimy, and then as military governor of Paris. He served as minister of war himself from October 1915 to February 1916. One of Galliéni's successors in this post was Marshal Lyautey, recalled temporarily from the residency-general of Morocco, to serve as war minister from December 1916 to April 1917.

Not all the top French commanders in World War I were colonial veterans. Several of them, Castelnau, Pétain, and Foch, to mention the greatest three, had no colonial experience at all. However, colonial and Army of Africa officers, particularly veterans of the Moroccan conquest, were disproportionately represented at the top.

In addition to requiring that French soldiers develop a talent for engaging in various forms of colonial warfare, thereby serving as a means of career advancement, Algeria and the colonies also challenged some officers to become developers, builders, urbanists, and teachers.

Large-scale private investment and development initially shied away from Algeria and France's other possessions. Therefore the armed forces, particularly the artillery and the engineers, executed a number of basic public works projects. In Algeria to attract colonists and to turn newly occupied strong points into real towns, French engineer officers planned and built Philippeville (Skikda), Orléansville (El Esnam), and Nemours (Ghazaouet). They added European quarters (and razed much of the indigenous quarters) in pre-colonial towns such as Algiers, Oran, and Constantine. An engineer officer, Poirel, extended the breakwater of Algiers with concrete blocks—an innovation for the period. Other engineer officers designed irrigation systems in several parts of Algeria, drilled artesian wells, and built roads. However, a common complaint made by opponents of the military regime was that the practice of using French soldiers to do much of the actual construction gave rise to an unacceptably high rate of sickness and death. In the tropical colonies where it was recognized in advance that Europeans could not generally engage in manual labor without very grave risks, the military builders made use of labor taxation and in some cases imported Asian coolies. The engineer corps surveyed most of France's colonial railways and actually built a few of them such as the Kayes-Bamako line in Mali and the southern penetration lines in Algeria.

The naval/colonial troops never had their own engineers; these were lent to them by the army engineer corps. But the naval artillery did perform some of the tasks of engineers. They planned and surveyed the colonial towns of Bamako, Saigon, Fort Lamy, and Bangui. The engineers, on the other hand, laid out Dakar and planned and built its first modern port facilities. Labor in the case of Dakar was provided by rented African captives and special disciplinary units lent from the army.

On both a formal and an informal basis French soldiers—often *sous-officiers* and young officers who might get bored with their normal assignments—became teachers. In Algeria, *Bureaux Arabes* officers made efforts to introduce new crops, sorghum for instance, and to modernize Algerian farming methods. In Senegal and other French colonies the first secular French primary schools were staffed by soldier-teachers. Finally, military doctors and other medical personnel taught hygiene and introduced the rudiments of European medicine to many of the indigenous peoples.

If officers and soldiers took on such tasks, first in Algeria and then in the tropical colonies, it was not only because they were responding to real needs but also as a response to ideological currents in France. One of these with roots going back to Louvois was that the army should be used in peacetime to undertake massive public works projects. In the nineteenth century this view was propagated by several writers and attained a degree of popularity particularly during the long periods of French disengagement in Europe. It seemed only logical to thinkers such as Emile de Girardin, General Schneider, General Morand, and Captain Durand that since armies would not be needed for their traditional purposes in what appeared in the 1820s, 1830s, and 1840s to be a dawning era of peace, they should be used to modernize France and its possessions. Algeria, which required both conquest and development, offered vast possibilities for both types of activities. Bugeaud's hope of settling Algeria with soldier-settlers was inspired both by this current of ideas and by his own self-conscious desire to emulate the Roman conquest of North Africa.[34] Indeed, he even proposed a colonization scheme in the environs of Oran in which European farmers and abandoned indigenous children would adopt a pastoral, semi-nomadic existence on the lands of tribes who had left them to join forces with Abd el-Kader.[35]

The use of the army, either directly or as a model of hierarchical collective organization, appealed to certain Fourrieristes and Saint-Simonians. The latter group was well represented in the Army of Africa and included such officers as La Moricière, Jourdan, Carette, and Poirel. These men, in particular La Moricière, were less interested in individual colonists as such, military or civilian, but in using the army to provide technical assistance to large-scale private enterprises. For La Moricière believed that "colonization in Africa was more a question of money than of men."[36]

A second current of thought that began during the Restoration and continued, if often on the periphery of French military thought, during the nineteenth century seemed to run counter to the ideal of development. Rather it reasserted the traditional role of the French army and eschewed the "spirit of industry."[37] Such was the conviction of Captain Pagézy de Bourdéliac, who wished to protect the army and its ideals from contamination by the mores of the industrial state. He even wished to move all major military installations into the countryside. On the other hand, he favored using the cadres of the army to moralize the conscripts who formed the mass of the French army and to teach them reading, writing, arithmetic, and basic skills. Bourdéliac did not realize that he was favoring modernization through the back door, so to speak, for "graduates" of his military "school" would not readily return to the illiterate peasant milieu from which they had come, and if by chance some did, they would demand radical changes.

The ideal of development did not take firm hold during the period under study so far as the army in metropolitan France was concerned; however, the ideal of education and moral and civic instruction did by the end of the nineteenth century. Both ideals were consciously pursued in the colonies because they answered major colonial needs. Their sway was expanded and more or less merged by the colonial actions of the Third Republic. By the early years of the twentieth century a young officer might be moved to take up a military career more in the hope of fulfilling these two ideals than of preparing himself to fight some future war.[38] Of course in the colonies the element of force could never disappear. Enlightened colonialists like Galliéni and Lyautey could switch from development to force with great ease when necessary.

Yet Lyautey was clearly sincere in his preference for peaceful solutions to colonial conflicts. In a letter to a friend he described enthusiastically his many responsibilities and activities in his sector in Madagascar. These included the supervision of a vocational school staffed by soldiers, a clinic headed by a military doctor, a primary school headed by a corporal, several experimental farms, a seed bank, and several land reclamation projects. He concluded, "here is the only kind of war which I like and understand, that which immediately produces greater wealth, more crops, and greater security."[39]

The man who wrote these words began his strictly colonial career rather late, at age forty, in 1894, after being virtually exiled from France for having published "Du Rôle social de l'officier" in the *Revue des Deux Mondes* in 1891. In this article he had evoked some of the ideas of Bourdéliac and of contemporary social Catholics such as Albert de Mun and La Tour du Pin. His principal argument was that France should use the newly enacted universal military service requirement (1889) as a means of educating and completing the moral and civic training of the young conscripts. As a secondary theme he recommended the humanizing of military routine. Above all he condemned certain traditional modes of behavior, for instance that by which a cavalry officer took pride in knowing everything about his horses but nothing about his men. He ended the article by evoking a military ideal of service rather than simply a quest for glory.

Lyautey, whose place of "exile" turned out to be Tonkin, found this French possession of recent acquisition to be an excellent laboratory in which he could test his ideas and adapt them to a colonial setting. They seemed to work—indeed, they won the approval of his superior, Colonel Galliéni, with whom he would later serve in Madagascar. The latter had elaborated and put into execution similar ideas during his periods of service in the Sudan and Martinique and probably also as a reaction to his period of study in the *Ecole Supérieure de Guerre* in Paris.

Having completed his colonial apprenticeship, Lyautey penned a sequel to "Rôle social," "Du Rôle colonial de l'officier," in 1900 which described in theoretical (and idealized) terms what he and Galliéni had been attempting to do in Tonkin and then in Madagascar.

Cautioning that repression in the style of the Algerian and Sudanese conquests was no longer to be held in favor, he warned against young officers "coming to the colonies to redo Austerlitz.''[40] Rather he suggested that in the new Colonial Army the rewardable *action d'éclat* be redefined to include such an action as inducing a hostile village to surrender without firing a shot or taking a life. As resident-general of Morocco, Lyautey would continue to be guided by these principles even if military reality required him to authorize a number of violent actions to subdue the country and to use the services of aggressive soldiers like Charles Mangin, ambitious in the traditional sense.

Meanwhile, Lyautey's suggestions for a reform of attitudes in the metropolitan forces took root. General André, liberal minister of war from 1900 to 1905, issued several new regulations requiring officers to become more familiar with their men and authorizing the creation of *cercles* (enlisted men's clubs) for troopers—places where they could spend their off hours. He also appointed Major Ebener to teach several courses at Saint-Cyr on the social mission of officers. Significantly, Ebener had been a sometime colonial. Detached to the colonial army he had served in the Sudan replacing Joffre as commandant of Timbuktu in 1896 when the latter was recalled to France. Unable to get along with the civilian governor of the Sudan, Albert Grodet, Ebener too had returned to France less than a year after his assignment to Timbuktu.

Unlike the Army of Africa which during the heyday of the Algerian conquest abused its troopers, the naval/colonial troops developed strong bonds between officers and men. These bonds owed their inception partly to the participation of officers and men in common undertakings, often non-military in nature, of the sort mentioned above and partly to the pragmatism of numerous colonial commanders. It was said of Galliéni that with him "subordination was a collaboration."[41] Such cooperation was no doubt also stimulated by a feeling of racial solidarity arising from the fact that in the tropical colonies French officers and men were but a tiny racial minority, often outnumbered by their indigenous troops. Nevertheless, when Galliéni ended his colonial career in 1905 to take up metropolitan commands, he published a book on the care of troops and made a point of bringing his men and officers closer together.[42]

If during the later years of the nineteenth century the French colonies provided an outlet for soldiers who wished to teach, develop, modernize, and govern non-Europeans, they also appealed to those who wished to get away from France but still serve France in a military capacity. Some wished to pursue a chivalric military ideal but found the metropolitan army, torn as it was by the Dreyfus affair and held in deep suspicion by much of the articulate French public, an unsatisfactory milieu in which to do so. But one could pursue such an ideal with some hope of satisfaction in an isolated outpost on the French colonial frontier.

Some officers had less idealistic motives for wishing to serve in the colonies. Some were frankly in search of a milieu in which to be authoritarian. Others simply wished to be presented with material and human obstacles to overcome. By the early years of the twentieth century, many French officers had read Kipling's works and consequently wished to take up their part of the "white man's burden.''

Lyautey admitted that he liked the "intense life of personal responsibility, of command, of bare-chested battle."[43] Ernest Renan's grandson, Ernest Piscari, who rebelled against his liberal and educated upbringing, joined the Colonial Army, abruptly ending his university studies. He asserted in several novels which he based on his colonial experiences that he was seeking the essence of the old professional army of pre-revolutionary France "for which battle meant more than simply homeland," and total commitment to an ideal.[44] He might have found part of this ideal in the French Foreign Legion. Piscari believed that he was rejecting the present—his present—for the past; Raoul Girardet suggests that he was in fact becoming a precursor of fascism.[45].

The major question remains to be answered: Did colonial involvement help or hinder the performance of the French armies in European wars? Although this essay cannot give a definite answer, it can suggest a few tentative conclusions.

Historians other than those dealing specifically with the French colonies condemn the influence of colonial warfare in the period under study primarily because of the French defeat in 1871. They overlook the French successes in Crimea, Italy, and World War I in which officers with colonial experience played major roles.

One must not forget that the Franco-Prussian War was brought on in the first place by the ineptitude of French diplomats and Bismarck's ability to outsmart Emperor Louis Napoleon. If the French army had lagged behind the Prussian army in terms of staff organization, armaments, development of universal conscription and military reserves, and the use of railways, one cannot blame the *algériens* for these deficiencies. Indeed, the French government and its ranking generals—some like Marshal Niel and General Trochu with Army of Africa backgrounds—realized that these deficiencies existed and were taking steps to rectify them. The Prussian victory at Sadowa stimulated many French officers to take a long, hard look at their army in comparison to that of Prussia. One outcome was the publication in 1867 of two influential critiques of the French army, *Les Institutions Militaires de la France* by the duke of Aumale, and *L'Armée française en 1867* by General Louis Trochu. Both authors were distinguished Algerian veterans. The former, an Orleanist prince, had served briefly as Algeria's governor-general in 1848; the latter had been a close collaborator of La Moricière and Bugeaud. But the war with Prussia came before France was really prepared to fight it.

A second reason that one should not be too harsh on the Algerian school is that the War of 1870 came thirteen years after the conclusion of the Kabylie campaigns had really closed the era of conquest in Algeria and more than twenty years after the war against Abd el-Kader. Moreover, political events in France had led to the removal of some of the most competent if not the first veterans of Algeria well before they would normally have retired: Bedeau, La Moricière, Changarnier, and Cavaignac, in 1851. Death had removed others: Bugeaud who had died prematurely of cholera in 1849, Duvivier and Négrier who had been killed during the events of 1848, and Bosquet who had died in 1861 as a result of injuries received in Crimea. Even Saint-Arnaud, the first French commander in Crimea and the victor at the Alma, died prematurely in September 1854. The latter, despite his age (he was born in 1798), was part of a group of less senior generals, at one point called *jeune Afrique*, who replacing their elders, led the French armies in Crimea, Italy, China, and Mexico. Should one not just as well blame these European and quasi-colonial campaigns for the defeat of 1871? They came closer in time to this main event than did the Algerian conquest. Finally, it has been said that the special conditions of Algerian warfare left French officers unfit to handle large commands—corps and whole armies. Yet ranking World War I generals with almost exclusively colonial and North African backgrounds did just that and did so quite well. One is on stronger ground if one blames the quality of some of the students who attended the Algerian/colonial school and the selection process by which the imperial regime chose its ranking generals in 1870 rather than blaming the quality of the school itself.

Algerian and colonial experience did stimulate an ability in officers to take the initiative, to improvise, and to develop eclectic interests. Such attitudes and talents were no doubt valuable to the handful of ranking officers of the army and navy who answered Gambetta's call and put together the armies of national defense. Faidherbe's experience both as a warrior and a colonial governor in Senegal and his later experience as a subdivisional commandant in Algeria helped him in his efforts to weld raw recruits and defeated soldiers from the imperial armies into an effective fighting force in a very short period of time. The resulting Army of the North comported itself honorably. Faidherbe found that organizing the *mobiles* in the departments under his jurisdiction was something like organizing the volunteers of Saint-Louis. In leading the Army of the North he borrowed some of the guerrilla tactics of his old foes, the Trarza Moors.[46]

Chanzy, the creator of the Second Army of the Loire, was a veteran of the Army of Africa. One of his able subordinates, Admiral Jauréguiberry, had commanded the naval troops which captured Saigon in 1859. In 1860, during the Franco-Chinese War, he had organized fluvial transport to connect Peking to the coast with light-draught, flat-bottomed boats. From 1861 to 1863 he had served as governor of Senegal. During the Franco-Prussian War, Jauréguiberry led naval and army forces with success at Coulmiers, Le Mans, and Jean-Erve.

After the war, officers like Lewel who took the initiative in bringing about important reforms in the French army were to a great extent men with at least some Algerian and other colonial experience. If they were able to swallow their pride, study the Prussians, and even adopt some of their methods including a similar staff system and war college, it was due to a great extent to their pragmatism born of colonial experience. Even the unpleasant stigma which was attached to colonial warfare served to goad a number of colonial officers, even very young ones, particularly those who served in the naval/colonial troops, into making a special effort to keep up with the latest metropolitan regulations and theories. Even an officer like Charles Mangin who embodied the older *beau sabreur* ideal made a point of earning the *brevet* of the *Ecole Supérieure de*

Guerre as did Galliéni, more the intellectual. Indeed Galliéni, who loudly proclaimed the superiority of a colonial career because it taught self-reliance and initiative, also felt sufficiently ill at ease about his own colonial background when he was called upon after 1905 to hold major metropolitan commands that he requested the loan of a recent *Ecole Supérieure de Guerre* graduate to teach him the latest principles of tactics and strategy.[47] One of his critics, the publicist Lieutenant-Colonel Mayer, indeed claimed that Galliéni, this iconoclast, known for his contempt for red tape and the minutiae of regulations emanating from the Paris bureaus, became a stickler for the enforcement of minor rules and regulations when exercising his commands at Clermont-Ferrand and Lyon—this to overcome what prejudice his metropolitan colleagues might have toward him because of his colonial background.[48] When the war came in 1914, Galliéni, recalled to active duty, displayed the best qualities of colonial and metropolitan officers.

Years earlier, Bugeaud had taken a middle ground on the question of the suitability of Algerian warfare as training for future European wars. Described by his aide-de-camp, Trochu, as being in a "permanent state of military professorate,"[49] Bugeaud believed that Algerian warfare was not sufficient by itself to train officers and soldiers for European warfare. But it could be an excellent "preparatory school" for chiefs and soldiers. He elaborated as follows:

It [Algerian warfare] permits one to study from a practical point of view...all the important questions relative to the well-being of soldiers: supply, transport, etc. One learns how to lead one's men without exceeding their endurance, to set up camp, to guard it, etc. Officers and men...become seasoned by incessant combat,...become accustomed to hunger, thirst, marching in all temperatures, and to all sorts of privations without becoming demoralized. The hardest part of warfare is not so much knowing how to die but how to live. Officers..., often engaged in actions in remote places with their batallions and their companies will become habituated to command and responsibility....[In Algeria]...we are only in primary school, but if we know how to profit from the lessons [which] we receive, we shall certainly become the best students in the secondary schools.[50]

This view would survive at least in some quarters. Writing after World War II, General Weygand, whose colonial experience began only after World War I, would write in 1961 that Algeria had been a "magnificent school for our young chiefs."[51]

There was unfortunately a major situation in which colonial practice and *Ecole Supérieure de Guerre* theories gave rise to a French military doctrine that had near-disastrous consequences for the French army in 1914—the *offensive à outrance* doctrine. Central to this doctrine was the belief that victory in battle was determined as much by psychological and moral factors and sheer bluff as by material factors. In other words, by continuing to advance, despite one's losses, one could compel one's enemy to retreat even if he had lost fewer men. Once one had imposed one's will upon one's enemy, one could dominate him by one's moral/psychological force and eventually force him to sue for peace.

The idea that the moral is more important that the physical had deep roots in the French national character. It had seen practical application in the revolutionary and Napoleonic wars. Men fighting for ideals in which they all believed fought better than those who had none or who did not wholeheartedly support their rulers' aims. The expression, "moral superiority" also came to designate the superiority of disciplined, well-trained men who trusted their officers and could maneuver effectively under fire.

After the close of the Napoleonic wars, the Prussian military philosopher and historian von Clausewitz distilled from the Napoleonic campaigns a dynamic theory of war which gave great importance to moral factors and to the value of offensive over defensive actions. But this was theory. The French army, on the other hand, kept the practice of the dynamic theory of war alive, even expanding it after 1830. Moral factors and offensive actions had become so thoroughly identified with colonial campaigns that Lieutenant-Colonel Mayer could write in 1928 that the *offensive à outrance* had been the "exclusive practice in colonial conquests where aggressiveness was the rule."[52]

Certainly in Algeria a basic element of Bugeaud's tactics was to keep the Army of Africa in a state of perpetual offensive both to give it a sense of moral ascendancy and to demoralize the indigenous Algerians not only by destroying their material resources but by outdoing them in terms of mobility, their particular strength. Even before Bugeaud became governor-general, he had propagated his belief that moral force was stronger than physical force,[53] and that "a good defensive must be offensive."[54] This attitude would be transferred to the tropical colonies. However, both in Algeria and in the colonies, as Mayer asserts, offensives were usually undertaken "with great care and accompanied with the minutest of precautions,"[55] not the case at the outbreak of World War I.

In Algeria, as mentioned earlier, much of the action consisted of raids by cavalry and semi-mounted infantry against property, indigenous encampments, and dispersed warriors. Efforts were made in Algeria and elsewhere to encourage the indigenous forces to concentrate so as to be more easily eliminated. Several towns in Algeria were taken by such methods, including Blida and Constantine (the latter on the second try in 1837). The typical reaction of colonial and Army of Africa forces to fortified indigenous towns was to breach the gates and weaker places in the walls, to direct infantry charges through the breaches, and to take the towns by storm and hand-to-hand combat in their streets and buildings. The West African settlements of Guémou, Nioro, Ségou, and Bissandougou, to mention a few, were taken in similar fashion. In such actions artillery was used more as battering rams than as anti-personnel devices. That such operations should be completed very rapidly was of utmost importance particularly in the tropical colonies, for the threat of disease and the precariousness of supply lines made long sieges very dangerous if not impossible for the French forces.

The essential lesson that the French learned was that offensive action could be counted upon to produce favorable results. What was not so easily retained, if ever learned, was that success in these instances was due to the organizational and material inferiority of the indigenous peoples. The transfer to France in the early twentieth century of a few officers with colonial backgrounds brought about a merger of colonial practice in the matter of the offensive and metropolitan theories.

Meanwhile, the *Ecole Supérieure de Guerre* had begun a systematic study of the French defeat of 1871 and the adversary's methods. One conclusion drawn by this study was that much of Von Moltke's strategy had been based on a study of von Clausewitz, who in fact had devised his teachings from studying Napoleon's campaigns. Von Moltke, therefore, had beaten the French with methods that the French army had developed and forgotten. Although the *Ecole Supérieure de Guerre* theoreticians did not deny the importance of the excellent Prussian staff system, their use of railways, and their conscription system, they were more taken by the Prussian use of the offensive which they believed Von Moltke had distilled through von Clausewitz from Napoleon.

Indeed, von Clausewitz's views on the subject can be summarized as follows: "War must be an utmost exertion of force, and especially of moral force, for the complete destruction of the enemy's armed resistance, and to this end the offensive should be undertaken whenever practicable and in its simplest, most direct, and most vigorous form."[56]

Unfortunately, some French theoreticians lost track of von Clausewitz's caveat, "whenever practicable."

Colonial and metropolitan theories of the offensive were also merged in the writings of Colonel Ardant du Picq whose *Battle Studies* (*Etudes sur le Combat*) had been written before the Franco-Prussian War (in which he was killed) but which did not appear until 1880. Essentially du Picq attempted to capture the essence of battle, to describe how troops react to certain combat situations, and to identify those elements which were conducive to victory.

He based his *Battle Studies* upon three principal sources. The first was his own military experience, which included service in the Crimea, Algeria, and Syria. Indeed it was during the Syrian intervention of 1860 that he was moved to begin the study of battle dynamics and psychology. His second major source was a questionnaire which he distributed among many of his colleagues. His third was a study of selected battles of antiquity.

For du Picq victory resulted from moral factors. Of course, he wisely defined "moral factors" to include organization, discipline, tactics, belief in one's cause, and the like,[57] all substantial warnings to the reader not to give "moral factors" too narrow a definition. But he subordinated material factors to moral factors because "one thing. . . [did] not change, man's heart."[58] Hence he concluded, "He will win who has the resolution to advance."[59] Too many of his latter-day disciples clutched at this last sentence and overlooked the fact that he only devoted three pages to the question of the use and effects of heavy artillery. As a consequence of theoretical studies such as these, an increasingly pro-offensive, anti-defensive bias crept into the French field service regulations after 1895.[60]

Then in the years immediately preceding World War I the idea of the *offensive à outrance* acquired yet another theoretical underpinning, that of the Bergsonian philosophical concept of the *élan vital*—the all-triumphant will transcends material and empirical considerations. It was an optimistic and anti-intellectual concept that provided civilian and secular reinforcement to the *offensive* doctrine. Then came Foch to the *Ecole Supérieure de Guerre*, as an instructor in 1895 and as the director in 1907. His "opportunism in execution" when the war began did not completely compensate for his earlier teachings to the effect that "the will to conquer sweeps all before it."[61]

Finally, just before the outbreak of the war came Colonel Louis de Grandmaison to head the Operations Branch of the General Staff. He had served in Tonkin under the orders of Galliéni as chief of post at Dong-Dang on the Chinese border. Here he earned Galliéni's praise. Later, in 1898 he published a book about his tour of duty, *L'Expansion française au Tonkin*. Fourteen years later he published his *Deux Conférences faites aux officiers de l'état-major de l'armée*, the extreme formulation of the *offensive à outrance* doctrine. It was a distillation of earlier *Ecole de Guerre* teachings on the subject, to which he added something of the mentality of his earlier colonial experience.

For Grandmaison, moral factors were not only the most important; they were the only factors which counted in war, "Others [were] important only to the extent that they affect[ed] morale." For when "one attack[ed] with full force, one always...[had] in front of one an adversary stricken with palsy."[62] If this were not enough for the faint of heart, he assured his readers concerned about security that "As far as the offensive is concerned, imprudence is the best security."[63]

Such foolishness contributed greatly to the elaboration of Plan 17 which presaged a German attack through the Franco-German border to be met by a massive French attack into the Rhineland that would throw back the Germans. Moral force was written into the French field regulations of 1913: "Battles are beyond everything else struggles of the morale. Defeat is inevitable as soon as the hope of conquering ceases to exist. Success comes to him whose will is firmest and morale strongest."[64]

In general, officers with colonial backgrounds supported the *offensive* doctrine and even Plan 17. A principal reason that War Minister Adolphe Messimy supported Joffre for the vice presidency of the War Council and generalissimo in time of war is that he endorsed both the plan and the doctrine as, for that matter, did Galliéni. Indeed, within the next year Gouraud and Mangin, also believers in the *offensive à outrance* doctrine, gave practical demonstrations of its applicability—in Morocco.

Galliéni, however, came to doubt both doctrine and plan. A spy had already revealed to the French authorities the essentials of the German Schlieffen Plan.

In 1914 Galliéni was so frightened by the results of a *Kriegspiel* which he had led at the *Ecole Supérieure de Guerre* that he made an urgent request for the reinforcement of the Belgian frontier. Already Galliéni had won a war game by using airplanes. In 1910, on the other hand, Foch had remarked that the airplane was "good sport, but for the Army...naught."[65]

As World War I got underway, Galliéni and other colonial officers brought to bear a pragmatic spirit typical of colonial officers that would in part compensate for earlier doctrinal excesses. Perhaps the most positive description of how the colonial frontier affected the intellectual scope of many officers and men, their sense of initiative and ability to innovate was that of Lyautey, who wrote at the beginning of his own colonial career:

There is not one...lieutenant, chief of post...who does not develop in six months more initiative, will, endurance, and personality than an officer in France during his whole career. And what maturity..., what confidence in one's self, what coming to grips with reality, the practical, the productive.[66]

In short, Lyautey had sketched "an aristocratic ethic of action."[67]

Certainly in terms of the personal development of the average colonial officer, these traits were very much worth having; however, they implied the inferiority of colonial subjects and an approval of paternalism and racial prejudice. Some of these qualities would lead to insubordination and many types of abuses such as the distinction which separated "initiative" from "indiscipline." Generally speaking, in Algeria and the tropical colonies, an act contrary to or in the absence of orders or an act undertaken without proper precautions qualified as a brilliant initiative—if it succeeded—and an act of indiscipline only if it failed. Even then it might be covered up and its protagonist given only a very light punishment.

This spirit of initiative-indiscipline was found in numbers of imperial army veterans, officers and men who served in the Army of Africa in its early days. The Algerian environment was another: The distance separating Paris from Algiers posed problems; added to this was the already poor communication system with Algeria itself. Hence, these conditions required that most problems be resolved locally. As the conquest of Algeria got underway, it attracted officers who were opposed to the routinization and spirit of blind obedience which increasingly characterized the metropolitan army. Such officers learned to profit from the possibilities, real and specious, for rapid promotion offered by the Soult Law and *actions d'éclat*.

Paradoxically, the attitude toward discipline mentioned above, which came to characterize the metropolitan army, also ended up stimulating initiative-indiscipline particularly in combat. The regulations became so rigid that when the fighting began, they had to be ignored if the combatants were to achieve any kind of success. Such an attitude reduced tactical considerations to a question of muddling through and gave the French soldier and officer a strong preference for hand-to-hand combat.[68]

In Algeria muddling through was not only practiced in combat; it became an accepted part of military planning. Indeed, General Trochu, who in his *Oeuvres posthumes* was highly critical of the let's-muddle-through mentality, holds the Algerian experience responsible for its ascendancy in the French army as a whole.[69] He traced the use of the common French expression, *débrouillez-vous*, meaning "let's muddle through," or as it is more frequently if vulgarly rendered in the army, *démerdez-vous*, to an Algerian Arabic expression, *Deubbeur rass eck*, meaning, "consult your head."[70]

According to General Azan, "Unauthorized initiatives...taken by the major colonials...contributed greatly to the constitution of the French colonial empire.[71] He cites the case of Bugeaud who went ahead with the Battle of Isly in 1844 despite orders from Paris, which he had received the day before, not to cross the frontier into Morocco. He also cites Bugeaud's refusal to halt his invasion of the Kabylie in 1847. Actions similar to these occurred in other colonial theaters. We can cite the unauthorized marches to Timbuktu in 1894 led by Lieutenant-Colonel Bonnier and Major Joffre. Although the first one of these ended in disaster, the second was a success. Not only did this begin the permanent occupation of Timbuktu by the French, but on a personal level, it contributed to the advancement of Joffre's career. Hindsight, however, suggests that none of these actions when they were taken were crucial. France would have been able to hold western Algeria, the Kabylie, and Timbuktu without their having been taken. The Bonnier-Joffre affair in fact had been stimulated by the murder of Captain Boiteux who, completely in violation of orders and common sense, had attempted a landing at Kabara (near Timbuktu) with a woefully inadequate force from the steamboat of which he was in command. With a small amount of effort he had hoped to achieve a great deal of glory.

An even more senseless disaster occurred much earlier in Algeria in 1845 at Sidi-Brahim. It was caused by the excessive ambition and negligence of Colonel Montagnac, commandant of the new French post of Nemours (Djemmaa Ghazaouat). Feeling "tired of playing the oyster in...[its] shell at Djemmaa,"[72] Montagnac wished to earn a little glory. He therefore sallied forth, without authorization from his immediate superior, Cavaignac, to *razzia* partisans of Abd el-Kader rumored to be encamped some fourteen kilometers to the southwest. But his column numbered only 423 officers and men; hence this action flew in the face of Bugeaud's general instructions never to operate in enemy territory with small columns. Moreover, Montagnac broke his column into small, separated sections, which also went against Bugeaud's instructions. The forces of Abd el-Kader attacked the column and killed all but fifteen participants.

There could be little doubt where the blame lay, but inasmuch as Montagnac was killed, we will never know his reasons. This attitude of "unauthorized initiatives" characterized not only the Army of Africa but even to some extent the whole French army. Montagnac and his men very quickly became heroes and examples of valor. A monument to them was raised near the Sidi-Brahim tomb where Montagnac himself had perished. In later years the title Sidi-Brahim was given to a military march of anonymous authorship which is still a favorite of French army bands.

The Soult Law, Algerian opportunities, high inflation, abysmally low military salaries, and various stimuli goaded many French officers into developing attitudes toward advancement similar to those of the *bourgeoisie des affaires* that came into dominance in France when the July Monarchy came into power. These officers abandoned an earlier conception, common during the Restoration, of a military career as service to the nation which was to a great extent its own reward. The new conception was one to the effect that "[one's] career was expected to advance at all costs, . . . to earn returns as if . . . [it were a business]."[73]

Writing in 1887, General Thoumas deplored this attitude:

We learned to inflate bulletins; we transformed into victories comparable to . . . Austerlitz situations in which our troops had pushed enemies forward who were [in fact] retreating so as to draw us into traps; we represented rear guard combats as smashing successes . . . [even though] as is vulgarly said, . . . [we] left lots of wool on the bushes. . . . [We] learned to succeed too well at the expense of our men, and . . . [I] still remember . . . Pélissier, . . . certainly not tender, . . . replying to a chief-of-column who was bragging of his success: "That's fine, but let us first take a look at the litters."[74]

The attitude of glory at all costs was transferred to the naval-colonial troops and goes far toward explaining their behavior in the Sudan from 1879 to 1899. The competitiveness in this theater was no doubt heightened by their poor reputation in France despite their heroism at Bazeilles and the smallness of their quota of rewards and promotions. Young Lieutenant Mangin bewailed this fact frequently during his first tour of duty in the Sudan. Ambition pushed to the point of psychosis led to the Voulet-Chanoine affair of 1899.

There fortunately remained the possibility, remote at first, but increasingly important for the Colonial Army after 1900, that ambitious officers might earn credit for promotions in non-destructive ways. Colonial officers transferred to France brought the spirit of initiative to the metropolitan army. A spectacular initiative was that taken by General Galliéni in September 1914, when he gave the order to General Manoury, commander of the Sixth Army, to move against General Von Kluck's First Army, thus beginning the First Battle of the Marne. He forced the hand of Joffre, who had been considering the situation and delaying. And as is of course general knowledge, Galliéni commandeered six hundred or so Paris taxis to move the Seventh Division, commanded by General de Trentinian, himself a former superior-commandant of the Haut-Sénégal-Niger, to the front.

Even Lieutenant-Colonel Mayer, who does find some fault with Galliéni in other respects praises his role in this famous battle and asserts that his colonial background had prepared him perfectly for this type of improvisation.[75] As military governor of Paris, Galliéni took other unorthodox but successful initiatives. For example, he authorized the use of oxen and plows borrowed from nearby farmers to dig artillery emplacements, something not included in the official military regulations.[76]

While World War I was going on, and of course after the war, critiques of the strategy and tactics of both sides blossomed. One cannot say that ex-colonials had any better insights than talented non-colonials although they may as a group have had special slants. In fact, Joffre's connections with the colonies did not help the collective reputation of colonial officers. It is important to remember that Joffre's colonial assignments had been fairly limited and that during his years as generalissimo he was dominated by an entourage of staff officers, few of whom had seen colonial service of any sort.

Excellent critical works were written by such officers as Lieutenant-Colonel Emile Mayer and the artillery officer Percin. The latter castigated the poor liaison between the French artillery and the infantry which he blamed for many accidental deaths.[77]

Galliéni and Mangin were two colonial officers who were highly critical of the way the French initially fought World War I. They had similar opinions about France's failures in the beginning days of the war that probably reflected a common colonial point of view. Both men were highly critical of the inability of the high command to improvise a plan of action quickly to go into effect once it had become evident that Plan 17 had failed. Both criticized the unsatisfactory nature of pre-war field training: "manoeuvres à l'eau de rose," scoffed Mangin, that had not trained anyone to real battlefield conditions. Both men deplored the excessive influence of the *Ecole Supérieure de Geurre*, "still with Napoleon and 1870." For Mangin, the difference between a professor of military art and a general was the same as that between an art critic and a painter. Galliéni accused the *Ecole Supérieure de Guerre* of teaching irrelevancies—concentrating too much on Napoleon and not enough on modern artillery and the recent wars in South Africa and Manchuria. After the war Galliéni suggested, much to the annoyance of Foch, that a small amount of dynamite should be set aside in order to blow up the *Ecole Supérieure de Guerre*.[78]

The colonial experience affected lighter aspects of the questions of decorum and discipline. There was the question of dress, too. As mentioned earlier, the special corps founded in Algeria after the French conquest evolved their own uniforms, the *zouaves* in particular basing theirs on a traditional Turkish-Algerian model. *Zouave* officers and for a while those of the *spahis* dressed in this fashion. The uniforms worn by the latter between 1839 and 1842 consisted of a red Turkish jacket covered with black braid, a blue vest, wide blue breeches, soft boots with screw-in spurs, a turban, and a red cape. General Du Barail confessed that this uniform could appear "quite attractive when one had a good line and grace; but [that] when one [had] acquired a [fat] stomach, it...immediately [gave] the impression...[that one was] a candy peddler on the rue de Rivoli."[79] Herein may lie the reason that *spahi* officers adopted in 1842 what was more or less the regulation French cavalry uniform.

But many officers serving in Algeria who were not specifically authorized to wear special uniforms made small changes in their regular uniforms anyway. Some, like General La Moricière, preferred to wear an Algerian *chéchia* rather than the standard *képi*. Others, like Duvivier and Daumas, both of whom were involved with the *Bureaux Arabes* and their predecessor organizations, wore full *zouave*-style uniforms which they personalized in various ways.

It became a common practice in the Army of Africa for officers and men to grow long beards both because it was convenient not to shave regularly and because they wanted to emulate the indigenous Algerians. Marshal Castellane, always the rigid disciplinarian, thought ill of this practice, particularly when it spread to metropolitan France. But there was little he could do; the Orleanist princes, Nemours and Aumâle, had adopted it as well as certain other particularities of dress. At least, thought Castellane, the regulations should be changed to reflect the royal practice.[80]

The ordinary French soldiers in Algeria increasingly ignored the uniform regulations. The distances over which columns operated, the scarcity of supply depots, Bugeaud's insistence on carrying only a minimum of supplies per column, and finally, the character of the marches and the terrain meant that uniforms deteriorated rapidly and could not be mended or replaced en route. So the soldiers improvised.

The naval colonial troops became equally casual about dress when in the bush on long marches. General Gouraud described an encounter between his detachment of *tirailleurs sénégalais* and British African troops while he was taking part in the delimitation of the Gold Coast-Upper Volta frontier in 1898. Observing that his men were envious of the clean, snappy uniforms of their English counterparts, he called them to attention and reminded them that the French, not the English, had captured Timbuktu, Djenné, Sikasso, and Oulé. He was gratified when an old *tirailleur* stepped out of line, banged the butt of his rifle on the ground, and exclaimed, "tout ça y a vrai...Anglais y a bon pour pantalon..., Français y a bon pour fusil."[81]

On the other hand, officers both of the Army of Africa and of the naval colonial troops could at times be fastidious, almost to an extreme, about questions of dress. In 1856 Governor Faidherbe of Senegal turned town the chance to have an audience with the emperor, Louis Napoleon, because he was ashamed at not owning a regulation governor's uniform.[82]

Colonial capitals could require a pronounced degree of dressiness even if they also permitted officers to add individual touches to their uniforms. Dressiness manifested itself even in remote areas on special occasions. Lyautey reminisced in "Du Rôle colonial" about how he was received at a remote post along the Chinese border by a recent graduate of Saint-Cyr who had donned "his most attractive uniform,...gloved, as if going to [a]...ball."[83] In 1909, Lieutenant Jacques Violet donned white gloves to lead his men into battle and to die at Ksar Teurchane in the Mauritanian Adrar; five years later hundreds of begloved young lieutenants and captains would die during the opening weeks of World War I.[84]

Colonial adaptations to uniforms gave rise to at least two innovations of some importance for the French armies as a whole. The first of these was the use of stripes on sleeves to indicate rank, done for the first time by the *zouaves*. Because of the prestige of this unit the practice spread to other units but did not become standard until 1870.[85]

The second innovation was the adoption of the khaki-colored uniform. On this question the naval/colonial troops were slightly ahead of the regular army. The word, *khaki* is Urdu for "dust-colored." The idea of coloring military uniforms khaki was introduced to the armies of western Europe by the British Indian army. French colonial officers began to experiment with khaki after 1900. Those officers who commanded indigenous troops wore khaki-colored uniforms in World War I.[86] However, the khaki-colored uniform was not generally adopted in either the Colonial Army or the regular army until 1918.

The point was made earlier in this essay that the colonial frontier stimulated greater closeness between officers and men than existed in France. Although this characteristic was less developed in the Army of Africa than in the naval/colonial troops, certain Army of Africa officers during the conquest of Algeria did permit a singular type of relaxation for their troops. When columns that had been on particularly long and arduous missions returned to their bases, their officers rewarded them by allowing them complete freedom in the towns where the bases were located. On the return of La Moricière's column to Oran from Mascara in 1841, the general, the commandant of Oran province, permitted his men two days of complete freedom in the city. "There were no serious disorders," reported General Du Barail.[87] Bugeaud permitted his troops to enjoy similar types of relaxation in Bougie in 1847 when they returned from their second raid into the Kabylie. During two days, called "saturnalia of Bougie" the men roamed freely, wined, and tried to wench at the expense of the civilian population. There was much fighting, pillaging of private homes, violence to the local gendarmes, and many loud cheers for "Père" Bugeaud.

Julien cites another case of indiscipline of a different sort in Oran. A civilian was being roughed up by two soldiers. He called for help when he saw General Létang approaching. But rather than helping the civilian, the general joined the two soldiers in beating up the civilian to teach him to "respect the proper rules of hierarchy." The fact that the civilian in question was the appointed mayor of Oran created a scandal of sorts.[88]

To a certain extent soldiers, and probably even some officers, stole from *colon* farmers. The legionnaires in fact were reputed to be highly skillful chicken thieves. Indeed, the Algerian experience gave the word *chaparder*, to pilfer, to the French language.[89]

Actions such as these were indicative not only of loose discipline but also of the contempt which numbers of Army of Africa officers and men came increasingly to feel for the civilian European population of Algeria. The sentiment, one must add, was reciprocated. Civilian military conflict was a recurring theme during the first forty years of the French regime, during which Algeria was ruled by the army. The differences between military and civilian conceptions of discipline, honor, and duty were bound to create misunderstandings and conflicts. Another major source of conflict was the role that the army would increasingly play as protectors of the indigenous peoples of Algeria.

Increasing numbers of officers and men resented risking their lives in the long, hard campaigns, suffering and dying in order to defend the doubtful activities of unscrupulous shopkeepers, incompetent farmers, and speculators, the latter perceived as avidly attempting to steal land from the indigenous Algerians only to be resold at windfall profits. They felt exploited by the saloon keepers and the pimps of the garrison towns. Some officers and men particularly resented the fact that a large proportion of the European settlers were not French at all but consisted of disparate Mediterranean elements, Spaniards predominating.

Civilians resented the whole idea of military rule and what they perceived as the anti-democratic, authoritarian biases of the soldiers. The civilians knew that their security depended upon the Army of Africa, but they resented this dependence.

There were, of course, many exceptions to the general rule of civilian-military conflict in Algeria. In the final years of military rule General Faidherbe served very successfully as subdivisional commandant of Bône and as interim divisional commandant of Constantine province in which Bône was located. In 1871, the radical deputy representing Constantine, Colas, wrote to the minister of war that Faidherbe ''[had] had the unanimous confidence of the army and the population'' and requested that he be appointed to head the division of Constantine on a permanent basis. Faidherbe's return would, in Colas's opinion, cause the province, at that time wracked by the revolt in the Kabylie, to ''return to order.''[90] Colas's request was all the more remarkable in that he was very anti-military.

Civilian-military relations in the tropical colonies tended to be closer and better than they were in Algeria. Part of the difference stemmed from the fact that the tropical colonies were not settler colonies and that there were relatively few civilians in them. Moreover, since the European garrisons were quite small, a feeling of racial solidarity was felt among all Europeans. In some colonies, Senegal for instance, and in other territories of French West and Equatorial Africa, there was such a shortage of European staff that some distinctions between military and civilian positions had to be blurred. Hence civilians, even non-officials, might serve as *chefs de poste* in supposedly military territories and, as already described, military men took up civilian duties. The problem in these colonies was that the indigenous troops were often permitted to run roughshod over the civilian indigenous populations in a way that was analogous to the behavior of the Army of Africa toward European civilians in Algeria.

The ranking officers in the colonies might look down on small settlers, what few there were, and retail merchants, but they recognized that the colonies needed to attract capital. Although there might be conflicts between the colonial wholesalers and the naval colonial authorities, there also existed a tradition of cooperation that had received a major boost when, in the 1850s, the Maurel and

Prom Company of Senegal played a major role in having Faidherbe appointed governor of Senegal and later helped him hold on to his post.

At the end of the century, Galliéni even saw a role for small colonists in Madagascar. He encouraged soldiers who had finished their terms of service to stay on as homesteaders.[91]

The colonial experience stimulated many small material and tactical innovations in the French army, some good, others bad, a few of which will be described below. Although the daily ration of wine continued to be considered essential for French troops in action, Bugeaud added hot coffee to the rations of his troops in Algeria. He found that they could march further in cold weather particularly at night when well dosed with this stimulant. Coffee was made available some of the time in France's European campaigns but never to the extent that wine was.

Weapons were developed and first tested in the colonies. One example was the Treuille de Beaulieu rifled mountain gun, a sort of light, animal-borne mortar which fired exploding shells. Several of these were tested in the Kabylie in 1857. In the 1870 War a few of them, equipped with new and improved shrapnel shells, were used on marshy or frozen ground where regular artillery could not go. Faidherbe's Army of the North made such good use of several Treuille de Beaulieu mortars that his principal opponent, General Von Goeben, believed that the Army of the North had used *mitrailleuses* (a French form of the Gatling gun), which had not been the case at all.[92]

A type of portable and disassembled French army tent had its origin in Algeria. French soldiers had been issued large duffle bags for use on certain types of long marches during which they were expected to sleep in the open. Several officers observed that groups of men would unstitch their bags at the end of a day's march and then stitch a few of them together to make a crude barrier to shelter them from wind and rain. Later, more sacks and some buttons were added, and a real tent was produced. In 1840 the duke of Orleans and Marshal Valée examined several varieties of these tents and chose one apparently made by several *Chasseurs à Pied*. It became the standard for what became known as the *sac tente-abri*, a regulation item.[93]

No doubt this arrangement worked well in Algeria and possibly even in Crimea where most members of tent groups had a fairly good chance of staying alive and together. One wonders how well these tents would serve in campaigns like those of the Franco-Prussian War in which one or more members of each tent group might be killed or separated from the other members of the group.

The Algerian conquest gave the Army of Africa valuable experience in logistics and long marches that, according to General Thoumas, was well demonstrated in Crimea.[94] But deterioration in these skills had obviously set in by the time of the Franco-Prussian War.

Michael Howard relates that as the Third, Fourth, and Fifth Corps of the French army marched toward Forbach in Alsace at the start of the war, their generals, following the Algerian practice, attempted to head up the column each night into divisional camps instead of permitting each regiment or battalion to bivouac along the way at an appropriate time. Consequently, the rear of the column could not reach the camp site until almost time to leave. Then having prepared to depart, the detachments at the rear were forced to wait hours until they could get underway.[95]

Many commanders in this war, with the notable exception of General Chanzy, continued the Algerian practice of bedding down their men at night in the open or in tents rather than in the readily available villages and farms. Therefore, in the cold months the Armies of National Defense suffered more from the cold than should have been the case.[96]

The Algerians and the colonial experiences reinforced the custom in the French armed forces that officers of even the highest ranks must personally lead their men in battle, often at the risk of their lives. Although there were always influential generals like the Marshal of Castellane who opposed the practice, it continued to have its practitioners, even some generals, despite what became the prevailing view by World War I that ranking officers were managers as well as warriors and should avoid unnecessary risks. That General Joffre and his headquarters remained far to the rear was bitterly criticized by Galliéni and Mangin.

Indeed, Mangin was one general who insisted on being where the action was and of displaying a maximum of panache and machismo. As commanding general of a division in the Fifth Army he would often inspect the front trenches. On such occasions he wore his *képi* and his rank insignia and would walk out in the open refusing to pass through the lateral approach trenches—"I might get dirty"—he explained.[97] Not only was he a good target for German sharpshooters on such occasions, but they could tell who and what he was. He was never hit.

Several encounters which Mangin had with General Pétain during World War I illustrate the differences between the colonial and the metropolitan military mentalities. In August 1914, while taking part in the retreat from the Belgian frontier, the two generals stopped for lunch by the roadside. Pétain took a piece of cold beef, a bit of bread, and some cheese out of a paper bag. Mangin, on the other hand, had his orderly serve up a meal of warm filet of beef, French fried potatoes, salad, and a bottle of wine. "What," exclaimed Pétain, "don't you realize we are at war?" "That is precisely why I want to be well fed," replied Mangin. "I have made war all my life, and I have never felt better. . . . You have been making war for a fortnight and you are nearly dead! Follow my example and eat properly."[98] Later the two men had differences over Mangin's role in the Aisne Offensives, Pétain considering that Mangin had been overly reckless and Mangin considering that Pétain was overly cautious.

In July 1918, when Mangin was preparing to lead the Tenth Army in the Battle of Villers-Cotterets, he moved his command headquarters from Bonneuil to a hill near the Soissons road where he built an observation post, camouflaged by a large tree, from which he could view the whole battlefield. When Pétain, now commander-in-chief of French forces, made an inspection on July 18, he ordered Mangin back to Bonneuil. Pétain justified that Mangin's improvisation was "too colonial."[99]

The experience of commanding African indigenous troops, particularly Blacks, on a long-term basis stimulated French officers to develop leadership qualities and charisma similar to those of indigenous war leaders. Their leadership styles became so personally linked to the men they commanded, the *esprit de corps* in their units so strongly tied to them, that a given unit might collapse or mutiny if its commander were changed too abruptly or if the unit were sent into battle before the new commander could establish a rapport with his men.

Leading indigenous troops reinforced in French officers a belief in the primacy of infantry and its expendability. Colonial expeditions in which large numbers of indigenous effectives were killed were considered successful if the objective was obtained without killing many French troops and officers. Since inter-African warfare of the middle and late nineteenth century was infantry-intensive and had high death rates, African recruits were not shocked by high death rates in French service and may even have considered them to be lower than what prevailed in African armies at war. At any rate, the African soldiers in French service who survived took great pride in their French commanders' victories. Knowing that "their" Africans greatly admired them lulled certain French commanders into accepting high infantry death rates as normal and even to think of themselves as superior if not invincible warriors. Later, in the metropolitan context of World War I, these commanders would find the *poilus* less understanding.

Success in African terms convinced several commanders of indigenous troops that they possessed *baraka*, a mystical trait, a sort of blessing, attributed to *marabouts*, holy men, in Muslim North and West Africa. They thought they had power to radiate holiness and good fortune to those around them, and of course, they would be fortunate themselves. Both Gouraud and Mangin came to believe that they possessed *baraka*. Mangin, in particular, seems to have allowed some of the decisions which he made in World War I to be swayed by this belief. It contributed along with his belief in the primacy and expendability of infantry to his continued faith in the *offensive à outrance* even after Galliéni and Gouraud had begun to have second thoughts.

Beginning with his recapture of Fort Douaumont and definitely after the failure of the Aisne Offensives, Mangin was known to many as "the butcher." He, of course, claimed that he did not deserve this sobriquet. In one of his books, *Comment finit la guerre*, he not only cited figures to the effect that the Aisne Offensives had taken fewer French lives than had earlier offensives (or Joffre's indecisive *grignotage*) but reiterated what became general knowledge, that the first statistics published about the Aisne Offensives had counted several categories of casualties twice. For Mangin this operation had failed because it had been badly executed and then aborted. After all, he argued, it had cost the French more lives to lose Fort Douaumont than to recapture it.[100] Mangin's points, although well taken, indicate that he had little sense of the straw that broke the camel's back.

On the other hand, Mangin's preoccupation with the infantry did make him an oracle in one very major instance. In 1910 when he wrote *La Force Noire*, he argued that the next Franco-German war would be a long one, not a short war as most strategists were claiming. He believed that since both of the competing alliances were of equal strength, they would create a stalemate that would only be broken after a long struggle and by the side with the greatest resources in manpower. His projected Black army would tip the scales in France's favor.[101] It is significant that among the English the most ranking officer with a similar disdain for the short-war theories was Lord Kitchener, Britain's greatest colonial soldier. Events proved both men right.

CONCLUSION

The proposals advanced in this essay must remain tentative pending further research particularly in the French military archives. One must go behind the numerous and recurring cliches and anecdotes about the Army of Africa and the use of indigenous troops that appear in one book after another. Many of them have their origins in a few sets of published officers' memoirs, those of General Du Barail and the marshal of Castellane for the Army of Africa, and the writings of Mangin and Gouraud for the *tirailleurs sénégalais*. One would like to broaden the selection.

Although the details remain to be clarified, one can definitely detect very broad influences which France's colonial possessions, particularly the African ones, had on the French armed forces during the period under study. To begin with, the colonies stimulated the development of indigenous troop formations which were of origins as varied as the colonies themselves. The first such formations were small and of only local importance. With the increasing use of indigenous troops from one possession to conquer and pacify others and, more importantly, the use of Algerian and colonial troops to reinforce France's defense posture in Europe, the indigenous troops took on great importance in France's total military strength. By the end of World War I, the French army was, in the popular mind, as much an institution of *turcos* and *tirailleurs sénégalais* as it was of metropolitan Frenchmen.

A second broad influence was the Africanization in appearance and spirit of certain purely European troop formations, particularly the *zouaves*, as well as the French officers of the various indigenous formations. Additionally and significantly, the most exotically uniformed of these units, the *zouaves*, was also the most prestigious and the most imitated outside France. The North African unit best known to foreigners, the one with the most romantic appeal was the

French Foreign Legion. The fact that General Mangin attributed the French recapture of Fort Douaumont to his *baraka* is illustrative of his Africanization.

Although the details remain to be clarified, it is obvious that the Algerian and colonial frontiers challenged the Army of Africa and the naval/colonial troops to develop forms of colonial warfare and to broaden the French officers' conceptions of their roles. It is equally obvious that beginning in 1848 men with such backgrounds who had been promoted rapidly came to occupy major positions in France's military hierarchy. This fact influenced the ways in which France would fight her future European wars. Army of Africa officers brought an Algerian stamp to the way the army repressed the insurrections in France in 1848 and 1871, and Army of Africa officers played major roles in giving Louis Napoleon dictatorial powers in December 1851.

The colonial influence touched on such aspects of the military way of life as discipline, decorum, dress, ability and willingness to take the initiative, ability to innovate, and attitudes toward civilians. In some cases this influence could be very pronounced.

Whether or not colonial influences were in the best interests of the French army is the hardest question to answer. In the case of the French defeat in 1871, the traditional view is that the Algerian conquest bears much of the blame for the defeat because it had failed to prepare the French army for serious European warfare. However, one must remember that the war itself was initiated not by the army but by the ineptitude of the French government. The army was caught unprepared. If it fought badly it was not so much the fault of the Algerian "school" but a result of its unpreparedness and the fact that during the imperial phase of the war it was led by poor graduates of the "Algerian" school who had been appointed to the highest positions for political reasons.

One can point to the disastrous *offensive à outrance* doctrine of World War I that in France had a partly colonial origin. But one must remember that the Germans formulated a similar doctrine at the same time without any colonial influence playing a part at all. And besides, in France, the highest ranking general to doubt the efficacy of the doctrine was Galliéni, a pure colonial. He was led to challenge it as a result of his empirical and pragmatic outlook, the result of his colonial experiences.

Military critics looking beyond the period covered by this essay can cite the Indochina and Algerian wars of the post-World War II era as perfect examples of the perniciousness of the colonial influence on the French army and the ultimate proof that the acquisition of colonies had never been in France's best interests. One can reply, however, that since both possessions had been under civilian rule for many years (the Japanese occupation of Indochina notwithstanding) prior to the outbreaks of the wars that led to independence in both cases and that civilian, not military, misrule had led to these wars, it seems fatuous to blame the military. In Algeria in particular the military were summoned by the civilians to deal with an intolerable situation of civilian making.

In short, the question of colonial influences on the French army is a major and poorly understood one which merits further study in all its aspects.

NOTES

1. The author would like to thank the following individuals and institutions for the financial support which enabled him to undertake this project: the 1975 Fellowship Committee of the French Colonial Historical Society and Dr. Peter Duignan of the Hoover Institution on War, Revolution, and Peace; Dr. Richard M. Hunt and the 1976-1977 awards committees of the Andrew W. Mellon Faculty Fellowships in the Humanities at Harvard University. For many favors and much moral support the author would like to thank Dr. Lester Brown, Dr. Kariuki Karei, and Mary Smalls, formerly of Voorhees College, Katie Kozack, formerly administrative assistant to the director of the Andrew W. Mellon Faculty Fellowships at Harvard University, and Nancy Capron of Paris, France.

2. The changing and overlapping jurisdictions of French colonial defense and administration can be very confusing. The reader should bear in mind the following points while proceeding:

Modern France inherited from its pre-revolutionary past the practice of administering the colonies through the Naval Ministry (*Ministère de la Marine*); however, Algeria and then Morocco and Tunisia were excluded from this pattern of authority. Algeria from the start of the conquest through 1870 was an appendage of the Ministry of War except during the three-year period, 1857-1860, when it and the colonies, taken temporarily from the navy, came under the aegis of a Ministry of Algeria and the Colonies. In 1870 *colon* pressure and a general discrediting of military rule led to the transfer of Algeria to the jurisdiction of the Ministry of the Interior. However, the primary task of defending and garrisoning Algeria after 1870 fell as before to the Ministry of War and the regular French army.

Later, when Tunisia and Morocco entered the French colonial picture they did so as protectorates administered by the Ministry of Foreign Affairs. But they were attached militarily to Algeria, and their pre-existing armies, reorganized and affiliated with the indigenous troops of Algeria.

The colonies proper, which by the early nineteenth century had dwindled to a few scattered sugar islands, fishing stations, and coastal trading enclaves, were administered and garrisoned by the Naval Ministry almost as if they were ships at sea. The emancipation of slaves in France and its possessions in 1848, the policy of assimilation that would be followed thereafter, particularly in the "old" colonies, and the beginnings of territorial expansion in tropical Africa and Asia in the 1850s would lead after several experiments to the creation of a Ministry of Colonies in 1894.

The responsibility for colonial defense had been passed back and forth between the Ministry of War and the Naval Ministry since before the eighteenth century. In 1831, when the Naval Ministry had once again received responsibility for colonial defense, it assigned battalions of the newly created Naval Infantry and Naval Artillery to constitute small garrisons in each colony. When by 1856 all the Naval Infantry units had been removed from France's war vessels (they were replaced by the Naval Fusiliers) and assigned exclusively to colonial garrisons and French coastal bases (including Algerian ones), they formed, along with the Naval Artillery, the nucleus of a veritable colonial army.

As units of indigenous troops were created in each colony, they were attached to the naval troops. By 1900, all of them, French and indigenous, were reorganized and renamed the Colonial Army. Although this new organization was attached to the Ministry of War, it remained administratively separate from the regular army. The individual garrisons of each colony were put under the specific authority of their governors for certain purposes.

The Colonial Army continued to perform in France and North Africa the functions which had been assigned to the naval troops—coastal defense and the like. In addition, units of colonial troops might be lent for combat service to regular army units in North Africa. Such was the case during the conquest of Morocco. Likewise, elements of the Nineteenth Corps, the permanent regular army garrison of North Africa, might be lent to the colonies as occurred, for instance, during the conquests of Tonkin, Dahomey, and Madagascar.

From 1893 to 1914 over half the effectives of the naval/colonial troops were stationed in France (conscripts exclusively so) where they hardly performed any of the functions of a colonial army. On the other hand, the regular army garrison of Algeria did perform colonial tasks and included indigenous soldiers but was not officially considered a colonial army.

3. Charles-André Julien, *Histoire de l'Algérie contemporaine: la conquête et les débuts de la colonisation (1827-1871)*, (Paris: Presses Universitaires de France, 1964), p. 276.

4. Or so was the opinion of a young lieutenant in the engineers, Louis Faidherbe, writing from Mostaganem, sometime between 1843 and 1846. Faidherbe to his mother, personal letter fragment, Ogé-Lamoitier Private Papers, Paris.

5. Jean Gottmann, "Bugeaud, Galliéni, Lyautey: The Development of French Colonial Warfare," in *Makers of Modern Strategy: Military Thought from Machiavelli to Hitler*, eds. Edward Mead Earle, Gordon A. Craig, and Felix Gilbert (Princeton, N.J., Princeton University Press, 1944), p. 236.

6. Ibid., and Jean Regnault, "Les Campagnes d'Algérie et leur influence de 1830 à 1870," *Revue Historique de l'Armée*, special supplement on Algeria 2, no. 4 (1953): 28-30.

7. Julien, *Histoire de l'Algérie*, pp. 188-189.

8. In western Algeria where Bugeaud fought arduous campaigns in order to destroy Abd el-Kader's hegemony, he designated the interior points of Médéa, Miliana, Mascara, and Tlemcen, the latter two which his forces occupied in 1841 and 1842 respectively, as major interior bases. Each was well stocked and occupied by at least seven thousand troops. They were paired and connected by road with coastal bases, the first two with Algiers, the third with Mostaganem, and the fourth with Oran. There remained a gap to be filled in the large valley separating the Dahra coastal range and the interior Ouarsenis. So to fill it and to create a fortified center six days' march from Mostaganem, Mascara, Miliana, and Médéa, Bugeaud founded the large French post, Orléansville, near the Roman encampment of Castellum Tingitanum, called El-Esnam by the Algerians. It was connected by road to the port of Ténès, forty-five kilometers to the north.

He abandoned some of the other posts such as Fondouk in the Mitidja and all the posts between Bône and Constantine despite there being *colons* and allied indigenous Algerians nearby who depended upon these posts for protection. He was persuaded only with difficulty not to abandon Guelma and Sétif. Finally, he ordered the complete destruction of Abd el-Kader's capital, Tagdempt, and his other towns, Boghar and Taza, thus earning the opprobrium of the Arabist, Pélissier de Reynaud, for his "brutal idea, an idea of destruction." (Cited in Julien, *Histoire de l'Algérie*, p. 192).

9. [France, Ministère de la Guerre], *Les Armées françaises d'Outre-Mer*, sect. 1, "Histoire militaire des colonies, pays de protectorat et pays sous mandat," vol. 1; Paul Azan, *Conquête et Pacification de l'Algérie* (Paris: Villain et Bar, 1936), p. 492; and Julien, *Histoire de l'Algérie*, p. 202.

10. See his report, "De la stratégie, de la tactique, des retraites et du passage des défilés dans les montagnes des Kabyles," cited in Gottman, "Bugeaud, Galliéni, Lyautey," p. 237.

11. Julian, *Histoire l'Algérie*, p. 299.

12. René Gallissot and Gilbert Badia, *Marx, Marxisme et Algérie: Textes de Marx-Engels* (Paris: Union Générale des Editions, 1976), pp. 52-53; Julian, *Histoire de l'Algérie*, pp. 270-278; and Kanya-Forstner, *The Conquest of the Western Sudan: A Study in French Military Imperialism* (London: Cambridge University Press, 1969), p. 10.

13. Bugeaud to Esclaibes, 26 May 1838, *Lettres Inédites du Maréchal Bugeaud Duc d'Isly: 1808-1849*, ed. Captain Tattet (Paris: Emile-Paul, 1923), pp. 179–182.

14. Ibid., pp. 180-182.

15. Cited in Julien, *Histoire de l'Algérie*, p. 316.

16. This phrase was the title which the anti-colonial publicist, the Count of Herisson, chose to give to his edited publication of a young, unnamed lieutenant's diary of his years as a young officer in Algeria in the 1840s. It had generally been used to describe the European occupation of North America, but Herisson was struck by the similarities between it and the French conquest of Algeria. Maurice d'Hérisson, *La Chasse à l'homme: Guerre d'Algérie* (Paris, Ollendorf, 1891), p. x.

17. Faidherbe to Chasseloup-Laubat, 29 April 1864, and 18 May 1864, ser. Sénégal I 50b, Section Outre-Mer des Archives Nationales de France, Paris.

18. Kanya-Forstner, *Conquest*, pp. 8, 9, 14, 15, and 273.

19. Julien, *Histoire de l'Algérie*, p. 226.

20. Bugeaud to Genty de Busy, 15 January 1847, *Lettres Inédites*, ed. Tattet, pp. 296-297.

21. Cited in Julien, *Histoire de l'Algérie*, p. 337.

22. Hubert Lyautey, "Du Rôle colonial de l'Armée," *Revue des Deux Mondes* 157 (1900): 311 and 315.

23. Ibid.

24. Julien, *Histoire de l'Algérie*, p. 300; and Pierre Chalmin, *L'Officier français de 1815 à 1870*, Bibliothèque d'Histoire Economique et Sociale (Paris: Librairie Marcel Rivière et Cie., 1957), pp. 133-135.

25. Kanya-Forstner, *Conquest*, pp. 1-14.

26. Chalmin, *L'Officier*, p. 92; and Julien, *Histoire de l'Algérie*, pp. 299-301.

27. It is the opinion of the historian Brison Gooch that one cannot say that Saint-Arnaud received command of the Kabylie expedition solely because Louis Napoleon wished to use him in his contemplated coup d'etat. The plan for the expedition had already been made and its commander-in-chief approved before Fleury visited Algeria in the spring of 1851 to sound out Saint-Arnaud about the possibility of his playing the major role in the coup. Nevertheless, Saint-Arnaud seems to have known that he would be well rewarded if he undertook this expedition. An obscure participant in the Kabylie expedition, Captain Faidherbe, indicated in a letter to his mother not only that Saint-Arnaud was totally negligent in the way he had led the expedition but that he clearly was more

interested in the effect that it would have in Paris than in giving it any permanent results so far as the Kabylie was concerned. He ended the expedition abruptly on 18 July 1851 as soon as it had served his purpose. Shortly thereafter, Saint-Arnaud received his promotion and returned to France, soon to be named minister of war. Brison Gooch, *The New Bonapartist Generals in the Crimean War: Distrust and Decision-making in the Anglo-French Alliance* (The Hague: Martinus Nijhoff, 1959), p. 26; Julien, *Histoire de l'Algérie*, p. 387, and Faidherbe to his mother, 30 October 1851, Ogé-Lamoitier Private Papers, Paris.

28. David B. Ralston, *The Army of the Republic: The Place of the Military in the Political Evolution of France, 1871-1914* (Cambridge, Mass.: M.I.T. Press, 1967), pp. 47-48 and 136-137.

29. Dallas Irvine, "The French Discovery of Clausewitz and Napoleon," *Military Affairs* (formerly *Journal of the American Military Institute*) 4 (1941): 152-156.

30. Ibid., p. 140.

31. Charles Bugnet, *Mangin* (Paris: Plon, 1934), p. 88.

32. Virgil Matthew, "Joseph Simon Galliéni 1849-1916: Marshal of France" (Ph.D. dissertation, UCLA, 1967), pp. 394-401.

33. Contrary to his critics at the time, Joffre believed that his colonial experience made him more, rather than less, qualified to serve as generalissimo. He made the following comments to Lieutenant-Colonel Mayer:

—J'avais plus de titres que n'importe lequel de mes collègues, ayant seul commandé devant l'ennemi un groupement de troupes de toutes armes, ayant seul eu sous mes ordres un groupe d'armes.

—Ah! bah!...

—Oui: j'ai eu sous mes ordres une colonne de toutes armes au Tonkin—six mille hommes—et, pour l'exécution d'un exercice qui avait pour objet les services de l'arrière, j'ai dû concevoir la manoeuvre d'un group d'armées, pour faire réaliser cette conception sur le terrain. Or aucun membre du conseil supérieur de guerre n'a eu l'occasion d'en faire autant. [Cited in Emile Mayer, *Trois Maréchaux: Joffre, Galliéni, Foch* (Paris: Gallimard, 1928), p. 34].

34. Raoul Girardet, *La société militaire dans la France contemporaine, 1815-1939* (Paris: Plon, 1953), pp. 147-148.

35. Julien, *Histoire de l'Algérie*, p. 233.

36. Cited in ibid., p. 246.

37. Pagézy de Bourdéliac cited in Girardet, p. 149.

38. Girardet, p. 295.

39. Ibid., p. 303.

40. Lyautey, "Du Rôle colonial," pp. 324-325.

41. Cited in Matthew, "Joseph Simon Galliéni," p. 170.

42. Lyautey, cited in Matthew, "Joseph Simon Galliéni," p. 170.

43. Ibid., p. 237.

44. Cited in Girardet, pp. 307-309.

45. Ibid., p. 337.

46. André Demaison, *Faidherbe*, Les Grandes Figures coloniales (Paris: Plon, 1932), pp. 206, 215, and 216.

47. Matthew, "Joseph Simon Galliéni," p. 391.

48. Mayer, *Trois Maréchaux*, pp. 75-76.

49. Cited in Julien, *Histoire de l'Algérie*, p. 175.

50. Cited in Paul Azan, *L'Armée d'Afrique de 1830 à 1852* (Collection du centenaire de l'Algérie, 1830-1930), (Paris: Plon, 1936), p. 362.

51. Maxime Weygand, *Histoire de l'Armée française* (Paris: Flammarion, 1961), p. 278.

52. Mayer, *Trois Maréchaux*, p. 71.

53. Weil, ed., *Oeuvres militaires du Maréchal Bugeaud, Duc d'Isly, réunis et mis à jour* (Paris: Librairie Militaire de L. Baudoin et Cie.), p. 49.

54. Ibid.

55. Mayer, *Trois Maréchaux*, p. 71.

56. Irvine, p. 164.

57. Colonel Ardant du Picq, *Etudes sur le combat: combat antique et combat moderne*, 8th ed. (Paris: Chapelot, 1914), p. 100.

58. Ibid.

59. Stefan T. Possony and Etienne Mantoux, "Du Picq and Foch: The French School," in *Makers of Modern Strategy*, ed. Earle, Craig, and Gilbert, pp. 216-217.

60. Irvine, pp. 160-161.

61. Foch, cited in Basil Liddell-Hart, *Reputations* (London: John Murray, 1928), p. 160.

62. Louis de Grandmaison, *Deux Conférences faites aux officiers de l'état-major de l'armée* (Paris: Berger-Levrault, 1912), p. 27.

63. Ibid., p. 28.

64. Cited in Barbara Tuchman, *The Guns of August* (New York: Dell Books, 1962), p. 51.

65. Cited in Liddell-Hart, *Reputations*, p. 162.

66. Cited in Girardet, p. 380.

67. Ibid.

68. Ibid., pp. 113-114. The practice of avoiding difficult decisions by relying on the ability of soldiers to muddle through still seems to be part of Western military strategy. A recent article on the NATO alliance in the *New Republic* (October 7, 1978) stressed the lack of unity among the various national armies comprising it. "One German officer declared that NATO is such a mess, the only thing that will save it in a war is the responsibility of the soldiers to disobey their orders."

69. Louis Jules Trochu, *Oeuvres Posthumes* (Tours: Alfred Mame, 1896), 2: 295.

70. Ibid., p. 290.

71. Azan, *Conquête et Pacification*, p. 506.

72. Montagnac, as cited in Julien, *Histoire de l'Algérie*, p. 202.

73. Pierre Chalmin, *L'officier français de 1815 à 1870* (Paris: M. Rivière, 1957), p. 28.

74. Général Charles-Antoine Thoumas, *Les transformations de l'armée française, essais d'histoire et de critique sur l'état militaire de la France* (Paris: Bérger-Levrault, 1887), 2: 632.

75. Mayer, *Trois Maréchaux*, p. 78.

76. Ibid., p. 164.

77. General Alexandre Percin, *Le Massacre do notre infanterie: 1914-1918* (Paris: Albin-Michel, 1921).

78. Charles Mangin, *Lettres de Guerre: 1914-1918* (Paris: Librairie Arthème Fayard, 1950), and Matthew, "Joseph Simon Galliéni," pp. 561-562. After the war when Foch

wrote his memoirs, he attributed the *offensive à outrance* doctrine to false deductions taken from "maneuvers and colonial expeditions." Ferdinand Foch, *Mémoires pour servir à l'histoire de la guerre de 1914-1918*, vol. 1 (Paris: Plon, 1931).

79. Cited in Azan, *L'Armée d'Afrique*, p. 268.

80. Maréchal Esprit de Castellane, *Journal du Maréchal de Castellane, 1804-1862* . . . (Publié par la comtesse de Beaulaincourt, née Castellane, et le P. Le Brethon), (Paris: E. Plon, Nourrit et Cie, 1895-1897), 3: 402-406.

81. Henri Gouraud, *Au Soudan* (Paris: Pierre Tisné, 1939), p. 181.

82. Louis Faidherbe, personal dossier, Naval Ministry, Archives Nationales de France, Paris.

83. Lyautey, "Du Rôle colonial," p. 322.

84. Girardet, p. 308.

85. Chalmin, *L'Officier*, p. 282.

86. *Histoire et Epopée*, p. 100.

87. Charles Du Barail, *Mes Souvenirs*, Vol. 1, (Paris: Plon, 1894), pp. 158-159.

88. Julien, *Histoire de l'Algérie*, p. 295.

89. Several other Algerian expressions which came into common use in France through the influence of the Army of Africa were *kif-kif* or *c'est du kif*, meaning "both choices are equal"; *bled*, to designate a small, isolated rural community; and *smala*, the entourage and family of an Algerian potentate, to designate anyone's large and cumbersome family.

90. Colas to Minister of War, 14 April 1871, in Faidherbe personal dossier, Ministry of War, Archives de l'Armée, Vincennes (France).

91. Matthew, "Joseph Simon Galliéni," pp. 320-324.

92. Louis Faidherbe, *Campagne de l'Armée du Nord* (Paris, 1871), pp. 95-97.

93. Thoumas, vol. 2, p. 306.

94. Ibid., pp. 391-394.

95. Michael Howard, *The Franco-Prussian War; the German invasion of France, 1870-1871* (London: R. Hart-Davis, 1961) p. 80.

96. Ibid., p. 309.

97. Cited in Bugnet, p. 152.

98. Cited in ibid., p. 144. In a sense, however, Pétain had the last word. He remained in excellent health and physical condition throughout his life and died in 1951 at the age of ninety-five. When Mangin died suddenly in 1925, he was only fifty-nine.

99. Pétain cited in Bugnet, p. 248.

100. Général Charles-M.-E. Mangin, *Comment finit la guerre* . . . (Paris: Plon-Nourrit, 1920), pp. 138-153 and 247.

101. Mangin, *La Force noire* (Paris: Hachette, 1910), pp. 88-89.

CHARLES BALESI

5

West African Influence on the French Army of World War I

The impact of the French military on Africa is relatively easy to examine, if not to measure. In contrast, measuring the influence of Africa on the French military is an elusive task. This essay deals with this task, focusing on the effects of the African experience on French military doctrine on the eve of World War I.

The beginning of French military involvement with Africa can be dated precisely to the organization on September 15, 1763, of the *Corps des Laptots de Gorée*, an auxiliary unit created to assist the marines in protecting France's modest outposts on the Senegalese coast. Yet, a century after France had lost most of its overseas possessions to England, it was from this unlikely starting point that it would rebuild a second, larger colonial empire. By the mid-1830s, the increase in colonial holdings in Algeria led the French command to recruit local troops, which were constituted into new corps, bearing exotic names which appealed to the imagination of the metropole. There were the *spahis*, the *zouaves*, and the *tirailleurs* who came to join the *chasseurs d'Afrique* and *légionnaires* in the conquest of North Africa. In West Africa, the first Black regulars appeared on the scene in 1838 when a royal decree ordered the formation of a company of *tirailleurs sénégalais*, which was to be attached to the Battalion of Marine Infantry of Senegal. From that day forward, the French Black troops continued to grow in size and in importance.

After the disaster of 1871 at the hands of the Prussian military machine, the Parisians could see morale-boosting detachments of colonial troops during the annual Bastille Day parade, while the rest of the nation read enthusiastic accounts in the provincial press.[1] During the last three decades of the nineteenth century, the growth in popularity of colonial campaigns seemed to lessen the humiliation of Sedan and the pain of the loss of Alsace and Lorraine. Young men who volunteered for the *troupes de marine* returned years later to their hometowns with the prestige of conquerors and were feted at the local *café du commerce*. They, too, had their part in the surreptitious shift of attention from the *ligne bleue des Vosges* (the mountain skyline which had become the new border with Germany) to unbounded colonial horizons.

First on these horizons, the conquest of Algeria was accomplished while military concepts were still rooted in the eighteenth century—and its harsh geographic environment was no surprise to an army which had known war in Spain, Portugal, southern Italy, and even Egypt in 1799. The absorption of Tunisia in 1881 had been a pure *promenade militaire*. Only the campaigns of the 1870s through the early 1900s in Black Africa and Morocco presented clearly different circumstances, circumstances which in turn had their effect on the participating French officers.

The French conquest of Africa—and for that matter, of all colonial territories— had the advantage of being spearheaded by a generally superior type of officer and non-commissioned officer, who in turn schooled their African levies with extraordinary success. The choice of a colonial military life had various motivations. Some, such as Lyautey, had escaped the ennui of French garrisons; another, Mangin, the future father of the *Force noire*, for example, had problems right from the start with rigid barracks regulations. For a Péroz, it was thirst for adventure; for many, faster advancement. Regardless of the circumstances which led them to overseas service, they had to fit the particular mold of the colonial officer, that is to say, they had to serve as instructors, schoolteachers, builders, diplomats, administrators, and sometimes soldiers, all at once, improvising with their own resourcefulness and the resources of the land they occupied. A French scholar in the field of military sociology, Jean-Paul Charnay, put it succinctly:

As a direct result, a segment of the army, the segment which served overseas . . . developed a particular mentality, habits of greater independence towards representatives of the civilian power . . . *la fonction crée l'organe* (the role creates the instrument).[2]

Officers had to show *élan*, a mixture of dash, impetus, enthusiasm; those who did not were shipped home by their *commandants supérieurs*, and quickly indeed if these commanders happened to be Galliéni or Archinard.

In the West African Sudan the French had, in addition to the rolling countryside of eastern France, a large terrain to rehearse the eventual war of revenge—*la revanche*—against Germany. However, the opportunity to apply military science in more realistic conditions than those of the *Grandes manoeuvres* did not meet with a completely favorable reception. The officers who chose to remain in the metropolitan army during their career regarded those who left for overseas postings as amateurs, whose sporting interest surpassed their commitment to preparing for the next war against Germany. In turn, the colonial officers, full of their own experiences, saw the metropolitans as useless theoreticians,[3] and answered the accusation of neglecting the Rhine for the Niger and the Congo by reaffirming at every opportunity their determination to meet the Germans in battle.[4]

Metropolitan or colonial, the French officer of the Third Republic certainly displayed a different attitude toward his profession from the officer of the Second Empire; the defeat of 1871 had brought a brutal end to the complacency into which the military establishment had sunk since 1815. In *Les Officiers*, a book published in 1960 as part of a historical survey of professional groups in France, the author observed:

The intellectual level of the French officer was generally superior between 1871 and 1914 to what it had been before the defeat. Galliéni kept, alternately in German, English, and Italian, what he called his *Erinnerungen of My Life di Ragazzo* (Memories of My Boyhood), where he showed an early interest in the campaigns of the British against the Ashanti, the Dutch in Sumatra, and the American General Stanley in Yellowstone. He learned Russian, *all* subjects interested him, everyday he needed his "brain bath."[5]

To quote another author who made a thorough study of the modern French army's political history:

Everywhere in the Army a veritable passion sprang up for military studies, for the history of warfare, and for the problems of strategy, tactics, and materiel.... Several periodicals were founded that specialized in military questions (*La Revue d'Histoire, Progres, Spectateur*) and the general press began to publish regular accounts of military matters.[6]

This military revival owed much to the stability enjoyed by the General Staff; in 1872 it had been reorganized along lines designed to make it independent of political pressures and changes. Politicians, from monarchists to radical socialists, were "both fully-conscious that public opinion remained passionately attached to the army and that the sole mission was to prepare France against the eventuality of a new conflict with the German Empire."[7]

Between 1883 and 1900, the major French campaigns in West Africa were conducted against five leading adversaries: Mahmadou-Lamine, Ahmadou, Samory, Béhanzin, and Rabah. These were leaders who had no formal military education and who depended on inferior and heteroclite armaments.[8] On the other hand, they had the advantage of superior numbers, extreme mobility, and of followers who showed a great determination and endurance. Yet, the outcome during these campaigns was monotonously the same: they lost battle after battle, usually to French troops about one-tenth the size of their armies.[9] The questions that arise, then, are the following: (1) What theories were espoused by the French colonial officers? and (2) what part did the Africans play in the development of these theories?

Of all the French officers who have written about the African campaigns, Marie-Etienne Péroz is by far the author who made the most detailed analysis of the factors for achieving victory in Africa when fighting native armies. In a book which began as a critical essay on an Italian colonel's work regarding tactics used in Eritrea and Upper Egypt, *La tactique dans le Soudan: quelques combats et épisodes de guerre remarquables*, Péroz examined errors and proposed remedies which he backed up with accounts of pertinent examples.[10] As the author saw it, the basic tactical procedure of large African armies in the Sahel was a division into three corps: an advance guard which engaged in frontal attack, and two flanks which would attempt to surround the enemy. Because the French were always outnumbered at least four to one, more often ten to one, any hesitation or loss of composure on the part of the officer in command was bound to be fatal. Consequently, during engagements, French troops observed strict firing discipline. Péroz wrote, "Firing at long distances must be forbidden to the artillery as well as to the infantry."[11] When the enemy's frontal attack would begin to lose impetus, the commanding officer must order bayonet counterattack. Péroz criticized strongly the lack of energetic use of *combat offensif*, emphasizing the psychological dangers of artificial defenses and involved entrenchments so favored by the Italians.[12] He also faulted the use of heavy columns, which were slowed down by hundreds of porters who had to be supervised and protected. He advised, instead, the classic French progression in square formation with lightly equipped scouts on all sides, while "The British dragged behind them approximately 200 pounds of baggage and supplies per man. Our column...never carried more than 30 pounds.[13] Péroz corrrectly foresaw the success some six years later of Marchand's expedition which traveled from the Atlantic seaboard to Fashoda on the Nile without the loss of a single man in combat:

We have read and we have often heard that 200 energetic men, well-commanded, amply supplied with ammunition, and well-in-hand of a completely self-controlled leader who is knowledgeable in the various aspects of African warfare, should be able to cross Africa in any direction without being defeated.[14]

Seventeen years later, a British officer, Lieutenant-Colonel Heneker, who wrote on the same subject of warfare in Africa, listed as standard procedure the system of "clearing volleys," where British columns systematically fired upon any dense vegetation encountered along the way. Heneker admitted that, "at...Dompoassi, 400 men firing 40,000 rounds in two and one-half hours had affected nothing."[15]

Famous lines have been written about colonial conquest by the Maxim gun. They could not have been more misapplied than to the French, who not only did not issue machine guns to their colonial troops, but paid dearly in the fall of 1914 for ignoring their impact in Europe as well.[16] The French, however, did use some artillery with the largest columns, mainly mountain guns, but found them to be more a nuisance than an effective weapon. Once the element of surprise wore off, the *sofas* took artillery fire in their stride[17] An anecdote from my own book on Black troops in the French army illustrates this point:

The psychological effect of the artillery was nil and its destructive power against which the rudimentary fortifications of the Africans were expected to be of no account, extremely limited. But perhaps of all the appreciations of the effect of guns in African warfare, the simplest and most powerful was the one given by a *sofa* captured after the engagement of Diaman-ko (January 1891). Shown a Lebel rifle and asked by Lieutenant-colonel Humbert, " 'Do you know what this is?' The *sofa* answered: 'When this touches me this death.' The colonel then turned about and rather dramatically unveiled a gun; unperturbed, the *sofa* shook his head and gravely replied: 'This, much noise, but never kills anyone.' "[18]

However, the same African armies, which invariably gave an honest account of themselves under artillery fire, broke when faced with French bayonet charges. All the literature—formal studies as well as entertaining memoirs—by French officers writing about war in West Africa agreed on the absolute superiority of bayonets over cannons.[19] In a voluminous study published in 1911, appropriately entitled *Le Tirailleur soudanais*, Captain Marceau summarized their thoughts on the subject in a concise axiom: "In Africa, more than anywhere else, naked steel is the *ultima ratio*."[20] This was not a reflection on the bravery of the Africans. Indeed, if there was also another unanimous opinion from the pen of the French, it concerned the heroism of their adversaries and their calm acceptance of death and defeat.[21] However brave the Africans were, even in instances where they had the help of deserters and Europeans and access to modern weapons, they were still able to reverse the outcome.[22] Péroz singled out the lack of training and good leadership as the essential reason for African defeat: "These *sofas* are really brave people. . . . Anyway they are the same men as our *tirailleurs* and *spahis*, only not well-trained and poorly led. This alone is the secret of their inferiority."[23]

Clearly, the French colonial officers learned rapidly to modify and refine their classical military education from the contact with their African armies in close-range combat; they also recognized very early in the conquest the importance of mobility as opposed to the false security of heavy supply convoys maintained close at hand. They learned to rely on products of the land, as scarce as they were, and on the endurance of their troops rather than on the diligence of quartermasters; that large armies surprised are armies defeated, that light, movable columns are better tools for victory than strongly garrisoned fortresses. We must express here a caveat: Africans were teachers of strategy to the French in spite of themselves. The French learned from the African leaders as much as from their own military educations. What the Sudan did in fact for the French colonial officers was to release them from the bondage of rigorous manuals. As mentioned above, the need to improvise and the need to adapt justified the *commandants supérieurs'* total disregard for regulations. To find Samory, or any of the other African leaders, to destroy their supplies, to win over their allies, made such disregard a *sine qua non* condition of warfare. In fact, the French officers in Africa purely and simply returned to Napoleonic tactics.

When several generations of colonial officers who had experienced combat not only in Africa but also—as in the case of Galliéni—in Indochina and in Madagascar, eventually returned to metropolitan postings, their opinions could not be ignored. In matters of tactics, Africa had taught them disdain for artillery, the cult of the bayonet, a trust in *élan* rather than in entrenchment, and perhaps also the arrogance of conquerors. The German foe, drilled in military life from cradle to grave, could hardly have been compared to the *sofa*; yet, the French colonial officers saw some similarity between the fanatically obedient, armed masses which attacked them in the Sabel in the name of their Almamy and the obedient masses of spike-helmeted Prussians, ready to die for their kaiser. Ironically, their views happened to coincide with the theory of *attaque à outrance*, or "continuous attack," which developed in the 1880s to become the supreme doctrine of the French General Staff on the eve of World War I.

In 1883, a newly appointed professor of tactics at the *Ecole Supérieure de Guerre* (equivalent to the War College), Major (later General) Louis Maillard, adopted as his own the concept that "to make war is to attack." This theory had in fact been originated that same year by the German military writer Von der Goltz. Maillard died in 1901, but his teachings were spread by two assistants, themselves later successively professors and directors of the *école*, Hippolyte Langlois and Henri Bonnal who had been a colonial officer in Indochina. Although *attaque à outrance* had its detractors, it gained ground rapidly. Ferdinand Foch—the future generalissimo of the Allied armies—who, as a young subaltern had been a student and later as general became director of the *école* in 1908, was a strong supporter of "offensive over defense as the means of victory."[24] But the most important proponent of the offensive was a colonial officer himself, Joseph Joffre, who had served in Indochina, West Africa (where he commanded the column which occupied Timbuktu), and Madagascar. Member of the *Conseil supérieur de la guerre* in 1910, chief of General Staff in 1911, he was to command the French armies in August 1914. It was then not surprising that:

In the ten years that preceded World War I, this whole generation of colonial officers came to occupy the Army's highest posts. Joffre may have played a decisive part in their advancement. He had a natural tendency to favor the officers from the overseas forces, for he knew that their service records, in the Colonial Army, were more outstanding or more convincing than the careers that the officers remaining in metropolitan France had tranquilly traversed. Galliéni acted in the same way. Little by little, the Army's upper echelons came to be populated by colonial officers. Just before war broke out, if we except Joffre and Galliéni, most of these officers were not yet in positions of the highest importance. But after the first few weeks of combat when the hour had come to make a pitiless selection among the general officers, Joffre gave most of the important commands to those whose careers had been spent overseas. Among them were Henrys, Guillaumat, Degoutte, Mangin, Gouraud and Franchet d'Esperey. In political circles there never arose the same prejudice against these men that still persisted against the generals from the "Jesuit warren."[25]

To these names we should add Archinard (who later organized the Polish army), Marchand, Largeau, and Baratier; the last two were killed while leading their respective divisions of colonial troops.

In 1917, three years after the ''Guns of August'' had inaugurated the age of industrial warfare with the decimation of hundreds of thousands of men, an American author reviewing for a military journal a book written by a veteran of the Moroccan campaign could still write that:

When one reads the description of those rare and longed-for moments when the French have their chance to rush in with the weapon that does not depend on supply trains, that does not wait to be reloaded, that cannot miss at close quarters—the ''arme blanche'', [bayonet] venerable, but ever young—one feels that one has been vouchsafed a flash of insight into the miracles of the Marne, of Verdun, and Chemin des Dames. Distant, obscure, unimportant as such a campaign as this may seem, Colonel Azan makes us realize that during the years of European peace, Africa was a great laboratory for the preparation of victories to come.[26]

An amazing comment, considering that France had lost 955,000 men, killed, wounded, or captured in 1914; 1,430,000 in 1915; 900,000 in 1916, and 546,000 in 1917. Included in these figures for 1914 were ten elite battalions of *tirailleurs sénégalais* annihilated in Belgium between October 25 and November 16. These ten battalions were the first manifestation of the participation of a quarter-million Black troops in the French war effort.

The idea of incorporating a large Black contingent into the French army first appeared in print in a nationalistic novel published in 1899;[27] reading the novel inspired a young colonial officer who had shared the glories and frustrations of the Fashoda expedition: Charles Mangin.[28] Eleven years later, in 1911, Mangin published *La Force noire*, the most controversial work dealing with French military questions since Lyautey's article on the social role of officers.[29] The debate which then engulfed France over the wisdom or the folly of recruiting and even drafting several regiments of Black African soldiers can only be mentioned here; suffice it to say that the Left saw the use of Black troops as a threat to the working class while the Right had images of German heads neatly cut off by the Senegalese.[30]. The different governments which ran France during the brief period of 1911 to 1914, pursued a middle-of-the-road policy, recruiting a few thousand more Blacks than warranted for the security of West and North Africa, the declining birth rate in France being the real spur in this issue.

After the initial shock of fall 1914, recruitment in West Africa was conducted at a very slow pace, due to a disenchantment over the destruction of the ten battalions mentioned above. But by September 1915 the incredibly high number of French casualties began to threaten the very ability of France to pursue the war. The General Staff, desperate for fresh troops, and remembering the promises of Mangin's book, ordered Clozel, the governor-general of *Afrique Occidentale Française*, to recruit 50,000 men without delay.

The Black troops brought to Europe were submitted to a different regime than their metropolitan comrades-in-arms. They were amalgamated into White units at battalion and often company level and benefited from the system of *hivernage* (from the French *hiver*, "winter"), which removed them from the front to southern France from October to May. Amalgamation was inspired by the General Staff's fear that hastily trained Africans with no previous close contact with Europeans would break under modern conditions of warfare. *Hivernage* was the direct result of the intense lobby of the *député* of Senegal, Blaise Diagne, on behalf of the Black troops for conditions to ease their adaptation to colder climates.

From strictly a tactical point of view, Black troops were utilized in circumstances not at all different from White or North African contingents. Contrary to common belief, the rate of attrition was not any higher in regiments of *tirailleurs* than in any other units. Standardized amalgamation with White units would have made the utilization of Blacks as "cannon fodder" impossible; further, their removal from the front for six to seven months out of the year statistically increased the odds in favor of survival in Senegalese troops. Therefore, as a whole, troops from Black Africa represented another comparatively limited positive factor for the French, but tactically speaking, their role and influence were not any different from any other similar contingent of the same size. In fact, their presence was often seen negatively by commanders of army corps and divisions who had to worry about their replacement during half of the year.

Not until 1918, when Mangin convinced General Foch and Clemenceau, the head of the government, that he could pierce the German lines with a massive thrust (with no artillery preparation) conducted by a corps composed uniquely of French and African colonial troops, did the impact of past West African campaigns and Black military valor exercise a maximum effect on the conduct of the war. "Sidi Bayonet," as Mangin had been nicknamed, had already proven on a smaller scale that war conditions had changed sufficiently to warrant a return to the surprise use of cold steel:

On August 30, 1918, the Direction of Colonial Troops had completed the project of organization of shock troops which was submitted to the general staff. Ten divisions *mixtes sénégalaises* were to be created with...regiments each including 1,485 Europeans and 1,341 Africans.[31]

Unknown to all protagonists, the war was nearing an end, and hostilities ceased before the shock army became operational.

Never had a European nation since the Roman Empire brought to its soil for the purpose of serving in its armies such a large number of soldiers from overseas. In the relatively narrow confines of the French territory (even more reduced by the infringement of war), the legions of black soldiers maintained a high level of visibility as the African component in the colonial empire of the Third Republic. The impact of Africa on World War I went far beyond tactics and the availability of effectives. It reached the emotional makeup of the nation, for the French reacted with affection and pride to the presence of Blacks in the metropole, childishly attributing to them all sorts of mystical military virtues. The myth of France as a nation of 100 million, from the northern sea to the equator, with an army of proportionate size, found a renewed energy through the image of Black regiments marching on the Rhine.[32] For the Germans, the myth attained even greater proportions as they cultivated irrational notions of unmitigated Black savagery.

The recruitment of this *Force noire* became then more than a game of numbers between the French and German general staffs. In the days when "propaganda" had yet to become an official part of the arsenals of nations, the picture of thousands of Blacks from Africa's interior, brought into the mainstream of civilization by France's *mission civilisatrice*, evoked a formidable psychological response from the Germans, ever expecting French decadence and anticipating its final fall. Thus, Black troops, seen by the French of 1918 not as mercenaries but as newly adopted children, continued, until 1940, to feel the myth of the invincible *Levée en masse*, born of the Revolution and against which the meticulous war machine of the Germans would be proven useless.

The French would probably have behaved as they did during the first months of World War I, with that wasted display of *élan* against machine gun concentrations and artillery barrages, regardless of their involvement in colonial wars. However, the tactical demands of the African campaigns, the type of warfare that Africans imposed on colonial troops, and the aptitude shown by these Africans once in French uniform reinforced military theories as developed in the aftermath of the Franco-Prussian War.

The famous long, triangular French bayonet had become the most unlikely bridge between Africa and Europe.

NOTES

1. The *tirailleurs sénégalais* were seen in Paris for the first time on July 14, 1899; they were the soldiers of the *Mission Marchand*, just returned from Fashoda.

2. Jean-Paul Charnay, *Société Militaire et suffrage politique en France depuis 1789*, Bibliothèque générale de l'école des Hautes Etudes, VIᵉ section (Paris, 1964), p. 56.

3. The rivalry between the two orientations, metropolitan and colonial, is illustrated by Captain (later General) Baratier's comments: "The newspapers which treat colonial battles with great emphasis are often read with a smile in France. I have myself often shrugged when seeing the word 'battle' applied to circumstances where the French had insignificant losses." However, once in the Sudan, he realized that "one fought and died in silence to avoid stirring public opinion." [*A travers l'Afrique* (Paris: Arthème Fayard, 1910), p. 89.] General Gouraud in *Zinder Tchad: souvenirs d'un Africain* (Paris: Plon, 1944), p. 132, recalled a discussion related to this rivalry with a fellow officer in a Paris cafe. Vincent Monteil also included in his study a story told by General Lyautey:

in a speech at the Sorbonne in 1923, [of] how he was greeted after nine years of colonial absence by a man who occupied one of the most important positions in our General Staff: he told me, "Finally you are coming back, you are re-entering the army!" "General, I have never left it." "Oh, for the past nine years you were a tourist." "Nine years ago I had never heard a shot, while for the past nine years, I have not spent a year without hearing fire." "Oh, shots from Negroes' rifles." "Yes, but they will kill anyway, sir."

[*Les Officiers* (Paris: Editions du Seuil, 1960), p. 37.]

Accusations claiming colonial officers to be incapable of European warfare are discussed and disputed by Paul Patureau in *L'armée coloniale*, a thesis for a Doctorate of Political Sciences (Paris: Arthur Rousseau, 1903); see pp. 96-98.

4. General Charles Mangin described the instance where Colonel Louis Archinard took leave of his staff; Archinard emphasized this commitment: "Struck by a grave attack of hepatitis, the Colonel had crossed the Niger on a stretcher and it was around his stretcher that he gathered all of us for his farewell. . . . The Colonel reminded us of the grandeur of the task we were pursuing in the Sudan . . . then, suddenly, he conjured up the European battlefields where he made an appointment to meet us." [Charles Mangin, *La Force noire*, Dedication to General Archinard, p. v (Paris: Librairie Hachette, 1910)]. The scene, which took place at Kankan, Sudan, April 12, 1891, is also mentioned by Gabriel Hanotaux in *Le Général Mangin* (Paris: Plon, 1925), pp. 40-41, and in "Le Général Mangin," *Revue des Deux Mondes*, June 15, 1925, p. 729. See also a similar feeling expressed by a dying officer, January 1881, reported by Edgar Malfere, ed., *L'épopée coloniale en Afrique Occidentale Française* (Paris, 1938), p. 100.

5. Vincent Monteil, *Les Officiers*, p. 31. David Ralston, dealing with the same period, quoted an excerpt from an older work which summarized well the attitudes of the French officers: "The French army was far more distinctly professional and therefore the interests of the officers were more immediately effective in army organization and doctrine." [*The Army of the Republic, the Place of the Military in Political Evolution of French, 1871-1914* (Cambridge, Mass.: M.I.T. Press, 1967), p. 58, quoting A. Vagts, *Militarism: A History* (New York: Norton, 1937), p. 240.]

6. Paul-Marie de la Gorce, *The French Army: A Military Political History*, trans. Kenneth Douglas (New York: George Braziller, 1963), p. 9.

7. Ibid., p. 6.

8. On Samory's armaments, see Martin Legassick, "Firearms, Horses and Samorian Army Organization: 1870-1898," *Journal of African History* 7, no. 50 (1966); on Rabah's army, see Pierre Gentil, *La Conquête du Tchad (1894-1916)*, 2 vols. (Vincennes: Ministère de la Défense Nationale, 1971). Samory and Béhanzin both received contraband armaments from other European powers, namely Britain and Germany. Concerning this curious aspect of colonial rivalry, see James J. Cooke, "Anglo-French Diplomacy and Contraband Arms Trade in Colonial Africa, 1894-1897," *African Studies Review* 18, no. 1 (April 1974): pp. 27-41. See also Jean Bern, contemporary of the conquest of Dahomey, *L'Expédition du Dahomey (Août-Decembre 1892): Notes ésparses d'un volontaire* (Sidi-Bel-Abbès, Algeria: Charles Lavenue, 1893), and Major Grandin, *A l'assaut du pays des noirs: Le Dahomey* (Paris: Haton, 1895).

9. For example, the combat of Kalé in 1890 where Captain Ruault and sixty *tirailleurs* attempting to progress toward Nioro faced two thousand of Ahmadou's *sofas*; see Charles Mangin, *Lettres de Soudan* (Paris: Edition des Portiques, 1930), pp. 71, 92.

10. Captain Marie-Etienne Péroz, *La Tactique dans le Soudan; quelques combats et*

épisodes de guerre remarquables (Paris: Librairie Militaire Beaudoin, 1890), quoting and analyzing Colonel Luciano, former chief of staff of General Baldissera during the Italian campaign in East Africa, 1887–1888, from *Rivista militare* (Rome, 1890).

11. Péroz, *La Tactique*, p. 46; see also General Joseph Galliéni, *Une colonne dans le Soudan français (1886-1887)* (Paris: R. Chapelot, 1905), "Fire should never begin at long range," p. 57; Mangin, *La Force noire*, p. 198, quoting Colonel Humbert's report on the combat of Sambiko and Diaman-ko: "Our firing discipline is remarkable; salvos are executed as during drills, therefore, consumption of ammunition is not considerable."

12. Péroz, *La Tactique*, pp. 41-42, fn. 1. The British, like the Italians, believed in reinforced entrenchments against African attacks; see Lieutenant-Colonel W.C.G. Heneker, *Bush Warfare* (London: Hugh Rees, 1907), p. 107.

13. Péroz, *La Tactique*, p. 24, fn. 1.

14. Ibid., p. 52.

15. Heneker, *Bush Warfare*, p. 6. The British system of using clearing volleys rather than scouts proved to be a complete failure in the Sierra Leone rebellion (1898) and at Karina (1897) as well as during the Benin expedition of 1897 and the Benin Territories expedition of 1899, p. 334.

16. In 1910 a pamphlet summarizing the role of machine guns in the French army amply demonstrated the reluctance of the General Staff to use this relatively new weapon. It seems incredible that only four years before World War I "The French army has not yet published a regulations book on machine guns." Lieutenant Amiel, *Etude sur la mitrailleuse et son emploi tactique* (Paris: R. Chapelot, 1910), p. 12.

17. Péroz told of the reaction of Samory's *sofas* at the battle of Kéniera, February 25, 1882, against a column led by Lieutenant-Colonel Bornis-Desbordes: "At the first gun shots, the *sofas* of Samory, although 10,000 in number, unaccustomed to this noisy language, gave way without fighting," but a few days later, "Samory...recovered from his alarm, gathered his warriors." [Péroz, *Au Soudan*, p. 10]. The incident is also related by Lieutenant-Colonel Mordacq, *Les Spahis soudanais* (Paris: Lavauzelle, 1912), p. 29.

18. Charles J. Balesi, *From Adversary to Comrades-in-arms: West Africans and the French Military 1885-1918* (Waltham, Mass.: Crossroads Press, Brandeis University, 1979), p. 20, quoting Baratier, *A travers l'Afrique*, p. 59. On the poor effects of artillery fire on Africans, see Edouard Thiriet, *Au Soudan français, Souvenirs, 1892-1894; Macina-Tombouctou* (Paris: Andre Lesot, 1932), p. 129; Mangin, *La Force noire*, p. 193; François Descostes, *Au Soudan, (1890–1891); Souvenirs d'un tirailleur sénégalais d'après sa corespondance inédite, extraits du "Correspondant"* (Paris: Picard et Perrin, 1893), p. 59; Péroz, *La Tactique*, p. 145.

19. Péroz, *Au Soudan français: Souvenirs de guerre et de mission* (Paris: Calmann-Levy, 1899), p. 282; Marie-Etienne Péroz, *Au Niger, Récits de campagnes: 1891-1892* (Paris: Calmann-Lévy, 1895), p. 32; *Par vocation: Vie et adventures d'un soldat de fortune 1870-1895* (Paris: Calmann-Lévy, n.d.); Colonel Henri Frey, *Campagne dans le Haut-Sénégal et dans le Haut-Niger 1885–1886* (Paris: Plon, 1888), p. 340.

20. Captain Marceau, *Le Tirailleur soudanais* (Paris: Berger-Levrault, 1911), p. 61.

21. Among many, see Descostes, *Au Soudan*; Frey, *Campagne dans le Haut Sénégal*; Péroz, *Au Soudan*; Thiriet, *Au Soudan français*; Péroz, *Au Niger*; General Henri-Eugène Gouraud, *Au Soudan, Souvenirs d'un Africain* (Paris: Pierre Tisné, 1939); Bern, *L'Expédition*; see also the works of Albert Baratier and Charles Mangin.

22. Péroz, *Au Niger*, p. 192.

23. See Grandin, *Le Dahomey*; also, Cooke, "Anglo-French Diplomacy and Contra-

band Arms Trade in Colonial Africa, 1894-1897.'' For the recruitment of deserters by African leaders, see Mangin, *Lettres du Soudan*; Baratier, *A travers l'Afrique* and *Epopées Africaines* (Paris: Perrin, 1913); Péroz, *Au Soudan, Au Niger*; Frey, *Campagne dans le Haut-Sénégal*.

24. Ralston, *The Army*, p. 350.

25. Gorce, *The French Army*, p. 89.

26. Book review of Paul Azan's *Souvenirs de Casablanca* (Paris: Hachette, 1911) in *The Military Historian and Economist*, July 1917, pp. 351-353. In his novel, *Les Hommes de bonne volonté*, vol. 16, *Verdun* (Paris: Flammarion, 1938), Jules Romains gives an ironic account of the almost divine power attributed to the bayonet: during the battle of Verdun two junior officers engaged in a comic routine at the expense of the French command's "famous recipe" for victory,

"Do you know this recipe?" "Yes, of course." "Pay close attention.... You throw yourself into the ranks of the enemy." "Yes." "Are you with me?" "Absolutely!" "And you cut through the maze," Jerphanion continued after a suspenseful pause, "with cold steel." "With cold steel, but that is wonderful!" exclaimed Fabre, feigning intense admiration.... Both then exploded into laughter. This was one of the latest routines they had invented. [pp. 101-102.]

See also an article published by a French writer in the United States during World War I, Emile Laloy, "French Military Theory," *The Military Historian and Economist*, vol. 2, July 1917, (Cambridge: Harvard University Press), pp. 267-286.

27. Viscount Emmanuel Melchoir de Vogüé, *Les Morts qui parlent: scènes de la vie parlementaire* (Paris: Plon, 1899).

28. *La Mission Congo-Nil*, led by Marchand, included Mangin and Baratier among others. To date, the most complete book on the subject has been published by a French scholar, Marc Michel, *La Mission Marchand 1895–1899* (The Hague: Mouton, 1972).

29. Captain Hubert Lyautey, "Du rôle social de l'officier dans le service militaire universel," *Revue des Deux Mondes* (Paris, 1891). It is significant that Lyautey wrote this revolutionary essay on the request of Melchior de Vogüé, who had been impressed "by the methods of Captain Lyautey and his ideas on the concept of the 'new army'." André Maurois, *Lyautey* (Paris: Plon, 1931), pp. 41-43.

30. From 1909 to 1911, 4,100 articles were published on the subject.

31. Balesi, *West Africans and the French Military*, p. 122.

32. The total number of Blacks recruited from October 1914 to March 1915 was 21,000. An attempt to determine precisely the number of Black Africans in the French army during World War I has been made by Marc Michel; the figure arrived at by Michel is 161,250 for the "soldiers who really came to France." Marc Michel, "Le recrutement de tirailleurs en *A.O.F.* pendant la première Guerre mondiale: essai de bilan statistique," *Revue française d'histoire d'outre-mer* 60 (1973): 644-660.

III

POLITICS IN THE METROPOLE AND THE COLONIES

The intimate relationship between Africans and the French military was a unique phenomenon in colonial history. To be sure, Britain did use African troops in African campaigns, but no Africans helped protect Britain during Hitler's Blitzkrieg. Another unique arena was that of political involvement of Africans in French politics—another sector without parallel in colonial history. Britain and Italy, Germany and Belgium did not ever entertain the notion of establishing African deputies; even Portugal, which approached France's policy of admitting *assimilés* into full citizenship, did not provide for systematic African participation in metropolitan government. The French case stands unique, and it gives the analyst looking for further evidence of double impact a fertile arena for investigation. The four essays which delve into politics will be divided into two parts; this part with emphasis on the formal political process, with case studies of Mali (formerly called French Soudan) and Senegal, with repercussions in France; and the next part, which will look in detail at France's policy toward African elites and the way in which African elites influenced France's African activities.

The policy of assimilation is the main reason France allowed local and regional political activity among its Black African colonies; Senegal, which had been able to have African electors participate in the 1848 elections to the French assembly, was also the first colony to have Africans as electoral candidates (Galandou Diouf for the General Council, Blaise Diagne for the deputyship). The rationale for allowing colonials to serve in French governmental institutions was that any man who accepted French culture, education, and outlook might qualify. The experience of Africans in politics in Senegal later spread to adjoining colonies, such as Soudan (Mali), where in the pre–World War II period of the Popular Front, Africans were influenced and tutored by the French Left in the art of politics, despite the fact that they did not get the vote and mandate to participate in the National Assembly in Paris until after the war.

The two essays in this section speak to the interface (in the best sense of that word) between French and African politicians. Charles Cutter, who spent many months doing field work in Mali, finding former political leaders to interview and discovering documents previously forgotten, shows how the political activity of the French Left, especially among the Socialists, was translated into activity in the colonies for the first time in the 1930s. Prior to the advent of the Popular Front in 1936 (which appointed its own minister of colonies and its own governors in African colonies) there was little extension of metropolitan politics into the Senegalese political arena, the only place formal elections were allowed. But 1936 was a political breakthrough, and elements already in the colonies now found a focus for their political aspirations, and new people, never allowed in the colonies before, now found it possible to seek work overseas. Senegal flourished under Popular Front leaders in both colonial administration and some local elected positions; this awakening also spilled over into neighboring colonies such as French Soudan.

Cutter is also concerned with the events of the late 1930s as the proximate causes for the nationalist activity that sprang up during and after the war. The literature on political developments during the inter-war period in French West Africa is singularly devoid of extended treatment of the origins of the later era of nationalism; Cutter's work is a path-breaking effort in this direction.

Janet Vaillant comes at double impact with an expanded treatment of Léopold Senghor and the participation of African leaders in the politics of the metropole. Senghor was the heir of Diagne, Diouf, and others who had prepared the way for Africans to participate in the political life of France; a great opponent of both the earlier deputies was Lamine Guèye, who after World War II took over Senegal's seat in the national Parliament. But post-war changes in the French constitution allowed more deputies from each colony to be sent to Paris, and Guèye soon found a protégé, Senghor, to join him in parliamentary maneuver. Senghor proved to be as gifted for politics as the older jurist and within several years had founded his own political party and upstaged Guèye. Vaillant's study looks mainly at Senghor but is suggestive of activity of other African deputies, which has never been studied in detail. While the position the African deputies found themselves in—helping to formulate legislation for the ruling country in addition to the colonies—was unique, the weakness of the Fourth Republic's political institutions meant that greater impact of a colonial group was limited. The very fact of Africans making laws in Paris, however, was suggestive of the double impact, even though limited in scale, that was possible during the last period of colonial rule.

CHARLES H. CUTTER

6

The Genesis of a Nationalist Elite: The Role of the Popular Front in the French Soudan (1936-1939)

The nationalist elite of the French Soudan, that group which brought the colony to independence as the sovereign state of Mali, had its genesis in the period of the Popular Front in French West Africa. Those who entered the political competitions of the 1940s and 1950s were the products of that short but intensely active period when French leftists and young educated Africans created the organizations and experiences which provided the basis for post-war political activity. For one member of that generation of men who created modern Mali the period of the Popular Front lit a "flame which could not be extinguished, not even by war."[1]

This essay explores the impact of the Popular Front on the French Soudan. For the Soudan, the Front represented a period of loosening up. Organizational freedom was permitted and the consequences of this were far-reaching. French leftists active during the period were the real catalysts of the post-war nationalist movement, but their success stemmed largely from the fact that the seeds they sowed fell on fertile ground. French West Africa in the late 1930s, despite the efforts of the entire apparatus of the colonial administration, had been infiltrated by a powerful stream of pan-African and nationalist ideas originating among left-wing African thinkers in Paris. In addition, the French Soudan had an experience unique among the colonies of the group: From December 1934 to November 1935 the Soudan was governed by a Black man. As acting governor during the period, Félix Eboué became a source of pride for young African intellectuals, a man whose achievement demonstrated their own possibilities and whose presence began a period of self-awareness for the educated elite of the colony.[2] Thus, at the outset of the period there was a developing affirmation of African personality which would blossom amid the encouragements of those representatives of the French Left who supported the government of the Popular Front.

Any study of the Popular Front's impact on the French Soudan must begin with an examination of the colonial bureaucracy and cleavages within it, for the interaction between French leftists and an emerging African elite is in large part the result of bureaucratic tensions sprung of structural differentiation combined with differences of class and political perspective. Most studies of colonial bureaucracy have generally focused on administrators, avoiding any scrutiny of specialists, those responsible for the actual implementation of policy. But in the French Soudan, it was precisely specialists, members of the technical corps of the colonial bureaucracy, who constituted the colony's political Left. It is they who reached out to involve young progressive Africans in a variety of voluntary associations and became thereby catalysts for the genesis of a nationalist elite.

POLITICAL ACTION WITHIN AN ADMINISTRATIVE STATE

A colony is an administrative state. The machinery of administration is an apparatus of domination, for the colonial subject is organized, ordered, and controlled by the colonial bureaucracy. As Cheikh Ahmadou Kane once noted: "Those who had shown fight and those who surrendered, those who had come to terms and those who had been obstinate—they all found themselves, when the day came, checked by census, divided up, classified, labeled, conscripted, administrated."[3] To the subject the apparatus of domination is monolithic, but administration demands hierarchy, and hierarchy implies stratification. It is impossible to speak of the colonial bureaucracy as a solidary unity, for the divisions of hierarchy produce differentials of status within the administrative structure. The period of the Popular Front in the French Soudan highlights the tensions and consequences which result from these bureaucratic cleavages, for in the Soudan, status differentials provided the basis for organization within and opposed to the colonial administration.

In French West Africa the Popular Front period can be conveniently dated from the appointment of a Socialist, Jules Marcel de Coppet, as governor-general of the federation in August 1936. While governor of Dahomey de Coppet had been recognized as a liberal administrator and his appointment confirmed the "immense hope" first generated among Africans by the Front's electoral victories in April and May 1936.[4] The appointment also encouraged local supporters of the Front to organize and pursue the coalition's goals within the individual colonies of the federation.

In the French Soudan supporters of the Popular Front first loosely coalesced in the fall of 1936 on the occasion of runoff elections to choose the colony's representative to the Superior Council of Overseas France (*Conseil Supérieur de la France d'Outre-mer*), a body advisory to the minister of colonies.[5] The initial election of October 4 had reduced the field of candidates to two: Adolph Vincent, a deputy and secretary of the Chamber of Deputy's Colonial Committee, and Ulbrich Guiberteau, a Bamako businessman and president of the local Chamber of Commerce.[6] To a group of assorted French leftists and African citizens, however, Vincent was a reactionary, "a man of Textiles du Nord," and a representative of the economic interests which had long exploited the indigenous population.[7] As a consequence they turned to Guiberteau, untainted by direct association with the agents of exploitation and sufficiently involved in the affairs of the Soudan to provide some representation of its views and problems. In the second round of balloting, Guiberteau received 344 votes, Vincent 266. For the supporters of the Popular Front who had worked against Vincent it was a personal victory, and they began to believe they could play a decisive role in the affairs of the colony.

A recognition of their political potential, a common commitment to the ideals of the Popular Front, and a desire to implement them in the Soudan all suggested the possibility, if not necessity, of formal organization to those who had rather loosely and spontaneously come together to defeat Adolph Vincent. Impetus for organization came with the assignment of a dynamic young inspector of schools, Charles Cros, to the Soudan in December 1936. Organization of an association supporting the Front—ultimately to be called *Les Amis du Rassemblement Populaire* (ARP) or Friends of the Popular Front—began in early 1937 under the direction of Cros, a number of his fellow teachers, and employees of the various technical services of the colonial bureaucracy.[8]

The colonial bureaucracy was divided into areas of general administration and specific or technical implementation. Generalists were the elite of the system, for they were responsible for the supervision and coordination of technical services within the colony. They were, properly speaking, the administrators. Governors, *administrateurs des colonies*, members of the *Secrétariat Général*, and members of the *Service Civil* each formed a separate corps, having internal hierarchy based on years of service, salary, and rank. The corps were formally differentiated from each other in terms of qualifications and functions; informally, they were differentiated in terms of prestige. More importantly, all administrative corps were significantly differentiated, formally and informally, from the technical corps.

Specialists, in contrast, were professionals assigned to perform a specific, technical task. The specialist was the station master or telegraph operator, the postmaster or postal clerk, the teacher, the engineer, the agricultural or public health technician. Like administrative corps, the technical services possessed an internal hierarchy and differential prestige vis-à-vis each other. Within the bureaucratic structure, however, specialists were formally subordinated to generalists, and this status differential was reinforced by differences of social origin, education and training, role perception, and political orientation.

In Bamako the group formed to support the goals of the Popular Front, *Les Amis du Rassemblement Populaire* (ARP), was founded by specialists working in the colonial bureaucracy. In part the organization may be viewed as a response to the authoritarian nature of that bureaucracy. The hierarchic nature of authority produces feelings of inequality.[9] When these institutionalized inequalities are reinforced by social imparities, the result may be tensions within the bureaucracy for which the structure is incapable of providing relief. Most obviously the coincidence of these inequalities may work to stifle the ventilation of grievances. Sealed off from vertical ventilation as a consequence of social and hierarchic stratification, tensions may seek relief in agencies external to the bureaucratic apparatus. In the Soudan these cumulative hierarchic and social inequalities sought resolution in the collective equality of the ARP. The individual *fonctionnaire*, powerless and inefficacious before the rigid formalism of the bureaucratic structure, turned to collective politics as a means of diminishing the tensions of institutionalized inequality.

In examining the activities of the ARP, one is struck by the predominance of teachers. Of the members of the five executive committees of which there is record, 48 percent were teachers. Charles Cros naturally became the organization's first secretary-general. Jean Le Gall, professor and director of the *Maison des Artisans Soudanais* (a technical school training local craftsmen) and member of the ARP's first executive committee, proposed the group's original manifesto of aims: (1) to gather in a "sentiment of close solidarity" all those French citizens who pursued the realization of the same ideal of justice, whether it be political, economic, or social; (2) to work for this realization and specifically to bring about the demands formulated by the Popular Front; (3) to furnish members of the groups, or organizations which might constitute it, all documentation and suggestions which appeared useful.[10] Despite the predominance of teachers in ARP leadership roles, however, the ARP was not a professional association, for teachers constituted only 16 percent of the group's initial members—those who joined while the organization was open only to French citizens, including those Africans holding French citizenship.[11] Teachers were certainly held together by ties of common professional interests, but in the ARP they joined with railway workers—numerically the greatest proportion of initial members (23 percent), postal employees, and others professionally unassociated with education. Significantly, teachers, railway and postal officials were all backed by strong unions in France and most were from metropolitan French technical services seconded to Africa, thus having a strong position to fall back to.[12] The common bond between teacher, postal or rail employee was a shared status within the colonial bureaucracy: specialists provided the organizational core of the ARP.[13]

As professionals specialists were concerned with technical performance, but their independence to perform was subject to the needs and desires of administrators. Specialists were institutionally subordinate to generalists and even though the administrator might have "sufficient general culture to respect the independence of real specialists and to leave their work to them,"[14] the administrator was officially responsible for the functioning and direction of public services in the colony. Administrative correspondence from teachers, for example, had to pass through the hierarchy of the educational service to the local administrator responsible for the coordination of the technical services—the *commandant de cercle*. If he thought it were warranted, the correspondence could then be passed on, with his observations, to his superiors.[15]

To the specialist the administrator represented the public authority of the colony, an authority to which he was subject—in ways differing but nevertheless similar to the African subject, for like the African, he too had no discretion in its exercise. On the basis of a personal investigation of the economic and agricultural organization of the West African colonies, Senator Henri Cosnier was convinced that "all authority, moral or effective, in all areas of human activity, is concentrated in the hands of the administrator."[16] Speaking of the *commandant de cercle*, Cosnier noted that he was at once the chief district administrator, judge, tax collector, and commander of the instruments of public force. In reality, suggested Cosnier, "he does not administer, he commands his district and no one, outside of himself should possess the slightest authority."[17] Earlier, Governor-General Van Vollenhoven had said it more succinctly: "The *commandant de cercle* alone is in command."[18]

As a professional the specialist might be the source of technical innovation, but change and improvement had to accord with the necessities of command, financial and otherwise. Because of administrative authority, innovation could be and often was stifled. Henry Zieglé had noticed this general phenomenon in French Equatorial Africa: "Les fonctionnaires de l'ordre technique des qu'ils n'opèrent plus dans les chefs lieux, se voient coiffés par des fonctionnaires d'autorité dont ils ne reconnaissent pas toujours la supériorité humaine, et qui sont tentés d'ajouter à la transmission des directives du chef leurs propres vues plus ou moin éclairées."[19] For Senator Cosnier the local administrator was the principal obstacle to the introduction of modern methods of agricultural production. As a consequence of this potential for administrative frustration, Cosnier clearly saw that the specialist, not a member of the administrative family and pretending to a certain independence, could form a core of opinion opposed to the authority of the administrator.[20].

At the very highest level of the colonial administration members of the ARP believed they had a sympathetic ear. Governor Ferdinand Rougier, an appointee of the Popular Front, had quickly approved the statutes of the new association and permitted a group representative a place in the official party which welcomed Minister of Colonies Marius Moutet to Bamako on 10 April 1937. Between the representative of the Popular Front and the organizers of a political group claiming ideological identity with it, however, there existed, in the words of Charles Cros, "la forteresse d'une administration bureaucratique inexpugnable et le mur d'un ordre solidement établi."[21] These barriers were in part institutional, a consequence of the structural distribution of authority within a centralized colonial bureaucracy. Specialists, whether they were teachers or postal clerks, engineers or agricultural technicians, shared a subordinate status within the administrative structure.[22]

This shared status was reinforced by other sociological factors which (1) worked to unify the members of the ARP, and (2) set them in opposition to the administration. In addition to institutional subordination, the specialist was separated from the administrator by all the aspects of class that characterized French social stratification: way of life, education, training, and outlook. Most fundamentally specialists and administrators were differentiated in terms of social origins and education, and consequent to these were the differences of political attachment and orientation.

Specialists tended to be recruited from the French working classes. To teach in colonial schools required only a *Brevet Supérieur*, marking the completion of primary (not to be confused with our "elementary") education, and a *Certificat d'Aptitude Pédagogique*, awarded at the conclusion of work at an *école normale*—a technical secondary school specifically devoted to teacher training.[23] A *commis stagiaire* (the lowest rank) just entering the corps of the *Service Civil* was required to have a *Diplôme de Bachelier*, signifying the completion of classical secondary education, plus a *Diplôme de Sortie* from either the *Institut Commercial de Paris* or the *Ecôle Coloniale du Hâvre* (much less prestigious than the *Ecôle coloniale* of Paris), or a *Certificat de Fin d'Etudes* from one of the higher commercial schools. Since the baccalaureat (*Diplôme de Bachelier*) did not prepare one for any specific career or assure any position, it was only a first step, after which further specialized training necessary for professional competence would be necessary. Those entering the administrative classes were thus those who could most easily postpone assuming a full-time job in order to continue their education. As a consequence administrators tended to be recruited from the French middle classes—the administration in general, the army, the professions—doctors, pharmacists, lawyers—and commerce and industry.[24]

According to Jean Surêt-Canale, a notably biased but suggestive writer, administrators were, with rare exceptions, men of the political Right and during the 1930s often sympathetic with, or supporters of, Fascist or pro-Fascist groups.[25] Teachers, rail and postal workers, and other specialists were men of the political Left in France: they made up the backbone of the Radical, Socialist, and Communist parties which had joined to support the Popular Front government of Léon Blum. In the Soudan, the leadership of the ARP accurately reflected the political spectrum of the Front. Robert Enard was a communist. Jean Barody was of the "extreme Left" and active in Socialist party activities in Senegal; Le Gall and Adolph Rançon were Socialists. And Robert Thiémonge was a member of the Radical party. Charles Cros states that he belonged to no party, being a political maverick (*sauvage*).[26] And in the Soudan the ARP was most conscious of its social origins and its ties with the working classes. The members of the ARP were, in the words of Secretary Cros, "men of the left, issued from the people and still of them," and, he added, "we follow with emotion the victories of the laboring classes in the metropole."[27] It was this perception of social origin that provided a common political orientation for the members of the ARP.

In the Soudan, as in France, the Left perceived itself as the defender of the

Republic and its traditions of popular representation and participation. In welcoming Colonial Minister Moutet to the colony, Secretary-General Cros had noted that it was the intention of the ARP, even at the risk of introducing politics into "ce pays calme du Soudan," "to bring to the Minister's attention those among them, citizens of France, either European or native, who had a right to expect an amelioration of their status."[28] The next evening the ARP hosted a dinner honoring the minister, and with Cros as their spokesman the group elaborated its demands. The purpose of the meeting, said Cros, was not merely to echo "the magnificent acts of the laboring classes of France which had extracted, step by step, decisive acts from capitalism which would give them the dignity to which they aspired and which they merited." Rather, he continued,

we intend that freemen, citizens of a free country, be treated here as French citizens, not as you well know we have been treated previously; in short, we demand the full and complete enjoyment of our rights. We do not want the Republic to be a monopoly within the metropolitan frontiers and that is why we demand an Overseas French Republic. Yes, we are concerned with the defense of our interests, and you have noticed that around you have gathered this evening, as if by an instinctive movement, the minor (*petit*) commercial employees, the small *colons*, the minor *fonctionnaires*, those modest men of conscience you know so well and [know too] how much they participate in the development of the colony. They have too often been forgotten and each time it is necessary, we will make our voices heard in order that they obtain just satisfaction of a material or moral nature to which they aspire.[29]

Although their principal concerns were personal and immediate, the Friends also proposed to study the problems of African non-citizens: housing for African civil servants, the role of women in the new native society, associations for former students, the problems of seasonal workers and their transportation. The inspiration for these studies would be the struggle for justice, said Cros, and they would result in the formation of logical and feasible demands requiring the collaboration of the government of the Popular Front.

This insistence on representation and participation was clearly opposed to the outlook of *étatisme* which characterized the administrators. The *étatisme* of the administrator was concerned with law and order, stable government and good, that is, efficient administration.[30] Such concerns produced an impatience with political controversy, conflicting ideologies and interests, and indeed, all party divisions. Even Governor Rougier, the appointee of the Popular Front, demonstrated this outlook. Addressing the members of the colonial administration upon taking office, he sounded a warning to those who might oppose the policies of the Popular Front, but more generally his words articulate the administrative mentality:

We are all here in the service of democratic France. The entire population will be required to respect the institutions and government that France has freely given itself. Have I any need of adding that the *fonctionnaires* owe them [the institutions and government] an unreserved cooperation.

Political discipline is an essential condition which has been delegated to them. For the *fonctionnaire*, as for the military man, there can be only one mission: in service there is no higher expression of authority.[31]

It was this tradition which shaped the role perceptions of colonial administrators. The demands of the ARP, for themselves as citizens and for African subjects, placed stress on the administrative system. For the administrator the formulation of participatory or policy demands, indeed, any activity which might "troubler l'esprit des populations indigènes" was suspect; his primary task was the preservation of order.[32] The commitment of the ARP, however, was such that they were willing to introduce politics into the affairs of the colony—basically an administrative state—and this was obviously disconcerting to administrators concerned with order and stability. Few would ever join the ARP.[33] Reticence or intransigence on the administration's part would only strengthen the opposition of the ARP, and hostility from those who thought their newspaper—*Le Soudan*— a broadside of revolutionaries and anarchists would further solidify the Friends.[34]

The ARP's opposition to the colonial administration was nowhere so total as this suggests, however. To those administrators ready to perform their tasks in good conscience and humility, the ARP offered its collaboration; but to those who had truckled to the vast economic interests, the "négriers de Bordeaux, de Marseilles," to those who represented a political tradition hostile to the representative and participatory tradition of the Popular Front, the ARP was implacably opposed. In short, the political traditions represented by the group could transcend the fissiparous tendencies of party attachment, bind the group together and set it in opposition to the traditions of the administrative ethos.[35] Those traditions would also lead to a linkage between French liberals and an emerging African elite—a group constantly watched by colonial security forces for any sign of anti-colonial, nationalist susceptibilities.

THE ADMINISTRATIVE MENTALITY IN ACTION: SURVEILLANCE OF SUBVERSIVE ACTIVITIES

Dissent and disagreement are virtually impossible in the administrative state, and the mere articulation of demands is frequently perceived as threatening. Thus one of the major preoccupations of the colonial administration during the 1920s was the surveillance of elements considered subversive to the colonial enterprise. In 1923 a special section for West Africa was added to the *Service de Contrôle et de Tutelle des Indigènes*, a branch of the Colonial Ministry devoted to infiltrating various anti-colonial, nationalist, and communist organizations which met in Paris and other French cities. For the colonial administration in West Africa, the principal concern was stopping communication between Parisian "subversives" and those Africans possessed of "un esprit indiscipliné." Correspondence to and from Paris was intercepted, and African correspondents subjected to careful and continuing surveillance; left-wing newspapers, legal in France, were declared "revolutionary propaganda" in Africa and systematically seized to prevent the spread of ideas considered anti-French.

"By secret circulars periodically addressed to the Lt. Governors," Governor-General Carde informed the Colonial Ministry in 1926, "I am endeavoring to keep their attention ever on guard to the imperious necessity of not allowing the slightest propaganda to be implanted and to intensify our measures of protection. It is only by this close surveillance that we can guarantee French West Africa against the contagion of subversive and anti-national ideas." Indeed, that "Bolshevik doctrines" had been so unsuccessful in the federation was due, the governor-general believed, not only to the "stability of native traditions which seem to defend them naturally," but to the "salutary fear of authority" those elements favorable to such propaganda continued to demonstrate.[36]

In the French Soudan, Lieutenant-Governor Terrasson de Fougères warned his *commandants de cercle* that "although French West Africa, and particularly the French Soudan, have hardly been touched to the present by Bolshevik propaganda under the diverse masques that it wears to achieve its ends, it is already insinuated into the immediate neighborhood—strike in Bathurst, riots in Nigeria." It would be vain to think, he continued, that the colonies of the federation could be indefinitely protected from this "propaganda of disorder" in the belief that "our natives are in general less inclined to submit to their influence." For the French Soudan, he thought, the attitude of certain categories of *évolués* was already significant, but more importantly, the administration was committing a grave error in losing sight of the fact that "the two principal leaders of the 'anti-colonialist' movement in Paris were born in French West Africa. One of the two, Tiémoko Kouyaté," he continued, "was even born in Ségou and educated in Bamako where his family still lives."[37] The two men referred to by Lieutenant-Governor Terrasson de Fougères were Lamine Senghor and Tiémoko Garan Kouyaté, leaders of the *Ligue de Défense de la Race Nègre.*

On March 26, 1926, Lamine Senghor, a Senegalese veteran of World War I and vehemently anti-colonial, met with a small group of like-minded people to found the *Comité de Défense de la Race Nègre.*[38] The group was nationalist and race-conscious, seeking to speak against injustices to Black people wherever they occurred. Vigorously anti-colonial, it sought a "permanent collaboration with those organizations which are genuinely struggling for the liberation of oppressed peoples and for world revolution."[39] Senghor became the group's first president, and Tiémoko Garan Kouyaté, assistant secretary-general. Given the close ties between the active leadership of the group and the Communist party (both Senghor and Kouyaté were members at one time), French authorities saw the group as part of a larger Bolshevik conspiracy. Its journal, *La Voix des Nègres*, was considered inflammatory and seized by colonial officials in Africa, while its subscribers and recipients were subjected to security investigations.[40]

Controversy within the group led to its reconstruction in May 1927 as the

Ligue de Défense de la Race Nègre; Kouyaté became secretary-general of the new organization and its newspaper was retitled *La Race Nègre*. With the death of Lamine Senghor later that year, Kouyaté assumed leadership and provided a vigorous and dynamic expression to its anti-colonial, pan-African, and nationalist views, within, it should be noted, the Republican democratic and participatory traditions of France. Writing to Raymond Poincaré, president of the Council of Ministers, to present the results of a recent *Ligue* protest meeting, Kouyaté stressed that as a "great republican," whose essential political goals had been "to preserve republican traditions against all attack" and to preserve the Republic itself, "one and indivisible," Poincaré could easily recognize the justice of the group's demands. The meeting, held 14 April 1928, had been called to protest the "inhuman actions" of the Colonial Ministry, that "Modern Bastille and plague of the Third Republic," and had appealed to north Africans, Indochinese, and colonial subjects of all races. "More than ever," the meeting's announcement read, "solidarity is indispensable between us." Not surprisingly the assembled participants declared, before all else, that colonization was "only a provisional state, and not definitive." They also affirmed their will "to defend in every way and everywhere the cause of the indigenous inhabitants in Africa, Asia, or America."[41]

In addition to its anti-colonial position the *Ligue*, under Kouyaté's direction, actively pursued its pan-African ideal. Writing to W.E.B. Du Bois, Kouyaté explained:

The goal of our *Ligue* is the political, economic, moral and intellectual emancipation of the black race in its entirety. It is a question of reconquering, by all means honorable, the national independence of the black peoples of French, English, Belgian, Italian, Spanish, Portuguese, etc. colonies...and to create in Black Africa a great black state.

In asking for the moral and financial support of American Black organizations, Kouyaté stressed the need for a pan-African unity that transcended continental limits: "The principal point lies in the unification of the world-wide black movement and the elaboration of a common program without ever losing sight of the details of differences."[42] Symbolically, the *Ligue*'s letterhead showed a Black woman bearing a great torch standing atop a globe, one foot planted firmly on Africa, the other on North America; freed of the manacles of oppression, she became the symbol of American freedom.

Freedom for the *Ligue de Défense de la Race Nègre (LDRN)* was clearly phrased in terms of national independence. Indeed the *Ligue* posed a dilemma to French citizens in its April manifesto: unrestricted assimilation with all its logical and political consequences, or acceptance "of the clearly national question of our peoples by provisional means of Dominion Status." And in 1929, writing to Léon Mba in Gabon, Kouyaté put it in the clearest possible terms:

"We are," he wrote of the *Ligue*, "partisans of a policy which prepares our countries, with little delay, for national independence."[43]

It was not these ideas alone that provided a constant source of irritation for the colonial administration, but the energy with which Kouyaté diffused them in a series of newspapers published by the various groups he led and the dedication with which he sought to organize new sections of those groups among the dispossessed of the colonial empire, whether living in France or in the colonies. In 1931 as a consequence of disagreements within the *LDRN*, Kouyaté was expelled, only to found the *Union des Travailleurs Nègres* in 1932. The *Union*'s newspaper, *Le Cri des Nègres* pursued the same anti-colonial, pan-African, and nationalist themes reporting on the activities of militant Black groups in America or the Caribbean, while focusing on the oppression of the colonial regime in Africa. Still later Kouyaté was to create *Africa* ("the most African independent journal for the defense of the interests of African peoples") whose columns were enriched by the reports of a well-developed network of correspondents throughout French Africa.[44]

Africa claimed to be openly sold on the streets of Dakar, Saint-Louis, and Kaolack, but it, like *La Voix des Nègres*, *La Race Nègre*, and *Le Cri des Nègres*, was inscribed on the colonial administration's list of suspect journals—its distribution subject to careful control and its subscribers subject to personal investigation and surveillance as part of the colonial administration's constant struggle against what it saw as "revolutionary propaganda" and "anti-French activity." In response to one such investigation, Amadou Thiam, one of the early adherents of the *LDRN* in the Soudan, told administrative officials that he read *La Voix des Nègres* in order to "inform himself." The journal was, he told his interrogators, "the only one to his knowledge which dealt with questions concerning French West Africa."[45]

Kouyaté had written to Thiam early in 1928 to say that his membership card in the *LDRN* would be sent as soon as a Bamako section of the *Ligue* could be created "by your devoted efforts"; in the meantime, he would be inscribed as a member of the Seine section. "Quickly form the Bamako section," wrote Kouyaté, but "[please] do nothing in secret, for the *Ligue* is a legal association."[46] Despite the *Ligue*'s legal standing in France, however, it had never been granted legal recognition in the colonies; indeed, no metropolitan law was ever immediately applicable to the colonial territories but required a special enabling decree. Thus Kouyaté's enjoinder to "Have no fear. Write us by airmail of the slightest manifestation of hostility on the part of the local administration," could have little substantive meaning in the colonial situation: Thiam was subject to continuing scrutiny and his correspondence apparently systematically opened; his ability to organize on behalf of the *Ligue* severely limited.

Kouyaté's influence in the French Soudan came less through such organizing efforts than through the steady infiltration of his ideas in the nationalist press. Among the young educated elite of the period, Kouyaté himself was not well known, but the newspapers associated with his name were. Despite administrative seizure copies managed to reach their intended audience and were eagerly passed from hand to hand, for the work of Tiémoko Garan Kouyaté, as one informant expressed it, "plaisait beaucoup dans les milieux africains."[47]

In French West Africa the administration seems to have been slow to recognize the nature of this audience, but once it did, it acted with swiftness and heavy-handedness. In 1930 the federation's *Political Report* noted:

Several évolués, for the most part known and discreetly watched, receive well such tendentious journals as *La Dépêche Africaine*, or extremist as *La Race Nègre* or *L'Ouvrier Nègre*, which usually reach them hidden in packets of large-edition newspapers or other publications of inoffensive appearance.

But it does not seem, in the present state of things, that this propaganda has any real chance of success outside of a few veterans, after a more or less extended stay overseas, and most especially seamen recruits who find promiscuities and detrimental contacts with certain of the most subversive and dangerous European elements in the great metropolitan ports and even in the ships' boiler rooms.[48]

Such limited perception of the potential audience for the nationalist press is surprising, for the governor-general in Dakar had been warned as early as 1928 by the lieutenant-governor of the Ivory Coast: "It is certain that the newspaper...*La Race Nègre* is presently read by a great part of the literate natives of the lower Coast and that an intense effort has been made to spread it throughout the colony."[49]

In the French Soudan several individuals were reported to have received "revolutionary propaganda" coming from France or Hamburg in 1931, but they had engaged in no propaganda activities in the interior of the colony, reported the lieutenant-governor. Aside from a number of *fonctionnaires indigènes*— African employees of the colonial bureaucracy—the Soudanese government felt there was little to be disturbed about for the moment. The literature had been mailed, the lieutenant-governor thought, at Kouyaté's direction to several of his former colleagues, and a number of them had already turned the material over to administrative officials.[50] Those who paid attention to the "subversive proposals held by metropolitan agitators," thought the Soudanese government in 1932, were only "isolated individuals whose action has had, to present, absolutely no repercussion in the colony and on the native population [*masse indigène*]."[51] Despite only isolated and inefficacious individuals, the colonial administration was quick to note that intelligence coming to the Security Services was "minutely verified" and the agitators thus signaled became "the object of a very close surveillance." New dossiers on the suspects were established, information gathered locally was transmitted to the Office of General Security in Dakar, and finally, the Soudanese government noted with some pride: "Photographs allow rapid identification and specific surveillance."[52]

By 1936 and the advent of the Popular Front government of Léon Blum, administrative officials in the French Soudan had begun to sense, at first somewhat dimly, that they were faced with a changing situation that they could only view with uneasiness if not alarm. "Without wanting to resort to a pessimism in bad form," wrote Bamako's *commandant de cercle*, "I will permit myself to say that if the populations of the District of Bamako live and develop in apparent calm, there are several indications which allow one to think that an entire mentality is in the processes of modification."[53] Particularly in the urban centers, the commandant thought one was watching "a transformation of society which can only cause the greatest vexations to a country where one has done much but where much remains to be done."[54] The comment suggests the end of one period of colonial history and beginning of another, and indeed, a mere six months later, just after the initial organizing activities of the ARP, the *commandant de cercle* of Bamako was to describe how disquieting the situation had become and to give vivid testimony to the administrative mentality when faced with rapid political change:

In the district and particularly in the city of Bamako, the evolution [of the African] has taken an anguishing ascent. New ideas, sown by emissaries coming from Senegal for the most part, have developed rapidly. These ideas are also spread by a certain press which...parades its information in often slanderous columns which are sold in Bamako by propagandists, several of whom are employed in the colonial service.

One will say that certain of them are excellent workers, punctual, deferential, intelligent, and "can assure the work of a European employee." I do not say "no," but I believe that it would be useful, even necessary, to eliminate from a country where the mass is attached to France, which recognizes that our work is completely beneficent, social, humanitarian, a rotten core that runs the risk of spoiling that which asks only to remain healthy.[55]

The agitators were known and "closely watched," he reported, but still "they obstruct our action...not only in the large centers, but even in distant *cantons* where they know how to find favorable ground." Sounding like some beleaguered counter-insurgency commander, the commandant continued:

It is difficult to react because the push is underhanded; it hesitates because it knows it runs the risk of being denounced if it attacks on too broad a front. It chooses its ground adroitly. And it surrounds us particularly; it is in our own entourage that we must watch most often.[56]

Such was the embattled feeling of the colonial administration in 1937, surrounded by "unfaithful" and "disloyal" employees who had begun to discuss and listen to ideas utterly subversive of the colonial enterprise itself. This was the setting for the activities of the Friends of the Popular Front and the environment that made those activities so successful.

ORGANIZING TO PURSUE POLITICAL OBJECTIVES

From its inception *Les Amis du Rassemblement Populaire* joined Europeans and Africans in common endeavor; indeed, one of the founding members of the group and its first treasurer, Isaac Diop, was one of the most active spokesmen of the Senegalese community in Bamako.[57] What the original members of the group shared, besides a common belief in the program of the Popular Front, was a common political status, for when first created, the ARP was open only to French citizens—those Frenchmen resident in the Soudan and that small number of Africans holding French citizenship. Its membership potential was thus exceedingly small: in Bamako, the colony's capital, there were only 529 resident Frenchmen in 1937, and 189 African citizens.[58] Such limitations were quickly noted—and criticized—by Tiémoko Garan Kouyaté who published the group's manifesto in *Africa* with an appended editorial note:

The first duty of the members of this group is to eliminate the dangerous barriers between white and black, between French citizens and "subjects"; if not, they will render the worst service to the Popular Front, of which they claim to be the Friends.[59]

As a matter of both ideology and practical politics, some members of the ARP began to urge that the group's membership restrictions be revised, its recruitment broadened to include African "subjects" as well as citizens.

It was, in part, an effort to develop effective pressure against the administration that caused the ARP to involve the emerging African elite in its affairs. At its meeting of 4 September 1937 (a date which commemorated the proclamation of the Third Republic), the ARP was presented a resolution to accept as members "all men and women of goodwill and firm conviction, without distinction of race, color, nationality, social condition or political status." The proposed reform meant that the group would cease to recognize the distinction between citizens and subjects; each would enjoy equal rights of membership and participation within the group. This change of regulations had been the personal initiative of Secretary Cros, believing that "a Friend of the Popular Front could not allow the door of the association to remain closed to subjects simply because they were subjects."[60] The meeting was lengthy and the proposal bitterly fought, both by moderate Frenchmen and African citizens, but in the end the motion carried. Within the ARP citizens and subjects—primarily the young educated elite—would work together in the pursuit of political goals.[61]

The association between ARP and emerging African elite was natural. The elite—teachers, administrative clerks, employees of local commerce—had all passed through the French educational system. It was they who spoke, read, and wrote French and had a touch of "la civilisation française"; of any Africans, they were the ones with whom the French felt most at home. It was they to whom the French Left had passed on the democratic and participatory ideals of Republican France, now resuscitated by the advent of the Popular Front. It was with this group that the French Left had, and continued to have, contact in both classrooms and offices.

The African educated elite, an emerging middle class, conscious of its own differentiation from both the French and the African masses and conscious too of the inferiority of its own working conditions and status when compared to European employees in the colony, was a group whose grievances could be mobilized by the French Left. By joining with the African *évolué*, French leftists sought to strengthen their pressure against the administration. For the Africans, it was their former teachers, men who had taught them the humanitarian political ideals of the Republic, the men who recognized the worst aspects of the colonial system, to whom (of any colonizer) they could feel closest, and to whom they might turn for aid to improve their situation. Even today the first two secretaries-general of the ARP, Charles Cros and Jean Barody, both teachers, are remembered as men of "generous ideas," genuinely interested in Africans. And when Cros left the Soudan, the young Modibo Keita had offered his esteem: "Thanks to you we know the true face of France; thanks to you we can hope that the words 'liberty, equality, fraternity' will no longer be mere words in the colonies."[62]

The organizational focus of the ARP was the *Ecole Primaire Supérieure* Terrasson de Fougères,[63] for it brought together not only politically progressive French and African teachers, but also other French leftists, specialist members of the technical corps who served as part-time teachers at the school. In each colony the *école primaire supérieure* stood at the apex of the territory's educational system, staffed by the best European and African teachers. Its students were the intellectual elite of the colony, carefully screened and selected in successive steps from village to region and finally at the level of the territory itself. Admission was competitive and highly restricted. The number admitted each year was the governor's estimation of administrative needs four years hence, for the graduates of the *école primaire supérieure* were exclusively trained to fill the needs of local administration, public and private. The most capable graduates were eligible for the competition to federal schools located at Dakar. If admitted to the *Ecole Normale* William Ponty, a student would be trained to be a teacher, given higher administrative training, or go on to the federation's medical school to emerge as a *médecin africain*.[64]

Training at the *école primaire supérieure* was divided into two parts, a general education given to all students and technical training in one of the school's specialized sections: administrative, railroad, or postal. While general instruction was dispensed by French and African teachers, professional courses were normally handled by technicians drawn from the specialized corps. Thus Henri Pérès and Antoine Peus, both early members of the ARP *comité directeur*, had taught the professional course on radio and telegraph operations, and Robert Thiémonge, another early ARP leader, had taught the railroad section of Terrasson de Fougères. Annexed to the school was an apprentice center whose object was the technical training of skilled workers, and to this center came Jean Le Gall, first director of the *Maison des Artisans Soudanais* and one of the ARP founders, and his successor Jacques Heuzey, later elected head of the ARP-inspired *Maison du Peuple*. Thus, other specialists, not members of the teaching corps, came within the orbit of Terrasson de Fougères. It was in the classrooms of Terrasson that the French Left established their contacts with the intellectual elite of the Soudan and through these students their influence would ramify throughout the organizational life of Bamako and the entire colony.

The teacher as leader was an institutionally conditioned role. Given the rigid nature of the educational system, the teacher had always occupied a position of leadership and had exercised authority over the students. The student population of Bamako was a group constantly manipulated by the teaching staff. The *Ecole Primaire Supérieure* Terrasson de Fougères was, according to Robert Delavignette "everywhere." Its students had been organized to build the *Maison des Artisans Soudanais*, to construct the *Vélodrom Frederick Assomption*, named after the director of education himself; it was the student body of the *école primaire supérieure* which had been organized to sing the "Marseillaise" for public celebrations; it was the student body which had been organized to greet minister of colonies Marius Moutet on his visit to the Soudan.[65] As a consequence, the emerging elite—local teachers, government clerks, and educated students—formed an ideal constituency to mobilize in opposition to the administration.

The influence of the French teacher-organizers of the ARP was in part communicated and reinforced by the African teachers with whom they worked. Among the youngest to be recruited to the ARP was Modibo Keita (later president of independent Mali), who graduated from William Ponty in 1936 and was assigned to the very important *école régionale* of Bamako. But perhaps even more important for the general spread of the political sentiments of the ARP were the older African teachers. Men like Fadiga Bouillagui and Séga Diallo, the deans of the African teaching corps, were not only those of the greatest seniority but also the most able and most respected teachers. In 1937 both had been awarded the French Legion of Honor; Diallo after thirty-two years of service and Bouillagui after thirty years. The younger Mamadou Konaté had taught at Terrasson until he was made director of the *école rurale* in 1933, but like them, he had built up a personal following among his students. Each of these men had in his own way served as an inspiration for the various classes to pass under his direction; each had become friend and counsellor to generations of educated elite and had extensive contacts not only with this group, but through their family connections with the uneducated population as well. As such they served as critical intermediaries within the communication network that joined the French Left and the emerging elite of the Soudan. But just as importantly, as more and more younger African teachers joined the ARP from the distant towns and villages of the Soudan—20 percent of the group's total membership was drawn from the teaching corps—they themselves became an important network for gathering and diffusing information and ideas.[66]

One of the first concerns of the ARP was the organization of the alumni of the *école primaire supérieure*, as Secretary Cros had informed Marius Moutet in April 1937. On the initiation of Cros the Amicale Terrasson de Fougères was organized and its statutes approved by the governor on December 23, 1937. The object of the new association was to tighten the bonds of friendship among former students of the school and to bring them closer to their former teachers, to the school, and to their young comrades currently in school.[67] The president and three vice-presidents of the new association were ex-officio—the director of education, the inspector of schools and the directors of Terrasson de Fougères and the *école régionale* of Bamako. At the general meeting of the group, the members chose as secretary-general Fadiga Bouillagui. Younger elements were represented by Amadou Doucouré, an employee of local commerce, and Siriman Mariko, a recent graduate of Terrasson who had served in the governor's cabinet and in the administration's military bureau. The Amicale Terrasson de Fougères tended to institutionalize links between the African elite and the French Left and to confirm the elite as an audience of the ARP, but in other areas of organizational life in Bamako the influence of the ARP was just as direct and even more political, as in the formation of professional unions.

In March 1937 rights concerning the organization of professional unions were applied to colonial territories by the government of the Popular Front.[68] With the encouragement of the local representatives of the French Left, unions were organized in the Soudan, but because of the requirement that members of professional unions must read, write, and speak French, the clientele of the unions was limited. It was, aside from resident Frenchmen, essentially the alumni of Terrasson de Fougères who would be allowed to form professional unions.

The professional union was quickly seen as a powerful means of organizing to seek change in the economic and social status of those exercising similar occupations. Among the first to organize in Bamako were African teachers, who were reported to have been organized under the direction of Mamby Sidibé, president and Mamadou Konaté, secretary-general, as early as July 1937.[69] Shortly afterwards, Konaté and Ouezzin Coulibaly, who served as director of studies at the *Ecole* William Ponty, organized a conference in Bamako to rally members to a federation-wide *Syndicat Professional des Instituteurs Indigènes*, for though the union already had a membership of nearly 200, only about 20 had joined from the Soudan. Coulibaly's speech highlighted many of the inequalities that existed between African teachers, members of a *cadre secondaire*, and European teachers, members of the *cadre supérieur*. In terms of salary, travel allowances, housing, leave time, or retirement benefits, the African teachers were treated differentially—to their disadvantage. The time had come to speak out against the injustice of their situation, Coulibaly told his audience, and that was the purpose of the union: alone, the teacher would be "crushed by the great bureaucratic system."[70] And in the Soudan African teachers apparently joined with their French colleagues to form a united front for the discussion and pursuit of common goals and problems; by 1938, Charles Mouriès, a leader of the ARP, was listed as secretary of the *Syndicat des Instituteurs*.[71]

Justifiably aggrieved as teachers were, employees of the private sector felt themselves even more disadvantaged than any member of the colonial civil service. The representative of Africans employed in the commercial sector stated their situation quite plainly to Marius Moutet on his visit to Bamako in April 1937:

The local administration, for its part, does not appear to treat us with all the goodwill we merit because we are not *fonctionnaires*; our rights are not equal to those of our comrades of the civil service who, however, have followed the same course of studies as we and share the same duties in the same social life as we.[72]

For those engaged in traditional African commerce, the appeal to the minister of colonies was direct and simple: "Help us to live." That, said the spokesman, required only a just and reciprocal aid to African commerce: "protect its products on the metropolitan market at least as much as metropolitan products are protected on the colonial market."[73] Given this sense of grievance and demand, many Africans employed in the commercial sector were attracted by the ARP's constant attack on colonial capitalism. They joined the ARP in large numbers—forming 17 percent of the group's total membership—and formed one of the first and most active unions of the Soudan with the encouragement of the French Left.[74] And again, the formation of the *Syndicat des Employés Indigènes de Commerce, Banque et Industrie du Soudan Français* demonstrated the ramifying influence of the *Ecole Primaire Supérieure* Terrasson de Fougères. Charles Cros himself attended the union's organizational meeting at the Chamber of Commerce, 21 November 1937, and two recent graduates of Terrasson de Fougères, Mar Diagne and Amadou Doucouré, assumed major leadership roles. Diagne became the union's first secretary-general, while Doucouré, already an officer of the *Amicale* Terasson de Fougères, was elected treasurer; less than a year later, in September 1938, he became the union's secretary-general.[75]

The influence of the French Left and Terrasson de Fougères also penetrated the various sporting associations which proliferated in Bamako during the period. In 1932, the *Amicale Sportive de Bamako* had been founded by a former student of the school, Makan Macoumba, and boxers of the association were trained by Jean Le Gall. Macoumba himself was later elected general commissioner of the *Amicale* Terrasson de Fougères and briefly served on the executive committee of the ARP. The sporting association provided institutional links between educated and non-educated Africans, and for the French Left, encouragement given to sporting activities could have political reward. In late 1938 the ARP organized a special sporting section known as *Les Flamboyants*, but its purpose was more than recreational: according to one early leader of the group, *Les Flamboyants* was created to guide, organize, and attract young Africans to the Popular Front, to make them militants of the Popular Front.[76]

Art, too, was encouraged by the French Left, with perhaps less overt political intent, but with highly important political consequences for the formation of a nationalist elite in the Soudan. *Art et Travail*, which became the artistic section of the ARP, had grown out of a loose grouping of young African intellectuals, mostly graduates of the *Ecole* William Ponty, who returned to the colony at the conclusion of their formal education only to learn that this indeed marked the end of learning as far as the colonial administration was concerned.[77] Once trained and integrated into his administrative post the young educated African found that his intellectual life had been forgotten, but from Ponty many young graduates brought back an enthusiasm for things artistic and cultural. There they explored the customs and history of their peoples and through this had begun a process of reevaluating African culture. Traditional songs and bits of folklore had been polished for the public performance, while legend and history had been creatively developed into plays performed by students from each of the colonies to celebrate the end of the academic year. The theatrical traditions of the *Ecole* William Ponty were continued in Bamako by the school's alumni, but with a shift of emphasis. At Ponty student plays had been subject to the "artistic criticism" of the colonizer; the colonial view of history and culture tended to predominate. In Bamako historical plays focused on different life episodes of the hero, highlighting African as opposed to French values and interpretations, while plays on contemporary themes examined the role of the *évolué*, a participant in two cultures—one African, the other European. As such, the plays became a means of self-evaluation, a means of questioning the assumptions of the colonial regime, and of validating self and culture.

In Bamako the theatrical activities of *Art et Travail* were exclusively in the hands of young Africans, graduates of Ponty and Terrasson de Fougères and even a few "demi-lettrés." Their offerings were meant to amuse and entertain, but at the same time there was a definite attempt to raise the consciousness of both players and audience; the plays frequently presented a critique of contemporary social values and institutions. "The Griot's Triumph," first produced by Soudanese students at the *Ecole* William Ponty, had criticized the musician who lied for money and inflated the vanity of his patrons with falsehood and puffery. Similarly, "La Sainte Louisienne" focused on the problems of marriage and criticized the excessive demands of a young girl which resulted in exorbitant expenditures for luxury items representing the good life, while "Le Bal de la Jeunesse d'orée," written by Modibo Keita, was an extended commentary on the pretensions of the young. In this play the object of satire was the young man who would ape his French masters and "faire le grand Monsieur." Such an individual, for many young educated Africans, was a fit object of ridicule—the African who had lost his sense of dignity, pride, and awareness of self. To restore this sense of self many plays sought to reconstruct and revalidate African history. At Ponty the story of Samory, the great resister to French military expansion in West Africa, had focused on more sanguinary aspects of the hero's life and on his dramatic encounter with the French; in Bamako, however, an earlier incident in Samory's life—his efforts to rescue his mother—became the focus of the play. Samory, the good son, the dutiful son, the son who loves and respects his mother, rather than Samory, the war leader, became the hero; French presence was ignored while African values were explored. Probably the most popular of the historical plays was that featuring the life of Sundiata, the near-legendary founder of the thirteenth-century empire of Mali, but again the play was a study of African history, culture, and values without reference to the colonizer. History in dramatic form was, for many members of the educated elite, an attempt to reestablish continuity with a past largely denied within the colonial context.[78]

With Charles Cros acting as head of the Soudanese Educational Service during the 1937-1938 school year, the theatrical efforts of *Art et Travail* were given full support by the local teaching staff. The refectory of Terrasson de Fougères was given over to provide a stage; the group was formally made the artistic section of the ARP shortly after African ''subjects'' were admitted to membership and Makan Macoumba became the first African non-citizen to serve on the executive committee of the group, representing *Art et Travail*.

Art et Travail was only one of several groups formed and developed with the aid and encouragement of French leftists in the Soudan. These organizations, representing a complex interpenetration on the part of the French Left, an overlapping of directorates and memberships, both French and African, were brought together in a collective enterprise, the *Maison du Peuple*, in February 1938. On February 12 Governor-General de Coppet, accompanied by Governor Rougier, officiated at the opening ceremonies. The *Maison* would serve as the headquarters for the ARP and all other organizations sharing the convictions of the ARP. These groups—sixteen in all—were both French and African and ranged from such ethnic associations as *La Société des Originaires du Ouassoulou* and the *Mutualité des Métis*, through sporting and social groups like the *Amicale Sportive de Bamako* and the *Foyer du Soudan*, through a number of professional unions to the *Association Républicaine des Anciens Combattants (ARAC)* and the *Fédération des Officiers de Réserve Républicaine* headed by Ulbrich Guiberteau, whom the ARP had helped elect as the colony's representative to the *Conseil Supérieur de la France d'Outre-mer*.[79]

By providing a common meeting place the *Maison* became a ''véritable foyer républicain du Soudan.'' For the ARP it provided an educational center, for it contained a library, reading tables, and places for seminars and discussions—implementing the educational desires of the ARP's dominant element—the teachers. The fact which joined the organizations together was simple, said Secretary Cros: ''We defend the Republic.'' The groups associated in the use of the *Maison* would maintain their individual identity and autonomy, but would be subject to ''republican discipline,'' and would each be required to respect the internal regulations of the *Maison*.[80]

In his inaugural speech Secretary Cros stressed the number of people represented by the associated groups and asserted their demands before the highest administrative officials of federation and colony: ''The workers of this territory, and notably the civil servants, count on your authority,'' he told the governor-general, "to end the liberalities taken with the budget in regard to certain capitalist enterprises." To subsidize such enterprises, he noted, represented a waste of resources which benefited only a small number of exploiters and as such must be eliminated. In turn, Governor-General de Coppet recognized the potential of the pressure group, but cautioned the indiscriminate use of political influence. "Today you are a force," he told those assembled, "a force which must be directed if you truly want to realize the ideal which animates us. Do not forget that the special interest must always give way to the general interest of the territory." Having thus suggested restraint before the demands of the group, the governor-general then offered immediate concession: "you will have your library, I promise you," he swore, responding to a request for funds to expand the holdings of the *Maison du Peuple*.[81] At the conclusion of the meeting the governor-general departed, saying farewell to the assembled and cheering group with the salute of the Popular Front—the raised fist.[82]

The gesture symbolized a changed political climate in the colony. As opposed to the statist traditions of the administrator, the groups assembled under the aegis of the *Maison du Peuple* represented the defenders of the Republican, representative traditions of French politics. They represented, too, a group whose interconnections could provide a collective pressure group against the administration, not only for the defense of the ideals of the Republic, but for an implementation of the policies of the Popular Front. Through the organizational impetus of the ARP the influence of the French Left was ramified through the structure of voluntary associations developing in the Soudan.[83] The organizational activities of the ARP linked the French Left with an African elite, organized that elite in a spirit of collective endeavor, and forged institutional links between the elite and non-elite African community.

With the organization of the *Maison du Peuple*, the ARP next concentrated on forming new sections in the principal towns of the colony and distributing its newspaper, *Le Soudan*, whose first issue was published just in time to cover the inauguration ceremonies of the *Maison*. In all, twenty ARP sections were organized throughout the Soudan and each consisted, by statute, of at least five members.[84] *Le Soudan* was actively and eagerly distributed by ARP members not only in those centers having several ARP members but also in surrounding villages.[85] Containing a continuing critique of administrative policies, featured frequently as "Les Scandales du Soudan," as well as news of interest from Europe, the newspaper proved attractive to many educated Africans: "The copies received by our agent are not sufficient for the population," wrote A. Ly from Sikasso. "Everyone wants to read the newspaper and the bush hasn't even been touched yet."[86]

Both the creation of new sections and the distribution of *Le Soudan* served to create a network of correspondents whose reports would enable the ARP to expose grievance and injustice, whether administrative abuse, misrule by traditional authorities, or highhandedness by petty bureaucrats. Such reports, carefully verified by ARP officials in Bamako, became the subject of written and personal interventions by the ARP leadership. Several meetings between ARP representatives and the governor of the Soudan himself are recorded, and when Jean Barody left the Soudan in February 1939 for a vacation in France, he asked and received permission to carry a thick dossier of grievances with him to the metropole.[87]

By 1939 the group was also looking forward to the elections of 1940 when a new delegate to the Superior Council of Overseas France would be chosen. Events in France, however, were to preclude any further electoral activities by the ARP. With the fall of the second Blum government in April 1938 the Socialist Marius Moutet was again removed from the Colonial Ministry; in his place the new premier appointed Georges Mandel, a sworn enemy of the unions and a man on whom the *colons* counted to suppress the excesses of union organization encouraged by Moutet and to reestablish *prestation* labor eliminated under Moutet.[88] After a lengthy campaign of hostilities organized by the political Right, Governor-General de Coppet was transferred from West Africa to the island of Madagascar in April 1939. When Barody returned to the Soudan in September, war had already begun in Europe, definitively ending the political experiments inspired in West Africa by the Popular Front and its sympathizers. Mobilization for the defense of the Republic could little tolerate the disruptions of local politics, and the government of Vichy officially eliminated the organizational freedom of the Popular Front era.

Under the Vichy government, associations were abolished and their members subject to surveillance and house arrest. Vichy was the triumph of the tradition of *étatisme*—the administrative spirit. But this repression and interdiction of activity only nourished the political appetites of educated Africans. For them the time of the Popular Front would be a period when "we were allowed to discover ourselves"; it had "opened the eyes of the Soudanese," allowed them to "take cognizance of their complexes," and "affirm an African personality."[89] In post-war Soudan there would exist, as a result of the catalytic activities of the French Left, a political elite sophisticated in doctrine and experienced in organizational technique. With them the nationalist and anti-colonial ideas of Tiémoko Garan Kouyaté would have common currency as a greater sense of self-confidence—an affirmation of an African personality—developed consequent to participation in those voluntary associations encouraged and supported by French liberals. Organizational experience gained in professional unions, alumni, or sporting associations, and in establishing the various sections of the ARP itself would provide the basis for creating political parties and trade unions in the post-war period. Publication and distribution of *Le Soudan* would provide experience in gathering grievances, articulating demands, and disseminating information. And theater, so important in shaping a sense of African personality, would become an instrument of propaganda and organization after the war. These skills and attitudes would be the legacy of the Popular Front period. Those in whom they had been cultivated, the educated elite of the French Soudan, the alumni of Terrasson de Fougères, would ultimately guide the destiny of an independent Soudan, symbolically renamed, as separation with the immediate past and as continuity with the distant past, the Republic of Mali.

NOTES

1. Abdoulaye Singaré, former minister of education of the Republic of Mali, personal interview, Bamako, June 1973.

2. "We were happy to learn that a man of our color could become Governor," recalled Jean Marie Koné, one of the principal leaders of the Union Soudanaise, Mali's governing party until 1968. While still a student at the *Ecole* William Ponty, Koné presented the "felicitations and benedictions of the Africans (*nègres*)" to Eboué during one of the governor's stops in Ségou. To this, Governor Eboué responded that one shouldn't despair, but there was "much to do." According to Koné, there was a "momentary stoppage of racism" while Eboué was acting governor. Personal interview, Bamako, June 1973. The life of Governor-General Eboué, born in French Guiana in 1884, is sympathetically surveyed in Brian Weinstein, *Eboué* (New York: Oxford, 1972). For coverage of Eboué's brief assignment to the French Soudan, see pp. 151-169. The impact of Eboué and other Antillais Blacks on their French colonial subjects has yet to be definitively studied. Lamine Senghor's *Ligue de Défense de la Race Nègre* carried a warning to "our antillais brothers, *fonctionnaires* in French colonies of black populations" in the first issue of *La Race Nègre*. These "sons of Africa," wrote the *Ligue*, have such a pride that they "believe themselves superior to the blacks of the ancient and direct African source." In letters from Bamako, Douala, and Siguiri, the warning continued, the same phrase appears: "Ils [les Antillais] sont pire que les blancs à l'égard des indigènes du pays." In Bamako, many Antillais *fonctionnaires* are remembered as "plus blanc que les blancs," with the notable exception of those in the judiciary whose commitment to equality before the law was deeply shocked by the racial distinctions and attitudes found among colonial administrators. After Eboué's departure from the Soudan a number of highly placed and sympathetic Antillais are alleged to have been transferred by the colonial administration.

3. Cheikh Ahmadou Kane, *Ambiguous Adventure* (New York: Collier, 1969), p. 45. Alexis de Tocqueville's comments on the French colonial bureaucracy in Canada are equally suggestive: "it preponderates, acts, regulates, controls, undertakes everything, knows far more about the subject's business than he does himself." *The Old Regime and the French Revolution* (Garden City, N.Y.: Doubleday Anchor, 1955), p. 57, note 24 and p. 253.

4. See, for example, the report of a meeting of the *Association pour la Défense et l'Emancipation des Peuples Colonisés*, 20 May 1936. "The Association signals to all the organizations of the Popular Front the immense hope that the electoral victory has given birth to among the indigenous populations of the French colonies." The group specifically called for an end to the *Indigénat* and for granting of various democratic liberties: freedom of the press, association, etc. *L'AOF*, 6 June 1936. The best history of the PF is that of Georges Lefranc, *Histoire du Front Populaire (1934-1938)*, (Paris: Payot, 1965). The elections of 1936 which brought forth the government of Léon Blum are discussed on pp. 111-136.

5. The *Conseil Supérieur de la France d'Outre-mer* met once a year, for eight days at the call of the minister of colonies. Colonies frequently elected members of the French

Parliament as their delegates in the hope that their political influence might be brought to bear in representing the interests of the colony. Precautions were carefully taken, however, to prevent the group from considering itself as a sort of colonial parliament. The colonial minister, for example, chose those questions which would be submitted to the council for its advice. In the Soudan, a colony of 3.5 million inhabitants, there were only 1,003 voters—the majority of the Europeans, either civil servants or merchants, and a few African citizens, mostly born in the four communes of Senegal. African subjects, who formed the bulk of the population, were, of course, not inscribed on the electoral roles, despite being subject to the weight of colonial fiscal demands. See *l'AOF*, 26 September 1936, for a comment on the injustice of the matter and the hope for some change with the advent of the Popular Front government of Léon Blum. The decree reorganizing the council was published in the *Journal Officiel de l'AOF*, 15 February 1936, pp. 134-136.

6. *Les Annales Coloniales*, no. 70 (11 September 1936) describes the seven candidates. No. 85 (3 November 1936) gives the final election results.

7. *Le Soudan*, no. 11 (December 1938). They would have preferred to support the candidacy of Aimé Quinson, a fellow socialist and former employee of the Soudanese Postal Service who had taken leave to campaign successfully for a parliamentary seat in the elections of 1936, but Quinson was ineligible.

8. The original *comité directeur* consisted of Adolf Rançon, a teacher at the *Ecole Primaire Supérieure* Terrasson de Fougères, assistant secretary; Isaac Diop, a Senegalese citizen employed by the treasury, treasurer; François Bros, a bureau chief of the Dakar-Niger stationed in Bamako; Emile Courrieu, the Bamako agent for the trading company Niger-Français; Jean Le Gall, professor of technical education and director of the *Maison des Artisans*; and Henry Pérès, station chief of the Radio Telegraphic Service in Bamako.

9. Peter Blau, *Bureaucracy in Modern Society* (New York: Random House, 1956), p. 69.

10. *Notre Voix, Organe du Parti Socialiste SFIO en Côte d'Ivoire*, no. 12 (25 May 1937). The one available source dealing with the ARP and the history of the Popular Front period, Frank Gregory Snyder's *One Party Government in Mali* (New Haven, Conn.: Yale University Press, 1965), pp. 9-35, misses much of the early organizational history of the group.

11. The sociological analysis of the ARP membership is based on the group's *Registry of Members*, located in the Diop Family Archives (DFA) in Bamako. For her gracious hospitality and generous access to these archives, I am indebted to Aminata Diop. The *Registry* lists 575 members as of 1939 when the group terminated its activities, although the pages covering members 151 through 330 have been removed, I was able to reconstruct all but 55 memberships through examination of the rosters of individual sections of the group. (Some of the 55 may be reconstructed from the pages of the ARP newspaper, *Le Soudan*.) The *Registry* and section rosters indicate the member's profession, location of membership or employment, and sometimes the date on which the member joined. The initial membership used as the basis for this analysis is 173, that number of members enrolled by September 1937 when the organization opened its doors to African non-citizens. Among these, there were 39 associated with the Dakar-Niger railroad, 28 teachers, 14 from the Posts and Telecommunications Service, 12 from the Radio Service. From the private sector, 24 were associated with local commerce.

12. I am indebted to Pierre Alexandre, *Ecole Pratique des Hautes Etudes*, Paris, for this and many other observations. Personal correspondence, 28 February 1972.

13. The emphasis here is on the active membership of the group, for there was a significant percentage of what Secretary-General Cros had called "minor employees of commerce" (14 percent). What employees of both the public and private sector share is a common status within the colonial society, but those working for private trading companies lacked the job protection enjoyed by some public employees.

14. Robert Delavignette, *Freedom and Authority in French West Africa* (New York: Oxford, 1950), p. 32.

15. *Journal Officiel de L'Afrique occidentale française* (hereafter, *JOAOF*), 10 May 1924, p. 67.

16. Henri Cosnier, *L'Ouest Africain français* (Paris: Larose, 1921), p. xiv. I am indebted to Richard Stryker, Indiana University, for bringing this work to my attention.

17. Ibid., p. 141.

18. "Circulaire au sujet des chefs indigènes," *JOAOF*, 1917, p. 472.

19. Henri Ziéglé, *Afrique équatoriale française* (Paris: Berger-Levrault, 1952), p. 176.

20. Cosnier, *L'Ouest Africain français*, pp. 141-142.

21. Personal correspondence. In a letter to the minister of colonies dated 7 May 1937, Cros indicated the nature of administrative resistance to even the symbolic aspects of the Popular Front during the May Day Festivities in Bamako:

Our comrades were painfully surprised for they believed the men whom you had designated to represent you in this territory would follow your policy and that at last under a government of the Popular Front Republicans would no longer appear as bad boys when they met to cry: "Vive la République." We hardly hoped that M. le_____, would come among us to sing the Internationale, but we had not imagined that he would not associate himself in any fashion with the national holiday, giving, once more, the impression that if the Minister commands from Paris, in the colonies, certain administrators (chefs) continue in large measure to do whatever pleases them. . . . Nothing has changed here.

Included with the letter was a summary of May Day activities in Bamako in which Cros described the nearly total abstention of the administration from decorating public buildings to celebrate the national holiday. "Not a single building in Bamako, with the exception of the *Sûreté*, the Post Office, and the *Artisanat*, which had their own flags and bunting (*pavillon*), not a single private building, with the exception of the Bank of West Africa and the Chamber of Commerce was decorated." This letter and accompanying summary of May Day activities are located in the records of the ARP in the DFA.

22. For a detailed discussion of administrative organization and relationships, see "Circulaire au sujet de l'administration des cercles," *JOAOF*, 1917, pp. 580-587.

23. The confusion between "primary" and "elementary" arises because of two parallel streams in French education before 1941: primary, conducted in *écoles communales*, *cours complémentaires*, and *écoles primaires supérieures*; and secondary, conducted in *lycées* and *collèges*. Alumni of the former were not allowed into the universities and could only go on to *écoles normales* to become school teachers. The secondary school system was elitist, restrictive, and to a large degree, private. In American usage, "academic high schools" or "college preparatory courses" might be the best equivalent to "secondary" education.

24. Delavignette, *Freedom and Authority*, p. 24. William B. Cohen, *Rulers of Empire: The French Colonial Service in Africa* (Stanford, Calif.: Hoover Institution Press, 1971), pp. 84-92, discusses the class origins of those recruited to the *Ecole Coloniale*. I have

profited immensely from a number of discussions over the years with Professor Cohen, Indiana University, on the problem of administrators and specialists.

25. Jean Surêt-Canale, *Afrique Noire: l'Ere Coloniale, 1900-1945* (Paris: Editions Sociales, 1964), p. 569.

26. Personnel Correspondence. In Bamako, Barody is remembered as "beaucoup plus communiste que socialiste" by Jean Marie Koné. I have used Charles Cros's description of Barody as "extreme Left."

27. *Notre Voix*, no. 12 (25 May 1937).

28. Ibid.

29. Ibid.

30. David Thompson, *Democracy in France Since 1870*, 4th ed. (New York: Oxford, 1964), p. 60.

31. *Journal Officiel du Soudan Français*, 1 May 1937, p. 267.

32. The colonial administration was traditionally sensitive to the demands made on it by resident Frenchmen. In 1926, Governor-General Carde wrote to the Colonial Ministry concerning the dangerous example offered by European civil servants: "The example given by European *fonctionnaires* by the form of their demands has not been without consequence on the state of mind of the African administrative employee [*agents indigènes*] who form, we should not forget, the intellectual elite of the local population, destined one day soon to be their spokesman." [Letter of 10 March 1926, SLOTFOM III, 95. Archives Nationales, Section d'Outre-mer (hereafter ANSOM).] And, again, during the economic crisis of the early 1930s, Governor-General Brévié was prompted to classify the articulation of citizen demands as a threat to public order in a *Circulaire* to the lieutenant-governors of the various colonies:

European merchants, individuals, businessmen, planters, individually or collectively, personally or by way of the Delegate to the *Conseil Supérieur*, believe themselves obliged to address the Ministry [of Colonies] directly by cabled petitions which seek to compel the high administration to take or impose measures which constitute in their mind a remedy for the actual crisis.

This was, the governor-general thought, "an inadmissible means of pressure and [a series of] provocations which could have the most fatal consequences if they lead, among the native population, to movements of insubordination or revolt as those which have just occurred in the Gold Goast and Togo." A public communication of demand and grievance was dangerous, according to the governor-general, because cables sent uncoded might fall into the hands of native telegraph operators and produce "more or less veiled threats against the public order." *Circulaire*, 19 April 1933. I D/145 "Etat d'Esprit des Populations Européens 1933-39." Archives Nationales du Mali (hereafter ANM). In an official telegram sent the day before, Governor-General Brévié suggested another reason to see European demands as threatening: they might "risk giving the mass of the population the impression of grave disagreements among European elements." *Télégramme officiel*, 18 April 1933 I D/145 ANM.

33. Only five members of the administrative services appear to have joined the ARP; the three earliest were each junior members of the *Service Civil*. The first to join, Robert Quod (member #15) reports a long family history of Socialist party support. (Personal interview, Paris, 1974). Much later members were two men who held extremely high positions in the colonial administration: Robert Salomon (#345) is identified as "Com-

missaire de Police,'' and Gonzalgue Parenteau (#444) was secretary-general, *par in-térim*—the second highest official of the colony.

34. *Le Soudan*, no. 8 (4 September 1938).

35. Shared political attachment and perceptions provided the basis of friendship ties which were in part strengthened by the operation of the colonial administration. As a consequence of the system of period rotation, Charles Cros and Adolph Rançon had both served at the *Ecole Régionale* at Kaolack, Senegal, and Paul Hilaire and Henri Toussaint had both served in the Kaolack Post Office. Indeed, Toussaint and Hilaire served at the same time, while the sojourn of Rançon and Hilaire similarly overlapped. Given the relatively restrained size of the French community, it is likely that Rançon and Hilaire, though of differing services, knew each other, and if not, the common experience would provide just another bond that would help to unite the ARP. In personal correspondence Charles Cros states that he had not met the other leaders of the ARP before arriving in Bamako.

36. Letter of 10 March 1926. SLOTFOM III, 95. ANSOM.

37. *Circulaire très confidentielle* 10 February 1930. ID/92. "Propagande Revolution-naire et anti-française, 1925-34." ANM.

38. Lamine Senghor (not to be confused with Léopold Senghor, the president of Senegal) was born in Kaolack, Senegal, in 1889, a member of the Serere people. He fought in the French army from 1915 to 1919, but apparently was partially disabled when his lungs sustained injury during a gas attack. After demobilization, he returned to Paris to study at the Sorbonne and became involved in radical politics. In 1923, he requested repatriation to Senegal for health reasons, but this request was rejected by the French government, fearful that he would be the agent of subversive ideas. He died on November 25, 1927, of tuberculosis. His biography appears in *La Race Nègre*, no. 5 (May 1928). Additional details on Senghor's life and the activities of the *Ligue de Défense de la Race Nègre* may be found in J. Ayodele Langley, *Pan Africanism and Nationalism in West Africa 1900-1945* (Oxford: Clarendon Press, 1973), pp. 286-235, which covers some of the groups active in Paris during the 1920s. Unfortunately, Langley's chapter does not cover the enormously active and influential career of Tiémoko Garan Kouyaté too much beyond his association with the *Ligue*. Kouyaté's life still awaits its biographer. He was born 27 April 1902 at Ségou, and apparently worked in the Ivory Coast as a teacher (1921-1923) before leaving to attend the *Ecole Normale* at Aix, from which he was expelled for conducting "Communist propaganda." He was executed by the Nazis during the occupation of France.

39. *La Voix des Nègres.*, no. 1 (January 1927).

40. Some colonial administrators were, however, able to make a distinction between "Bolshevik propaganda" and the nationalist aspirations of colonial subjects. In writing to the governor-general concerning those Dahomeans to whom copies of *La Voix des Nègres* had been addressed, the colony's lieutenant-governor observed, "If the militant Danae has addressed them copies of *La Voix des Nègres*, it is because they have been nominally designated by Dahomeans in Paris as susceptible to being interested *not in bolshevik conspiracies but rather in the demands of black nationalism*. They have, in principle, an undisciplined spirit." [Letter of 1 September 1927. SLOTFOM V, 3. ANSOM. Emphasis added.]

41. The letter, dated 26 April 1928, announcement of the meeting and summary of actions is to be found in SLOTFOM III, 111; and SLOTFOM III, 78. ANSOM.

42. Letter of 29 April 1929, SLOTFOM III, 78. ANSOM.

43. Letter of 30 May 1929, SLOTFOM III, 58. ANSOM.

44. *La Voix des Nègres*, the journal of the *Comité de Défense de la Race Nègre*, was first published in January 1927 and had at least two issues. It was soon replaced by *La Race Nègre*, first published in June 1927 as the official voice of the *Ligue de Défense de la Race Nègre*. Publication and distribution figures for the newspapers have not been located, but the lieutenant-governor of the Ivory Coast noted that a packet containing 600 copies of *La Race Nègre* had been intercepted. (Letter of 8 February 1928; SLOTFOM III, 58 ANSOM.) *Le Cri des Nègres*, presumably first published in 1931, followed such events as the Scottsboro trial in America and published articles in vernacular writing—Cameroonian and Malgache languages appear, for example. French intelligence sources indicated that *Le Cri* had a press run of 3,000, of which 300 were sent to Bordeaux and Marseilles; 100 to Dunkirk; 50 to Rouen, 150 to Le Havre; 150 to the Belgian Congo; 100 to the Cameroons; 400 to French West and French Equatorial Africa; 100 to Reunion; 250 to Guadaloupe; 200 to Martinique; 50 to Guyana; 50 to Berlin; 50 to Haiti; 200 to South Africa, with the remainder sold or distributed in Paris and its suburbs. ("Note sur la propagande révolutionnaire intéressant les pays d'outre-mer," no. 246 (31 January 1932), p. 7. ID/160. ANM). *Africa*, the last of the Kouyaté newspapers, probably devoted more of its columns to affairs in the French Soudan than any other. One of the men most active in the activities of the Popular Front period, Makan Macoumba Diabaté, was president of a "Committee of Friends of *Africa*" in Bamako. Macoumba had been a Soudanese stringer for a variety of West African newspapers, but for *Africa*, he appears to be only one of several, including one anonymously called "Barakela Telegraphiste"—an African employee of the Postal Service. *Africa* was first published in December 1935.

45. Letter of 20 June 1928, Lt. Gov., Soudan to Governor-General. SLOTFOM III, 58. ANSOM. Thiam had been born in 1902 at Bafoulabé, Soudan, the son of a local merchant. After attending the *Ecole* Pinet Laprade, Dakar, he worked for the *Service de la Navigation du Niger*, quitting there to work for the *Société Commerciale de l'Ouest Africain* in October 1924. In 1926, he went to work for the Syrian firm of Naja Frères in Bamako where he had the reputation of being a "serious employee." For the colonial administration, however, he was classified as "a militant" of the *Ligue de Défense de la Race Nègre*. (See the letter of 3 January 1931, Governor-General Brévié to Lt. Governor, Soudan, ID/92, "Propagande révolutionnaire et anti-français, 1925-34." ANM.)

46. Letter of 24 March 1928, Kouyaté to Thiam. The emphasis is Kouyaté's. SLOTFOM 11, 78. ANSOM.

47. Personal interviews, Abdoulaye Singaré, Assane Sèye, Fousseyni Diarra, Jean Marie Koné, and Sane Moussa Diallo, Bamako, June 1973. The quoted comment is that of M. Diarra, who was an early leader of a sports association created by the Friends of the Popular Front. The newspaper most frequently recalled by my informants was *Le Cri des Nègres*. Significantly, Kouyaté himself had written an article on the fiftieth anniversary of the conquest of the Soudan in which he commented, "What they [les indigènes du Soudan] want is the possibility of being able to evolve and develop within the framework of their own nationality. . . . They want their independence. They will fight for it." [*Le Cri des Nègres*, N.S. 3ième année No. 4 (January 1934).]

48. *Rapport Politique d'Ensemble annuel*, 1930. p. 21. 2G30/6. Archives Nationales du Senegal (hereafter ANS).

49. Letter of February 1928. SLOTFOM III, 48. ANSOM.

50. *Rapport Politique annuel du Soudan français*, 1931, p. 28.

51. *Rapport Politique annuel du Soudan français*, 1932, p. 26.

52. Ibid., p. 27.

53. Cercle de Bamako, *Rapport Politique*, 1936, p. 20. ANM.

54. Ibid., p. 27.

55. Cercle de Bamako, *Rapport Politique*, 2ième trimestre, 1937, p. 10. The *Commandant* makes specific reference to an article in *Africa* when discussing what he perceived as unfounded criticism of the administration. ANM.

56. Ibid., p. 12.

57. Born in 1889 in the commune of Saint-Louis, Senegal, Diop proved an excellent student (accomplished in French, Arabic, and English) and after graduation was employed as a clerk by the government of Senegal in 1906. In 1907 he was admitted provisionally to the teaching corps, completing his probationary period in January 1909. In 1919 he joined the prestigious financial corps for French West Africa, but opposed Blaise Diagne, the Senegalese deputy to the French Parliament in the elections of that year and as a consequence was dismissed from his Treasuries post. Shortly afterwards, he was employed on a contractual basis by the government of the French Soudan, a type of employment that carried few of the fringe benefits of a regular civil service appointment as well as a smaller salary. In December 1937 the *Trésorier Payeur* of the Soudan wrote to the colony's governor praising Diop's work: "I must also add that among his *camarades titulaires* [those holding regular civil service appointments] presently in service at the Treasury, none can be found to perform the work given to M. Diop with as much competence." [Letter of 16 December 1937. DFA] This was a letter, Diop was to later write, that "unleashed many intrigues against me" on the part of his co-workers and even several "*chefs*." Long noted as an articulate spokesman for African interests, Diop is more than likely one of those "agents of new ideas" so vehemently criticized by Bamako's *commandant de cercle* in 1937. See note 55.

58. Soudan français, *Rapport Politique annuel*, 1937. The total population of Bamako was reported to be 24,404, and the colony's total civilian population was listed as 3,627,076. In 1938 there were 542 Frenchmen reportedly in the city, but only 178 African citizens. Most Africans holding French citizenship were born in one of the four communes of Senegal: Saint-Louis, Gorée, Dakar, or Rufisque. For details on the process of naturalization, see "Circulaire relative à l'accession des indigènes a la qualité de citoyen français," 19 January 1933. *JOAOF*, 1933, pp. 158-160.

59. *Africa*, no. 12 (June 1957).

60. Secretary Cros, personal correspondence with the author.

61. Secretary Cros, in personal correspondence with author, denies the suggestion that this linkage with the educated elite might be an attempt to bring pressure on the administration, citing the sanctions at the disposal of the government. The evidence suggests a faith in support at the highest levels of the administration (de Coppet, Moutet) which might protect against such action. Indeed Jean Barody wrote, while secretary-general of the group, to deny a rumor that the group's newspaper, *Le Soudan*, had been suppressed and stressed the political (as opposed to administrative) support the group had: "The newspaper is not at all suppressed; *no one has the right to do it*; moreover, this would create a pretty scandal [*joli tapage*] in France where we have numerous friends both in the Chamber of Deputies and in the Senate." [Letter of 6 August 1938 (No. 103/ARP), Barody to Couillet Coulibaly, Commerçant à Gao. Emphasis in the original. DFA.]

62. *Le Soudan*, no. 4 (May 1938). "Barody interested himself in us," commented Jean Marie Koné, and "always defended students in administrative councils." (Personal

interview, Bamako, June 1973). In general teachers seem to have been the least tainted with racism among the specialists of the colonial bureaucracy.

63. "Given the considerable service rendered to the education of the natives of the Soudan by Governor Terrasson de Fougères," it was decided to name the local *Ecole Primaire Supérieure* after him as a posthumous honor in June 1931. Born in 1881, Jean Henri Terrason de Fougères had died 5 May 1931 of injuries suffered in an auto accident in France. See the *Journal Officiel du Soudan français*, 15 June 1931, p. 272.

64. For a most interesting contemporary examination of the French educational system in French West Africa, see W. Bryant Mumford, *Africans Learn to Be French* (London: Evans Brothers, Ltd. 1936), a work which includes several translations of official statements regarding education. Peggy Sabatier's "Elite Education in French West Africa: The Era of Limits, 1903-1945," *The International Journal of African Historical Studies* 11, no. 2 (1978): 247-266, provides a fine study of pre-World War II education in French West Africa and shows how restricted access to higher education was in the federation.

65. Robert Delavignette, *Soudan-Paris-Bourgogne* (Paris: Editions Bernard Grasset, 1935), pp. 43-44.

66. While secretary-general of the ARP, Jean Barody wrote to teachers in outlying districts to aid in the creation of a distribution system for the group's newspaper, *Le Soudan*: "We do not doubt that henceforth you will be able to serve us as an intermediary with the population of your center...[but] a word of caution; do not have the newspaper sold by the school children." [Letter of 8 August 1938 (111 through 122/L.S.) DFA.] Considering the number of persons employed and their geographical distribution, it is clear that the Educational Service of the colony was potentially one of the most effective communication networks possible. Inspection tours by Charles Cros as an *inspecteur des ecoles* could also facilitate private communication among members of the ARP belonging to the teaching corps. The ARP *Registry of Members* lists 102 members as teachers, and frequently a teacher served as a leader of a local section of the ARP.

67. *Paris-Dakar*, 16 February 1938. According to a later description, the group also concerned itself with "finding employment for educated young people, adherents or not, or with bettering the situation of those whose employment is precarious." *Le Soudan*, no. 6 (26 June 1938). At this date, the group had 130 active members.

68. The discussions surrounding application of the decree granting the right to organize professional unions in French West Africa illuminate both the colonial and administrative mentality. Bernard Sal, director of finances for the federation, is quoted as saying, "A professional union can be useful to Europeans and certain evolved Africans; I doubt if it is useful to the bulk of Africans who know so poorly how to defend themselves and who are assured, under our tutelage, of a protection to which legislation on native labor is striking testimonial." [*Procès-verbal*, 9 July 1936, p. 6, K171/26, Fonds Modernes. ANS.] Within the ranks of *administrateurs*, there was bitter dissension concerning the possibility of *fonctionnaires d'autorité* obeying a call for a general strike of union members. Indeed, a West African section of the *Syndicat National des Administrateurs des Colonies* associated with the left-wing *Confédération Générale du Travail* (G.C.T.) was formed and actively recruited among administrators, but less than 25 percent of those eligible appear to have joined, primarily, according to Pierre Casset, secretary-general of the local union, because of the strike issue. In a letter to the secretary-general of the GCT, Casset gave eloquent expression to administrative self-perceptions:

the administration is the natural tutor of the native populations, and that the administrator of a territorial district obey an order for a general strike would mean for the African populations the end of cultivations with famine for a consequence; the extension of epidemics—plague, smallpox, etc. . . . ; the cessation of teaching services and postal services; the nonfunctioning of a justice to which our overseas subjects are passionately attached because of the guarantees of impartiality to be found there; this would finally mean, in conclusion, the end of public order; strong tribes would fall on weaker tribes, theft, brigandage, etc., etc. *Can the Administrateur des Colonies, in such conditions, plunge the entire populations subject to his tutelage into misery and insecurity?* [Letter of 16 June 1937. Emphasis in the original. K 4/1. Fonds Moderns. ANS.]

69. *Africa*, no. 13 (July 1937).

70. *Africa*, no. 16 (October 1937).

71. *Africa*, no. 11 (May 1937). For a criticism of unequal application of Popular Front labor legislation to Black and White workers in the Soudan, see *Le Périscope*, no. 409 (29 October 1938).

72. Details on the activities of the *Syndicat des Instituteurs* are extremely limited. Mouriès is listed as a representative of the union, along with Konaté, Séga Diallo, and Madiba Dansoko at one of the organization's meetings for the *Maison du Peuple*. See *Le Soudan*, no. 3 (10 April 1938), p. 2. At Charles Cros's departure from the Soudan, Mouriès acted as spokesman for the various unions associated with the *Maison du Peuple*, praising Cros for his encouragement of union formation. At this time, Mouriès is referred to as secretary of the *Syndicat des Instituteurs*. *Le Soudan*, no. 4 (1 May 1938), p. 2.

73. *Africa*, no. 11 (May 1937).

74. Of the 520 members of the ARP whose professions are listed in the *Registry of Members*, 90 can be identified as employed in the private commercial sector.

75. African merchants had a history of formal organization in the Soudan. Since 1930 they had been grouped in an *Association Mutuelle de Secours et la Prévoyance*. See the *Journal Officiel du Soudan français*, 1930, pp. 608-609, for the statutes of the group. Two *Association Mutuelle* leaders, Aly Niangado and Ousmane El Madane were also prominent in the *Syndicat des Employés Indigènes de Commerce*. Niangado was assistant secretary while Ousmane El Madane served as a councillor. Not only was there an overlap of membership, but the *Syndicat* seems to have taken over some of the mutual assistance functions of *Association Mutuelle*. See the *Syndicat* dossier in the files of the Direction de l'Intérieur, Bamako.

76. Personal interview, Fousseyni Diarra, Bamako, 1973. Just *how* political *Les Flamboyants* appeared to the colonial administration is suggested by correspondence in the ARP records. In July 1938 Jean Barody wrote to Robert Percept, a fellow teacher:

The article in *Le Soudan* announcing that *Les Flamboyants* would adhere to the F.S.G.T. [*Fédération Sportive et Gymnique du Travail*] has provoked a letter from de Coppet to Desanta [governor of the Soudan]. This letter was communicated to me despite the classification "confidential." It warns the Governor about affiliation to an organization created in June 1934 by the Socialist and Communist parties. I told the Governor that our society sought a moral and material support in the F.S.G.T. and not an occasion to play politics. [Letter of 31 July 1938, No. 56/ARP. DFA.]

Snyder, *One Party Government in Mali*, errs in calling Barody president of *Les Flamboyants*, having confused those who presided over the group's organizational meeting with the actual executive committee elected by the group. The organization meeting is discussed in *Le Soudan*, no. 6 (26 June 1938); the definitive executive committee lists Diarra Thiagame as president. *Le Soudan*, no. 10 (November 1938).

77. *Art et Travail* grew out of the concerns of Jean Le Gall, director of *Maison des*

Artisans Soudanais, and Modibo Keita, recently returned to the colony from his education at Ponty. For Le Gall, the idea was to offer design courses to the youth of the capital to develop their interests in art. For Keita, it was to provide a form of intellectual and recreational activity for the educated young. Despite the oral tradition surrounding Keita's exclusive role in the formation, Le Gall's role is admitted by most participants. At Charles Cros's departure from the Soudan, Modibo Keita commented: "Yes, the group *Art et Travail*, embryo of that educational program sketched out by Comrade Le Gall, created by you with the help of Comrades Huezey and Ardouin and all the ARP, lives, will live." *Le Soudan*, no. 4 (1 May 1938).

78. My knowledge of the early theatrical activities of *Art et Travail* is principally based on interviews with Assane Sèye and Ibrahima Sall, Bamako, 1966; and Tiémoko Sangaré and Jean Marie Koné, 1973. For an extended discussion of the theater of William Ponty in French Soudan, see Charles H. Cutter, "Nation-Building in Mali: Art, Radio, Leadership in a Pre-Literate Society" (Ph.D. dissertation, UCLA, 1971), pp. 244-257.

79. In addition to those cited, the *Maison du Peuple* linked the following: *Syndicat des Travailleurs du Rail de France et des Colonies*; *Syndicat des Agents des PTT*; *Syndicat des TP*; *Syndicat de la Police*; *Syndicat des Trésoriers*; *Syndicat des Instituteurs*; *Syndicat des Agents de l'Agriculture, des Eaux et Forêts et de l'Elévage*; *Mutuelle des Employés de Commerce Indigène*; and the *Syndicat des Employés de Commerce Indigène*.

80. The affairs of the *Maison du Peuple* were governed by a thirty-three-member commission representing each of the constituent groups on some presumably proportional basis: eight delegates from the ARP; six from the ARAC; four from the *Foyer du Soudan*; two each from the *Syndicat des Travailleurs du Rail* and the *Syndicat des Instituteurs*; and one each from the remaining groups. The Executive Committee consisted of Jacques Heuzey (ARAC), secretary; Henri Toussaint (*Syndicat des PTT*), assistant secretary; Ousmane El Madane (*Foyer du Soudan*), treasurer; Tiemoko Diarra (*Syndicat des PTT*), assistant treasurer; and Modibo Keita (ARP), librarian.

81. *Le Soudan*, no. 2 (6 March 1938).

82. In Paris, the government opposition was quick to react. In the Chamber, one of the deputies, Henri Ponsard, placed a demand for interpellation, asking what sanctions the government planned to take against a governor-general of the colonies who had officially presided at a ceremony under the symbols of a foreign state. (*JORF, Débats Parlementaires*, 1938, séance du 31 mai, p. 1210). To this the ARP darkly remarked that "le capitalisme coloniale" was guiding the hand of its enemies.

83. This is not to say that all voluntary associations were created by French influence nor that French leftists were involved in all those groups existing in Bamako. As early as 1932 the government recognized a *Société d'Anciens Elèves Indigènes de l'Ecole Française* at Gao. See the *JOSF*, 1932, p. 148. In addition, many groups operated without government recognition. Among the most important African groups not brought into the *Maison du Peuple* was the primarily social organization *l'Espérance*, a group which organized Saturday-evening dances for Bamako's young people and brought together both Soudanese and non-Soudanese young people in a spirit of African solidarity. *L'Espérance* was officially recognized by the government in July 1936 (*JOSF*, 1936, p. 450) but had been formed in 1931 and had remained active since its creation. Aside from its social orientation, the major reason *l'Espérance* did not join in the *Maison du Peuple* was that it already had its own meeting place, equipped with electrical lighting and a radio receiver.

84. Sections of the ARP were created in Baloulablé, Bandiagara, Bougouni, Gao, Goundam, Kayes, Kita, Kolokani, Koutiala, Niafunké, Nioro, Mourdiah, Ouahigouya,

San, Ségou, Sikasso, Sofara, Tougan, and Toukoto. The largest and first organized of the sections was Koulikoro, with seventy-seven members as of late 1938. The smallest was that of Bougouni with six members. An ARP section in Niamey, Niger, also maintained contact with the Bamako group.

The formation of ARP sections throughout the colony had apparently begun in early 1938. In a letter dated 15 March 1938, Governor Rougier wrote to Charles Cros:

I have been notified that meetings of members sympathizing with the Friends of the Popular Front, including French subjects, have been held outside of Bamako. Since the statutes of your association indicate that it is constituted among citizens and that its social seat is Bamako, please supply information concerning:

(1) the admission of French subjects to your association
(2) the extension of your group outside of Bamako and the organization of sections thus envisioned.

[Letter No. 267 APAI (15 March 1938), Rougier to Cros, DFA.]

85. According to ARP records, 2,000 copies of Le Soudan were published for the first five issues, with the exception of issue no. 3 (10 April 1938), for which there was a press run of only 1,800. Jean Barody reported that the government of the Soudan subscribed to forty-four copies, and the governor-general in Dakar took ten copies. Le Soudan, no. 13 (February 1939).

86. Letter of A. Ly to Barody. No date, but after 7 May 1938. DFA.

87. The request was to carry back "un fort dossier qu'il voudrait pouvoir solutionner." Le Soudan, no. 14 (March 1939).

88. For the attitude of the colons, see Marcel Homet, Afrique Noire: Terre Inquiète; Garderons-nous nos Colonies d'Afrique? (Paris: J. Peyronnet, n.d.). Nicole Bernard-Duquenet's "Le Front populaire et le problème des prestations en AOF," Cahiers d'Etudes Africaines 16, nos. 1-2 (1976): 159-172, is a splendid examination of Governor-General de Coppet's difficulties in transforming the prestation system in French West Africa.

89. The evaluations of the Popular Front are those of Abdoulaye Singaré, Assane Sèye, and Jean Marie Kone, to whom, with many others cited and not cited, I am deeply indebted for their willingness to share their experiences so generously.

JANET G. VAILLANT

7

African Deputies in Paris: The Political Role of Léopold Senghor in the Fourth Republic

The political impact of France on its Black African colonies is easily visible in the history of these territories from the late eighteenth century until their independence in the 1960s, and in the legacy of attitudes and political institutions that characterize these African nations today. What is perhaps less obvious is that the colonies, in turn, have had a reciprocal and enduring influence on France. Today, as a direct result of its colonial past, France possesses an African immigrant population that has brought to France many of the problems of an ethnically diverse community. Even more dramatically, however, the African colonies played a decisive role in French politics after World War II. Failure to resolve the colonial problem led to the collapse of the Fourth Republic in 1958.

The Fourth Republic had expanded a unique feature of French metropolitan political institutions. During the life of the Republic, from 1946 to 1958, deputies elected from the colonies sat in the National Assembly in Paris. The most distinguished among them held cabinet posts and appeared to be fully integrated into the French political process. Nonetheless, the Black African deputies proved powerless to bring about significant changes in France's Africa policy. The political career of Léopold Sédar Senghor, poet, university graduate, and deputy from Senegal during the life of the Fourth Republic, illustrates both the extent and limitations of African influence on French politics during this period.[1]

The fall of France to the Nazis in 1940 and the sordid aspects of the Vichy administration revealed grave weaknesses in the French body politic. This led, not unexpectedly, to a great surge of nationalist sentiment after the Liberation. Inspired by de Gaulle's vision of France as a world power, France developed the aspirations of a great imperial power after the war, but lacked altogether the

I would like to thank the American Philosophical Society for their support of this research.

necessary resources. The government refused to recognize its limitations. It would not sacrifice one colony to hold another. It would not devote its energies to integration with the colonies at the expense of European unity, nor would it seek closer ties with Europe at the cost of looser ones with its colonies. Perhaps most serious of all, the government could not reach a consensus as to the speed and manner by which to modernize its economy.[2] Unable to pull back overseas, and lacking all realism about its capabilities, the Fourth Republic was characterized by its indecisiveness. Charles de Gaulle, with the clarity of hindsight, captured the essence of the situation:

The multiplicity of viewpoints which is peculiar to our people by reason of our individualism (and) our diversity. . . would once again reduce the State to being no more than a stage for the confrontation of amorphous ideologies, sectional rivalries, semblances of domestic and external action without continuity or consequence.[3]

Under such circumstances, articulate competent deputies from Africa merely added to the clamor.

One of the most able of these deputies, Léopold Sédar Senghor, had first gone to Paris as a student twenty years earlier, in the fall of 1928. A scholarship from the colonial administration was his reward for a brilliant academic record in mission and state schools in Senegal. He entered the top Paris *lycée*, Louis-le-Grand, competed, unsuccessfully, for that most prestigious of all Paris institutions, the *Ecole Normale Supérieure*, and then studied at the Sorbonne where he became the first black African *Agrégé de l'université*, roughly the equivalent of the American Ph.D. During these student days he developed friendships with many of France's future leaders, among them, René Brouillet, de Gaulle's first advisor on Algeria, and Georges Pompidou, de Gaulle's envoy to the first tenuous secret meetings with Algerian nationalists in Geneva and later prime minister and president of France under the Fifth Republic. His education and personal friendships gained Senghor a natural place in that informal elite, which, recent study has shown,[4] ruled France during the Fourth Republic. It is argued that those who attended certain elite educational institutions formed a web of informal contacts and personal trust that remained hidden from the public eye but proved decisive for many political alliances in the post-war period.[5]

Senghor was a writer and teacher by education and temperament, and had at first no intention of entering politics. In the 1940s and 1950s, he published four collections of poetry and was hailed as the authentic voice of Africa, a ''noble example of what France and Africa can do when they mutually enliven each other's genius.''[6] Jean Paul Sartre, then dean of Paris intellectuals, recognized his importance by writing a long introduction to Senghor's *Anthology of the New Black Poetry*, in which he discussed Senghor's theory of *négritude* and Black distinctiveness.[7] That same year, 1948, Sartre and Gide joined Senghor, Alioune Diop, and a group of African and French intellectuals in launching *Présence Africaine*, a journal designed to bring information about Africa to the Paris public. Senghor also became active among the Catholics who gathered around Emmanuel Mounier, the journal *Esprit*, and France's large Catholic center party, the *Mouvement Républicain Populaire*.[8] In poetry and essays and personal encounter with Paris intellectuals, Senghor provided an interpretive link between his culture and theirs. Mounier and Sartre, colonial administrators such as Robert Delavignette, and politician-publicists such as Paul Alduy all cited Senghor as their expert source of information about Africa.

Senghor's explicitly political career began in 1945 when he was appointed to serve on the Monnerville Commission, which was charged to study overseas representation in the upcoming Constitutional Assembly. As the first Black African *agrégé*, he was sought out as the symbol of French colonialism at its generous best. In 1945 he had his first collection of poetry in press and a job at a *lycée* near Paris, and he was also lecturing at the National School of Overseas France, the training institute for colonial administrators. What impact Senghor may have had on the final form of the Monnerville Commission's report is impossible to determine, as the proceedings were closed. Judging from the content of the report, a mirror image of the recommendations of the colonial administrators' conference held at Brazzaville the year before, and the fact that Senghor skipped its final sessions, his influence must have been minimal.[9] Nonetheless, Senghor was sought out again by the French Socialist party (SFIO) to stand for a seat from Senegal to the Constituent Assembly that fall. He won easily. Thereafter, he climbed steadily in political position, first as a symbolic Black face, but soon, after breaking with the SFIO, a political force in his own right.[10]

With a fine sense of theater, the constitutional drafting committee chose Senghor as its official grammarian. The draft constitution of April 1946 pleased Senghor by its creation of the French Union to replace the former empire. The constitution was rejected by French voters, however, for reasons that had nothing to do with its colonial provisions. This vote worried Senghor, despite public assurances from the minister of colonies, Marius Moutet, that the sections establishing the French Union would be carried forward unchanged. As it turned out, Senghor's apprehension was justified for the new Constituent Assembly, elected in June 1946, had moved to the Right. The euphoria of Liberation was over. A group of French colonists and right-wing politicians met in Paris on July 30 to accuse the colonies of ingratitude and urge France to keep tight control of its overseas investments. They accused the African delegates of representing no one but themselves, with separatism and hostility to France.[11] Dismayed by this shift in mood, Senghor acted in good French political style by giving a public interview to vent his disappointment. In harsh words, out of keeping with his more usual conciliatory tone, he warned:

We do not wish any longer to be subjects, nor to submit to a regime of occupation . . . while waiting for complete independence, we advocate federation in the context of the French Union. . . . I would like in conclusion to assure the Whites of our unshakable will to win our independence and that it would be stupid as well as dangerous for them to wish to make the clock march backwards. We are ready, if necessary, as a last resort to conquer liberty by any means, even violent.[12]

Senghor made it clear that he was not about to accept a casual thank you for the Africans' war effort and live happily with the status quo.[13] Such warnings failed to convince the new Constituent Assembly. Finally the overseas delegates called on Lamine Guèye, their senior member, to convey to the president of the Assembly their intention to resign en masse unless their views were taken seriously. Only then did hasty conferencing push the Assembly to create a French Union along the lines of the earlier draft.[14] Nonetheless, Senghor thought that the new Constitution represented a step backwards. For example, the statement that the Union of France and its colonies was formed by free consent was withdrawn, and no change in the status of any Union member was permitted without the consent of the French National Assembly. As a result, any talk of independence by Africans implied an attack on the Constitution. Furthermore, the details of colonial administration were left to future organic laws, opening up the possibility that the conservative trend gathering in France might leave promised local assemblies stillborn. In pointing out these potential problems with the Constitution, Senghor also warned that only the vigilance of the African delegates had prevented it from treating the African colonies even more unfavorably.[15]

The Constitution of the Fourth Republic placed power squarely in the National Assembly. There was no provision for a strong executive, and governments fell with regularity, as no party was able to gain a clear majority or form a stable coalition. In the first parliamentary session from December 1946 to June 1951, for example, eight ministries served an average of seven months each. An upper chamber, the Council of the Republic, could delay but not change legislation and the much-discussed Assembly of the French Union was a consultative body only and in fact powerless. Every provision of the Constitution seemed designed to support the French citizen in his desire to answer "*non*" to any change suggested by the government. As for the Black African colonies, the Constitution provided that the most important decisions would continue to be made in Paris, either by the National Assembly or by career officials at the Ministry for Overseas Territories. The one concession granted to Black Africans was the right of the overseas colonies to elect deputies to the National Assembly. While Senegal had had a deputy intermittently since the nineteenth century, Black Africa was now granted twenty-five seats (increased to thirty-three in 1951) out of a total of approximately six hundred. Complicated franchise rules limited the representation of ethnic Africans somewhat further—twenty-one in 1946, thirty in 1956.[16] These few men thus became the spokesmen for African interests, responsible for trying to shape French policy to meet the needs of their territories.

In fact, the National Assembly found little time for African questions. Serious inflation, strikes, a draining war in Indochina, and the worrisome machinations of a strong Communist party kept most deputies far too busy to attend to remote questions about which they knew next to nothing. This left career officials in the Overseas Ministry a free hand. In 1950, to pick a year at random, the transcript of Assembly debate runs to more than 13,500 pages, of which less than a hundred mention French West Africa specifically, and under thirty-five have a comment by Senghor.[17]

Nonetheless, once in the Assembly, Senghor and his African colleagues set about trying to learn the rules of the parliamentary game. They were all bound in theory by the discipline of the political party to which they were affiliated: Senghor and Guèye by the SFIO, Felix Houphouët-Boigny, the deputy from the Ivory Coast who emerged as Senghor's chief rival for African leadership, by the Communist party, and other Africans by a variety of smaller groups. To a point such dispersal was an advantage in that it provided an African voice in several party circles, so argued Houphouët-Boigny,[18] but it had the disadvantage that no party put colonial issues high on its list of priorities. After two years of trying to work within the SFIO and a brief flirtation with a new left-wing splinter group of SFIO intellectuals which took a more compatible stand on colonial issues, Senghor resigned from the SFIO in 1948.[19] He was stung by SFIO interference and support of Lamine Guèye in a local quarrel, and more significantly by the fact that "instead of being ends in ourselves, we have become means in the often sterile game of metropolitan politics."[20] Briefly without party, Senghor joined and then led a loose grouping of overseas deputies, the Independents from Overseas. He tried to create a single African party or, at the very least, an informal parliamentary grouping to coordinate policy. This effort failed, partly because of the small number of African deputies and a rule requiring fourteen members minimum for a totally independent party, and partly because affiliation with a large party was a prerequisite for cabinet appointment and hence a share of executive power.

A solid bloc of African votes could have had an important voice in the Assembly of the 1950s. No metropolitan party had a clear majority, with the result that small groups could often control the deciding votes and thus wield power out of all proportion to their size. Mindful perhaps of the argument originally used against allowing them membership in the National Assembly, namely that France would become the colony of its colonies, the African deputies chose not to take this route. They adhered instead to an unwritten rule that overseas deputies should not interfere in metropolitan affairs. Scrutiny of their voting records indicates that they almost always voted with the metropolitan party to which they were affiliated, even when, as in votes on Algeria, they privately opposed their party's position. There were several instances when the African deputies, voting as a bloc, could have swung the vote for or against investiture of a particular prime minister, presumably in return for a concession on the colonies.[21] They chose not to do this, in part because of the parliamentary rules mentioned earlier, and in part because of strong, if subtle, pressures to behave like good Frenchmen. Their overarching strategy was to influence from within: join parties, join ministries, join public forums; accept the good faith of France, educate France about its colonies, and assume that the ideals of equality and fraternity would eventually prevail. These were good reasons for avoiding militancy, but perhaps the most important reason why the Black Africans failed to act effectively as a bloc was that the two most prominent African deputies, Senghor and Houphouët-Boigny, were frozen into a rivalry for leadership fostered by colonial administrators and fueled by conflicting strategies, priorities, and personal ambitions. The effect of their rivalry was to divide the others and reduce their combined effectiveness.

Senghor's campaign to change colonial educational policy typifies the possibilities and limitations of African ability to influence French policy. Senghor quickly recognized that though in theory, initiative on colonial policy came from the Council of Ministers responsible to the Assembly, in fact most decisions continued to be made, as they always had been, by career bureaucrats of the Overseas Ministry from their office on Rue Oudinot. To that office, he turned his attention. He was already known there as an expert on education because he had served them as a consultant before the war.

In Senghor's view, improved education was a precondition of all African development and required not only more schools but better pay for the teachers, the creation of institutes of higher learning in West Africa, course material adapted to African needs, and most crucial of all, transfer of the control of education from the Overseas Ministry to the Ministry of National Education. To this end, Senghor spoke in the National Assembly, published articles, and gave interviews. Simultaneously he sent numerous letters to Rue Oudinot and worked directly with Ministry officials to show that he had studied even the most minute problems, understood the difficulty of change, and was prepared to make positive proposals as well as criticize the existing situation. The private letters show Senghor a model of respect, tact, and almost pedantic thoroughness;[22] the public ones a loyal patriot of France.[23] His correspondents reacted favorably to his high tone, but replied politely that there was no money, times were hard, and they could do little. On the questions of more schools, teachers' pay, and even the creation of new institutes in West Africa, the ministry finally took limited action. On the broader question of administrative control, however, Senghor met a brick wall. The Overseas Ministry would not give up control of Africa's education to specialists who "would not understand," so they said, the delicate requirements of the colonial situation. They did not, obviously, wish to lose control of the preparation of West Africa's future elite.[24]

Such efforts to work through the system became increasingly frustrating for Senghor. So long as he played the game by French rules, details of policy changed but its essence and spirit remained intact. There were, of course, personal rewards for playing so nicely. In September 1950, Senghor was sent to represent France at the Council of Europe in Strasbourg, later to the United Nations Trusteeship Council and then to UNESCO, and in 1955 he was appointed a secretary of state in Edgar Faure's government. In this capacity he helped in the delicate negotiations between France and nationalist groups on Morocco and Tunisia. Houphouët-Boigny was similarly rewarded. Loyal Africans were very useful for defending France's Algeria policy before international audiences. Senghor lived in a fine apartment, published his poems with leading publishers, and even received a literary prize. His was a familiar face on the Paris intellectual scene. All this, however, had little visible impact on France's policy toward West Africa in the late 1940s and early 1950s.

What finally pushed the Fourth Republic into action on the colonies was not the pleadings and maneuverings of the well-mannered deputies in Paris but developments overseas. After the fall of Dien Bien Phu in May 1954 the colonial focus shifted from Indochina to Algeria. Teetering back and forth between resistance and concession to Algerian nationalists, a succession of insecure governments finally realized that comparable movements for autonomy elsewhere in their empire could not be ignored forever. To ease the situation in West Africa, the so-called *loi cadre* was passed in 1956. It promised to extend the power of local assemblies in West Africa through a future series of decrees, and to create territorial executives for the first time. Most important, it reflected a new attempt to meet African demands for autonomy in time and in such a way as to prevent the total dissolution of the French Union. Senghor greeted this effort enthusiastically as a step toward true federation, but vehemently opposed an important facet of the new arrangement: there was no provision for an executive at the level of the old West African Federation. He believed, correctly as it turned out, that this would lead to the balkanization of Africa, the creation of many states too small to possess significant bargaining power with France or to be viable on their own. On this issue, he divided with his rival, Houphouët-Boigny, who was only too glad to support the French administration in a policy that would weaken Senghor's capital, Dakar, the administrative seat of the old West African Federation, and also free the relatively rich Ivory Coast from subsidizing its poorer neighbors. In the struggle over this issue, Houphouët-Boigny, or more accurately the French administration, overruled Senghor.

Thereafter events in Black Africa moved very fast. Local politicians accused the French of refusing to implement the *loi cadre* in good faith, for French administrators on the spot ignored the new executives and bypassed the local assemblies.[25] Pushed by the growing militance of his local supporters in Senegal, Senghor called for a very loose, confederal arrangement: independence at once, to be followed by negotiation of special ties between the former colonies and France. While France continued to hesitate, events in Algeria grew more threatening and violent, culminating in an abortive military revolt, the recall of de Gaulle to power, the abolition of the Fourth Republic and the creation of a new, Fifth Republic in June of 1958.

De Gaulle, with characteristic certainty, ruled out the idea of a loose confederation for which Senghor argued passionately before the Constitutional Committee for the Fifth Republic.[26] De Gaulle refused to grant independence under pressure or on terms that did not originate with him. He offered the colonies a stark choice: "yes," unity with France, or "no," independence in isolation from France. For a time Senghor and the Senegalese leaders hesitated, arranging to be away from Dakar when de Gaulle visited to solicit support for a "yes" vote. Persuaded in the end by fear of France's economic withdrawal, Senegal and all of French West Africa, except for Guinea, fell into line. A bare two years later, partly as a reward for his loyalty, and partly because de Gaulle finally recognized the determination of West Africans to be independent, Senghor persuaded de Gaulle to grant independence to the Federation of Mali, Senghor's attempt to recreate the old West African Federation which managed to attract only Senegal and the Soudan. In 1960 the Mali Federation fell apart, and Senegal became a small independent state. The political history of the relationship between Black Africa and France thereafter is that of the relations between juridically independent nations. A special relationship has remained, particularly in the economic and military realms, but no longer is African influence on France's Africa policy exercised primarily through metropolitan political institutions.

The Fourth Republic provided an unusual opportunity for representatives from colonies overseas to take part in a metropolitan government with the same rights and duties as representatives of metropolitan origin. There is no evidence, for example, that Senghor's participation in the National Assembly was less than complete. Yet this participation by itself did not secure an enlightened or evolutionary colonial policy. The African deputies were too few in number and too divided among themselves to act effectively. French understanding of colonial views was too limited and its tradition of centralization too strong to listen to talk of federation, and finally the government was too weak to take any decisive or controversial action. The result was drift, at a time when the situation in the colonies was changing very rapidly.

The pressures responsible for the final collapse of the Fourth Republic did not originate at home but overseas. They were not created by intransigent African representatives in Paris. They built up because of French indecisiveness and flaws in the very structure of the Fourth Republic. African deputies such as Senghor tried to act as interpreters and compromisers between increasingly militant constituencies at home and Parisian administrators who were ambivalent, ignorant, and often unduly influenced by small business and settler lobbies. The fears expressed at the Constituent Assemblies of 1945 and 1946 that France might become the creature of its colonies proved utterly groundless, because electoral rules kept Africans vastly underrepresented in the National Assembly and the overseas deputies carefully refrained from meddling in metropolitan affairs. They did not form a militant bloc in pursuit of their narrow colonial interest, but tied themselves loyally into what was, at best, an ineffective political system.

The influence that the Black African deputies did exert on the Fourth Republic is difficult to estimate and impossible to quantify in the sense of determining to what extent how many deputies or administrators acted differently as a direct result of their presence. The clearest instance of direct and successful pressure by the African deputies was a group action, their threat of mass resignation from the Second Constituent Assembly. This drastic measure succeeded in causing a suspension of proceedings and hasty attention to their grievances. Even here, however, the result was compromise, not capitulation by metropolitan interests. For Senghor, as an individual, his greatest political successes came on educational matters where he put most of his energy and on which he was an acknowledged expert. Here too, however, he did not get the major changes he wanted. So long as he and his African colleagues worked within the French system, lobbying bureaucrats, making speeches in the National Assembly, and giving interviews to the French press, they could obtain changes in detail only. They never succeeded in forcing an essential policy change. Their greatest success came when they were united and militant, which was rare, but even then they had to be satisfied with half-measures. Indeed, one might even argue that the presence of Black deputies in the National Assembly lulled French policy makers into thinking that the deputies' patience and good manners would be echoed in the colonies.

Senghor's most important contribution to France's Africa policy probably lies in the intangible realm of influencing the way the French elite thought about Africa. His visibility, obvious competence, and gentle manner led to complete acceptance by his colleagues who then found it difficult to sustain the view that Africans would never be able to govern themselves. Eloquent with his pen and at home in French literary and historical traditions, Senghor explained Africa and African aspirations in language educated Frenchmen could understand. It is ironic that Senghor reluctantly gave up the life of the intellectual to serve Senegal as a politician, and that as a politician his greatest influence resulted from his intellectual accomplishments. Senghor himself believes that he influenced French colonial policy most effectively not through his explicitly political activity but indirectly, through his lifelong friendship with Georges Pompidou and others of the French elite. His friendship with Pompidou, he believes, sensitized Pompidou to developments in Africa and so enabled him to develop informed policies while serving as de Gaulle's most trusted advisor. Presumably, this same sensitivity influenced Pompidou's policy later when he became president of France.[27] Senghor apparently shares the view of post-war French politics suggested earlier, namely that personal ties formed in certain Paris schools are the key to understanding the politics in that period. Few Africans were likely to have such ties, but if they did, they had the same opportunity to influence events as their metropolitan counterparts.

In terms of his most important political goals, however, Senghor failed. He was unable to get France to move, as he first hoped it might, toward true political integration with the colonies or later to form a loose federal union. Such a federal arrangement flew too directly in the face of the Napoleonic heritage of administrative centralization, a heritage that lives on to plague France today. It required blood spilled in Indochina and Algeria to make French society face the seriousness of overseas demands for more autonomy; no amount of rhetoric, however eloquent, was able to achieve this. As the situation in Algeria worsened, French public opinion polarized, African constituencies grew increasingly militant, and the African deputies proved powerless to deliver what their constituents demanded. Only after an abortive revolution and the recall of de Gaulle to power with strong executive prerogatives was the impasse broken. After de Gaulle returned to power and, advised by Pompidou and others, recognized the need to offer independence to the sub-Saharan colonies, Senghor at last found some success. Though he failed to see the establishment of a West African Federation as he had hoped, he did succeed in gaining independence in friendship with France. The fact that he and other African national leaders were well known and respected in Paris circles because of previous service in the National Assembly no doubt smoothed these final negotiations.

The major problem faced by Africans in their effort to shape colonial policy lay with the very structure of the Fourth Republic and the deep divisions within the French polity. The Republic lacked a strong executive capable of taking controversial action. Full acceptance into the French political process for an individual African deputy meant only that he shared the frustrations of his metropolitan colleagues. The African deputies' lack of impact on French colonial policy mirrored the overall difficulty of the French government in formulating any policy when public opinion was divided. While many pressing problems simply drifted unresolved, the situation in the colonies was changing so rapidly and raised such passion and division that it demanded decisive action—action the Fourth Republic was incapable of taking. The weight of colonial demands overloaded a defective system and provided the occasion, not the underlying cause, of its collapse. Thus the colonies hastened the evolution of the French political regime toward a presidential system with a stronger executive than had existed under either the Third or Fourth Republics and forced upon the French public a more realistic view of their place in the post-war world.

NOTES

1. For Senghor's biography with emphasis on his political contributions see Irving L. Markovitz, *Leopold Sedar Senghor and the Politics of Negritude* (New York, 1969); Jacques-Louis Hymans, *Leopold Sedar Senghor: An Intellectual Biography* (Edinburgh, 1971), and Ernest Milcent and Monique Sordet, *Léopold Sédar Senghor et la Naissance de l'Afrique Moderne* (Paris, 1969).

2. Raymond Aron, *France Steadfast and Changing* (Cambridge, Mass., 1960), p. 166.

3. Charles de Gaulle, *Memoirs of Hope: Renewal and Endeavor* (New York, 1971), pp. 5-6.

4. Ezra Suleiman, *Politics, Power and Bureaucracy in France: The Administrative Elite* (Princeton, N.J., 1974).

5. For example, René Brouillet suggested Pompidou to de Gaulle when he was looking for an advisor in the 1940s; Senghor made the initial contacts with the Algerians for Pompidou in 1961. All three knew each other from Louis-le-Grand. Interviews with René Brouillet and André Guillabert by the author, Paris, June 1975.

6. Pierre Emmanuel in *Temps Présent* (March 8, 1945): Authier in *Nouvelles Littéraires* (September 9, 1948). These and similar reviews are in the private collection of Armand Guibert, Paris. Senghor's publisher, Le Seuil, also has a collection of the reviews of Senghor's early poetry.

7. Jean Paul Sartre, "Orphée Noir," in Léopold Sédar Senghor, *Anthologie de la Nouvelle Poésie Nègre et Malgache de Langue Française* (Paris, 1948), pp. xl-xliv.

8. One of Senghor's first published essays appeared in *Esprit*, "Défense de L'Afrique Noire," *Esprit* 13, no. 112 (July 1, 1945): 237-248.

9. The speech by commissioner for the colonies, René Pleven, at Brazzaville was published in the Dakar daily *Afrique en Guerre* (February 24, 1944), p. 1. For a total account of the conference, see Commissariat aux Colonies, *La Conférence Africaine Française, Brazzaville* (Algiers, 1944). The report of the Monnerville Commission is in *Journal Officiel, Assemblée Consultative Provisiore, Documents* (Paris, November-August 1944-1945), pp. 484 ff. For details, Gaston Monnerville, *Témoinage* (Paris, 1975), pp. 365-367.

10. Lamine Guèye had unsuccessfully sought to represent Senegal in the Assembly of the Third Republic.

11. *Marchés Coloniaux* (July 27, 1946), p. 748; ibid. (August 24, 1946), p. 859. Michel Deveze, *La France d'Outre-Mer* (Paris, 1948), pp. 266-267.

12. Léopold Sédar Senghor, "Nous ne voulons plus être des sujets," *Gavroche* 102 (August 8, 1946).

13. Ibid., Monnerville, *Témoinage*, p. 388.

14. Monnerville, *Témoinage*, pp. 392-393; Lamine Guèye, *Itineraire Africain* (Paris, 1966), pp. 147-170.

15. The text of the relevant portions of both constitutions, as well as an excellent discussion of the issues involved, is in Ruth Shachter Morgenthau, *Political Parties in French Speaking West Africa* (Oxford, 1964), Appendix 11, pp. 379-392. See also Léopold Sédar Senghor, "Les Nègro-Africains et l'Union Français," *Revue Politiques et Parlementaire* 49, no. 468 (June 1947): 205-208.

16. Philippe Guilleman, "Les Elus d'Afrique Noire à l'Assemblée Nationale sous la Quatrième République," *Revue Française de Science Politique* 8, no. 4 (December 1958): 861-877.

17. "Table Analytique" and "Table des Noms," *Tables du Journal Officiel de la République*, 1950 (Paris 1951), pp. 74-75, 56.

18. Paul-Henri Siriez, *Félix Houphouet Boigny* (Paris and Dakar, 1975), p. 81.

19. Sartre was the most distinguished member of this short-lived group, the *Rassemblement Démocratique Revolutionnaire*, the left wing of the SFIO.

20. Senghor's letter of resignation to Guy Mollet is reprinted in *Condition Humaine*, no. 14, (October 5, 1948), p. 1.

21. Party discipline held on most colonial issues. Some African deputies supported government policies on Algeria in contradiction to their private opinions, hoping thereby to prove loyalty and gain support for their positions on West Africa. Guilleman, "Les Elus d'Afrique Noire."

22. "Enseignement en France d'Outre-Mer, Projet de Loi, Senghor," Direction de la Cooperation avec la Communauté et l'Etranger, Archive, Paris. This dossier contains letters from Senghor and replies and notes of various French administrators.

23. "Débats de l'Assemblée Nationale Constituante," *Journal Officiel de la Répub-*

lique Française, no. 29 (March 1946), pp. 944-947, and Senghor's articles in early editions of *Condition Humaine*, Dakar, February and March 1948.

24. Direction de la Cooperation avec la Communauté et l'Etranger.

25. Mamadou Dia, "Bilan de 8 Mois d'Autogestion," speech to the Territorial Assembly, Saint-Louis, December 20, 1957 (Saint-Louis, 1957) and his article in *Afrique Nouvelle*, no. 511 (May 21, 1957).

26. Maurice Duverger saw merit in Senghor's proposal. See his *La 5ᵉ République* (Paris, 1960), pp. 268-269.

27. Léopold Sédar Senghor, interview with the author, Dakar, March 1976. Mamadou Dia, president of the territorial government in Senegal prior to independence, later Senghor's arch political enemy, agrees with this assessment. Interview with the author, March 1976.

IV

FRANCE AND THE AFRICAN ELITES

The African elites that grew up under French tutelage were encouraged by the French for several reasons: first, for the egalitarian notion of promoting the revolutionary ideals of fraternity and liberty (those who embraced French culture and French codes could become *assimilés* regardless of color). Second, were coldly pragmatic needs of finding auxiliaries to staff the empire in Black Africa, since persuading home-loving French people to emigrate, even for short durations, was difficult. Third were educational reasons: part of the rationale for France's conquest was to spread *la mission civilisatrice*, and this meant sending thousands of teachers to help Africans evolve out of what was perceived to be a non-historical, savage human condition. Official rhetoric spoke of a thousand years for the Gauls to become civilized, but hopefully, with France's aid, Africans would not have to wait quite so long.

Britain needed auxiliaries, too, and training colleges such as Achimota in what was Gold Coast made a significant contribution in helping create a Ghanaian elite. But in contrast to the British, who accepted the growing African elite only reluctantly (and often referred to them as the "verandah boys"), France lavished much care and planning in nurturing its African wards, especially in Senegal in the nineteenth century.

By 1900, however, the situation began to change and François Carpot, the mulatto deputy from Senegal, heralded the change: Africans were no longer willing to be treated in a paternalistic way, and now began to talk of "equal pay for equal work." The *Jeunes Sénégalais*, who supported Carpot and later abandoned him when Blaise Diagne promised more, were a vanguard movement that established an agenda for reform that other African elites, in all of French West Africa, French Equatorial Africa, and Togo and Cameroun, would eventually adopt. The chapter by Wesley Johnson looks at the continuity among leaders of the Senegalese over five decades and the way the elites made an impact upon not only the French in Senegal and West Africa, but also in France. This includes also the traditional elite, represented by Bouna N'Diaye, Senegal's leading chief of the early twentieth century, who was sought out by the French administration to help formulate policy. Whereas Vaillant, in her essay on Senghor and the Fourth Republic was more skeptical about African influence in the Parisian political arena, Johnson takes a longer look at elite influence and suggests that the cumulative effect was considerable within the areas of contact.

The other side of the coin is examined by Peggy Sabatier who spent time in French-speaking Africa looking at records of the William Ponty School and interviewing some of its graduates. The Ponty School was the premier training institution for Africans during the inter-war period and maintained its influence immediately after the war; but with France's desire to hold on to her colonies, more scholarships were made available for students to study in the metropole by 1950. The elite formed at Ponty conducted the nationalist phase of African politics in the 1950s and became the heirs of France as the leaders of the new countries granted independence in the next decade. Sabatier looks at complex questions such as life-style and what the ultimate impact on these Africans was, after living through colonial domination and neo-colonial times: "The colonial administration trained, used, rewarded and at times frustrated and humiliated them." There was no doubt that Ponty graduates emerged with something that set them apart; they were the first group with a self-identity beyond the Senegalese communes (and possibly some Africans in the military) to think of themselves as an elite, as a group set apart. From the French perspective, they succeeded in creating a Francophile group of Africans committed to perpetuating certain aspects of France's intellectual and cultural life in the years to come. From the perspective of neo-colonial critics, France succeeded in creating a compliant elite modeled in its own image that would cooperate with French foreign and economic aims in the post-independence period.

It is probably no accident that two of Africa's most durable leaders since independence were Léopold Senghor and Félix Houphouët-Boigny, both of whom were trained in politics and served as cabinet-level officials during the Fourth Republic. A third leader, whose durability equaled these two, was Sekou Touré, whose training ground was French labor and politics. All three emerged as part of France's colonial elite, and all three managed to stay in power by creating and manipulating their own national elites for more than two decades.

It is also worth noting that French foreign policy has been anchored solidly during the past decade to the concept of *Francophonie*, that is, orchestrating the political and cultural activities of French-speaking nations. The Black African nations are in the majority in such an endeavor; hence sustained efforts of the *Quai d'Orsay* are targeted on keeping a francophone community very much alive. It is within this context that double impact, born in the days of the Senegalese communes, lives today.

G. WESLEY JOHNSON

8

The Impact of the Senegalese Elite upon the French, 1900-1940

At first glance, one greets with skepticism the notion that an assimilated people such as the Senegalese might have had an impact upon the colonizing French. The essence of assimilation, we are told, is to cast aside one's own culture and become acculturated within the fold of the host nation. In theory, this is precisely what occurred in Senegal between 1900 and 1940; in the process, the Senegalese earned a reputation for being the most assimilated people under European colonial rule in Africa. The names of Senegalese politicians and men of letters—Blaise Diagne, Lamine Guèye, Léopold Senghor—have become synonymous with French culture and the French policy of assimilation. It was because of the supposed success of this policy in Senegal that in 1945-1946 France expanded its assimilation policy to all other colonies of French West and Equatorial Africa and brought in more than two dozen deputies to sit in the French Parliament.

What was the reality of assimilation in Senegal before World War II? In another study, we have examined the thesis that the Senegalese became assimilated to the French for pragmatic reasons, rather than any inherent interest in becoming Black Frenchmen; that they were mainly concerned with preserving the right to vote and to gain equal access to jobs.[1] The supposition that the assimilator devoured the *assimilée* therefore is open to question in the case of Senegal; in fact, the reality of the situation suggests that in many cases, the assimilated group actually exercised some impact upon the colonizing power, both in Senegal and in France. Senegalese who became prominent in public life, journalism, and education maintained an influence on the French that is perhaps unique in African colonial history. One is reminded of the "born again" convert who joined the crusading evangelical church; he was baptized and assimilated into the fold of his new faith. The church members, however, found in due course that their new adept had brought with him a number of beliefs and ideas that ultimately made an impact upon the congregation. Our purpose in this essay is to examine the proposition that the Senegalese converts may have exercised some influence on the French "mother church."

THE ERA OF CARPOT AND DIAGNE

Senegal was well known in France as the oldest colony in Africa; since the seventeenth century, France had held sway in Saint-Louis and later on the island of Gorée. In both places, which were primarily trading comptoirs, a population of mixed African and European ancestry grew quickly, and by the time of the French Revolution they controlled local matters: these were the Creoles, or as they were often called, *les métis*. Few French people cared to live for long periods in the tropics before the day when quinine was discovered as a prophylaxis for malaria; home tours were frequent, and once one had made a small fortune, or at least enough to serve as a "grubstake" back home, most returned to France. This meant that it was necessary to have a group of trusted individuals to watch over trading firms, warehouses, and commerce with the interior during absences in France. The Creole population naturally took over that role and managed it so successfully that by the nineteenth century it was apparent that local affairs in the Senegalese communes were to be dominated by the Creoles. Thus in 1848 when France sent for a representative to the new Republic's Parliament, the Senegalese sent Durand Valantin, scion of an old *métis* family. As Dakar and Rufisque were added to the *communes de plein exercise* (places with full voting rights and the power to have a municipal council and mayor), the Creole families dominated the lists that were elected. This continued to be true despite a French resurgence after the growth of the New Imperialism and the arrival of new trading firms in Senegal to do business in the expanded French empire that soon became the myriad colonies of French West Africa and French Equatorial Africa. Senegal, as the first of France's Black African colonies, presided over this expansion; and vying with the French merchants for this expanded trade were the old Creole families—the Devès, Descemets, Guillaberts, and Pattersons among others. Some families concentrated on managing politics, and here the Creole family of Carpot excelled: Théodore Carpot was elected head of the local General Council (a quasi-legislative council), and his brother, François Carpot, became deputy from Senegal to the national parliament.

François served in the *Chambre des Députés* from 1902 to 1914 and pioneered the cause of local interests seeking redress in Paris. Despite Creole success in electing council members and mayors in the Four Communes, and Theodore Carpot's success as president of the General Council, the deputyship had eluded the Creole party since the days of Durand Valantin.[2] In 1902, however, after a spirited campaign in which he benefited from a strong Catholic vote on his behalf, François Carpot was elected as the first Creole deputy in half a century.[3] The tide seemed to be running strong in the direction of the *métis* for control of France's richest Sub-Saharan African colony.[4] The chief opponents to the Creoles were the large French trading firms, whose interests were similar but whose politics were fragmented. The French administration, preoccupied with building an empire from Dakar to Lake Chad, let affairs drift. Into such a situation came François Carpot, a French-educated lawyer who resolved to make an impact on Paris. Upon his election, which surprised officialdom, Governor-General Ernest Roume wrote to the minister of colonies:

That which really characterizes the election of April 27 is the complete triumph of local influences, especially those of the old mulatto families of the country, over the metropolitan forces, the great commercial houses.[5]

Carpot had studied law in Paris after earlier studies in Bordeaux, the traditional home of Senegalese students; by 1898 he was back in Saint-Louis, winning a local election for membership on the General Council. His career in colonial politics was launched.

Carpot's sights were focused on a return to Paris, where he had practiced law briefly after his studies. Winning against the French candidates in 1902 meant a return to familiar quarters, and it is in this context one must examine his political achievements. His campaign in 1902 was unusual because Carpot fought against the idea then current that all voters could be bribed (practiced for years by the French on the majority Black African electorate); his platform caught the imagination of younger voters especially. Carpot stood for more local authority, favored vacations and salary levels to match those of France, and criticized France for putting tariffs too high in the colonies. He also favored greater respect for indigenous political traditions and institutions. In fact, Carpot, as most Creole leaders, was proficient in speaking Wolof, the African language which had become the lingua franca of Senegal. Carpot cut a new political figure in Senegal, where for years the deputy had been a "parachuted" French candidate—that is, someone authorized by a powerful party to stand for election in the constituency, but who had little, if any, interest in the affairs of Senegal.[6]

Carpot was not the only person of African descent to sit in the French Chamber during these years: Gratien Candace, the outspoken Black deputy from Martinique, was also active in the national assembly. But it was Carpot who reestablished the idea, lost with the end of Valantin's deputyship in 1850, that an African colony should be represented by a man "of color." François was warmly welcomed into the Radical party, with whom he initially affiliated, and served on several of its committees until he affiliated with the Radical-Socialist party. He found no exclusionary politics practiced; to the contrary, the contending French parties were delighted to embrace him.

Carpot's *profession de foi*, or platform, suggests the range of his interests and his determination to make the metropole aware of problems in the African colonies. It should be mentioned that Carpot did not attempt to mask his origins or to trade on his French culture; though he was "integrated" in parliamentary life, he put forth local issues that affected his African constituents. Through the efforts of Carpot many French deputies were made aware for the first time that there was a major French colony in Africa, that it had problems, and that the assembly should take an interest in its future. He wanted to establish the secret ballot in Senegal's elections (adopted in France, it had not yet been promulgated in the colony); he favored a progressive income tax; and he argued for abolition of the death penalty, a move that won him the enmity of the ministry of colonies, which needed the ultimate sanction to keep order in the newly conquered African dominions. Carpot was a great believer in civil administration and argued that the days of the military conquest were over, that Senegal deserved to be under civil rule like other colonies.[7]

Carpot, a product of assimilation and a prize specimen of its fruits (according to his French supporters), favored the new policy of association that was announced by France after the turn of the century. This meant that France would no longer aspire to assimilate all the indigenous peoples it had newly conquered, but rather would hold them at arm's distance. Carpot, a good member of the intellectual elite trained in French schools, separated himself here from his African constituents and took the basic position of evolution—that is, that eventually all people could aspire to assimilation, but not just now. His lukewarm support of assimilation policies would later contribute to his defeat at the polls in 1914, when he fell out of touch with his Senegalese constituents, who were fighting for their rights under France's assimilation policies. But for most of the time he served in Paris, Carpot was a sounding board for local concerns, and he conscientiously strove to carry these to Paris.

When Carpot stood for reelection in 1910, he listed a number of accomplishments: he had served as secretary of the Chamber of Deputies; he had presided over the Petitions Committee; had sat on the naval, colonial, and parliamentary initiative committees; and had even served on the Executive Committee of the merged Radical and Radical-Socialist party. He had sponsored a plan to reorganize the Ministry of Colonies, which he believed operated in an autocratic manner, incompatible with a Republic; he favored allowing the Senegalese to organize labor unions and cooperatives as they had been authorized in France. He also favored tolerance for Muslims, knowing that the majority of his constituents were in fact under Islam; he argued that young Frenchwomen should be allowed to teach in Senegal—that it was safe and that their services as teachers would be invaluable. He suggested that economies in colonial governance could be effected if France would educate young Africans for government jobs rather than importing expensive Frenchmen. This blunt approach made him popular with the young elite in Senegal which was just emerging at this time. In fact, Carpot made the French aware, through his presence and his arguments, that there was a growing African elite, well educated and ambitious, that wanted to find its place under the sun. Carpot's campaign posters in Senegal were warmly endorsed by such luminaries as Henry Brisson, president of the Chamber; Léon Bourgeois, member of the Senate; and General André.[8]

Carpot also showed real courage to oppose a major development in French national security policy, and occupied front-page newspaper coverage for his arguments. The question was that of whether or not to begin recruiting Black African troops for the *Armée Noire* that General Charles Mangin favored for France's military depth. By 1910 rumors of war had caused France's high command to consider various alternatives for greater manpower; building up an African army was one proposal that rapidly gained support in France and from the governor-general of French West Africa, William Ponty. But François Carpot vehemently argued against this idea from the speaker's rostrum of the Chamber in 1910: he felt that "the liberty of engagements for blacks [was] not always strictly maintained; that the economic consequences of a vast recruiting program would be funereal."[9] By 1912, when some recruiting had already begun, Carpot still opposed it, joining forces with Jean Jaurès and the Socialists to mount an attack upon the expanded proposal in the Chamber:

To impose obligatory military service on natives who are vanquished men and subjects?...France has been generous and accommodating to the weak, but she can't require the natives to participate in the defense of her territory while the natives believe, right or wrong, that they have been dispossessed of their homeland.[10]

Carpot vigorously fought the initiatives of the army and Ministry of Colonies, which favored the scheme. But his coalition, even supported by Jaurès and his compatriots on the Left, was not enough to stop the French army. Recruiting was increased during the next two years, and the groundwork was laid for conscription of Africans that took place after the war started in 1914. Ironically, Carpot's opposition, lauded by many Africans who wanted to stay out of any potential intramural quarrels in Europe, later won him the ill will of the young Senegalese elite (young educated men of Saint-Louis and Dakar) who sought the right to enlist in the army in order to clarify their status as French citizens rather than as French subjects.[11] The net result of Carpot's defense of Africa's manpower potential contributed to his defeat at the polls in Senegal in 1914. The urban elites wanted to serve in the army, whereas the non-urbanized peoples, who could not vote for Carpot, were opposed to service.

Carpot was defeated in 1914 by Blaise Diagne, who favored Africans serving in the French armed forces. In fact, Diagne was later during the war catapulted into the French public eye because of his activities on behalf of recruiting more Africans for the army. Carpot never gave up hope of being reelected; he ran again in 1919 but was once again defeated. He then retired from public office. But during his twelve-year stay in the Chamber, he had pioneered the concept of furnishing the assembly with an authentic voice of concern from Black Africa—the first since Valantin. Carpot was in a unique position as a colonial to participate fully in the political life of the ruling country. If one looks at Britain, Belgium, Germany, or Portugal during these years, there is no comparable example of a colonial coming to the capitol of the metropole to vote, lobby, and become a valued member of one of the ruling parties. To be sure, France at this time had representatives in Parliament from Algeria, but these were *colons* (Frenchmen transplanted from France to North Africa, such as Eugene Etienne) and not a colonial who had roots in the colony. Carpot prepared the way for a deputy who also would give the assembly an African voice; this one stronger and louder and more authentically African.

Whereas the admission of François Carpot, a mulatto, to the French Parliament created a ripple, the election in 1914 and admission of Blaise Diagne, a full-blooded African, caused a tidal wave of protest. Diagne, who was well educated in French schools in Senegal and France, had served for almost twenty years in the French customs corps in various overseas colonies. Intelligent, shrewd, audacious to a fault, Diagne determined that Senegal needed an authentic African representative, since he believed the Creoles, such as Carpot, were increasingly ignoring the needs of Africans and siding with the French. Diagne returned to Senegal in 1914 and made the question of military service an issue; he correctly perceived that the Senegalese elite, often called the *originaires*, were worried by suggestions from some French officials that they no longer be allowed to vote; the franchise had been theirs since 1848. Diagne campaigned on other issues, such as equal pay for equal work (an implied criticism of double pay scales for French and Africans in government). He favored returning key lands to the Lebou ethnic group, which had been dispossessed by the French when they built the new capital of Dakar in the mid-nineteenth century. He also courted the *petit colon*, or marginal French worker, whose interests in Senegal had been overlooked by both Creole and French business candidates in the past. By forging a coalition of young elites, Lebous, and marginal French workers, Diagne was able to overcome Carpot's incumbency and be elected deputy of Senegal.

Diagne's victory was not well received in several circles: the Creoles realized that a full-blooded African would unleash the floodgates of entry into politics for other Africans. In the past, the Creoles had posed as "elder brothers" of the Africans, arguing that they possessed the acumen and expertise to manage local political affairs. Diagne's victory would set in motion the wheels of change, and the Creoles attempted to have Diagne's victory quashed.[12] Carpot brought a complaint against Diagne to a special commission appointed by the Parliament in Paris to look into alleged irregularities in Diagne's election. Indirectly, Carpot had the support of the French administration, which was electrified by Diagne's victory. Neither the governor of Senegal in Saint-Louis nor the governor-general in Dakar had foreseen the possibility of an African winning the election; the French colonial government had adjusted to having its most important African colony represented by a *métis*, who had studied in Paris and who seemed approachable, despite his calls to reorganize the Ministry of Colonies; but to face a full-blooded Black, who seemed to emerge from nowhere, with no apparent family connections to the old Creole oligarchy of Saint-Louis, created a malaise in official circles. Governor Raphaël Antonetti who wrote from Saint-Louis to Ponty after the election, deftly suggested that Diagne might be done away with, but then noted that "we shouldn't do this." This was an open invitation to Ponty to give Antonetti orders to prevent Diagne from leaving Senegal for Paris. Ponty, who was known to be a disciple of Lugard in supporting traditional chiefs, was usually hostile to the new urban elites, whom he failed to understand; but in this instance, since Diagne had supported the idea of military service, and Ponty was the prime backer of General Mangin's idea of the *Armée Noire*, Ponty opted for not tampering with the election. Moreover, as a good Republican, Ponty undoubtedly knew that Diagne had won a fair election (there was no evidence of voting irregularities) and that if he were removed from the scene, an inquiry from Paris was bound to follow.[13]

Diagne's fate as the new deputy from Senegal, the new African voice in the Chamber, was held in the balance by the Leredu Commission, empowered to decide Diagne's acceptability to be seated. The attack was mounted on Diagne as a possible African subject not having the right to run for office; the commission sidestepped the niceties of jurisprudence and held that Diagne had won an election, that he had exercised his option as a voter during his assignments overseas, and the fact that he had never been registered for a Senegalese election should not be held against him. Carpot made a last-ditch stand against Diagne, arguing that he had unleashed a racial war in Senegal, pitting Whites and Coloreds against Blacks. The Leredu Commission, sifting through a mountain of evidence, decided that no hard proof of irregularities existed and that Diagne should be seated.[14]

The French colonial establishment, the Ministry of Colonies, and the big French businesses from Bordeaux and Paris all had favored excluding Diagne in some way. Diagne's knack for survival in the French customs corps, however (where he was threatened numerous times for his aggressive pro-Black political attitudes) stood him in good stead, and he outwitted an effort to quarantine him in Senegal and escaped to France, to show visibly who he was and that he was an educated African fully capable of filling a seat in the Chamber. Diagne had debated in public no less an important "establishment" figure as Victor Augagneur, former governor-general of Madagascar, on the problems in French colonial policy. He established a reputation very quickly as an accomplished orator and skillful debater; Diagne felt as though he were "in his milieu" upon entering the Chamber. His colleagues there reserved a welcome for him just as warm as that given Carpot a dozen years before, for was not Diagne, like Carpot, a living example of the wisdom of France's assimilation policies?

Diagne was not, as some had supposed, an ignorant African emerging from the masses. He was born on the island of Gorée of African parents, but when a child was taken under the wing of the Crespin family, which had distinguished itself among local Creole families by furnishing high-level functionaries to the French colonial system. The young Blaise grew up in an atmosphere of achievement and education; what more natural in later years for him to aspire to a post in the customs corps—and eventually to sit in France's assembly? When it came time to marry, Diagne married the French girl he had met during a leave in Paris, Odette Villain of Orleans. And socially, Diagne was received in a number of important residences in France upon arrival, because he was a member of the *Grand Orient*, France's leading order of freemasonry. During his overseas service, Diagne was befriended by French people who appreciated his wit, culture, and ambition and persuaded him to become a mason, which was the inner circle of colonial officials. In one sense, Diagne's admission to the *Grand Orient* almost overshadowed his admission to Parliament; the lodge was admission to the private circuit of power behind the scenes that often made crucial decisions during the Third Republic. Diagne entered that world when he entered the lodge; his entry into Parliament confirmed his right to an important place in lodge councils.[15]

The outbreak of war in August of that year drew Diagne into military questions quickly. His constituents in Senegal still wanted the right to enlist in the army, but they specified the *regular* French army, not the *colonial* troops, into which the Africans recruited by Mangin's disciples had been placed. Diagne cabled to Dakar to his lieutenants to hold firm, that only when the citizenship rights (franchise) of the Senegalese urban dwellers was clarified could the question be resolved. This took place the next year when Diagne, after adroit maneuvering and lobbying, persuaded the Chamber to give a voice vote on the legality of the four communes of Senegal's inhabitants (about 90 percent African) conserving citizenship rights. The Chamber, mindful that this would pave the way for more military recruits, supported Diagne.[16] The so-called Diagne Laws of 1915 confirmed that all Senegalese born in the four communes were French citizens; in return, Diagne gave the signal for the enlistments in Senegal to begin. A wave of patriotism to save "the mother country" swept over the urban Africans, who earnestly went forth to fight for France and Senegal against the "German barbarian."

Diagne's status grew quickly with his colleagues because he had helped the war effort. In 1917 Georges Clemenceau, who had just become prime minister of France, called in Diagne and asked if he would undertake a special recruiting mission to find more African troops. The situation on the Western Front was critical; France had suffered tragic losses in manpower, and it was a matter of speculation when the Americans would arrive. This made more African troops crucial to France's survival in trench warfare. Would Diagne be willing to persuade African chiefs and parents to send more sons to fight for France? This set in motion another struggle of personalities far stranger than the Carpot-Diagne battle, when Carpot had opposed Africans in the French army and Diagne had supported the idea to gain confirmation of citizenship. Now Diagne faced the official and personal wrath of Joost Van Vollenhoven, the brilliant young governor-general of West Africa who was viewed by the Ministry of Colonies as the brightest star on the colonial establishment horizon. Van Vollenhoven immediately filed a report to Paris arguing that France's West African dominions could not furnish any more soldiers; that Africans were sick of a long war in which they had little stake; and that in fact, many areas of French dominion were on the verge of revolt (Mali, Dahomey, Ivory Coast). Added authority was lent to Van Vollenhoven's observations by the fact that they were prepared by his chief assistant, Maurice Delafosse, France's most famous and respected anthropologist of Africa.[17]

Diagne's political future and effectiveness were at stake. Clemenceau presumed because Diagne was Black that he could approach Africans in Soudan (now Mali and Upper Volta), Guinea, Dahomey, and Ivory Coast and persuade them to send more men—something that French governors and district officers had been unable to do. Once the Africans understood that recruitment meant fighting in combat rather than lucrative garrison or guard duty, there was little interest across French West Africa in serving in France's troops. Diagne, after all, was an elected official only in Senegal, and in fact was representative only of the urban dwellers in that colony who had the franchise. Rural Senegalese and other Africans in France's other colonies that made up French West Africa only knew of him dimly, if at all. What would be the reaction of the great traditional chiefs of eastern Senegal, the Soudan, the Mossi of Upper Volta? Clemenceau knew little if anything of the political situation in West Africa, where only someone of personal charm and long service in Africa, such as William Ponty, who numbered many Africans as his intimate friends, could possibly hope to sway the traditional chiefs. But Ponty had died in 1915, and his successor in office, Van Vollenhoven, was now taking the line that the Africans had suffered enough because of the war and should be left alone.

Diagne as a consummate politician decided he would risk his political future by making the recruiting trip, hoping that his prestige as high commissioner of recruiting, a cabinet-level job that Clemenceau designed for him, would give him enough clout to change the attitude of both Van Vollenhoven and the chiefs. He insisted on a number of conditions, which Clemenceau agreed to. First, West Africa would be given more hospitals and clinics, *lycées* would be established for the benefit of African students, African soldiers would be exempt from taxation, especially free from the hated *indigénat* (native code), African veterans would receive decent pensions, and after the war, a new medical school would be built in Dakar and good jobs reserved for veterans. Diagne shrewdly insisted that these promises be spelled out in a memorandum decree to be issued by the minister of colonies, Chamber colleague Henri Simon, in the *Journal Officiel de la République Française* on January 14, 1918, for all the world to see. Only then would he consent to leave for Dakar as head of the recruiting mission. Van Vollenhoven, miffed because his expert advice was ignored, resigned his post; there was also the hint that the governor-general preferred not to give full honors to an African, even one of cabinet level.[18]

Diagne's recruiting trip proved a great success. As a direct result of his efforts, more than 60,000 men were eventually incorporated into the army. He was well received by most chiefs and French administrators, although exaggerated stories of his demands upon French colonial officers gave the impression that Diagne traveled in imperial style. Diagne was a stickler for official protocol. When arriving in Dakar, for example, he refused to leave his ship until the new governor-general came first to see him. In his view, as a cabinet-level officer, the governor-general was obligated to do the welcoming, and Diagne had his way. For his efforts, Diagne was offered the *Légion d'Honneur* by Clemenceau but realizing that his efforts had resulted in African men joining the ranks of the war weary, he declined. He was painfully aware that many West Africans resented his trip, that they grudgingly admitted his authority, and that they wondered why an African would champion the cause of sending more men to France when the Frenchman Van Vollenhoven was against it. This proved to be the high point of Diagne's impact upon the French, who gave him the title of commissar of colonial troops after his cabinet mission expired. All France was beholden to the deputy from Senegal who had arisen to help France in its darkest hour.[19]

After the war, Diagne ran for office again in Senegal and founded the first effective political party in French West Africa, patterned on French party lines. This victory in 1919 over rival François Carpot settled Diagne into a twenty-year stay at the Chamber and brought him constantly before the French public during the 1920s and early 1930s. When William E. B. Du Bois decided to organize the first Pan-African congress in France at the Versailles peace conference in 1919, he asked Diagne to chair the sessions. Diagne's prestige as a loyal colonial subject, leader of the international Pan-African congress, and commissar of colonial troops led to his selection by colleagues in the Chamber as head of the Committee on Colonies.[20] Diagne was now in the unusual position of chairing the parliamentary commission charged with overseeing the activities and policy of the Ministry of Colonies. He carried the African voice started by Carpot forward and became one of the arbiters of colonial policy.

The Merlin affair illustrates the power that Diagne amassed during the early 1920s in these positions. Martial Merlin was a conservative and old-school colonial governor who was installed as the new governor-general of French West Africa in 1919 by reactionary officials at the Ministry of Colonies, who feared the rising power of Blaise Diagne and the possibility of eventual subversion from the Bolsheviks in the Soviet Union. Merlin gave notice that he looked with a jaundiced eye upon the activities of the Diagne political party in Senegal. Multiple harassments and provoking incidents led to a confrontation between Diagne and Merlin, and they became bitter enemies. Merlin launched a campaign to discredit Diagne, to have him branded as a dangerous radical in France, charging that Diagne spoke with a forked tongue, making statements disloyal to France in Senegal, and covering his real intentions with pious utterances of loyalty in France. There was some truth to these accusations, since Diagne viewed his mandate from the Senegalese to bring about greater participation in local governance; he was perfectly clear about his demands but in France added rhetoric that would retain his friends and shore up his alliances in the Chamber. Merlin's campaign of vilification and harassment was stepped up in 1920 and 1921. Finally, in 1923, Diagne acted: he arranged for the transfer of Merlin and his replacement by *Grand Orient* colleague Jules Carde the year following.[21]

Diagne's reputation soared both in France and Senegal: in France as the most powerful deputy on colonial matters; in Senegal as the African who dared deal with the French on their own terms. It was acknowledged by Fernand Levecque and Maurice Beurnier that they both owed their appointments as governor of Senegal (at different periods) to the influence of Diagne.[22] Diagne soon gained a reputation as one of the most effective speakers in the Chamber and was courted by other deputies to support legislation. During the early 1920s, he founded and edited a colonial weekly newspaper in Paris, *L'Effort Colonial*, to broadcast his views.[23] The paper did not survive (Diagne also founded the leading paper in Senegal, *La France Coloniale*, which did flourish until his death in 1934) but indicated the scale of his activities and the depth of his ambition.[24] Diagne's name was sought by tobacco companies for endorsements, he backed a wholesale trading company in Senegal that might have become a major concern but for the complications of wartime trading regulations, and he fostered experiments with new types of marine propulsion on the Senegal River.[25]

Diagne lived his career to the hilt. He occasionally played tennis and enjoyed taking his three sons and one daughter to the beaches or mountains for holidays. He had few hobbies and spent what free time he had writing letters or editorials for his newspapers. He was what today would be termed a "political animal" in the sense of his total devotion to the Chamber and his responsibilities there; he understood the nuances of the French political system and brilliantly exploited them on behalf of his African constituents. He was frequently invited to speak in Paris and the provinces, and he became a familiar figure on the lecture and debate circuit. At Rouen in 1922 he told his audience of 3,000, assembled in the Circus amphitheatre:

Other countries (such as India and Egypt) may harvest bitter fruits of a utilitarian colonization, but France...has understood her duty is not limited to colonizing but includes that of liberating an oppressed race.[26]

Diagne lauded France's educational and economic policies in Africa, criticized American Blacks for ideas that were "too revolutionary" and not practical, and reminded his listeners of the almost 35,000 Africans who died for France during the war and more than 40,000 who were wounded. This was received with an enthusiastic outburst of applause, a military band concert, and civic and regional authorities crowding around to congratulate him.

Diagne heralded a new phase in French culture after the war: that of taking great interest in Black culture, personalities, music, art, and literature. This had been spear-headed by the very real impact made upon the French public by the Senegalese *tirailleurs*, as the French called the Blacks who had served in the army (despite the fact that the majority of West Africans serving in the French forces were from other colonies than Senegal). There were joyful parades through Paris and down the Champs Elysées, inspections at the *Ecole Militaire* to honor the Black troops after the war. In a sense, they became fashionable, with their red caps and colorful uniforms; they jammed the cafes and added a dimension of color in Paris that was totally new. In the midst of this glory was Diagne, as commissioner of African troops, who soon became the self-appointed spokesman for all things black in France.[27]

This was the 1920s, a time when an American Black entertainer, Josephine Baker, became the toast of Paris; when a new generation of African expatriates (seeking greater freedom in France than they had in France's colonies), joined with other Blacks from the West Indies and the United States, who sought greater freedom too. Paris has always been a cultural mecca for expatriates and exiles; this decade saw a new group emerge in its cafes, streets, and journals: the Blacks. Among this group, Diagne was persona non grata; he was the establishment figure who was coopted by the French. This world of expatriates was dominated by such proto-nationalists as Garan Kouyaté of Soudan, Lamine Senghor of Senegal, and Tovalou Quénum of Dahomey. These men sought to modify the colonial regime in Africa and set in motion the possibility of self-government. Many were ideologues (some were Marxists), some were cultural nationalists, anticipating the *négritude* philosophies of the 1930s; many of them were watched closely by the French police and were obliged to disappear at times in the *demi-monde* of Paris to survive. But on the whole, Paris was a free city, and the traffic in ideas was great among Black peoples from both the old and new worlds. The French art world had by now, thanks to Picasso, Braque, and others dis-covered the glory of traditional African peasant art; American jazz, *le jazz hot*, made Black musicians welcome at Parisian bistros; and by the end of the period, Raoul Diagne, son of the deputy, became one of France's soccer idols, a Black hero for the sports fans of the nation. One could fairly say that the Senegalese were in the vanguard of this Black cultural awareness that spread across France.[28]

By the end of the 1920s, however, Diagne fell out of favor with many Sen-egalese and fought for his life in the parliamentary elections of 1928. Only the fact that his colleague in the *Grand Orient*, Jules Carde, had become governor-general in Dakar partially through Diagne's influence saved him. One has the impression of managed elections; the opposition, former Diagne lieutenants Gal-andou Diouf and Lamine Guèye, came to Paris to contest the outcome. They challenged not only the election but the idea that Diagne was the filter through which Africa was interpreted to the French Parliament and public. They found willing listeners at the French Socialist party (SFIO). The era of Blaise Diagne as the primary influence of the Senegalese elite on France was rapidly drawing to a close.[29]

THE CHALLENGE OF GALANDOU DIOUF

Blaise Diagne did not die until 1934. After his friend Carde managed to "arrange" his election in 1928 and forestall investigations, Diagne went on to win reelection in 1932. But it was apparent he had lost his appeal to his Senegalese constituents, which at one time had bordered on the charismatic, in the true sense of that word. There were new men, hungry for recognition, eager to taste the fruits of public acclaim too, who were waiting in the wings, ready to make their mark on the world of France. Galandou Diouf and Lamine Guèye were the leaders of this Diagne opposition. They were two very different individuals, and in this essay we will consider Diouf first and then Guèye .

Galandou Diouf could possibly claim to be the elder Senegalese full-blooded African politician, because for several years before Diagne arrived home in Senegal to win the election of 1914, Diouf had served in the General Council and had become a thorn in the side of the French government with his critical remarks in council meetings. Diouf might have flirted with the idea of running for deputy himself, but he lacked the educational advantages of a Diagne and the milieu of Creole elitism and achievement in which Diagne had matured. When Diagne appeared in Senegal, Diouf deferred to him and became his chief lieutenant and campaign manager. A large, powerful man, garrulous and good natured, Diouf had a natural flair for politics and learned quickly from the more experienced Diagne, who had seen metropolitan political campaigns and knew how to conduct one. Diouf basked in Diagne's election; he stayed in Senegal and managed local politics for Diagne while he was in Paris. When the 1915 laws were passed confirming citizenship, Diouf was one of the first to enlist and was made a lieutenant in the regular French army. He fought in the war as a surrogate for Diagne, who stayed on the job in the Chamber. When the war was over, Diouf personally orchestrated the great Diagne victory in 1919, which put his party in control of Senegal's cities, General Council, and deputyship. Diouf became mayor of Rufisque and continued in the General Council.[30]

By the mid-1920s, however, Diouf was breaking away from his mentor. They differed on Diagne's rapprochement with the large business firms of Bordeaux— Diouf agreed with the expatriate leaders in France, such as Lamine Senghor, that Diagne had compromised himself. Diouf believed it was impossible to serve both the Senegalese and the French business monopoly at the same time. More-over, he was not helped by Diagne when he ran into trouble for fiscal irregularities at Rufisque city hall; the so-called "*affaire des charbons*" in which Diouf supposedly profited from delivery of coal to the city tarnished his image with some officials. Among the Senegalese people it was a different matter, for Diouf had a personal touch which drew voters to him regardless of his behavior. "Galandou" was a man who came to power as a member of the young elite of Saint-Louis, but who now drew his greatest strength from non-educated voters, who were willing to forgive his excesses or failings. Diouf had attempted school teaching but was suspended by the French because of his outspoken manner. He had tried business after his tenure as mayor of Rufisque, but was driven into bankruptcy by the French, who feared his opposition to Diagne (who by the late 1920s appeared to be pro-French compared with the populist Diouf).[31]

The election of 1928 found Diouf mounting an effective campaign, charging that Diagne was so preoccupied with life in Paris that he was ignoring his constituents in Africa; that Diagne had shored up his liaison with Bordeaux commerce and was no longer an independent man; and that Diagne could no longer represent African demands, since he was out of touch with what Africans wanted the French to hear. As mentioned above, the evidence suggests that he won the election, and when the governor-general refused to have a recount, Diouf and his manager, Lamine Guèye, sailed to France. There they were cordially received by the French Socialists, who at that time were beginning to take an interest in France's African colonies—an interest that would grow steadily and culminate in 1936 during the Popular Front with the appointment of party member Marius Moutet as minister of colonies.[32]

Diouf's most promising host was Pierre Taittinger, member of the famous champagne family, who was now head of the Chamber's Committee on Colonies that Diagne had once chaired. He promised to look into Diouf's complaints if Diouf would help spread some of Taittinger's ideas to Senegal. He had founded the *Ligue Patriote* and Diouf promptly joined it. Diouf took no chances, however, and left Paris with excellent contacts in hand with both Taittinger and the Socialists. During the next year in Senegal, Diouf served as a local director for Taittinger's interests; but when the powerful deputy was unable to buck the colonial establishment in order to inquire into the election of 1928, Diouf lost confidence and moved to his SFIO friends. By early 1930, Diouf and many followers had joined a fledgling group of French Socialists in Dakar and established the base from which the Socialists would eventually become the most powerful party in Senegal. This took courage in 1930 because at that period colonial officers considered Socialists "*agents de Moscou*" and Diouf was openly branded a Communist by the press, business, and government interests.[33]

Galandou Diouf was no stranger to France. He had served in the war there and afterwards was Diagne's chief assistant during Diagne's appointment as commissar of colonial troops, and he had made useful future contacts during his 1928 visit. Although Diouf stood for reelection and lost in 1932, when Diagne died two years later, the populace of the colony was agreed that he should be the new deputy. His ex-manager Lamine Guèye, who had become reconciled with Diagne in 1931 in order to accept a provincial magistrateship, opposed him but lost. Diouf now readied himself to take on Diagne's mantle in the Chamber by shoring up his position in Senegal. Not trusting some of his followers, who had deserted him after the 1932 loss, Diouf decided to make Alfred Goux, an ambitious French businessman, his prime lieutenant for political affairs in Senegal. Goux had access to funds from the main business houses of Senegal; Diouf, who now broke his ties with the SFIO, was presented as a reasonable man, with a long record of activity in business and farming. Goux provided a solid financial base for Diouf, who now abandoned his earlier rhetoric of castigating Diagne for being too closely aligned with the French business houses.

There was considerable debate on how Diouf would perform in Parliament. No stranger to Paris, no stranger to legislative bodies, Diouf still lacked the polish, self-assurance, and cosmopolitan outlook that had made Diagne so popular with both Parisians and provincials alike. Diouf proved quickly that he was not a naive rustic in the city; having several wives under Muslim law, he decided he would take a new, younger wife to serve as his hostess in Paris. Asked if the French would complain about his wives, he said if necessary he would legalize just one of them and keep the others "as mistresses, just as the French do."[34] The young Mme Diouf made an immediate impact upon Paris; her photos were printed everywhere because she decided to remain in *boubou* and traditional Senegalese dress. Her grace and charm made her a favorite of Parisian society, and her dress was widely copied and even exercised a subtle influence upon the Parisian salons. Far from appearing an obscure rustic, Diouf was thrust into the public eye, too, because of his connections with French veterans of World War I, of which he was one. There were fond memories of the Senegalese troops and Diouf was immediately cast into the role of Parliament's Black representative. Diouf had little trouble accepting the theoretical mandate to speak for millions of West Africans who were neither in his jurisdiction in Senegal nor particularly interested in his politics.[35]

Diouf was bombarded by appeals from different political groups to affiliate; his acquaintance with Taittinger, who was still head of the Committee on Colonies, now paid off, and the champagne magnate wrote on 20 September 1934 to the governor-general at Dakar:

I received a letter from Galandou at the same time I received your note....He tells me he has now rallied to your point of view. Upon my personal assurances, he has discarded his attitude of being persecuted, and he tells me he is now ready to cordially work closely with you, and follow your advice, which at the beginning of his political career could be terribly helpful.[36]

Diouf had undoubtedly had his head turned by so much attention, especially being courted by the head of the Committee on Colonies. His Socialist friends courted him also, but Diouf preferred to create his own political party in Senegal, known popularly as the Dioufist party, which would be loosely affiliated with Taittinger's allies. On 10 May 1935 he gave a speech at a reception in his honor, after also (in good French tradition) being elected mayor of Dakar: "It's not just 400,000, but a million men who would march tomorrow to defend the Fatherland in Danger!" Diouf repeated this speech countless times during the next four years, until the war actually did break out, and West African soldiers again marched off to help France in another European war. This was the secret of Diouf's great popularity in France: no one doubted that he, Galandou Diouf, former chief assistant to the great Diagne, former first lieutenant of the French Army, could persuade the Africans once again to leave their tropical homeland to defend France in the trenches. The Senegalese veterans' organization endorsed this point of view, and Diouf soon found himself a featured speaker all over France, renewing a distant camaraderie with World War I veterans.[37]

Diouf was homespun, gruff, lovable, and human; the French overlooked the fact that he had few of Diagne's qualities of sophistication that had made him the ideal specimen of assimilation. In 1934 Diouf quickly found his political base: the old-boy network of the *anciens combattants*; he shrewdly exploited it and found politicians courting him rather than, as many in Senegal had supposed, he courting politicians in France. Diouf became an independent and did as he pleased while Alfred Goux managed his political base in Dakar and his assistants ran the Dakar city hall in his absence. Diouf did not hesitate to lend his prestige to the cause of North African Islam and on 9 March 1935 spoke at a banquet in Paris organized by *Ligue de Défense des Musulmans Nord-Africains*; he organized an informal grouping of 210 deputies in the Chamber called *Groupe Parlementaire de Défense des Intérêts de l'A.O.F.* to protect and lobby bills affecting French West Africa. On 22 June 1936, speaking in the prestigious *Salle des Sociétés Savantes* in Paris, Diouf told his audience of French businessmen, members of the *Comité de Défense des Intérêts des Colonies et des Coloniaux*, "I am neither radical, socialist, nor communist, but tomorrow I can put 400,000 Negroes at the call of France!"[38]

Diouf signed a contract with the textile magnate Boussac giving his company exclusive rights to make textiles for the African market with Galandou's photo or likeness printed on a variety of cloth destined to be made into table cloths, sheets, and especially to be worn by fashionable African ladies. Thus Diouf pioneered the practice that became standard in most West African countries after World War II during the nationalist period of having politicians' likenesses adorning textiles.[39]

Diouf further anchored his power base in Senegal by cementing good relations with the Mouride religious group, one of Senegal's largest Muslim orders and probably its most powerful religious group. When Diouf had been forced into bankruptcy in the early 1930s by his French opponents, he had survived only thanks to loans from Cheikh Anta M'Backé, brother of the leader of the Mourides. M'Backé had run afoul of the French administration, so that when he became deputy, one of Diouf's first acts was to arrange for the end of M'Backé's house arrest. M'Backé reciprocated by putting the political clout and wealth of the Mouride group at Diouf's disposal. In an analysis made in secret by the French *Sûreté-Général* in 1938, the question was asked, "What are the sources of Diouf's popularity?" The document gave these responses:

Galandou Diouf est considéré par tous les autochtones (citoyens ou sujets) comme leur émanation directe. Proche d'eux par le niveau d'instruction, son manque de prévoyance et ses difficultés financières permanentes, son mode de vie, son attachement aux traditions religieuses et au pays, dont il se proclame avec fierté "cultivateur," ses qualités et ses défauts (réactions et inimitiés, spontanées, mais sans rancune et sans arrière-pensée), Galandou représente la race.[40]

The document also pointed out that Diouf obtained the respect and loyalty of all older Africans, even those who opposed him politically, because of his fidelity to Senegalese traditions and values. He also was respected for not being *grisé* by his political successes in France and remaining accessible to all his constituents when in Senegal.

By 1936 the Popular Front had come to power in France and Léon Blum had appointed a Socialist as governor-general of French West Africa, Marcel de Coppet. The new leader was particularly solicitous of pleasing Diouf, whom he had known for thirty years, and de Coppet wrote to his minister, Marius Moutet, on 16 July 1937 apologizing for any implication that he opposed Diouf; he pledged to do everything in his power to aid the deputy.[41] Diouf's impact upon the French administration was made manifest in numerous ways during the late 1930s. For example, he became the protector of the Moroccan and Lebanese communities in Dakar, who controlled a brisk trade as middlemen that French wholesale firms ignored; these expatriates were rumored to give generously to Diouf's political coffers in return. Diouf became a firm friend of Robert Delmas, shipping magnate who lived in Senegal but who represented Bordeaux commercial interests and managed his own shipping line. Galandou ordered investigations into the conduct of Mr. Fil, who was director of the *Ecole Blanchot*, an important secondary school in Dakar; he also demanded that a number of SFIO sympathizers should be watched and quizzed for possible disloyalty to France by spreading subversive literature. And for his mythical constituency of all French West Africa, Diouf lobbied in Paris and Dakar for reforms on the *prestations* or forced labor service: he argued that decent shelter should always be provided for work crews and that they should receive a balanced diet, the same quality of food given to soldiers while on campaign.[42]

Diouf's moment of glory came in 1939 when the war got under way and African troops again marched off—although not as readily and quickly as he had predicted. Diouf's protestations of continued loyalty of Africans were not quite accurate, but on the other hand, reports as to potential Nazi plans for French West Africa if France were conquered circulated in Senegal and spurred cooperation. The Senegalese had already experienced one war against the Germans and needed no particular prompting to understand the dire situation which France and its colonies were in. Diouf traveled back and forth between Senegal and France as the troops left, but he wrote to the Ministry of Colonies in late 1939 that he hoped they would not take too many men, since able-bodied men were needed to get in the groundnut harvest, which was vital for the war effort. Diouf was looking forward to a long war, much like the 1914-1918 conflict, and did not suspect that France would crumble by spring of 1940. When the Vichy government took over, Diouf cooperated at first but increasingly became hostile, especially as rumors persisted in Vichy that Pétain was going to bargain away French West Africa to Hitler for concessions in France. He died in 1941, his faith in the French nation shaken after years of loyalty and commitment to the "ideals of 1789" that he now saw rejected.[43]

THE IMPACT OF OTHER SENEGALESE ELITES

While the period 1900 to 1940 was dominated by Carpot, Diagne, and Diouf, there were a number of other Senegalese who influenced the French in Senegal and in France. A thorough discussion is not possible in this study, but several names should be discussed, such as Bouna N'Diaye, Lamine Guèye, and Léopold Senghor. The most respected traditional chief of Senegal during these years was Bouna N'Diaye, claimant to the hereditary throne of Djolof, one of Senegal's last traditional states to resist the French conquest. Bouna had received military training with the French as a young boy, and when the call went out to serve France during World War I, he responded by ordering a number of his subordinates and dependents to go to war—with him at their head. His example of personal bravery won him the respect of French military and citizens alike, for in most instances, African chiefs would send criminals or vagrants from their dominions to fight the war in Europe.

After the war Chief N'Diaye was rewarded with a new post in the revamped General Council in Senegal, now called the *Conseil Colonial*, in which 50 percent of the elected members were replaced with government-appointed chiefs. This was a move on the part of the French administration to undercut the power of the new elites; its principal architect, Governor-General Merlin, foe of Diagne, personally recruited the prestigious N'Diaye, titular claimant of the throne of the Wolof empire, to be his principal advisor. N'Diaye accepted because a lot of chiefs in Senegal had suffered under the French doctrine of direct rule, in which paramount and other major chiefs were killed, pensioned off, or given reduced commands. He hoped that if he entered the new legislative council with other prestigious chiefs, the balance could be tipped toward the chiefly sector and that traditional authorities might be constituted and recognized. This was, after all, the great period of acclaim for Lord Lugard's policy of indirect rule in Nigeria, which safeguarded many powers and privileges for traditional leaders. In fact, on the surface it appeared as though he needed Merlin, when in reality it was Merlin who desperately needed the support of the Wolof sovereign.[44]

Merlin seemed to win the first round of battle to reduce the urban elites and Diagne forces; the spectacle of Bouna N'Diaye, Moctar Diop, who was the heir of the Damel of Cayor and son of the courageous resistance hero, Lat Dior Dop, and a dozen other chiefs taking their new places in the council overawed the urban representatives. A new era of chiefly influence, spearheaded by the two most prestigious traditional chiefs, N'Diaye and Diop, working hand in hand with Merlin seemed to be dawning. Diagne himself seemed impotent to react. N'Diaye had frequent meetings in Dakar to advise the governor-general personally; Merlin solicited his advice constantly and kept his door open when it was generally closed to most Africans.

The ascendancy of N'Diaye and his impact on Merlin and the general influence of the resuscitated traditional leaders continued for several years; but there were two main reasons why this new development in Senegal and French colonial relations (and potential reorientation of French colonial doctrine) became a failure by 1925. First, N'Diaye and Merlin needed each other. As long as Merlin was commanding at Dakar, N'Diaye was able to serve as an *eminence grise*. But in 1924, Blaise Diagne finally outmaneuvered his old foe Merlin by helping to arrange his transfer outside West Africa to another colonial post. In his stead

Diagne lobbied for the appointment of Jules Carde, an outstanding administrator in Algeria, who just happened to be a member of the *Grand Orient*. Within a year of taking office, Carde restructured the council by dropping four chiefs and replacing them with elected urban elite members. The balance was tipped in favor of the representatives of the communes and the experiment in chiefly power declined. To be sure, chiefs stayed in the council until war broke out in 1939, but they never had the support they enjoyed under Merlin. The second reason the chiefs lost out was the fact that the urban Africans eventually outflanked the chiefs in the niceties of legislative council procedure, despite the persistent influence and support of the French administration. The elected members were veterans of many political campaigns and found maneuvering and tactical moves to be second nature, whereas the chiefs were used to commanding, not debating or compromising. In the final analysis, many of them proved to be ineffectual as members of the council. For his part, Bouna N'Diaye continued to be an effective member of the council and in a survey taken in 1933, was ranked at the top of the ten most influential chiefs in Senegal. His prestige survived Merlin's experiment and he continued to be a trusted advisor to the French, who rewarded him with a handsome pension, trips to Paris, and the highest order of the *Légion d'Honneur*.[45]

Turning from an examination of a traditional elite member who influenced the French, let us look at the case of Lamine Guèye, who was the first Black African to take a law degree in France. Lamine Guèye sprang from an esteemed old Saint-Louis family; his ancestor, Bâcre-Waly, had been a distinguished African merchant and leader in that city. Young Lamine early joined the Young Senegalese action group that supported Blaise Diagne in the election of 1914; he deftly avoided being sent to the front lines after being drafted for military duty and convinced Diagne that he should back him in obtaining a law degree in France. The deputy took a personal interest in this articulate young man; having an African lieutenant trained in French law could be extremely valuable. By 1923, however, Lamine Guèye had returned to Senegal and by 1924 had left Diagne and was supporting the French lawyer Paul Defferre for deputy. Guèye's actions surprised many loyal Diagnists, who knew the deputy had placed great store in training him as a top aide, but Lamine Guèye was, above all, independent and interested in advancing his own career, not that of a deputy who was losing touch with his political base.[46]

Defferre lost, but Lamine Guèye was launched as a force to be reckoned with. He served a term as mayor of Saint-Louis and flirted with the idea of opposing Diagne in 1928; but Senegal, as a traditional society, tended to defer to age, and Lamine Guèye had barely celebrated his thirtieth birthday. He decided instead to back Galandou Diouf, managed his campaign, and made the historic visit to Paris in 1928 with Diouf. In Diouf's case, the contact with Taittinger proved to be fruitful for later politics; in the case of Lamine, it was the contact with the French Socialists that set the course of his political career for the next three decades. Feeling the pinch of the depression years, Guèye patched up his differences with Diagne, accepted a magistrate post in the French West Indies, and left the Senegalese scene until 1934, when he surfaced after the death of Diagne to oppose Diouf. Despite an intelligent campaign, and rallying around him the brightest, best educated elements of the communes, Guèye was unable to overcome Diouf's attraction to former Diagnists, who fondly remembered Galandou, and his entente with the Lebou elders, who controlled most of the African vote in Dakar and Rufisque. Lamine's power base was Saint-Louis, but that old capital, which was the arbiter of Senegal's political fortunes, was now in decline and no match for the faster-growing southern cities.[47]

Lamine Guèye founded the *Parti Socialist Sénégalais* (*PSS*) in 1934; it soon became affiliated with the SFIO, and when the French Socialists came to power in 1936 as part of the Popular Front, Lamine Guèye was put in the position to become the party's expert on African affairs. He ran unsuccessfully against an entrenched and popular Diouf for the deputyship that year and was tapped by Minister of Colonies Moutet to move to Paris. Guèye became the first African since Diagne to work closely with the French administration on policy matters. His expertise was brought to bear on the ministry's Commission on Review of African Law. Interviewed in Paris amidst his work in 1938 by *Les Annales Coloniales*, Guèye observed that there was no uniform system of justice for indigenous persons; that in his opinion, there had been too much reliance on oral traditions or customs, and that it would be advantageous to have a code written down which would be fair to everyone. He felt that the present definition of what constituted a crime or wrongdoing was far too vague; that this lack of precision gave too much latitude to magistrates, who often abused their power.[48]

Lamine Guèye's Paris sojourn, where he was fêted and welcomed into the councils of the SFIO, prepared him well for his parliamentary career after World War II: when Charles de Gaulle decided in 1945 to expand the franchise and representation in the Chamber beyond Senegal, Paris witnessed a new band of African deputies arriving from the colonies of French West Africa, French Equatorial Africa, and Madagascar. Lamine Guèye was by common consent the *doyen* of the group; even though he had not served in the Chamber in the 1930s, his experience in Paris with Moutet, the Ministry of Colonies, and his long association with the SFIO, dating from the 1928 trip, meant that he was the best known Black African in France. To many Frenchmen, he was the successor to Diagne as the best example of assimilation. Like Diouf, Guèye found a special constituency to relate to in the metropole—not the veterans, but members of the legal profession, who admired this pioneer African lawyer who spoke and wrote French with precision and clarity. He remained loyal to the SFIO party in Parliament in the 1940s even though his African colleagues decided to form their own party—the Rassemblement Démocratique Africain (RDA) under Houphouët-Boigny. Ernest Milcent, a veteran French journalist who lived in Senegal for many years, summed up Guèye as follows:

He represented an era of Senegalese life, the period between the days of traditional colonialism and the advance toward independence. This was the period that began in

1936, reached its apex immediately after World War II, and ended in 1956. It was the era of the SFIO, the incarnation of the assimilation policy and of the political control of the bourgeoisie of the four old communes.[49]

Any analysis of the impact of Senegal elites would not be complete without a mention of Léopold Senghor. While Senghor was much younger than Guèye, he first surfaced publicly during the Popular Front era and was offered the directorship of education for French West Africa during a visit to Dakar. Senghor, like Guèye, had been a protégé of Diagne's in Paris, where during the late 1920s and early 1930s he completed his studies in language and literature and became Black Africa's first *agrégé*, one of France's most difficult degrees. Senghor's fame grew in Senegal, but he refused the post and returned to teaching in France instead, sensing he would be caught in a political maelstrom. It was during the late 1930s that he and Aimé Césaire laid the foundation for the *négritude* school of thought in their poetry, which would become *le dernier cri* of Paris after the war. Senghor would then become Guèye's protégé, be asked by the French government to serve as grammarian for the official texts of the new constitution for the Fourth Republic, and would eventually break from Guèye and found his own African party, the *Bloc Sénégalais*. He and Guèye would be the dominant political figures for the next several decades in Senegal, where Guèye eventually became president of the national assembly and Senghor president of the republic. Both carried to a logical conclusion the activity begun in the Chamber by Carpot almost a half century before.

There is no question that the majority of French people during the years 1900-1940 knew little about Senegal or French Black Africa. While it is true that eminent literati such as André Gide and René Maran caused many French to take note of tropical Africa and its problems, and the illustrious Dr. Albert Schweitzer conveyed a different type of African world to the French, the facts are that the most effective spokesmen for Africa, who made a small but mea-surable impact upon France's ruling class, were the deputies who represented Senegal in the Chamber of Deputies. Carpot, Diagne, and Diouf all had important and influential parliamentary careers; Guèye and Senghor both made their mark in France and helped to create the notion of the Senegalese elite; and Bouna N'Diaye, member of the traditional elite, made an impact upon French rule in Senegal at a time when France elsewhere had downgraded chiefly rule. France aspired to rule and assimilate its colonial charges, and at one level of analysis, succeeded very well—even in the case of Bouna N'Diaye, a traditional chief who gave his loyalty to the French Republic. But at another level of analysis, which we have attempted to consider in this essay, the French also set in motion an elite that learned to play the rules of assimilation so effectively that they became prime instruments in bringing about a reverse impact upon the French and used these skills eventually to gain independence. Even the special character of that post-colonial period, whether in Senegal or Ivory Coast or Mali, was determined by the reciprocal relationships growing out of the African elite's colonial activities. For in the final analysis, everywhere in French Africa, it was this same elite (whether a Senghor, Touré, Houphouët-Boigny, Keita, or Ahidjo) who took power—and who wield it today. It was they who were given seats of honor on the front rows at the funeral of the greatest Frenchman of the century, Charles de Gaulle, a testament to their influence. And it is they who today help define and formulate the foreign policy of France toward the underdeveloped world, and who are given full honors at the Elysée Palace in Paris. They are the heirs of Carpot, Diagne, and Diouf and the early Senegalese elite.

NOTES

1. See my monograph *The Emergence of Black Politics in Senegal* (Stanford, Calif., 1971) which covers the period 1900-1920 and a forthcoming monograph entitled *In Search of Equality* for the period 1920-1940. In these works I suggest that the stereotype notion of the Senegalese striving to become a Black Frenchman is false; that in fact Wolof culture became the dominant cultural force in modern Senegal during this period; and that Senegalese urban elites were primarily interested in keeping the vote they had procured in 1848 and maintaining equal access to jobs.

2. On Durand Valantin, see Johnson, *Emergence*, pp. 27, 43, 49ff.

3. See Archives of the Republic of Senegal (hereafter ARS) 20-G-12, for detailed reports of French spies and police observers of Carpot's electoral campaign.

4. A cogent analysis on the breakdown of the French-Creole entente in local politics is furnished by Hezei O. Idowu in an Ibadan, Ph.D thesis, unpublished, "The Conseil Général in Senegal, 1879-1920," 1966, pp. 358, 377.

5. Governor General E. Roume to Minister of Colonies, 30 April 1903, in Archives Nationales, Section Outre-Mer (hereafter, ANSOM), Sénégal VII-7bis.

6. See my description of this situation in Johnson, *Emergence*, pp.110-113.

7. Johnson, *Emergence*, pp. 112-113; see also materials on Carpot's political ideas in ARS, 20-G-19, including the materials clipped from *Le Radical Sénégalais*.

8. See political endorsements in Carpot materials, ARS, 20-G-17.

9. Shelby Cullom Davis, *Reservoirs of Men* (Chambéry, France, 1934), pp. 114-115.

10. Ibid., pp. 136-137.

11. See my description and analysis in Johnson, *Emergence*, pp. 178-195; see also the debates in the *Journal Officiel de la République française, Chambre des Députés, débats*, 1915, pp. 948-949, 986-987, 991, and 1072-1076.

12. There is not space here to discuss the other Creole complaint, launched by the Justin Devès forces, which had supported Frenchman Henri Heimburger, another "parachuted" candidate. See materials in ARS, 20-G-21 and the Leredu report, cited below.

13. Governor Raphaël Antonetti to Governor-General William Ponty, 10 June 1914; Ponty to Minister of Colonies, 24 June 1914—both in ARS, 20-G-21.

14. See copy of the Leredu Commission report, taken from the debates and supplementary hearings in the Chamber, séance of 7 July 1914, in ARS, 20-G-21.

15. When the one hundredth anniversary celebrations on the birth of Blaise Diagne were held in Senegal in December 1972, an important part of the week's activities was commemorating Diagne's activities with the *Grand Orient*. For references on Diagne's

private life, see "Centenaire de Blaise Diagne," special issue of *Notes Africaines* (Dakar, Bulletin de l'IFAN, No. 135, 1972) of which I was editor, as well as the catalogue on Blaise Diagne issued by the Archives of the Republic of Senegal, *Blaise Diagne*, edited by Jean-François Maurel (Dakar, 1972).

16. See the debates in the Chamber cited in note 11 above.

17. See Report of Governor-General Van Vollenhoven to Minister of Colonies, July (no date given) 1917, ANSOM, Series AOF, 533-2.

18. The question of Van Vollenhoven's motives has never been resolved, and probably never will, since he died a hero's death on the battlefield. But there is no doubt that he believed he had his African charges' best interests at stake. See Johnson, *Emergence*, pp. 193-194; Joost Van Vollenhoven, *Une âme de chef* (Paris, 1920).

19. Johnson, *Emergence*, pp. 194-195; Raymond Leslie Buell, *The Native Problem in Africa*, 2 vols. (New York, 1928), 1: 955; 2: 9; see also special report on African recruiting in ARS, 17-G-241-108.

20. On Diagne and the Pan-African congresses, see Johnson, ed., "Centenaire de Blaise Diagne," *Notes Africaines*, no. 135, pp. 90-92, and articles in *L'A.O.F.* (Dakar), July 24, 1919. For a full analysis of Diagne's reelection in 1919 (and his party's victories in 1920), see ANSOM, AOF Affaires Politiques, 595-1.

21. For an example of Merlin's activity, see memoir on Diagne's politics for 1921 in ARS 17-G-237-108.

22. Johnson, ed., "Centenaire de Blaise Diagne," p. 69.

23. *L'A.O.F.*, March 8, 1922.

24. Diagne's Senegal newspaper flourished from 1928 to 1934, but at his death, Lieutenant Duguay-Clédor found it impossible to continue, since the base of Diagne's organization had been destroyed with his death. A full run of *La France Coloniale* can be found at the library of IFAN-Université in Dakar.

25. See description of commercial endorsements in ARS, 17-G-234-108.

26. Described in *L'Ouest Africain Français* (Dakar), January 15, 1922.

27. See materials on various incidents and reactions to the Black troops after the war in ANSOM, AOF, Affaires Politiques, 534-10. See also *Le Courrier Colonial* (Paris), October 28, 1921, for Diagne's proposals for an Unknown Soldier to represent all Africans who fought in the war.

28. Personal communication from General Adolphe Diagne, eldest son of Blaise Diagne, June 22, 1975.

29. On Galandou Diouf's break with Diagne, see analysis in *L'Ouest Africain Français*, March 10, 1928, partly written by Diouf; see also *La France Coloniale*, April 5, 1928, for article by Governor Camille Guy, who labeled Diouf's opposition as the "Anti-French party." Governor-General Carde's perspective on the election is set out in his report to Paris in ARS, 20-G-82-23, dated May 12, 1928.

30. "Notice Concernant M. Galandou Diouf, Député du Sénégal," a special document prepared by the *Sureté-General* of French West Africa, July 11, 1938, in ARS, 13-G-17/18-17.

31. Ibid.

32. See analysis of elections and Diouf's visit to Paris in ARS, 20-G-82-23, especially those of the local police, which give a chronology of the events leading up to the mission to France.

33. See general dossiers on Diouf's career in politics in ARS, 13-G-17/18-17.

34. Personal communication from Moustapha Diouf, son of Galandou Diouf, interview in Dakar, May 28, 1972.

35. See response to question, "How to Explain Popularity of Diouf?" in *Clarté* (Dakar), April 18, 1935.

36. Letter from P. Taittinger to Governor-General J. Brévié, September 20, 1934, in Diouf dossier, ARS, 13-G-17/18-17.

37. Speech by Diouf, reported in local police reports, on May 10, 1935, in ARS, 13-G-17/18-17.

38. Speech by Diouf in Paris at the Salle des Sociétés Savantes, June 22, 1936, reported in *Le Populaire* (Paris).

39. See "Notice Concernant M. Galandou Diouf," in ARS, 13-G-17/18-17.

40. See note on "Causes de la Popularité de Galandou Diouf," in "Notice Concernant M. Galandou Diouf."

41. Letter from Governor-General Marcel de Coppet to Minister Marius Moutet, July 16, 1937, quoted in Diouf dossiers, materials for 1937, Ibid.

42. Galandou Diouf to Governor-General of French West Africa, March 23, 1940, Diouf dossiers for 1940, Ibid.

43. Diouf died on August 6, 1941, leaving more than 30,000 francs in medical debts, which Governor-General Boisson agreed to pay. See Diouf Dossiers for 1941, Ibid.

44. Materials on the House of N'Diaye, ARS, 13-G-15-2.

45. Ibid.

46. On April 30, 1925, a dinner-rally was held in Dakar by Lamine Guèye for Defferre; the Frenchman's campaign platform, as reported by the police who attended the rally, was most likely written by Guèye, since it followed a general line Guèye himself followed for the next ten years. See Police Reports on 1924 Legislative Elections, Senegal, in ARS, 20-F-100-100.

47. See analysis of why even many young Senegalese turned against Lamine Guèye in Police reports of political rally at Wagane Diouf's residence, June 22, 1934, in ARS, 20-G-89-23.

48. *Les Annales Coloniales* (Paris), January 3, 1938.

49. Ernest Milcent, article on Senegal in Gwendolen M. Carter, ed., *African One Party States* (Ithaca, N.Y., 1962), p. 125. See also the article written by Lamine Guèye on his own political thought, "Politique d'Idées ou de Personnes," *L'Ouest Africain Français*, March 24, 1928.

9

Did Africans Really Learn to Be French? The Francophone Elite of the Ecole William Ponty

Since William Mumford in 1935 (*Africans Learn to Be French*), Western observers of the African scene have frequently contrasted French and British education systems and the educated products of these systems in terms of "assimilation" (French) versus "adaptation" (British). Although recent literature has laid to rest the myth that education in French West Africa was a replica of that of the metropole,[1] there has been little research either on how educated francophone Africans themselves perceived their education and their relationship to France in the colonial period, or on specific French policy toward the educated African *fonctionnaires*. While a study of these two issues does not answer the question of the French impact on African elites, it nevertheless seems a necessary precondition for answering it. Finally I will mention briefly certain aspects of colonial-trained elite life styles and values in the early 1970s which give some indication of both the extent and the limitations of Western influence.

The term "elite," although I am somewhat uncomfortable with it, refers to any French-speaking African person before World War II.[2] As a group the men I am studying come closer than anyone else to elite status in the colonial period. They are the graduates of the William Ponty School in Senegal, a federal institution which for all practical purposes was the apex of the French colonial educational system in French West Africa for almost fifty years, from 1903 to about 1950. Students who had completed the three-year *école primaire supérieure*, itself the culmination of a severe selection process, were eligible for the Ponty competitive entrance exam. If accepted, they faced three more years of intensive education, including specific training for a teaching, administrative, or medical career.[3] Their schooling was crowned by a local diploma, with no officially recognized equivalent in the metropole. My purpose here is not to discuss in any detail the education offered at Ponty; but rather the impact of this education and that of their subsequent bureaucratic careers on a group of Ponty graduates and, in more detail, on certain individuals in the presentation. Much of the following material necessarily comes from interviews, about half of them from the class of 1945.

The degree of admiration and even identification many of these men had felt for France as schoolboys was striking. Of those interviewed, almost half had considered themselves French or had had a deep affection for France, and another quarter had thought of it with admiration and/or gratitude. Several reported tears at the news of the fall of France in 1940, and a larger number would have volunteered on the spot had they been old enough. (Of those who were no longer in school, however, none whom I interviewed had volunteered.) Later in their careers many became disillusioned by discrimination and difficult working conditions encountered in military service or in the administration,[4] but among older graduates especially, emotional ties to France are often still strong.

What we are today we must recognize that we owe to France. . . . It was only the French who educated us, built schools and hospitals. A comparison—someone who has lost his father and mother; there is someone who takes care of him, raises him, finds him a good job—he can only consider that person like his father. Feelings toward France—with us of an older generation they haven't changed. For example when I look at a magazine which deals with international issues I always look for France. "Here it is. Why not in the first rank!" [a 1926 graduate]

However, such feelings, which would certainly have pleased French administrators and teachers, should not be confused with a total adoption of French culture.[5]

In the first place the French opposed the wholesale adoption of French culture and especially French prerogatives by Ponty graduates. There are four main areas in which policy was deliberately designed to prevent large numbers of Western-educated Africans from becoming too French: the educational system itself, military service, careers in the colonial administration and naturalization (citizenship).

ELITE EDUCATION

I do not want to linger on the first here. Perhaps most significant was that students graduating from the highest school in French West Africa, after six years of post-primary education, received only a local Ponty diploma which was never recognized in France. The exam for the *brevet élémentaire* (the diploma in France), usually considered its closest metropolitan equivalent, was not given in French West Africa until after World War II, and the *baccalauréat* (*bac*) exam was given only in Dakar and Saint-Louis and required knowledge of a foreign language, never studied at Ponty. Except for the brief Aix experiment in the early 1920s, which involved sending the best Ponty graduates for three or four years of study in the metropolitan normal school of Aix-en-Provence, a Ponty degree was a dead end educationally throughout the inter-war period, with a few notable exceptions.[6] In addition the school administration by the mid-1930s was deliberately enlarging the place of Africa in the Ponty curriculum beyond the earlier cursory look at African history and geography. Individually researched studies of aspects of the student's own culture, the *cahiers*, became an important part of the final exam grade; perhaps equally time-consuming although never part of the formal curriculum were student-written and produced plays, also about African themes.

Most graduates pointed out that while at Ponty they had no basis for comparing their education with that of France and on the whole were well satisfied with their "French" schooling. However an abortive attempt to introduce the metropolitan *brevet élémentaire* in the late 1920s resulted in "awakened ambitions and disillusionment among students,"[7] and some graduates in the 1930s continued to send off for *brevet* textbooks on their own. A few stubborn Senegalese even managed to gain the *bac*.

MILITARY SERVICE

In 1927 the term of military service for graduates of federal schools was reduced from three years to eighteen months, and a presidential decree in 1933 further reduced actual service to one year.[8] However, within the army there was a clear distinction between those Ponty graduates who were citizens (either from the communes or naturalized) and the majority who were subjects. Much to their dismay the latter were expected to wear the clearly non-European uniform of the *tirailleurs sénégalais*, sleep on mats instead of beds and eat the simplest African fare (such as boiled corn gruel or manioc with sauce) instead of the meat and bread they were used to at Ponty. However, perhaps the greatest indignity was that, like the *tirailleurs*, they were often expected to go barefoot.[9]

I want to look more closely at one Dahomean graduate, Christophe Gbaguidi (teaching section, 1934), whose military career exemplified both the use which the army made of its educated recruits and the careful limitations put on African subjects' advancement, the deliberate policy not to treat them as French. Although eligible for the draft when he turned twenty, in 1933 Gbaguidi received the customary student deferment until his graduation and then was not taken until 1934. Like many Ponty graduates he was promoted to corporal after four months of training and given a desk job as well as responsibility for teaching elementary French and other primary school subjects to some of the *tirailleurs*. Released in 1936, he was recalled when war broke out in 1939 and with about forty other Ponty graduates (all subjects like himself) was sent to a special training course in Abidjan, supposedly to be trained as officers. But within a week of their arrival, word came down that they were only to be trained as sergeants, a change that Gbaguidi ascribed to the "jealousy" of certain French officers and non-commissioned officers. During the six-month training session the group was still clothed *en tirailleur*, although Gbaguidi and his Ponty-educated brother had received a special medical dispensation (for "sensitive" feet) to wear shoes at all times. Posted to northern Dahomey as a sergeant, he was demobilized soon after the armistice of 1940, only to be briefly called back that same year under Vichy.[10]

It is clear from official correspondence that Ponty graduates were seen as important additions to the largely uneducated *tirailleur* forces,[11] and there are repeated instances of Pontins successfully demanding greater privileges and more European-type living conditions. Nevertheless, many graduates date the beginning of a disillusionment with France from their brief military experiences where it was clear that the dominant policy was to use their special skills while treating them as close to ordinary *tirailleur* Africans as possible.[12] Even citizens, whose treatment was far better, were often stripped of their self-perceived French identity by prolonged exposure to the *Français moyen* enlisted man.

CAREERS IN THE COLONIAL ADMINISTRATION

The same pattern is clear in graduates' careers as *fonctionnaires*, although here the distinction was between European and African rather than between subject and citizen—and thus more acceptable, at least in the inter-war period. At the most fundamental level Africans were placed in an aptly named "*cadre secondaire*," with the salary scale and indemnities considerably lower than those of their European counterparts in teaching, administration, and medicine.[13] Although housing was supposed to be provided for teachers, it often was only on the most rudimentary scale, and if a European teacher left a house, it might not be available to the African who followed him in the post.[14] Colonial authorities were often skeptical about the capability of Ponty-trained Africans to serve in the *écoles primaires supérieures* or direct large regional primary schools, though in fact they often did so. Likewise a *médecin africain* might be in sole charge of a medical center for a large district, and an administrative section graduate responsible for a customs post—both with only cursory long-distance supervision. In fact, once he graduated from Ponty or the Dakar Medical School, a graduate's contact with Frenchmen might well be limited to infrequent inspection visits from his superior and, in any case to professional rather than personal relationships.[15] Graduates of the teaching section especially, who were the most likely to be in isolated posts, rarely, if ever, became friendly with the only other educated person in their village—the French administrative officer.[16]

NATURALIZATION

Finally, the French were reluctant to grant citizenship to substantial numbers of educated Africans outside the four communes, although in the late 1920s there was some discussion in Paris of a status intermediate between that of a subject and a citizen. These "associates" would have most of the rights of naturalized citizens except that of voting in French parliamentary elections. However, the members of the *Conseil de législation coloniale* (a part of the advisory *Conseil Supérieur des Colonies* in the Colonial Ministry) could not agree on whether this new status would be automatic for those fulfilling certain conditions of education, assessed taxes, or administrative positions (in which case all Ponty graduates would have undoubtedly been included), or whether it would be at the discretion of the governor. Nor could they decide if the associate status should be connected to that of citizenship as a sort of preliminary stage. The most vocal exponent of a totally separate associate status was Bernard Lavergne, who noted in a report in 1927 that "we can't hope that except in the rarest cases even our most évolué natives can become like us, our equals...the Africans that very few generations separate from the most primitive savagery."[17] In any case the associate status was never introduced.

Few Ponty graduates outside the four communes tried to acquire citizenship in the inter-war period, and those who gained it (sometimes through their fathers) stressed its practical advantages.[18] They emphatically denied that it made them more "French" than their comrades who were subjects. However, the conditions for naturalization did include a rather arbitrarily judged "civilized way of life" and monogamy, and at least one Muslim citizen waited until independence before taking a second wife.

Turning to this colonial-trained elite group today, many of whom are retired or near retirement, what can one say of the lasting French impact on them? Most obvious is the language itself—the French which they speak so fluently and with such pride. On numerous occasions graduates point out that while their education at Ponty was deficient in some areas, their French was better than that of most post-independence secondary school graduates, in large measure because they spent so much time on it at the expense of other subjects. In interview situations they seemed perfectly at ease and spontaneous in French (at least with an anglophone), exceptions to the "basically pathological," eternal apprenticeship typical of most educated Africans as described by the Dahomean Paulin Hountondji.[19]

To what extent do Ponty graduates speak French at home? Of those to whom I asked this question, 24 percent from all classes and 14 percent from the class of 1945 reported that they spoke only French, with another 6 percent in each group speaking "mostly" French. Twenty-four and 29 percent respectively spoke mainly or entirely in an African language (usually but not always their maternal tongue) and the remainder, about one-third, used both languages.[20] Hountondji has noted that African intellectuals often use a language which is in itself a mixture, predominantly African but using many French words.[21] This is undoubtedly true, but it is much more likely to happen when a Western-educated person is speaking Wolof, for example, than when he is speaking in French, that "universal language" which must be kept pure.

Many times graduates said they would have liked to speak French at home for the sake of their children, but could not do so because of the illiteracy or simply the opposition of a wife. Uneducated wives were in fact a major limiting factor in the adoption of a Western life-style, often deliberately chosen as such by Muslim graduates or, at least in Senegal, chosen for them by their families. About three-fourths of the graduates had only one wife, the remainder two (with one exception who had three). Most of the men with two wives were Senegalese Muslims; interestingly enough the equally Muslim Malians generally had only one wife, perhaps a reflection of different economic circumstances. Wives tended either to be quite well educated (beyond the primary certificate) or to have had no French education at all; in the 1945 group 58 percent of the wives had had some post-primary training, but fully 29 percent were illiterate. The educated wives were mainly in the teaching and medical professions,[22] although between one-fifth and one-quarter were or had been secretaries.

Although many Pontins had wanted a "traditional" wife, or at least had accepted one, they were all determined that their children would have a Western education. However, Muslims were generally still sending their children to Koranic school first, and sometimes continued their older children's Koranic training after school or during vacations. Also the large size of most families[23] meant that the father had concerned himself personally only with the education of his older sons and daughters, many of whom already have impressive higher education credentials.

Most large households were further enlarged by the addition of other children whom relatives or friends had asked the Ponty graduate to raise and educate. Although characterizing themselves as a "sacrificed generation"[24] and knowing full well that their own children were unlikely to honor such extended family obligations, about 85 percent of them, from both the class of 1945 and the group as a whole, had taken on such obligations.[25] It is a fittingly ambivalent action—at the same time reaffirming traditional obligations and helping to expose a new generation to Western (essentially still French-dominated) education.

One last aspect of the Ponty graduates' life-styles and values is that of their continuing attachment to the land, not merely in some abstract sense but in the actual ownership and supervision of cultivated fields or orchards. Graduates interviewed in 1972-1973 virtually all lived in urban areas, but about three-quarters of those from whom this information was gathered also owned farmland, either inherited or bought. Several others, including a Dahomean who had served most of his professional life in Mauritania, voiced their intention of buying land before or at their retirement. Many who own land now are not personally involved in its exploitation and even allow it to lie fallow, but others manage to make weekly visits for inspection and supervision, and most plan to become more involved at retirement.

The French impact on these men is a complex and perhaps ultimately unanswerable issue. The colonial administration trained, used, rewarded, and at times frustrated and humiliated them. For many of the older ones their entire careers were as colonial civil servants, and relatively few left the service for which they were first designated at Ponty. But if Ponty (or extended French education generally) in the colonial period has transformed their professional careers, it has not done so for their private lives. Much as the French intended, most Ponty graduates are not "Black Frenchmen" but Black Africans with a deep if sometimes reluctant admiration for France.

NOTES

1. See especially Prosser Gifford and Timothy Weiskel, "African Education in a Colonial Context: French and British Styles," in Gifford and William Roger Louis, eds., *France and Britain in Africa: Imperial Rivalry and Colonial Rule* (New Haven, Conn., 1971), pp. 663-711; Weiskel has also written a useful thesis, "Education and Colonial Rule in French West Africa, 1890-1945," Yale University, Scholar of the House Program, 1969.

2. Most importantly, until the 1950s educated Africans lacked the power component which is essential for elite status; their preeminent position was qualified by their dependence on and subordination to the French. See J. E. Goldthorpe, "The Educated African: Conceptual and Terminological Problems," in A. W. Southall, ed., *Social Change in Modern Africa* (London, 1961), p. 146.

3. Until 1940 medical preparatory section students spent only two years at Ponty before taking the entrance exam for the four-year Dakar Medical School, from which they graduated as *médecins africains*.

4. One response to this disillusionment was to contrast the many "unworthy" Frenchmen in the colonies with the good Frenchmen in France. It did not begin with the Ponty graduates, cf. Mody M'Baye's article in *La Démocratie*, 25 December 1913, cited in G. Wesley Johnson, "The Senegalese Urban Elite, 1900-1945," in Philip Curtin, ed., *Africa and the West: Intellectual Responses to European Culture* (Madison, Wisc., 1972), p. 161.

5. See G. Wesley Johnson, "Senegalese Urban Elite," p. 154, on the pride of young *originaire* Wolof in their African dress and language.

6. One was the Senegalese writer Ousmane Socé Diop, who graduated from Ponty in 1928, managed to complete the *bac* on his own in 1931, and then was sent to the veterinary medical school at Alfort. *Journal Officiel de l'Afrique Occidentale Française* (hereafter, *JOAOF*) (1931): 478, 767.

7. France, Archives Afrique Occidentale Française (hereafter, AAOF), *Annual Report*, Inspector of Education Charton to Governor-General re 1931-1932, 23 August 1932, 0-303-49.

8. AAOF, *Decree*, 16 October 1927, 9-295-45; *JOAOF*, "Decree No. 1018 Promulgating Presidential Decree of 29 March 1933, Art. 14," *JOAOF* (1933): 468.

9. As late as October 1946 Ponty graduate citizens and subjects were still being treated differently, although determined individuals and groups had managed in scattered instances to improve their own conditions. In that month Governor-General R. Barthes wrote the minister of Overseas France (FOM) that there were still "shocking inequalities" which ought to be remedied immediately, before the election campaigns. AAOF, 19 October 1946, 5D/29/14.

10. Interview with Gbaguidi, Savalou, Dahomey, 29 March 1973; personal correspondence with Gbaguidi, 2 November 1973.

11. Telegram from FOM to Dakar, 20 February 1945, and answer; the minister was

concerned that the educational reforms of Brazzaville would be compromised by the wholesale induction of the graduating class of 1945, but he was assured that they would provide vitally important *cadres* to the army and be released after only one year. AAOF, "Service Militaire," 20 February 1945, 0-304-49.

12. The *médecin africain* graduates of the Dakar Medical School were an exception. Although called officially "sergeant nurses," they worked as doctors and were respected as such. Interview with Koffi Allangba, Abidjan, 8 March 1973; see also Mamadou Gologo, *Le Rescapé de l'Ethylos* (Paris, 1963), pp. 130-133.

13. For instance, in 1921 European teachers' salaries in *Afrique Occidentale Française* (*AOF*) ranged from 4,500 to 11,000 francs, plus an indemnity of seven-tenths for serving in the colonies. An African's salary ranged from 3,000 to 9,200 francs (if he passed a professional exam, the D.A.P.), but he did not benefit from the same colonial indemnity.

14. AAOF, Charles Béart, "Culture des Maîtres Indigènes Niveau de Vie, Revendications," 18 February 1939, 0-285-49, p. 24.

15. AAOF, Béart, "Culture des Maitres," p. 5; this lack of social contact did not change for those rare Ponty students who reached the mainly European *cadre supérieur* and *cadre général*. One noted of his work in the Treasury: "In general I was on good terms with my colleagues but no visiting back and forth. We respected each other at work; after work each went his own way. And then there are those [at work] who don't even want to come near you." Interview with Théo Diara, Dakar, 4 February 1973.

16. AAOF, Béart, "Culture des Maitres," p. 19.

17. FOM Archives, Conseil Supérieur des Colonies, Bernard Lavergne, "L'Accession des Indigènes de nos Colonies à Qualité de Citoyen," 4 June 1927, p. 26.

18. For example, citizenship was extremely useful if they were in trouble with the authorities. Interview with Adélakoun Germain, Cotonou, Dahomey, April 1973.

19. Paulin Hountondji, "Charabia et Mauvaise Conscience: Psychologie du Langage chez les Intellectuels Colonisés," *Présence Africaine*, n.s. 61 (First Trimester 1967): 11-31; however, on one memorable occasion in 1973, at a reunion and meeting to discuss the constitution of a newly formed alumni association, graduates engaged in lengthy and heated discussion not only on the substantive content of the eighteen articles but on minute details of their exact wording.

20. Although the numbers were very small, Ivorien families were the most likely to use French, those from Mali least likely. Senegalese graduates also spoke mainly Wolof or both French and Wolof.

21. Hountondji, "Charabia et Mauvaise Conscience," p. 27.

22. The latter were either nurses or (more frequently) midwives. Together these categories made up about one-third of known wives' professions, in both the 1945 and the larger group. Teachers made up 37 percent and 36 percent of the two groups, respectively, divided between *institutrices* who had attended a post-primary normal course and *monitrices* who had only a primary education and short training session.

23. Only 16 percent of all graduates had three or fewer children, 40 percent had four to seven, 31 percent eight to eleven, and 14 percent twelve or more. The figures are comparable for the class of 1945, with 46 percent having four to seven children and 29 percent eight to eleven. See Barbara Lloyd's study of elite Yoruba in Ibadan, which noted that a "surprising feature of educated families is their large size," six children being common. Barbara Lloyd, "Education and Family Life in the Development of Class Identification among the Yoruba," *The New Elites of Tropical Africa*, ed. P. C. Lloyd, (London, 1966), p. 166.

24. One teacher used this term in a 1938-1939 investigation of African teachers. AAOF, Béart, "Culture des Maîtres," pp. 11-12; it was spontaneously repeated in many interviews.

25. The majority of those from whom data was gathered also felt free to refuse a child on occasion, however, usually alleging lack of room. Barbara Lloyd documented a similar phenomenon in Ibadan in the early 1960s; she found twenty-seven "permanent visitors" in the thirty elite households she studied, two-thirds of them children and adolescent relatives. Lloyd, "Education and Family," p. 165. n.5.

V

THE ARCHITECTURAL DILEMMA

We now shift to the cultural sphere for consideration of double impact in architecture, art, and literature. France after all lost its most potent settler colony when Montcalm was defeated in Quebec in 1763; it had a chance to recoup with Louisiana but Napoleon, hard pressed for credits to meet the British blockade of the continent, sold it to Thomas Jefferson. Algeria became the only focal point for immense numbers of French emigrants; the rest of the empire that France gained during the nineteenth century was not designed for nor receptive to settlement. This characterized all of France's dominions in Black Africa—yet even though the French who governed as colonial masters would come and go, the French were determined to build in a permanent way that would indicate their regime had come to stay for a long time. This sense of permanency did not emerge at once, since the empire grew like Topsy almost overnight and many towns reflected their garrison origins. Marshal Lyautey, French proconsul in Morocco, reflected this point of view, and it is significant that Lyautey's Morocco was often looked to as a model by other French officials and planners.

Raymond Betts, the distinguished historian of the French empire, has taken Dakar, a city he knows well from first-hand study and observation, as a foil for examining the policy of architecture and urban development carried out during the colonial regime. Betts suggests that a "disharmony" characterized many cities, both in North and Black Africa, as French planners struggled to cope with the realities of urban African populations who were in the majority. Betts tells us of the change that came to West African cities after the introduction of French women and children, left at home in an earlier era of conquest: new shops, cafes, boutiques, and residential areas were needed. Only belatedly did French planners begin to realize their cities could not be composed solely of chic European *quartiers*, such as the Plateau in Dakar, ringed by shanty towns such as the

Medina; this gave birth to such experiments as SICAP, which are still continuing in the suburbs of Dakar, as subsidized and planned housing areas for African families multiply.

Labelle Prussin's essay reflects some of these concerns, but she takes us back in time to the first contacts between France and Africa, and the images that were conveyed to the French public. Prussin, who has traveled extensively over all of francophone West Africa investigating both indigenous African and French colonial architectural styles and monuments, suggests that French architects conveyed their own interpretation of traditional African models, and these in turn became prototypes for some of the colonial buildings later built in West Africa. The apex of French efforts was found in the Neo-Sudanese style, used especially in markets constructed in Bamako and Dakar, and in the planning and building of new mosques for Islamic congregations. The net result is a synthesis of "an *élan* coming out of a long French cultural tradition and an *ethos* derived from the indigenous African milieu."

10

Imperial Designs: French Colonial Architecture and Urban Planning in Sub-Saharan Africa

Among the statements of critical acclaim about France's urban efforts in the colonial empire, few were inspired by the settlements found south of the Sahara. If there was a familiar comment about the cityscape in that colonial region, it was the allusion to the indistinguishable small towns that languished in southern France. The novelist Paul Nizan described inter-war Djibouti in just such a way:

Djibouti has no past. It is a sub-prefecture of the south of France that was built forty years ago. It is just old enough for the pink wash of the houses to have begun to peel and for trees in the governor's garden to look like trees.[1]

At the time that Nizan made this remark, Djibouti was more than geographically removed from the urban settings left in the New World by the Old Regime. The little port also stood apart in cultural contrast with what had earlier been achieved. The modest beauty of the Place d'Armes in Montreal and the pleasing dimensions of the cathedral square in New Orleans endowed these colonial cities with an urban grace and charm which have been widely praised—and which have made them historic settings of perennial appeal to the tourist.

No one today would visit the former French colonial cities in Sub-Saharan Africa for the same reason. Only Abidjan among them, the new urban creation of the inter-war period, was considered to have great merit, "urbanism of the highest quality."[2] Dakar, in sombre contrast, was usually described in words of disappointment. At the moment of its first triumph as the major French port in Africa south of the Sahara and, then, in its twilight hour, when it stood as an "imperial city," Dakar moved no commentator to admiration. On the first occasion, in 1912, a visitor wrote:

Dakar is only a little provincial town quickly developed on African soil. The countryside is not pretty, vegetation is rare, the colonial style, if it may be so described, is directed toward the useful, not the beautiful.[3]

On the second occasion, in 1950, the French sociologist Jacques Dresch described the city as "this composite monster, without any immediately sensed charm, despite the scale and majesty of its site."[4]

French commentary on urban settings located elsewhere contained more gracious remarks in general. Saigon, Tunis, and Fez, for instance, were all seen as examples of wise and often imaginative planning: the juxtaposition of the old and the new, the local and the colonial. Even Algiers, a city which the French military had badly mutilated in the early nineteenth century, emerged in the twentieth as an urban center of great appeal.[5] However, it was Rabat, Morocco, which became something of a colonial showcase in the interwar years.

Rabat proved to be a most suitable, indeed an alluring setting for realization of the new "International Style" with which the name of Le Corbusier is identified. After a brief flirtation with the Neo-Moorish, noticeable in the Residence-General, for instance, the bolder architects enthusiastically accepted the stark simplicity and the clean form which were the marks of the new style. Both public buildings and private villas gave reality to Le Corbusier's generalization that culture is the art of selection and that selection requires "the clear and naked emergence of the Essential."[6]

The "Essential" was nowhere to be found in the urban settlements south of the Sahara and most certainly not along the streets of Dakar at this time. On the contrary, that city's style was, at best, eclectic and was treated to special metaphor by an English sociologist:

The greater part of the public buildings look as if they had been made after models confected by a pastry-cook on one of the luxury Italian boats, who had paid a hurried visit to the French Colonial Exhibition.[7]

The obvious contrast between Rabat and Dakar was proof that the French had not lost their architectural genius but seemed to have geographically restricted its exercise. The reasons for which one portion of the empire seemed to fare so well in urban development and another so poorly is an interesting historical question.

A heroic interpretation would no doubt conclude that personality made the difference. The author Claude Farrère did offer just such a conclusion by stating that General Hubert Lyautey had accomplished in a quarter of a century in Morocco what had not yet been accomplished after five centuries of colonization in Senegal.[8] There is no denying the incredible influence, derived from the intense commitment, that Lyautey brought to urban development in Morocco. Moreover, his commitment was given fine realization through the well-trained efforts of Henri Prost, who served the Residency as chief architect and urban planner and who later continued his distinguished career by serving the city of Paris in the same capacity.

Yet, of equal importance was the manner in which these men worked together. Lyautey was an incredible manager, and he organized a half-dozen able and well-trained architects and urbanists into a team which was given responsibility for designing Morocco's urban future, city by city. That the first French metropolitan law on urban planning, that of March 14, 1919, was inspired by the one operative in Morocco, is some indication of the success and range of influence of this urban team. No other French territory was so well invested with dedicated and cooperative talent. Nevertheless, Lyautey was not the first to see the need for such regulation and planning in urban matters.

Were a general history of French colonial urban planning to be written, it might start with the early efforts of Lieutenant Pinet-Laprade, who did draw up a plan for Dakar in 1856, one that was considered outscaled for its time. Such early planning was, however, chiefly concerned with the alignment of streets, the installation of sewer and water systems. The qualities which would later be identified with the urban schemes of the Austrian architect Camille Sitte, with the Town Planning movement in Great Britain, and the City Beautiful movement in the United States, were then lacking. The concern with form, with architecture, with scale and harmony, those elements which made a city a work of art, was sensed later in the French colonial world. Such concern seems first to have been aroused in Indochina, where Governor-General de Lanessan established a *Service des batiments civils* in 1893, separated from the usual *Service des travaux publics*, so that architecture would be reserved for the architects.[9] A decade later, Governor-General Jonnart of Algeria moved in a similar direction with the creation of a *Service d'architecture*, which was to be responsible for the supervision of all public buildings constructed with public funds.[10] Lyautey's own organization, the *Service central des plans de ville*, set up in 1914, was bolder yet: it was the first to envision urban planning as such. Through its initiative, the idea of the *plan-directeur* was introduced—years before Le Corbusier would claim the idea and the term as his own inspiration.[11]

South of the equator, French urban planning emerged more slowly and erratically. Moreover, it was not on the African continent as such, but on the island of Madagascar that the first and most important initiatives were undertaken. On December 4, 1918, a *Commission d'urbanisme* was created for the city of Tananarive. Then, on December 24, 1926, a *Conseil d'urbanisme* was established and charged with the responsibility of drawing up plans for all major urban agglomerations, an action taken in imitation of what Prost had done in Morocco. Urban planning on the island even included projects for the creation of garden cities, the then-fashionable mode of combining the verdant with the urban to assure nicely landscaped domestic settings.[12]

Neither French West Africa nor French Equatorial Africa made such institutional advances. It was only in 1931 that Governor-General Antonetti created an independent *Service d'architecture* in the AEF while even more belatedly, the governor-general of the AOF formed a *Commission d'urbanisme* for Dakar in 1938.[13] The tardiness of this last institution may perhaps be excused on the grounds that steps had earlier been taken to assure control of urban growth. An official report of 1931 claimed that the city's form had been regulated since Dakar had attained autonomous administrative status as a *circonscription* in 1924. Supposedly, this change allowed the *Service des travaux publics* to operate more forcefully, because independently, and thus to guarantee "to create a new city from which would be excluded everything that was banal and provisional."[14]

No such exclusion seems to have occurred, if one can believe the words of an urban planner appointed by the Governor-General, a few years later. According to H. L. Hoyez, writing in 1938, "Dakar has no character, let alone a colonial character."[15] Hoyez complained of the private entrepreneurs who acted as their own architects, but he suggested the possibility of reworking the facades of public and commercial buildings to make them distinctively colonial. He also urged the preparation of a *plan directeur* so as to assure more effective urban planning in the future. The presence of Hoyez was certainly proof of that need, but it also was suggestive of the fitful way in which urban development was carried on at this late date, in this part of the colonial empire. Hoyez seemed to represent the imaginary person, the *urbaniste en mission*, about whom Guillaume Tarde, a member of Lyautey's "team," had earlier complained:

A governor-general requests the talents of a highly recognized technician . . . and charges him to prepare an overall plan after a few weeks of tourism in the country. The expert lays out the plan, prepares some beautiful drawings, places them on the desk of the governor-general, and then leaves. From that . . . nothing of value ever comes.[16]

The authorities in Dakar might well have heeded these words. Hoyez was one of three *urbanistes en mission* who offered advice and provided plans in the 1930s. Their efforts created more immediate confusion than long-range urban order.[17] Moreover, their collective knowledge of Dakar's urban condition was not impressive. They were of the same mind as most individuals who accepted architectural commissions for buildings in Sub-Saharan Africa: unschooled in the history and environment of the region, disposed to import ideas rather than to generate them on African soil. Few individuals uttered the words of architect Barbier, who turned down the commission to design the cathedral of Dakar because "I do not know the region well enough."[18]

The monumental results in Dakar stood as some proof of this fact, if the visual interpretation of one Frenchman with a keen eye is accepted:

Dakar is not a city, but a disorderly construction site where tasteless buildings badly decorated with pilasters and balustrades are haphazardly arranged: the town hall, the port authority building, the palace of justice, the market, and who knows what else? . . . The governor-general's palace, enormous and pretentious, has the air . . . of a funeral monument designed for American Southerners.[19]

Figure 10-1
The Governor-General's Palace in a photograph taken in the 1930s.

Photograph courtesy of IFAN, Dakar.

The lack of talented residential architects remained a persistent problem. In 1945 Jean Alaurent, who was then head of urban planning in the Ministry of Colonies, complained that "architectural specialists were and remain rare" in this part of the empire.[20] His contention was historically supported by some small statistical proof: there were eight governmental architects in Indochina in 1908; there was none in Equatorial Africa in 1934.[21]

Discontinuity and disinterest in architectural design, both conditions the direct result of the high turnover of administrative personnel, were aggravated by the restricted vision the French seemed to have of the urban forms found in their African empire. They saw much in North Africa, but little in Africa south of the Sahara. The richness of the urban tradition in the one region was seemingly contrasted by the paucity of such a tradition in the other. As a modern author described the Sub-Saharan urban scene, urban form seemed to be "something that had been imported."[22]

Modern urban planning in North Africa was undertaken by Frenchmen who were fully cognizant of the richness of the architectural legacy they found there. They were also sensitive to the fact that the French military had caused dreadful

Figure 10-2
The monumental iron gates of the Governor-General's Palace in Dakar. The gates were exhibited, as part of the French exhibition, at the St. Louis Exhibition of 1904.

Photograph by the author.

Figure 10-3
The Moorish motif effected in the early twentieth century, here shown in the wrought iron work of the Marché Kermel, the central Dakarois market before World War I.

Photograph by the author.

depredations in the early years of the occupation of Algeria. They therefore took care to embellish and to preserve. The effort to effect a harmonious architectural style between old and new through the introduction of the Neo-Moorish is one example of this concern. The establishment, in 1905, of a *Comité du Vieil Alger*, in imitation of like historic preservation organizations in Bruges and Nuremberg, is another example.[23] The growing caution in approaching urban change is sensed in the words of Lyautey, who said, ''nothing is worse for the originality and charm of Algerian cities, as for all those in the Orient, than their penetration by modern European installations.''[24]

Such an opinion was never uttered about any urban site in Sub-Saharan Africa. To the French eye of the time there was little about the region that merited serious architectural consideration. As the director of public services for Pointe Noire put it at the Congress of Colonial Urbanism in 1931, ''Native art at the time of our occupation of the region did not have any true architecture that was worth preserving.''[25]

His argument was certainly not unreasonable. There was little to be seen or imitated because there was little that had endured for long periods of time. The lack of durable building materials was a major factor in accounting for French conclusions about regional architecture. The lack was also a problem to modern urban planners who were confronted with the threat of fire and plague in crowded residential areas constructed of straw, mud, and wood. Although the first brick kiln made its appearance in Dakar in 1866, brick structures remained expensive to build, particularly in French Equatorial Africa, where a shortage of cheap fuel with which to fire the kilns was a considerable problem. The appearance of nineteenth-century French urban settlements in West Africa both as "boom towns" and as provincial towns was in large measure attributable to walls of wood and roofs of imported clay tiles.

Such an appearance changed sharply after World War I, when reinforced concrete was widely introduced as a building material, one that had the double advantage of being relatively cheap and accessible. This new building material was first tried in the colonial world in Jamaica in 1911, but it was most pleasingly employed by Auguste Perret in the docks he designed for Casablanca in 1915. The range of possibilities that the material offered was quickly appreciated by Le Corbusier and by some of the architects working in Morocco, where a dramatic break with previous colonial styles was successfully made.

There was experimentation south of the Sahara as well, but it was of a more eclectic nature. What soon emerged as a romanticized and popular idiom was described by one architect as the *style AOF*.[26] The more generally employed terms for the style were Neo-Sudanese and Nigerian, but the first term gives a hint of the conscious search undertaken by French architects to find an architectural expression that would provide a symbolic unity and harmony for the various territories under French rule in this part of the continent.

When it was first introduced in West Africa, however, reinforced concrete seemed to add to the architectural pastiche about which so many critics complained. The new Chamber of Commerce building in Dakar, for instance, was done in the Ionic order of the Style Louis XVI. The new cathedral, begun in 1923, was mixed in style, with the Byzantine and the Neo-Sudanese blended with an insouciance that today seems remarkable. Yet the governor's palace in Abidjan was constructed along simple and modern lines, its dome gracefully done in reinforced concrete.[27]

If there was a dominant interwar style, it was indeed the *style AOF*. Not surprisingly, the style was inspired by religious edifices, the mosques found in places like Djenné. This was not the first time that religious structures lent their architecture to secular purposes in the colonial world. The famous Victoria Terminus in Bombay was a Gothic-Saracenic blend that was described as churchlike in appearance. The railroad station in Oran was little more than a mosque serving new technology. The Neo-Sudanese had a different center of triumph, however, and that was on the grounds of the several international expositions held in France, where the style was employed in every pavilion put up to house exhibits from Black Africa. First appearing in the Colonial Exposition of Mar-

Figure 10-4
Portion of the façade of the Chamber of Commerce in Dakar, the first major building constructed of reinforced concrete.

Photograph by the author.

seilles in 1906, the Neo-Sudanese grew bolder in expression through every exposition up to, and including, the Parisian one of 1937.[28]

Actually fashioned in France, the Neo-Sudanese soon went overseas where it appeared in many of the public buildings that went up in the inter-war period. It appeared in the maternity hospital in Dakar, the public market at Bamako, the railroad station at Bobo-Dialosso. It even appeared in administration buildings and gasoline stations. In each expression, it provided a rhythmic combination of the vertical and the horizontal, with its postlike columns—the adapted form of the wattle and wood minarets of a countryside mosque—being the most pronounced feature. Moreover, the ochre coloring generally employed in these buildings visibly evoked a tropical environment in which the pastoral dominated.

Most of these buildings still stand in compelling attitudes today, for they join the *art deco* creations of the time as new expressions, perhaps whole experimentations with form. An anonymous critic said of the colonial section of the Exposition of Decorative Arts in 1925, "The proper concern of modern art is

Figure 10-5
The Maternity Hospital of Dakar in the Neo-Sudanese style of architecture.

Photograph by the author.

not to invent anew, but rather to employ elements borrowed from the most diverse traditions with new feeling.''[29]

The Neo-Sudanese was such an example. It was timely and hence a short-lived style, fashionable in those years when African empire seemed secure and when the colonial city was acquiring civic functions that called for new emblems. The style quietly left the scene after World War II,[30] when the "International Style" lived up to its name. At the time most African cities, regardless of location or European background, began to acquire that rectangular, vertical look identified with Los Angeles, Miami, and Casablanca. Even before this time, however, the colonial city was undergoing a transformation which made it a European city, its shape and environment conforming to the new commercial and residential functions of a place where European investments, residence, and tourism were jointly increasing.

Whether the term "colonial city" is even an appropriate way of defining the French settlements in Sub-Saharan Africa is a question that has been raised. One critic distinguishes between the "colonial city" and the "tropical city," the latter primarily distinguished by its spatial proportions.[31] There, the small number

Figure 10-6
The *Building administratif*, constructed after World War II to house the administrative offices of the French West African Federation. An example of the newer "international style."

Photograph by the author.

Figure 10-7
A modern street scene of Dakar, showing a typical two-story structure, with living space above the shops.

Photograph by the author.

of residential Europeans occupy a large amount of space, while the large number of Africans are confined to spatially restricted quarters. Because the French did consider climate the major factor in architectural and urban considerations, the city in a tropical environment tended to sprawl. The location of private villas on large lots, the provision of green space between residential sectors, the use of the verandah as a major architectural element—these were the characteristics of urban development introduced to alleviate the effects of a climate that the French considered undesirable and unhealthy.[32]

The resulting disparity between European spaciousness and African congestion was probably the most striking feature of inter-war French Africa. This disparity was further intensified by the growing practice of sectorialization. What Lyautey had elevated into an aesthetic principle—the need to establish the European city away from the indigenous one so as not to disturb or destroy the latter's appearance and folkways—was, in more basic terms, a form of racial discrimination. Yet the justification for the separation was described as hygienic, economic, and cultural, therefore without any racial intent. The argument was made that

Figure 10-8
A view of Dakar in the 1930s, with the Governor-General's Palace on the high land known as *Le Plateau*.

Photograph courtesy of IFAN, Dakar.

any African so desiring could live in the European sector, if he were financially able to do so. But de facto segregation occurred nevertheless.[33]

Of the several plans establishing the sectorialization of Dakar, Hoyez's was the most interesting. He retained the Medina, that indigenous quarter recently established as a response to the bubonic plague of 1914, but he added to the residential distinctions by creating two new categories of residence. The "First Category" was to be newly reserved territory for European settlement. The "Second Category" was something of a mediating zone, fixed between the business zone and Medina on one side, the European residential zone on the other. There those Africans desirous of adopting the European way of life would live with those Frenchmen "of a less privileged condition."[34]

This practice of sectorialization—what would be called "zoning" in American municipal parlance—made the Sub-Saharan cities larger than they need have been, more spacious than populated. The introduction of the automobile made distances less imposing, at least for the Europeans, and thus the luxury of space was quite affordable. The Sub-Saharan "city" consequently was more a set of geographical configurations than it was a center of dense population. An urban agglomeration was defined as existing wherever a few hundred or a few thousand Europeans congregated. In 1926 the "city" of Abidjan had a total population of 9,126, of whom 431 were Europeans.[35] Yet this was the very time when Dakar was popularly described as a *ville impériale*, the hub of an expanding economic and transportation network, perhaps, but surely not a metropolitan center.[36]

Urbanism, as a French expression in Sub-Saharan Africa, was a combination of pretension and anticipation, the planning of structures that would idealize the colonial situation and the preparation for that awaited moment when the city would indeed be the impressive center of French culture and influence in Black Africa. The conditions of the contest held in 1914 for the post office of Dakar reflect this mood:

The planned building should be one of the most important monuments in Dakar. It will be visible from every part of the harbor and the lower city. . . . It is thus desirable from an architectural point of view that the building offer an imposing and original exterior.[37]

An expression of the monumental, which was desired in the building, was to be a characteristic of colonial urban planning everywhere, not in Dakar alone. Although the French Sub-Saharan efforts were never realized, new cities of grand proportions added to the colonial landscape in the early twentieth century. New Delhi and Canberra appeared as totally planned cities, the former representing British imperial ideals, the latter new Australian federal ones. Lyautey was at this time supervising the majestical layout of Rabat, and the English architect S. D Adshead was preparing his plans for Lusaka as an impressive variation of a garden city. Le Corbusier came up with bold designs for Algiers, plans that so astonished the mayor of that city that he described them as being "for the next century."[38]

As the principal city of the French territories in Sub-Saharan Africa, Dakar was the natural recipient of similar plans, though somewhat more modestly proportioned and less imaginative in projection. All told, five major sets of plans were prepared in the inter-war years, but none was more monumental—and less suitable to the environment—than that drawn up by Toussaint in 1931. The descriptive aspects of the plan are worth considering briefly, because they do demonstrate that the French were interested in making an architectural impression, a mark in durable materials, that would celebrate their colonial achievements.

When it is remembered that Toussaint's plans were initiated in the same year that Le Corbusier was beginning his work in Algiers, the former are clearly seen as belonging to another time and another place, neither of which was the future. Toussaint's plans were more suitable for a nineteenth-century French city than for modern Africa in transition. Architecturally, they offered little that was new and nothing that was daring. They were grand for all that. The architect's attention centered, as it should have, on the Place Protet, the center of the European commercial sector of the city, which he would convert into a grand Place de France, surrounded by arcaded buildings which would provide shelter from the sun for pedestrians. The roads leading into the Place de France would be defined by monumental archways, each rich in allegorical figures and African animals, and the arches themselves done in the *style AOF*. The center of this urban piece would be:

a monumental fountain representing France bringing abundance to the West African colonies. . . . This monument will be composed of a large circular basin in white stone, in the middle of which will be the eight colonies of the federation stylized as eight female figures carrying calabashes in which water will flow from a higher-placed basin, in turn fed by a cornucopia held by a France larger than life and made of white stone.[39]

It is doubtful that Toussaint or any other Frenchman seriously thought of exporting Versailles to the colonies. The grandly proportioned imperial city, with its monumental vistas and wide roadways, was a British dream realized in the plans Sir Edwin Lutyens drew up for New Delhi. Rabat, however elegant, was of different proportions. Efforts to embellish Hanoi and Saigon in the interwar period were not so grandly conceived, although quite as successfully realized.

There is no such urban history to recount French efforts south of the Sahara. There the French colonial city grew more erratically and never quite lost the appearance of the provisional until after World War II. Alaurent described this haphazard development well:

The small urban center, often an outgrowth of a landing, grew in numbers of shops and bungalows, without anyone taking the opportunity to intervene intelligently. The hesitation lay between the thought that "it was hardly worth the effort" and the thought that "it is too late."[40]

It was too late. Urban development after World War II was of a different order and with a different purpose. Moreover, the chief activities were scarcely realized before the empire was over: the remarkable *plan directeur* for Dakar and Cape Verde, outlined in 1945, was completed in large measure by 1961, the year after Senegal gained its independence.

There may be many lessons, but no single one, to be learned from a study of French urbanism and architecture in Africa south of the Sahara. However, there is an element of irony in it, which provides a conclusion. The people who so regularly prided themselves on being the heirs to Rome in modern colonial policy and practice left behind in Africa—and in every other part of their empire—few signs of that architectural greatness by which the Romans in Carthage and the Romans in Gaul are still remembered today.

NOTES

1. Paul Nizan, *Aden, Arabie*, trans. Joan Pinkham (New York, 1968), p. 121.

2. "Un Nouveau Casablanca: Abidjan et la Côte d'Ivoire," *L'Illustration*, March 2, 1935, p. 256.

3. Dr. d'Anfreville de la Salle, "Dakar et la colonisation française," *La Revue*, June 15, 1921, p. 500.

4. Jacques Dresch, "Les Villes d'Afrique occidentale française," *Cahiers d'outre-mer*, no. 11 (July-September 1950).

5. See, for instance, the commentary of Louis Bertrand, "Du Vieil Alger romantique à Fez la mystérieuse," *Revue des deux mondes*, September 1928, p. 9.

6. Le Corbusier, *Towards a New Architecture*, trans. F. Etchells (New York, 1960), p. 128.

7. Geoffrey Gorer, *Africa Dances* (New York, 1939), pp. 24-25.

8. Claude Farrère, *L'Atlantique en ronde* (Paris, 1933), p. 66.

9. See Henri Vildieu, "Rapport sur les Bâtiments civils," dated June 1899, Archives d'Outre-mer: Indochine, Folder 6899, pp. 16-17.

10. See the certified copy of the *Arrêt* of December 12, 1905, in Archives d'Outre-mer, Alger, 4M 26.

11. See Le Corbusier's claim in *Poésie en Alger* (Paris, 1950), p. 12.

12. See Colonel E. Withas, "L'Urbanisme en Afrique tropicale," in Jean Royer, ed., *L'Urbanisme aux colonies et dans les pays tropicaux* (La Charité-sur-Loire, 1932), p. 112.

13. On its initial activities, see the "Procès-Verbal de la 1ère séance, Commission d'urbanisme," February 2, 1938. Archives de la République du Sénégal, 4P 400 (32).

14. See "La Circonscription de Dakar et dépendances," Gouvernement-général de l'A.O.F. (Paris, 1931), p. 65.

15. L. H. Hoyez, "Regards sur Dakar" (typescript, n.p.) dated Dakar, May 6 1936. Archives de la République du Sénégal, 4P 1 (4).

16. Guillaume Tarde, "L'Urbanisme en Afrique du nord," in Royer, ed., *Urbanisme*, p. 28.

17. On the complications ensuing with two urbanists working for two different agencies—the government-general and the mayoralty—see the letter signed by Canet, inspector-general of colonies, dated October 28, 1946, in the Archives de la République du Sénégal, 4P 776/165; and the letter signed by Ponzio, administrator of Dakar, dated August 8, 1936, in the Archives de la République du Sénégal, 3G 2/6 (28).

18. Cited in René Vanlande, *Dakar!* (Paris, 1931), p. 14.

19. J. Rouch, *Sur les Côtes du Sénégal et de la Guinée* (Paris, 1925), p. 31.

20. Jean Alaurent, "Vers la transformation du cadre de la vie coloniale, *L'Architecture d'aujourd'hui* 16, no. 3 (1945): 4.

21. On the architects in Indochina, see "Notes pour Monsieur le Gouverneur-général," dated Saigon, October 5, 1908, in Archives d'Outre-mer, Indochine: Folder 15, 355. On the situation in Equatorial Africa, see the typed report entitled, "Etat numérique du personnel européen des travaux-publics proposé en raison de la réforme administrative," dated Brazzaville, October 29, 1934, in Archives d'Outre-mer: A.E.F., 7B 151.

22. Pierre George, *La ville, le fait urbain à travers le monde* (Paris, 1952), p. 311.

23. See H. Klein, *Le Comité du Vieil Alger* (Algiers, 1910).

24. Hubert Lyautey, Speech delivered to the Université des Annales, December 10, 1926, and printed in *Paroles d'action* (Paris, 1927), p. 450.

25. Nicolau, "La Ville de Pointe Noire au point de vue de l'hygiène et de l'urbanisme," in Royer, ed., *Urbanisme*, p. 168.

26. Toussaint, "Ville de Dakar: Programme général de l'urbanisme," (typescript, n.p.), Archives de la République du Sénégal, 4P 400 (32).

27. "Un nouveau Casablanca," p. 256.

28. See the chapter by Labelle Prussin in this volume for the history of architecture in the French expositions.

29. "La Section coloniale," *L'Illustration*, September 19, 1925, p. 291.

30. Jacques Dresch provides a very brief summary of architectural evolution in his "Villes de l'Afrique occidentale," p. 204. Hoyez said of the Neo-Sudanese in Dakar: "these buildings cast about some African color and this is not displeasing." See his "Regards sur Dakar."

31. Assane Seck, "Introduction a l'étude des villes tropicales," *Tiers-Monde* 6 (1965): 176.

32. A good example of this concern and its effect on architectural considerations is G.-R. Pigusson, "Pointe Noire," *L'Architecture d'aujourd'hui* 16, no. 3 (1945): 84-85.

33. For Lyautey's defense against the accusation of racial segregation in Moroccan urbanization, see L. Ladreit de Lachorrière, "L'Urbanisme colonial français et ses réalisations au Maroc," *Afrique française* 42 (1932): 161-163.

34. Hoyez, "Rapport général sur le plan directeur," copy dated Paris, July 27, 1938, in Archives de la République du Sénégal: 4P 408 (32), pp. 13-14.

35. The figures are from the 1926 census and are reprinted in Robert Delavignette, *Afrique occidentale française* (Paris, 1931), p. 177.

36. See Raymond Betts, "Dakar, Ville impériale," in Robert Ross, ed., *Colonial Cities*, forthcoming.

37. "Programme pour la construction d'un hôtel monumental des postes et télégraphes à Dakar," dated February 1914, in Archives de la République du Sénégal, 4P 32/104.

38. Quoted in a letter to M. Brunel, dated December 1933, and reprinted in Willy Boesinger, ed., *Corbusier: oeuvre complete, 1929-1934*, 4th ed. (Zurich, 1964), p. 174.

39. Toussaint, "Ville de Dakar."

40. Alaurent, "Vers la transformation," p. 4.

LABELLE PRUSSIN[1]

11

The Image of African Architecture in France

Architectural development in French-speaking West Africa can only be understood, first, within the broader historical context of French imperialism and, secondly, through consideration of particular aspects of the resultant expansion. These particular aspects in turn help explain the unique quality of what I have chosen to call the ''Neo-Sudanese'' style. The term ''Sudanese,'' coined by the French at the turn of this century, carried far more than a stylistic reference— it designated a visual, architectural symbol for the entire *élan* of the French colonial effort.

Those aspects which appear to be particularly relevant are as follows:

1. The strong presence of an exotic literary and visual imagery in nineteenth-century France which, while growing out of its involvement in North Africa, was subsequently projected onto a select region of West Africa.

2. The concomitant development of Rationalist architectural theory and training whose canons imbued the thinking of the French corps of Military Engineers engaged in North and West African campaigns.

3. The French obsession with geography which contributed to environmental determinism and decision making in building technologies.

4. The rotational nature of the French civil and military administration overseas.

5. The dichotomous but contradictory growth of industrialization and technology in late nineteenth-century France, which generated concern for the potential uses of new building materials and technology in the colonial network.

In this paper, I focus on material relevant to the first factor.

The metropolitan image of late nineteenth-century French colonial expansion can only be fully appreciated in the context of the vast literature of Romanticism and Exoticism which inundated France during the first decades of the century. Not only did that literature strongly influence public opinion, but by fanning the public's imagination through fantasy, it created a continuing demand. The humble, isolated preoccupation with African exoticism voiced by Rabelais in his first volume of *Pantagruel* gradually swelled to tidal proportions by the turn of the twentieth century just as French expansion in West Africa was riding the crest of colonial conquest. The fertile soil of West Africa provided a vast new realm of subject matter in which the fantasy world of science fiction could flourish.

The literary foundation had been well laid by the mid-nineteenth century. Authors and artists such as Victor Hugo, Alexandre Dumas, Delacroix, and Fromentin, reflecting French politics of the time, drew heavily on North African sources, that is, Algeria and Morocco, for their inspiration.[2] The base they laid colored the lens through which subsequent West African expansion was viewed. For example, one has only to compare Delacroix's *Femme d'Algers* at the Salon of 1834, or Gérome's *Belly Dancer* of the Salon of 1863 with the languorous ladies of Senegal which appeared in *La Tour du Monde* in 1862 (Figure 11-1).

In the second half of the nineteenth century, their counterpart in juvenile literature was Jules Verne. Writing in an age of geographic fervor and scientific discovery, his works of marvel and adventure fired the imagination of the young— the future colonizers of West Africa. Between 1863 and 1900 over sixty *Voyages Extraordinaires* appeared in print, both serially and as bound volumes. The first of these voyages, *Cinq Semaines en Ballon* became his passport to fame and fortune.[3] Drawing heavily on the accounts of Réne Caillié and the newly published volumes of discovery by Heinrich Barth, Verne took his readers on an adventurous and suspense-filled balloon trip across West Africa, in the course of which its heroes sailed over Kouka, Djenné, and the Inland Niger Delta, barely avoided a forced landing at Timbuktu, and introduced the geography of a whole new sub-continent to his French juvenile readership.[4]

The Verne novel, while it was perhaps the first of a corpus of fictionalized travel in a West African setting, was hardly the last. Nor was the literature of Exoticism limited to fiction. The vast enterprise of military conquest which filled the last decade of the nineteenth century itself created a prolific literature of *true* adventure. Much of this literature, dealing with the conquest itself, was written by military officers directly involved in the political, geographic, and exploratory missions which beat a path across the western Sudan. Their accounts, evoking images of a hitherto unknown world of royal kingdoms and great rivers, were as much a tale of romantic adventure as a catalyst for national pride, prestige, and patriotism. The words of Col. P. L. Monteil which "caused the heart to vibrate, because one followed anxiously, behind the caravan, the shadow of the fatherland which threw itself on lands ignorant of our name," were matched by the excitement conveyed in a rendering of the capture of Ségou-Sikoro in *Le Journal Illustré* in 1891. (Figure 11-2).[5]

The literature was not confined to repeated editions of hardbound volumes. In fact, much of what eventually appeared in book form was first serialized in

Figure 11-1

A *Signara* from Saint-Louis and her attendant. "Voyages et expé-
ditions au Sénégal," *Le Tour du Monde*, 3, 1 (1861), p. 25.

Figure 11-2
The expedition of Colonel Archinard: The capture of the town of Segou-Sikoro, capital of Soudan. *Journal Illustre*, March 8, 1891.

journals and reviews of popular interest addressed to the general reader, as well as in journals devoted specifically to colonization.[6] Frequently, it was the journals themselves which financed voyages of reportage and exploration.

In all cases, verbal accounts were accompanied by lavish and imaginative illustration. In the early nineteenth century, illustrations were rendered by recognized artists who were frequently invited to accompany political missions. Such, for example, was the case for Delacroix. Since photographic illustration in the mass media did not come into its own until after the turn of the century, the tradition continued until that time.[7] Visual images obviously had a decided effect on molding the French attitude toward its colonial holdings.

What emerges most clearly from careful scrutiny of the illustrative material associated with colonial expansion is a dichotomy in the rendition of both the African physiognomy and the environment. The Romanticism and Exoticism so eloquently conveyed by Delacroix, Gérome, Fromentin, and Loti which first enveloped the Senegalese-Mauretanian coastline was subsequently projected into the Sudan. The denigrating Black caricature, perhaps an extension of New World racism, was applied to non-Islamized peoples along the Guinea Coast rainforest.[8] The bias in rendering the African physiognomy had its counterpart in architectural and environmental representation: just as the Black African on the Guinea coast lived in a savage, barbarous milieu, so the White, Islamized African of Haut-Sénégal-Niger lived in a "civilized" setting, closely associated with North Africa and the Near East. One has only to compare the way in which each was presented through the pen of the same illustrator, Riou, in accounts by Mage, Galliéni, Binger, or Monteil.

As the century drew to a close, the spirit of military conquest had a full-time companion in the politics of colonization, a devoted patron in the name of Victor Hugo, and an ardent advocate in the pen of Emile Zola.[9] Zola, inspired by the glowing accounts of Félix Dubois and the latter's frequent allusions to the fertility of the Niger Valley, wrote *Fécondité*, a brilliant piece of propaganda for the colonization of the Inland Niger Delta.[10] His enthusiastic description may perhaps have truly been dictated by an ardent desire to see France prosper as an imperial power, a power whose great hope lay in population growth and successful colonization. The Inland Niger Delta was, for Zola (and many others), the future breadbasket of France.[11] The choice of site, in the environs of Djenné, was no coincidence; it reflected the maturation of an environmental imagery which the instantaneous success of Félix Dubois's *Tombouctou la Mystérieuse* had crystallized into architectural reality.

The moment Archinard camped on the Pondori Plains facing the city of Djenné on April 11, 1893, he set the stage for all subsequent imagery of the so-called "Soudanese" style. The vision which unfolded in front of his officers' eyes evoked immediate comparison with North Africa, and he subsequently wrote, "The officers of the column who had been in Tunisia say that Djienné resembles Kairouan, our blacks have compared it to St. Louis."[12] Continuing, he noted that,

For me, [it] is the richest and most commercial city which I have seen in the Soudan, it is one which, for an European, resembles a city most, and it differs absolutely from the other great black centers which are already familiar to us, Sansanding, Segou, Nyamina...or some large villages south of Siguiri.

In the light of Colonel Archinards's reaction and its rapid transmission to the French mass media, one can easily understand *Le Figaro*'s decision to send one of its seasoned reporters into the field.

Félix Dubois was first and foremost a journalist, or, as he called himself, a "*publiciste*." His contributions to *L'Illustration* prior to 1892 were brief, one- or two-page articles dealing with religious matter and the Near East.[13] But, as he himself noted, "the entire world now has its eyes turned towards central Africa," and at the end of 1890 he and Adrien-Marie, a painter, were sent by *L'Illustration* to accompany the Brosselard-Faidherbe mission, financed by the *Comité de l'Afrique Française*. While the purpose of the mission was to reach the source of the Niger in the Futa Djallon, Dubois's presence more appropriately served the cause of publicizing the colonial effort. The account of his trip appeared in serial form late in 1892 as "La vie Noire."[14] Its subject matter was the heavy rainforest area between Benty (near Conakry) and the base of the Futa Djallon Range—non-Islamized Black Africa—and each of the new serial installments was beautifully and lavishly illustrated with double-page aquarelles by Adrien-Marie. Shortly afterwards, Hetzel (Verne's publisher) printed the serial in book form, replacing the original water colors with hardline cartoons by Riou.[15] On his return from this first West African trip, Dubois went to Jerusalem, where he authored a special Noel supplement on Christmas in Bethlehem.[16] Equipped with a knowledge of both West Africa and the Near East, he was the logical choice for assignment to Timbuktu. Fresh from travels in a milieu not unlike that of the sub-Saharan savannah-sahel, one can assume that the impressions of his Near Eastern trip would certainly have colored his next major reportage, "Tombouctou la Mystérieuse."[17]

Prior to the appearance of the major serial itself, Dubois authored a number of preamble articles for Le Figaro, all of which undoubtedly whetted the public's appetite. Using Egypt as his frame of reference, Dubois first wrote a brief note on the Sudan in June 1895.[18] The description and comparison between the Nile Valley and the Niger Basin laid the basis for a hypothesis which persisted until this day—the Egyptian origin for Djennenke (that is, Sudanese) architecture. In describing the Sudan, he referred to the great system of natural channels in the Inland Niger Delta, to the abundance of millet, rice, and corn which covered the plains, to a fertility comparable only to the Nile Delta. "The entire middle Niger valley," he wrote, "is another valley of the Lower Nile, but even vaster and more opulent." A month later Le Figaro devoted a glossy Supplément Illustré to a single article by Dubois and a back page of "cartoons" with advice on dress, supplies, and equipment required by any reader planning a trip to Timbuktu.[19] Finally, the serial itself appeared in the fall of 1896. In his introductory remarks Dubois apologized for his lack of poetic genius needed to paint an adequate picture of the greatness of the Niger River. Then, lauding the military officers who had taken their role as civilizers to heart, he suggested that the Dienneri (the flood plain around the city itself) was "par excellence, the extraordinary image of Egyptian soil, a golden earth." The city of Djenné itself, he noted, was a city which had come down to us intact from its Songhay heritage, a heritage which, he suggested, had its origins in Egypt.

The serial was published immediately afterwards as an Edition du Figaro. Unquestionably a bestseller, it was promptly translated into English and appeared the same year in both the United States and England.[20] Perhaps more than any other publication of its time, the account reflected the spirit of French colonialism at its apogee. By the same token, its innumerable well-executed and accurate drawings of the architecture of Djenné, particularly its ancient mosque, set the scene for African architectural imagery in metropolitan France. Yet, despite the fact that the book was intended primarily as a piece of sensational journalism, and Dubois insisted that he was no more than a "publiciste" for the colonial effort, the book was, and still is, cited by many Africanist scholars as an emi-nently acceptable piece of scholarly research.[21]

In 1897 Dubois left once again for West Africa, this time as second-in-command to the Cazemajou Mission, also sponsored by the *Comité de l'Afrique Française*. What is less well known is that Dubois was dismissed from the mission during its trek into Upper Volta for meddling in political affairs which were none of his business—presumably a stroke of luck, considering the demise of the mission shortly thereafter.[22] During the next decade, very little appeared over Dubois's signature, but in 1911 he accompanied a trans-Saharan expedition whose purpose was to explore again the possibilities of a rail link between North and West Africa, and in 1911 *Notre Beau Niger* appeared.[23] Much of it is a justification of what was then a timely French political concern: a trans-Saharan railroad link. However, the trip also afforded Dubois the opportunity of revisiting Djenné, and the pages devoted to his return provide a fascinating contrast with his earlier reportage. Now supremely disillusioned with the city, he condemned the newly built Great Mosque and the "improvements" made by the French administrators and mourned the declining bustle of the city's life. Djenné, he noted, "is a city on the road to decline," and "after twelve centuries...the fatal hour has struck."[24] Thus, he sounded the death knell for a city which he himself had been instrumental in bringing to life for the French public, a city which he had projected as an architectural prototype for the French Sudan.[25] But although Dubois chose to announce Djenné's death watch, his earlier writings as well as his own involvement in efforts at colonization had already set in motion a whole new development. In the decades to follow, the imagery of the "Sudanese" style in metropolitan France evolved into a symbol for the whole of French West Africa and for much of Northwest Africa as well.

Among the most fascinating subjects in the architectural history of the Western world are the periodically sponsored World Expositions and Fairs. "Exposi-tions," Ada Luise Huxtable noted, "were (and are) a catalyst of taste and style."[26] Exhibitions are also a competitive, public revelation of national self-image. To paraphrase Goffman, they are a presentation of national self, revealing not only reality but aspiration. In the course of the nineteenth century, national consciousness and identity among European powers used overseas holdings as a major measure of national status and worth. Consequently, their physical presence and display came to constitute larger and larger components of the international fairs.

France, perhaps because it was a relative latecomer to the field of successful colonization, was obviously strongly motivated to stage these matches of colonial and national strength. Certainly, the splendor and frequency with which it staged expositions remains unmatched on a world scale.[27] France's self-image of its African holdings was mirrored not only in the architectural settings of its own expositions, but in the architectural imagery which it presented through partic-ipation in the world expositions of neighboring powers.

During the first decades of the nineteenth century, France had, with the exception of Algeria, few possessions to feed its appetite for Romanticism and Exoticism. A reviewer of the *Exposition Universelle* of 1855 in Paris noted with regret that Senegal and the Gabon were hardly represented, and their scattered products difficult to appreciate.[28] In contrast to the paucity of its West African possessions, Algeria appeared, in the eyes of the observer, to have a great future. "Algeria will be a second France, young, fertile, populated by the overflow of the mother country. Its success is now certain." This Algerian focus provided a visual envelope for subsequent West African architectural imagery.

The *Exposition Universelle* of 1867, staged at the apogee of the Second Empire, reflected a more general interest in antiquities, geographical exploration, and the nascent international armaments race. The exposition included a host of pavilions which most visitors were perhaps familiar with only through the romanticized engravings of travelogues and geographical encyclopedias—a Dutch farmhouse, a Russian *izba*, a Hindu pagoda, even a temple of the Nile replete with sphinxes to round out one's *tour de monde*. One could also inspect the enormous Krupp cannon which subsequently was turned on Paris itself in 1870.[29]

In 1878 another world's fair was staged to announce France's arrival on the world scene of colonial expansion. From the heights of the Trocadero (built precisely on the site which Napoleon had originally earmarked for a palace for the king of Rome), one could gaze down and out toward the Ecole Militaire, along a Champs de Mars lined once again with the pavilions of far-off lands. In addition there was now an Algerian Palace and a *"Galerie de l'Egypte Ancienne,"* whose purpose was to show by contemporary monuments the state of Egyptian civilization under the Pharaohs, under the Arabs and the Ottomans and under the reigning dynasty.[30] Within the *galerie*, against a backdrop of the great pyramids and tombs of Memphis, Saqqara, and Thebes, one could examine the archaeological artifacts acquired during France's Egyptian campaigns. The pronounced emphasis on Egypt and its heritage, reflecting France's previous involvement on Egyptian soil, contributed in some measure to subsequent theories which saw in Egyptian soil the seeds of West African Savannah architecture. The basis for the theory, tangentially suggested by the renowned French architect-engineer Viollet-le-Duc, lay in the environmental similarities between the Egyptian milieu and that of the Upper Niger Delta and the assumption that the basic elements of any architectural style derive from the exigencies of climate, the nature of materials, and the habits of their creators.[31]

The Centennial Exposition of 1889 marked France's full emergence from her metropolitan cocoon. Although the primary theme of the exposition was the Age of Mechanization—symbolized by the Eiffel Tower and the *Galerie des Machines*—France's colonial activities occupied a position almost as important, albeit less publicized. Between the Quai d'Orsay and the Esplanade des Invalides rose an auxiliary exposition complex announcing France's increased colonial concern—the *Exposition Coloniale*. Against the setting of a Palace of the Colonies, which faced the War Ministry, rose the pavilions of Cochin China, Mar-

Figure 11-3
Mohammedan house in the Sudan, Universal Exposition
of 1889. Drawing after Henry de Parville, *L'Exposition
Universelle de 1889*, Fig. 137 (Paris: Rothschild, 1890).

tinique, Caledonia, Annam and Tonkin, Tunisia, Algeria, and Senegal.[32] While
the architectural style of the Palace of the French Colonies is a complete enigma,
one thing is certain: there is nothing African in it. The Senegalese Pavilion,
however, recalls various illustrations rendered by Riou in the Binger volumes.
A third exposition complex, located along the Seine directly in front of the Eiffel
Tower (as if to emphasize, by comparison, the historical advances of technology
and civilization) was entitled "*Histoire de l'Habitation.*" A more mature version
of its predecessor at the 1878 exposition inspired by the success of Viollet-le-
Duc's treatise of the history of architecture, it included replicas of an ancient
Swiss lake dwelling, an Eskimo igloo, Aztec, Assyrian, Egyptian, and Arabic
domestic architecture, and finally, a "*soudanienne*" dwelling with inclined projecting pilasters.[33] Whether M. Charles Garnier was an adherent to Viollet-le-
Duc's tenets of architectural theory is difficult to say, but adherence was certainly
implied in the series of articles which reported on this aspect of the exposition.
What is more relevant to our interest however is the obvious conceptual distinction between the supposedly historical, superior Sudanese house, and the
rainforest "huts." The Sudanese house in the company of respectable historical
replicas with inverted lotus columns and a parapet of merlons, vividly recalls
an illustration by Emile Bayard for Mage's volumes—the house belonging to
the daughter of the last king of Ségou at Yamina[34] (Fig. 11-3).
The last decade of the nineteenth century witnessed the greatest frenzy of

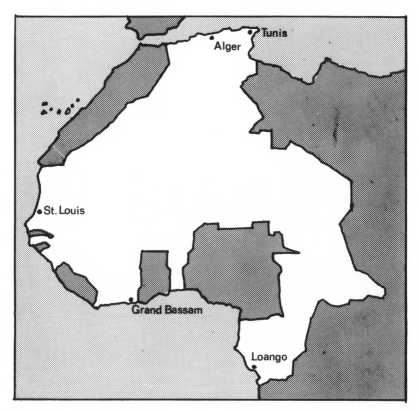

Map 5
The French African Empire, 1900

French expansion in Africa. By 1900, France's possessions on that continent far
outweighed those of all her competitors combined. Its African colonial empire
extended from Cape Verde to Lake Chad, from the Mediterranean to the Guinea
Coast, from Algiers to the Congo, (Map 5). The *Exposition Universelle* of 1900
in Paris ushered in the optimism of a new century of progress as France emerged
victorious from the colonial competition. It is not surprising, therefore, that the
Exposition Coloniale, originally conceived in 1896 as only an adjunct to the
Exposition Universelle, became its largest component.[35] At the gateway to the
Exposition Coloniale, on the western summit of the gardens of the Trocadero,
stood the *Palais du Ministère des Colonies*, an egregious example of Neo-Classic
classicism. M. G. Scellier de Gisors, the architect-in-chief of the Colonial Exposition, in justification of his design, suggested that, "The Palace of the Ministry
of the Colonies. . . dominating the pavilions of the colonies and the protectorate
countries, should represent to the World Exposition the central power, director
and organizer of our colonial expansion."[36] And indeed, the architectural *pas-*

Figure 11-4
Pavilion of Senegal-Soudan at the Exposition of 1900. *Le Pav-
illon du Sénégal-Soudan a l'Exposition de 1900*, frontispiece
(Paris: (Alcan-Levy, 1901).

tiche was little less than a combination of the flamboyant elements of a decadent
Roman Imperial age, complete with festoons, composite columns, acroteria, and
broken pediments, in the language of the *Ecole des Beaux-Arts*. Within the
cluster of colonial pavilions, in a most prominent position, stood the Senegal-
Soudan Pavilion[37] (Fig. 11-4). Behind it were arranged those of Madagascar,
the French Congo, Dahomey, Ivory Coast, French Guinea, Tunisia, the CFAO,
and the Alliance Française.

The inspiration for the design of the Senegal-Soudan Pavilion, wrote the chief
architect, was the architecture of Djenné and Timbuktu.[38] The documents referred
to were the numerous drawings and photographs brought back by various voy-
agers during the preceding decade, and it was claimed that the pavilion was

"truly original and had no predecessor in any previous Exposition."[39] The Egyptian origin of the architecture was widely accepted and publicized. The Songhay art and architecture "possesses the characteristic essentials of Egyptian art: the pyramidal form, the absence of windows, the triangular crenellations and pylons."[40] Dubois himself, writing a decade later, insisted, however, that he was the author of the design concept.[41] Egotism notwithstanding, there can be no doubt that Dubois, as commissioner for the Sudan, played a considerable role in the creation of this new imagery.

The two domes evoked the characteristic *pain de sucre* pinnacles so characteristic of the Dyula mosques which explorers and military reconnaissance, had encountered on their marches through the Voltaic Basin. However, the traditional asymmetrical clustering of buttresses had been ordered into symmetrical alignment and balance. Wooden *toron* (projecting wooden scaffolds) were replaced with simulated curving "horns"; the domes themselves were graced with an ogee curve at their apex. The total *gestalt* of the form differs little from the *Beaux-Arts* axial symmetry which dictated other exposition buildings.

In point of fact, the domes themselves are non-existent either in western Soudanese facades or the Dyula mosques—even as interpreted by Dubois himself. The transformation suggests a parallel which had already begun in the French Soudan itself, as the 1893 French reconstruction of the Palace of Ahmadu at Ségou into La Residence illustrates so well (Fig. 11-5). There *in situ* the basic Sudanese contreforts had been "organized" into the mold of Western symmetry.[42] Thus, the Senegal-Soudan pavilion at the *Exposition Universelle* of 1900 did indeed mark the genesis of a new prototype which ultimately found its way back, under the aegis of French administration, to the western Sudan.

The architectural expression of the conceptual dichotomy between Black Equatorial Africa and White Muslim Africa in the French mind suggested above, emerges clearly in the adjacent Dahomean pavilion (Fig. 11-6). In contrast to the ordered regularity and balance which characterizes the Senegal-Soudan pavilion, the irregular, supporting pillars encircled with serpents, the abstracted non-structural balustrade, and the thatch roof echo the "primitive savagery" of the Amazon portrayed decades ago in articles by Répin, Burton, and others.[43]

The Colonial Exposition made its debut as an independent entity in 1906 at Marseilles.[44] By 1906, there were also more resources and information on which the planners of the *Exposition Coloniale de Nogent-sur-Marne* in the Bois de Vincennes could draw for their architectural model, and the *Palais de l'Afrique Occidentale Française* reflected a more realistic, perhaps more sober representation of the newly established "Sudanese style." Once again, inspiration for the design was attributed to indigenous sources.[45] Once again the assemblage was a *pastiche*, conceived with French verve: the style of Timbuktu and Djenné, capped by a formidable "*tata*, chateau-forteresse des rois noirs."[46] True, the sophisticated elegance of 1900 had been replaced by a nascent "brutalism" and the pierced parapets and facade more accurately reflected elements of monumental West African architecture, but the underlying design *gestalt* remained

Figure 11-5
Façade of the Residence at Segou. Drawing by Riou. Lt. Col. P. L. Monteil, *De Saint-Louis a Tripoli par Lac Tchad* (Paris: Alcan, 1894), p. 21.

Western. The elements of reality (if it is ever possible to recreate "reality") could be attributed perhaps to the indigenous builders employed in its construction.[47] Despite the importation of "local" materials and labor, and despite the claim that "European labor never touched the work," one has only to compare the neighboring *Pavillon Cinématographique* with the drawing of a Somono communal house recorded by Mage at Ségou to realize the covert design role of the French architect.

The Colonial Exposition at Marseilles was designed to convey to its viewers a microcosm of the colonial empire.[48] The West African complex, its most spectacular fantasy, was symbolically presented in Sudanese garb. Henceforth, the Sudanese style was used as the symbol for West Africa in every subsequent exposition, French or otherwise. Thus, at the 1910 World Exposition in Brussels, for example, the *Palais de l'Afrique Occidentale*, which was designed by Charles Lefebre and which housed the de la Nezière paintings from the 1906 Marseilles Exposition, was no more than a modified version of its predecessor.[49]

Another colonial exposition was mounted in Marseilles in 1922, following World War I and the resultant redistribution of European colonial holdings in West Africa. This exposition was a far more ambitious attempt to replicate the indigenous West African savannah monuments in a French setting. Its iconog-

Figure 11-6
Dahomeyan Pavilion in the Exposition of 1900. *The Parisian Dream City* (St. Louis: N. D. Thompson, 1900).

raphy began to reflect the architectural impact which French colonial administration had already had in West Africa itself, as well as the metropolitan imagery of the African savannah setting. The "colossal" *tata*, a streamlined, more precisely articulated version of its 1906 predecessor, more accurately represented the minaret of the great Timbuktu mosques of Sankore and Djingueré Ber (Fig. 11-7). A Western interpretation of the traditional Djennenke facade was grafted onto this elongated composite of a minaret.[50] In combination, the two became in the French mind the stylized prototype for the entire Sudanese style. The efficacy of the symbol can be measured by its appearance on the title page of every publication associated with that exposition.

The Marseilles Exposition marked another interesting phenomenon: its architects were awarded the contract for the design of all subsequent West African exposition buildings. The Olivier firm, with various partners, was not only responsible for the 1922 Marseilles Exposition, but also for the West African Pavillon at the 1925 *Exposition des Arts Décoratifs*, the 1931 *Exposition Co-*

Figure 11-7
The "tata" at the Colonial Exposition in Marseilles, 1922. *L'Illustration* 159,
4134 (1922), p. 506.

loniale, and the 1937 World Exposition in Paris. The variations in the symbolic form reflect only a matter of personal preference by the French architect assigned to the project, since the formal image had by now become ossified, as can be seen in the *Pavillon de l'Afrique Occidentale* at the *Exposition des Arts Décoratifs*, 1925, Paris, harbinger of the Art Deco movement in Europe.

Since this single structure was called upon to represent the *whole* of West Africa, however, several additional travesties were considered necessary. Animal representation, perhaps reflecting the acceptance of the Abomey bas-reliefs as a respectable art form, was grafted onto the facade. In addition, the earthen dome with projecting pickets, which had made its appearance at the 1922 exposition in Marseilles, was now combined with conical Musgu housing from the Cameroons to create a rather bizarre, stylistically and structurally inaccurate representation.

By 1931, the year in which the great *Exposition Coloniale* was held, the world had changed considerably. Colonial empires were solidified, trans-continental air and surface transport had been firmly established and the solution to the world's economic disaster was optimistically sought in colonial development. The World Colonial Exposition was the first (and one might add, the last) of its kind. Conceived in 1919 to commemorate the centennial of French involvement in Algeria and to celebrate fifty years of the Tunisian Protectorate, its planning matured during the 1920s—a decade heavily imbued with what Laude has termed *"négrophilie."* Plans for a trans-Saharan railroad were being revived, irrigation schemes and colonization programs for the Upper Niger Delta were actually begun, and the financing of the Mission Dakar-Djibouti had been allocated. Once again the hope of France lay in its West African, and more specifically, savannah holdings. Its 10 million square kilometers appeared to be the golden key to recovery and the reestablishment of France as a world power.[51] The West African complex attempted to reconstruct "as perfectly as possible" indigenous life "in the land of the Blacks." Visitors descending the elevator of the tower of the Grand Palais would find themselves "transported to the heart of Black Africa through the narrow streets of Djenné, faithfully reproduced, with its terraced and storied housing, to the thick walls of red *pisé* such as one meets on the banks of the Bani." And further, the "Sudanese style was the single truly original one through which the Niger flowed," and its hallmark was the *tata*, "once the ordinary residence of black kings, now the residence of great chiefs." Its traditions and typical character had been preciously preserved and it is in "the mosques and other monuments of Timbuktu and Djenné that the most faithful and best-known examples are realized." Thus, the *Afrique Occidentale Française* complex represented an attempt to replicate, in a ten-acre microcosm at the Bois de Vincennes in Paris, the 10 million square kilometers of French Africa. This replication was symbolically expressed through a now Neo-Sudanese style. Judging from the press reports, not only was the West African montage, particularly its Grand Palais, one of the two most spectacular components of the entire exposition (the other was the *Palais d'Ankor*, Cambodia); it received the greatest accolades. The imposing mass of brilliant, red-sienna hues against a verdant background of the Bois de Vincennes, the inclined walls and heavy buttressing of its fifty-foot high *enceinte*, out of which rose the 150-foot high *donjon* or tower, unquestionably produced a most awe-inspiring sight "in itself, a symbol of French West Africa."[52]

Designed by the firm of Olivier and Lambert, the Grand Palais and its related buildings were a greatly exaggerated version of their predecessors. The variations which were incorporated only reflected a decade of change in the field of French arts and architecture itself and in French building activity in the West African savannah. Carefully regulated masses and well-ordered fenestration were combined to simulate "environmental integrity"; wooden door grilles were carved into "fetiches"; framed panels of bas-relief, "inspired by the fauna and ethnography" were rendered in Art Deco, and the miniature of the Great Mosque at Djenné served as a permanent cinema.[53]

Apparently, the honesty of representation was questioned by some, since the press felt called upon to justify the travesties.[54] "If the tower had not been as high, if the ensemble it animated were less powerful, one would no longer have a work of art, but merely an exercise in African construction." One ought not to quibble with the "architect-poets," because by their travesties "they have given us the sense of French West Africa." But even more important to our interest, "those who have never been to Africa find it original and natural and the *colonials and indigenes who know there is nothing similar there* will discover with joy that *it is truth* to them" (my italics).[55] The architecture of the Expositions had matured beyond its original Exoticism into a new reality of its own.

The hope and optimism expressed in the 1931 exposition was dissipated by the depression years which followed, and the international scene tolled the early warning of ultimate colonial demise. One more attempt was made to stage an exposition with a colonial component, but the 1937 exposition was no more than an echo of its predecessors. True, the AOF component was still extensive, but neither effort nor finances existed to match the magnificence of 1931.[56] The entire *Centre des Colonies* was located on the Ile des Cygnes in the Seine, and near the Pont de Passy rose a "monumental Sudanese gate," which in turn opened onto a central alley leading to "an exact reproduction" of the Sankoré mosque at Timbuktu, designed by none other than the architects Olivier, Lambert, and Hoyez.[57] The replica of the Sankoré mosque housed the Museum of Ethnographic Arts and Culture, whose collections were subsequently transferred to the newly reorganized Trocadero—the *Musée de l'Homme*.

In retrospect, as one scans the architectural imagery created by the various colonial expositions, what clearly emerges is a process by which a myth of suprareality unfolded and in turn enveloped the traditional architecture of francophone West Africa. Overt and covert elements of a Western, and more specifically, a French aesthetic found their way back to the African continent in the course of the twentieth century. The imagery of the metropolitan myth, unfolding concurrently with the realities of architectural development in Africa, was conveyed by those who went to settle and to administer, as well as by African visitors to, and participants in, the expositions. The penultimate impact was not on France, but on Africa itself. It resulted in the "Neo-Sudanese" style.

Reference was previously made to the reconstruction of the Palace of Ahmadou at Ségou by Underberg and its conversion into a residence for the commandant of the Cercle. It was this remodeled version which was popularized in France by Charles Monteil, Félix Dubois, and others. The balanced, symmetrical arrangement of buttresses and towers, reflecting the formal Neo-Classicism espoused by the *Ecole des Beaux-Arts*, became the prototype for the new twentieth century style. That a concern with order and symmetry was paramount in the minds of French administrators is evidenced by comments in the general reports. Perignon, the commandant of the Cercle of Ségou, wrote that "there is neither order nor symmetry in the construction or ensemble of housing; hence the eye is not agreeably impressed. A Bambara village, from the distance, resembles a village in ruins. Thus we are attempting, at Segou, to encourage the inhabitants by means of 'cadeaux,' to build their houses on the ancient Egyptian model."[58] In describing the plans of a *tata* constructed by one of (his) better interpreters in 1898, Tellier wrote, "It is interesting in the sense that it represents the sum of perfection of indigenous habitat, because the builder guarded the observances of all his customs as regards the distribution (of spaces), but in substituting our rectilinear alignments for the habitual irregular forms...it is a new type, an indigenous construction built 'à l'Européenne,' as Samba Ibrahima Diawara admitted himself."[59]

When it was decided to rebuild the mosque at Djenné in 1907, a revised francophone model was already at hand. The new mosque at Djenné followed the style of La Résidence at Ségou as much as it followed Dubois's reconstruction of the ancient mosque. Sponsored by the French government, funded with French francs, built under the direction of a French military engineer-administrator, it was acclaimed as "the most important monument of Sudanese art in our African empire"[60] (Fig. 11-8). While the complexity of French politics which were involved in sponsoring and funding the mosque are outside our immediate concern, the construction reality clearly suggests the nature of the interface between traditional, Islamic, and French interests.

The *qibla* wall, the accepted facade of the mosque fronting onto the market square, closely follows the model established by La Résidence at Ségou. The entrance facade with its two deeply set recesses echoes, however, the much more characteristic formal arrangement of indigenous doorways, and as has been frequently suggested, a system of proportions found in much of the Mande-Dogon sculptural tradition. To all but the *Western* eye, the entrance facade, reflecting an indigenous emphasis on openings, remains the dominant face. For all intents and purposes the *qibla* wall is a fake, and the two flanking towers which establish the symmetry serve no function. Only the central tower, behind which the *mihrab* sits, is functional. The market facade became, in turn, a new prototype for all major mosques in the western Soudan.

Figure 11-8
The mosque of Djenné. The most important monument of Sudanese art in the French African Empire. *L'Illustration* 138, 3586 (18 November 1911), pp. 390-391.

The Great Mosque at Mopti was built in 1935 under the aegis of M. Cocheteux, its Civil Service administrator. His description of its design and construction is equally enlightening. M. Cocheteux suggested that he "was inspired principally by the mosques at Djenné, of Goundham, and of Gourao, now extinct." Further,

despite an inquiry effected in the course of numerous trips, in the Cercle of Mopti as well as in neighboring Cercles, it was impossible to obtain any information from the *indigènes*. For the notables and the Imam, the single imperative was an eastern orientation and the minaret. . . . I had designed the principal facade, [to be] the most beautiful, but the required eastern orientation made it invisible from the *digue* of Sevaré and the entrance from Komoguel, both of which were necessary from a tourist point of view. In order to mitigate this inconvenience, I built two identical facades.

Thus, for the sake of Western tourism and its emphasis on perspective, the very organization of both Muslim and indigenous space was violated.

One needs only to review, *en masse*, the subsequent proliferation of structures built under the aegis of the French administration in its various Cercles to appreciate the impact: the Mosque at San; the Résidence, the dispensary and the former Post Office (now the residence of the chief justice) at Djenné itself; the old market at Bondoukou, the railroad station at Bobo Dioulasso; the market at

Bamako; and the laboratories built by the *Office du Niger* at Ségou (Fig. 11-9). All represent the maturation of what could be termed a "Neo-Sudanese" style in the former French Sudan. All reflect stages of development in the interface process. All are an architectural synthesis of the *élan* derivative of a long French cultural tradition and the *ethos* which prevails in the indigenous West African milieu. The employment of stylistic elements—four earthen pinnacles—in a recently constructed gas station at Dakar is striking testimony to the ultimate development in that synthesis: its popularization (Fig. 11-10).

NOTES

1. This paper is based on data collected during the course of research on the architecture of Djenné and the greater Inland Niger Delta. The research was funded by a Kress Foundation Grant from the Department of the History of Art, Yale University, and a field research grant from the African Studies Program, Yale University, 1970-1971. I am grateful to Professor Raymond Mauny for his helpful comments on this draft.

2. Victor Hugo, *Bug-Jargal* (Paris, 1826); Alexandre Dumas, *Le Véloce* (Paris, 1848) is an account of his visit to Tangiers, Algiers, and Tunis; Eugene Fromentin, *Un été dans le Sahara* (Paris, 1856) and *Une année dans le Sachel* (Paris, 1858). Fromentin traveled to North Africa as a painter, but his North African travels inspired him to write, so that he used prose as well as visual imagery to convey the spirit of North African Exoticism.

Today, political missions always include journalists, photographers, and cinematographers, all molders of public opinion and servants of the mass media. A century ago it was equally common for literati and artists to accompany such missions. Delacroix, for example, was an official member of M. de Mornay's embassy to Morocco in 1832. His impressions came back to us in sketches, paintings, notes from his journey, and extensive correspondence. Although his *Journal du Voyage au Maroc* was written during his residence in Morocco, it is interesting to note that the *Journal* was not published until 1893 during the height of French colonial activity in West Africa.

For a comprehensive survey of the exotic attraction that North Africa exerted over metropolitan France see Pierre Jourda, *Du Romanticisme à 1939* (Paris, 1956), 2: 59-75; Roland Lebel, *Histoire de la Littérature Coloniale en France* (Paris, 1931); Roland Lebel, *Les Establissements Française d'Outre Mer et Leur Reflet dans la Littérature Française* (Paris, 1952); Roland Lebel, *L'Afrique Occidentale dans la Littérature Française (depuis 1870)* (Paris, 1925).

3. Jules Verne, *Cinq Semaines en Ballon*, illustrations by Edouard Riou (Paris, 1863); an English translation appeared in 1885 in New York. The romance was a phenomenal success, and Hetzel's decision to publish this first volume was a turning point in Verne's career. Within five years, *Voyage au Centre de la Terre* and *De la Terre à la Lune* appeared. This trilogy clearly reflects the dual preoccupation with geography and technology which gripped the French reading public.

4. His description of Djenné (p. 344), while it was no more than a paraphrasing of Caillié's modest description, echoed the nascent spirit of fascination for West Africa in general and the French Sudan in particular.

The country became more marshy towards evening; the forests dwindled to isolated clumps of trees; and on the banks of the river could be seen tobacco plantations and swampy meadowlands fat with

Figure 11-9
The central market at Bamako, Mali, photographed c. 1935. Courtesy of the Ministere de la France d'Outre-Mer, Documentation Francaise.

Figure 11-10
Total gas station, Dakar, Senegal, photographed
by Labelle Prussin, c. 1970.

forage. At last the city of Djenné, on a large island, came in sight, with the two towers of its clay-built mosque, and the putrid odor of millions of swallow nests accumulated in its walls. The tops of baobabs, mimosas and date trees peeped between the houses; and even at night the activity of the place seemed very great. Djenné is, in fact, quite a commercial city; it supplies all the wants of Timbucktu. Its boats on the river, and its caravans along the shaded roads, bear thither the various products of its industry.

5. Roland Lebel, *L'Afrique Occidentale*, p. 24.

6. See, for example, weekly journals such as *L'Explorateur*, *L'Universel*, *Le Tour du Monde*, *A Travers le Monde*, *Le Journal des Voyages*, and among the most popular magazines, *Revue des Deux-Mondes*, *Les Débats*, and *Les Temps*. Some of the journals specifically devoted to the subject of colonization were *Le Monde Colonial Illustré*, *Le Journal des Coloniaux*, *L'Afrique Française* and *La Dépêche Coloniale*. Newspapers such as *Le Figaro* carried weekly, lavishly illustrated supplements, and the magazine *L'Illustration* devoted much of its pictorial content to the colonial conquest. The writings of Barth, Binger, Mage, Galliéni, and Lenfant, to mention only a few, all appeared in serial form in *Le Tour du Monde* prior to book publication.

7. For example, the journal *Les Temps*, owned by Hetzel, Verne's publisher, sent Adrien-Marie, a painter, and Félix Dubois, a journalist, to accompany the Brosselard-Faidherbe mission into what is now Guinée, in 1891.

8. During the last decades of the nineteenth century, the illustrations in published works on West Africa were in the hands of only a few illustrators, of whom the most prolific was Riou. It is his illustrations which accompany the writings of military explorers and administrators such as Mage, Galliéni, Binger, and Monteil.

Edouard Riou (1833-1900) made his debut at the Salon of 1859 with some early landscape painting of Egyptian subject matter. Apparently his work was mediocre, and it was only as an illustrator that he eventually made a name for himself. The style which characterizes his illustration had its beginnings in a set of drawings executed in collaboration with Biard for a serial which the latter wrote on Brazil and which was published in 1862 in *Le Tour du Monde*. The comic, disparaging representation of the African physiognomy, already clearly evident, persisted in the decades which followed.

Whether it was his newly acquired expertise or the publisher's ties with *Le Tour du Monde* which provided the entrée is difficult to assess, but when Hetzel decided to publish Verne's *Cinq Semaines*, Riou was commissioned to do the illustrations. Careful scrutiny reveals an already distorted representation as well as the emergent dichotomy in rendition.

The early association with Verne and Hetzel also explains the Riou illustrations in a number of other Voyages Extraordinaires, such as *Voyage au Centre de la Terre*, Capitaine Hatteras, and *Le Tour du Monde en Quatre-Vingt Jours*. Since Hetzel was also the publisher of *Les Temps*, a journal which subsequently carried the writings of Forbes, Burton, Dubois, and Monteil in serial form, it is logical to assume that the earlier association accounted for many subsequent commissions.

Perhaps the best example of the nature of insidious visual influence is the publication sequence of one of Dubois's books. Although the illustrations to his "La Vie Noire," serialized in *L'Illustration* in 1892, were done by Adrien-Marie who accompanied him on the Brosselard-Faidherbe mission, when the serial was published in book form by Hetzel in 1893 as *La Vie au Continent Noir*, the illustrations were by Riou, "according to the Marie documents." One has only to compare the romantic, soft-toned, and imaginative water colors of Adrien-Marie with the distorted, hardline caricature of Riou to recognize the heavy racist overtones which pervaded all of Riou's work.

His caricature style was subsequently reinforced with illustrations which accompanied an account of a voyage to French Guiana in 1879 by Dr. Jules Crevaux, and the sharp distinctions between Black Africa and White Africa made by Riou himself clearly can be seen in his drawings for the Mage volumes. Riou's interpretation of the Islamized "Maures" varies considerably from his rendition of the Bambara notables. A similar parallel emerges from the Galliéni volumes.

A kind of "specialization" evolved, whereby Riou was called upon to illustrate all works dealing with "Black Africa," while the Delacroix tradition appears to have been relegated to illustrators such as Emile Bayard.

9. Victor Hugo was a member of a "comité de patronage" set up to found a French colony at Timbo (Guinea) in 1882. H. Brunschwig, "Politique et Economie dans L'Empire Français d'Afrique Noire 1870-1914," *Journal of African History* 11, no. 3 (1970): 405.

10. Emile Zola, *Fécondité* (Paris, 1899), translated as *Fruitfulness* (New York, 1900).

11. The following quotes from the English edition convey the spirit of Zola's writing:

The Niger, the good giant, the father of all over yonder. (p. 474)

He spoke of Djenny, the ancient queen city, whose people and whose monuments came from Egypt, the city which even yet reigns over the valley...big villages which would some day be great towns. (p. 475)

We are the pioneers, the vanguard, the riskers full of hope and faith....We are opening the road, we are carrying our dear old France yonder, taking to ourselves a huge expanse of virgin land, which will become a province. . . . Thus we shall swarm and swarm, and fill the world! (pp. 479-480)

12. Colonel Archinard, "La Prise de Dienné," *Le Figaro, Supplément Littéraire* (23 March 1895). Parenthetically, it is also of interest that to the Senegalese *tirailleurs* it was not the visual imagery which dictated comparison, but functional association. Djenné was, in their minds, the African counterpart to Saint-Louis, in all respects a "European city."

13. See *L'Illustration* 1 (1890): 486-487, 506, 507, etc.; 2 (1891): 326-327; 3 (1892): 507.

14. *L'Illustration* 2586, 2588, 2589, 2591, 2593, 2595, 2596 (1892). The purpose of his trip is succinctly noted by Dubois himself, when he wrote "the moment has come to ask of artists a living and complete picture of the impressions of a Frenchman who found himself transported to black country." *L'Illustration* 2586 (1892): 227.

15. Félix Dubois, *La Vie au Continent Noir* (Paris, 1893). The volume is dedicated to Lucien Marc, the director of *L'Illustration* who sent Dubois on the original trip.

16. *L'Illustration* 2597 (1892).

17. Félix Dubois, "Tombouctou la Mystérieuse," *L'Illustration* 2788-2796 (1896).

18. Félix Dubois, "Le Soudan," *Le Figaro* (29 June 1895): 2.

19. Félix Dubois, "Figaro à Tombouctou," *Le Figaro, Supplément Illustré* (27 July 1895).

20. Félix Dubois, *Tombouctou la Mystérieuse* (Paris, 1897); Félix Dubois, *Timbucktoo the Mysterious*, trans. Diana White (London, 1897).

21. The scholarly attribution derives perhaps from Dubois's paraphrasing and "translation" of portions of the *Tarikhs* and other Arabic manuscripts found at Timbuktu and his archeological "reconstruction" of the ancient mosque at Djenné. It has been suggested that Dubois drew heavily on information provided by Dupuis-Yakouba, a White Father then resident at Timbuktu, without acknowledgment. Roland Lebel, *L'Afrique Occidentale*, p. 81.

One is also tempted to wonder why, in the light of reader interest, Charles Monteil's modest but erudite ethnography of Djenné, published shortly afterwards in 1903, was of such limited issue and barely reached the eye of the public or scholar.

22. Senegal, Archives, *Letter*, "From Le Capitaine Cazemajou to Félix Dubois," 27 August 1897, Dossier 1G222.

23. Félix Dubois, *Notre Beau Niger* (Paris, 1911).

24. Félix Dubois, *Notre Beau*, pp. 182-189. For example, "in many quarters, abandoned houses, crumbling walls, dying streets, dead corners"; "imagine Mont Saint-Michel surrounded by a flat and banal road in place of its picturesque belt of ramparts"; and, "in place of a *pastiche* of Djenné architecture, it is a caricature that one sees today under pretext of a mosque."

25. The negative tenor of his writing, however, was not surprising, when viewed in the perspective of current decisions being made at precisely the same time by the French colonial administration. By 1913 the city was demoted to a *cercle*; the military and administrative interests found its location totally inadequate for their needs, and it was replaced by Mopti, originally a small village at the confluence of the Niger and the Bani rivers. The Medersa was shut down in 1913 and its holdings moved to Timbuktu as a result of French politics. Another tangential point of interest was the posthumous appearance in 1913 of a two-volume *Voyage Extraordinaire* by Jules Verne, entitled *La*

Mission Barsac. This last romance, with its story of Blackland's ignominious existence and subsequent destruction north of Gao, appears to echo the sentiments voiced by Dubois.

26. "You Can't Go Home to Those Fairs Again," *The New York Times* (28 October 1973): Arts and Leisure Section.

27. During the nineteenth century alone there were a number of *Expositions Universelles* staged in Paris: 1797, 1801, 1802, 1819, 1823, 1827, 1839, 1844, 1849, 1855, 1867, 1878, 1889, and finally 1900.

28. Henri E. Tresca, *Visite à l'Exposition Universelle de Paris en 1855* (Paris, 1855), pp. 72-73.

29. Georges Pillement, *Paris en Fête* (Paris, 1972).

30. Auguste Mariette-Bey, *La Galerie de l'Egypte Ancienne à la Exposition Retrospective du Tracadero* (Paris, 1878), pp. 1, 48ff; George Augustus Sala, *Paris Herself Again*, 2 vols., 5th ed. (London, 1880).

31. Viollet-le-Duc, "Construction," *Dictionnaire Raisonné de l'Architecture* (Paris, 1859); Viollet-le-Duc, *The Habitation of Man in All Ages*, trans. Benj. Bucknall (Boston, 1876).

32. F. G. Dumas and L. de Fourcaud, *Revue de l'Exposition Universelle de 1889*, vol. 1 (Paris, 1889).

33. Ibid., pp. 115ff; "L'Habitation Humaine," *Figaro Exposition, l'Exposition de Paris*, Supp. to 12 (1889): 120ff.

34. As previously noted, there is a specialization of labor in Mage's olumes: drawings illustrating events and people in the rainforest were executed by Riou, those of the savannah by Bayard.

35. The establishment of an *Office Coloniale* by the minister for the colonies in 1899 also provided further impetus to the scale of the *Exposition Coloniale*. The purpose of this office was to encourage colonization by centralizing, distributing, and publicizing information on agricultural, industrial, and commercial investment prospects in the newly established colonies.

36. Charles-Roux, et al., *Colonies et pays du Protectorat, Exposition Universelle de 1900* (Paris, 1900), p. 49.

37. The combined pavilion apparently reflects the fact that in 1900 Haut-Sénégal-Niger still constituted a single administrative unit.

38. Charles-Roux, et al., *Les Colonies Françaises, Exposition Universelle de 1900* (Paris, 1902), p. 132: "For the elements of detail of the building, we have drawn upon the reported documents from Djenné and Timbucktu which the director of the Colonial Office has obligingly put at our disposition."

39. *Le Pavillon du Sénégal-Soudan* (Paris, 1901), p. 19.

40. Ibid., p. 19.

41. Dubois, *Notre Beau*, p. 186:

Charged with building a part of the colonial constructions, M. Scelliers de Gisors had presented a project for the pavilion of the Senegal-Soudan which. . .equally well could have been used as an entrance hall to a railroad station.

In the capacity of Commissioner of the Soudan, I refused this project and communicated my photographs of Dienne to the eminent architect, which inspired him. We had thus a pavilion which was cited among the most singular and original.

The director-general of the Colonial Exposition, M. M. Charles-Roux, elaborated further:

The two extremities [of the pavilion], East and West, are surmounted by pointed domes whose form has been given to us by the mosques of Dienne. The simple exterior decoration is composed only of profiles [animal representation being forbidden] and the curious system of contreforts [buttressing] used in the Soudan.

The two lateral porches [are] preceded by pylons tied by means of a framework of savage aspect....On the exterior and at the extremities of the building, two indigenous houses of an amusing profile, where the Senegalese artisans, blacksmiths, goldsmiths, and weavers work under the eyes of the visitors. [J. Charles-Roux, *Les Colonies Françaises*, p. 132.]

42. The process of reconstruction was clearly described by P. L. Monteil:

Underberg, who formerly had studied architecture, was in the process of constructing the Residence on the ruins of the ancient Dionfoutou [palace] of Ahmadu; he had maintained respect for the local architecture and, as one can judge by the reproduction, the Residence had a very great air, with its conical ornaments which set off the copings. [Monteil, *De Saint-Louis à Tripoli*, p. 20.]

43. See, for example, M. le Dr. Répin, "Voyage au Dahomey," *Le Tour du Monde* 7 (1863): 65, 96, etc.

44. The choice of Marseilles was of course not accidental. Sea transport was the only communication link with Africa's West Coast, and Marseilles was the primary French shipping port on the Mediterranean involved in the African trade.

45. "Inauguration de l'Exposition Coloniale de Marseille," *La Dépêche Coloniale Illustrée* 6, no. 8 (1906): 90; the architect was M. Deglane.

46. "This palace of the African king, whose high profile dominates the whole of the African countryside, is one of the most beautiful things of the Exposition. It is assuredly the most stunning, unexpected, impressive architectural work of the Exposition." Ibid., p. 90.

47. *A Travers le Monde* 21 (25 May 1907): 161.

48. Ibid.

49. The architect was inspired "by some of the constructions in *pisé* from the cities on the banks of the Niger." "Les Colonies Françaises à l'Exposition Universelle de Bruxelles," *Bull, de Comité de l'Afrique Française. Renseignements Coloniaux* 10 (1910): 313; see also Georges Schwob, *Les Colonies Françaises, Exposition Universelle et Internationale, Bruxelles, 1910* (Paris, n.d.); interestingly, the adjunct delegate of French West Africa to the exposition was M. Olivier, and one is tempted to wonder whether he was responsible for the design of subsequent West African exposition buildings.

50. Comparison with the traditional Djennenke facade clearly reveals the travesties of its aesthetic and of the meanings attached to its component parts.

51. The strength of conviction led Blaise Diagne, a Senegalese under-secretary of state to the colonies to cry out with hope, "But I tell it to you, the era of miracles has not ended; the French colonial genius will yet be that which will regenerate [France]!" Cited by Robert Delavignette, *Bulletin du Comité de l'Afrique Française. Rens. Coloniaux* 11 (November 1931): 634.

52. Delavignette, *Bulletin*, p. 634.

53. The bas-reliefs were the work of Baudry and Jonchere. Other decorative panels on the exterior facade were designed by Quinquaux, Cezolles, Garnier, Monier, and Scriba.

54. *L'Illustration* 4603 (23 May 9931): n.p.

55. Delavignette, *Bulletin*, p. 620.

56. Jean Gallotti, "Voyage dans l'Ille des Cygnes," *L'Illustration. Exposition 1937* (29 May 1937).

57. Paul Dupays, *Voyage Autour du Monde, Pavillons Etrangers et Pavillons Coloniaux à l'Exposition de 1937* (Paris, 1938), p. 248.

58. Senegal, Archives, Capitain Perignon, "Généralities sur les Régions du Haut-Sénégal et du Moyen-Niger, 1900," Dossier 1G248, p. 263.

59. Tellier, *Autour de Kita* (Paris, 1893), p. 234.

60. *L'Illustration* 138, no. 3586 (1911): 390-391; the initial cost of the Great Mosque and its facing Medersa was 14,000 French francs. The construction works were under the direction of first the administrator M. Blanc, and then M. Bleu. Immediately afterwards, the Résidence and the dispensary were built, then the post office. With the exception of the Medersa, all remain standing today. Senegal, Archives, "Rapport fait par M. Saurie, Cercle de Djenné," 28 October 1901, 4G10.

61. Personal communication with M. A. Cocheteux, Nice, 27 June 1968.

VI

FRENCH AND AFRICANS IN ART

African art has now achieved in the mid and later twentieth century the international reputation that African music acquired earlier in the century with the emergence of jazz and related musical forms of African origin and inspiration. African art had languished in the natural history museums of Europe from the time of the earliest explorers; it had to await a new century and a new esthetic. In fact, African art helped to create a new esthetic, for the climate in Paris during the late impressionists was one of change; restlessness and boredom with *Beaux-Arts* parameters, excitement with new dimensions furnished by *les fauves*, the impact of the camera, which now made representational art less fashionable and desirable.

It was in this setting of cultural upheaval and a searching for new means of expression that African art was discovered in Paris, not by the critics, but by European artists themselves. Gerard Le Coat's essay looks at this crucial period, important for the founding of modern art and crucial for the European acceptance and understanding of an old, traditional esthetic of non-representational art that had grown firmly in Africa's soil. Recast, adapted, and refined for European tastes, this esthetic would inform the works of Picasso, Braque, Modigliani, and others. Soon a confrontation developed between what Le Coat calls *art nègre* and *art moderne*, with *art nègre* becoming part of the general spirit of *négrophilie* characteristic of Paris in the 1920s. Le Coat then pinpoints the period just before World War I when the *prise de conscience* took place among such artists as Vlaminck and Picasso. Le Coat relates his findings to other cultural manifestations also influenced by discovery of things African: the writings of Blaise Cendrars, the music of Milhaud, and the great exposition of Africa's colonies in Paris in 1931. Le Coat demonstrates the potent impact of African culture in France, and the resulting influence on selected artists.

At the same time, Senegal was producing a group of expert craftsmen, the goldsmiths of Wolof and Toucouleur origin, whose complex and sophisticated creations were winning a place for them in the continuing parade of colonial expositions that started in the mid-nineteenth century and continued until the end of the colonial regime. Marian Ashby Johnson shows in her essay, based upon extensive interviews in Senegal, that a tradition of fine craftsmen who had artistic and esthetic ideals dating from pre-European contact was refined and influenced by French patronage, both in buying objects in Senegal and in recognizing and giving a place of honor to goldsmiths at the many colonial expositions. Here was double impact, with the French recognizing the validity of African art and giving it a showcase, even before the recognition of African sculpture; and the reverse process, with the *bijoutiers* from Saint-Louis and Dakar traveling to the capitals of France and other European countries, learning from European techniques and models, and broadening the repertory of traditional African jewelry making.

GERARD G. LE COAT

12

Art Nègre and *Esprit Moderne* in France (1907–1911)

Picasso's so-called *période nègre* begins in the spring of 1907, when he undertakes *Les Demoiselles d'Avignon*, and ends during the fall of 1909, when he works on a group of portraits which is to lead to what will later be known as *cubisme*, that is, after the opening of the *Salon des Artistes Indépendants* in April 1911. As early as 1905, however, African artifacts had already come to the attention of several painters, poets, and *amateurs d'art* of the Parisian circles, among them *les fauves* Matisse, Vlaminck, Derain, and their friends Max Jacob, Apollinaire, Carco, and Gertrude and Sarah Stein.

From 1905 until the beginning of World War I, the *afficionados* of the *art nègre* are to remain few. They are for the most part artists defending the *esprit moderne*, or collectors such as André Level, Léonce Rosenberg, and Paul Guillaume. The situation is to change progressively during the war years. In 1914, the *Société des Amis du Trocadéro* is created. The *Musée d'Ethnographie* of the Trocadero, which had been founded at the time of the *Exposition Universelle* of 1878, opens new halls and attempts to attract a larger public. In 1917, Paul Guillaume and Guillaume Apollinaire publish *Sculptures nègres*, the first documentary work written in French on the subject (only sixty copies were issued, however). At the same time, avant-garde composers, recently converted to jazz (a music, it is worth noting, that they considered essentially Black African) begin to associate themselves with the movement. Francis Poulenc's Opus No. 1, first played at the *Vieux Colombier* in December 1917, is entitled *Rhapsodie nègre*; on Armistice day, Stravinsky writes a *Ragtime* for eleven instruments.[1] Moreover, the movement becomes international. In 1915, the German Carl Einstein publishes *Negerplastik*, the first scholarly work to focus on African sculpture. In 1916 Marius de Zayas, critic of art and literature, publishes in New York his *African Art: Its Influence on Modern Art*.

Immediately after the war, the public at large becomes conscious of the confrontation *art nègre–art moderne*, and a new period of expansion begins, characterized by what Jean Laude calls *la négrophilie*.[2] In 1919 an *Exposition d'Art nègre* takes place for the first time in Paris, in the halls of the Galerie Dewanbez. For the occasion, a *fête nègre* is organized. In the spring of 1920, the magazine *Action* publishes a series of interviews entitled *Opinions sur l'art nègre*. In 1921 the writer Blaise Cendrars presents to the public his *Anthologie nègre*, the twenty-one chapters of which group cosmogenic and historical legends, traditional and modern folktales, fables, pieces of poetry, songs, and dances. The seriousness of the project is attested by the introductory notice:

The present volume is a compilation. For this reason, I have been careful to indicate with exactitude in the bibliography the date and place of publication of the works that I have consulted. I have reproduced the tales as missionaries and explorers have brought them back to us in Europe. . . . It is to be regretted that literary accuracy is not always the only concern of these travelers. In effect, the study of the languages and literatures of primitive races [sic] is one of the most valuable sources for the knowledge of the history of the human mind and the best illustration of the law of intellectual constants perceived by Remy de Gourmont.[3]

This last remark is significant: it reveals a new viewpoint on the so-called primitive art forms, and anticipates the concept of an a-historical man proposed by Lévi-Strauss in *La Pensée sauvage* in 1962. In 1923, the *Légendes cosmogeniques* presented by Cendrars will inspire the ballet *La Création du monde*, with music by Darius Milhaud and decor by Fernand Léger (as well as costumes, masks, and stage curtain). Performed by the *Ballets suédois*, the work is indicative of this new effort of rehabilitation. Fernand Léger borrows from genuine African objects: Baule and Bushonge masks, ritual costumes.

La Revue Nègre, the great hit of the *Théâtre des Champs-Elysées* in 1925, marks the highpoint of the *négrophilie* in France. Nevertheless, this fad does not exclude a more serious consideration of the African arts. Studies and exhibitions multiply, the logical outgrowth being the prestigious *Exposition Coloniale* of 1931, which coincides with the foundation of a *Musée des Colonies*. In music, a similar evolution occurs. African instruments are now being collected and classified. In his atelier of rue Bonaparte, Derain gathers Senegalese instruments that he knows how to tune and play. The pianist and composer Jean Wiéner is especially interested by Cameroonese and Gabonese instruments. André Schaeffner, who was later in charge of the section of musical ethnology at the *Musée d'Ethnographie* du Trocadero publishes his *Notes sur la Musique des Afro-américains* and, in 1926, in collaboration with André Coeuroy, the first methodical study on jazz.[4]

The years 1932–1939 are equally fertile in ethnographical research, a decisive step being the reorganization of the Trocadero museum, which becomes in 1937 *Le Musée de l'Homme*. However, regarding the pictorial production that is of

Figure 12-1
Baule mask from Ivory Coast. 42 cms., painted wood. Musée Barbier-Müller, Geneva.
Photograph by P. A. Ferrazzini. This type of mask influenced Picasso in color treatment,
formal schematization, and tridimensional treatment of space (cf. the protruding eye
retained for some of the *constructions*, notably the *Construction à la guitare*, 1911).

Figure 12-2
Dogon statuette from Mali. 76 cms., wood. Such *bois nègres* were admired and closely studied by Parisian artists, *fauves* and protocubists alike, as early as 1905 (cf. Matisse's *Nus* of 1907-1909 and Picasso's human figures of the same period, notably the *Dancer* of 1907). Photograph by P. A. Ferrazzini. Musée Barbier-Müller.

Figure 12-3

Kota reliquary figure from Gabon. 63 cms., red and yellow copper over wood. Musée Barbier-Müller. Photograph by P. A. Ferrazzini. As a rule, Western artists did not try to learn about the cultural ascriptions which validated the artifacts that they admired. What fascinated them was the total estrangement from the Hellenistic models characteristic of the academic tradition.

Figure 12-4
Fang reliquary head from Gabon. 22 cms., wood. Musée Barbier-Müller. Photograph by
P. A. Ferrazzini. The question of the borrowings is made complex by the fact that Western
artists, more often than not, used tridimensional artifacts in order to solve problems
involving a bidimensional treatment of space.

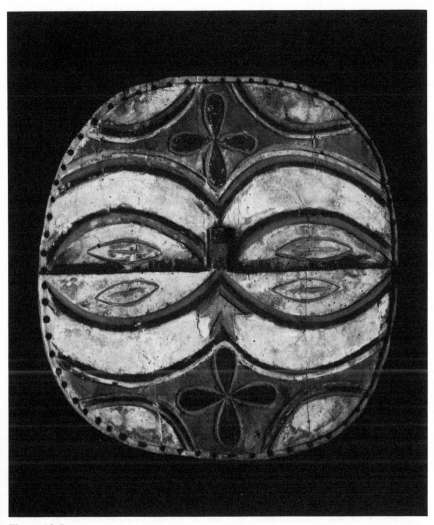

Figure 12-5

Teke (Tsaye?) mask from Congo. 34 cms., painted wood, white, red and black. Musée
Barbier-Müller. Photograph by P. A. Ferrazzini. A number of artists of French origin or
living in Paris in the early twentieth century began collecting artifacts imported from the
French colonies. This exceptional piece of craftsmanship belonged to the *fauve* painter
André Derain. Noteworthy is the recourse to a double axis of symmetry, vertical and
horizontal.

interest to us here, the *art nègre* is no longer the catalyzing force. In fact, the most significant moment in this respect is that of the initial impact, which occurs between 1907 and 1911. It is this moment on which we shall focus now, with special reference to (1) the circumstances of the discovery, (2) the nature of the borrowings, and (3) the contribution to the stylistic evolution of *l'art moderne* of the time.[5]

There exist various accounts relative to the first discoveries of the *bois nègres*. A number of artists have written about their initial encounter with African art. There are also accounts of *amateurs d'art* who, around 1905, frequented the *cénacles* of the avant-garde. The problem is that many such reports are contradictory as to precise dates, places, and circumstances. Various reasons explain this. First, they were written much later and published as memoires. Thus, those of Carco, Max Jacob, and Vlaminck appear in 1927, 1928, and 1929 respectively, more than twenty years after the occurrence of the event; that of Gertrude Stein is dated 1938. Secondly, these recollections are marked by nostalgia: the essential preoccupation is to recapture a bygone youth, the heroic times of an intense interrogation, a preoccupation confirmed by such titles as Carco's *Mémoires d'une autre vie* and Vlaminck's *Tournant dangereux*. And above all, their tone is impassioned. The writers generally present a highly personalized interpretation of the facts.

Vlaminck, who takes credit for the initial *prise de conscience*, describes on several occasions (and each time with noticeable differences in the scenario) his "feeling of wonder" when he first saw African sculptures "on a shelf over the counter of a *bistrot*, standing between bottles of Picon and Vermouth"[6] (in the most complete account, he mentions two statuettes painted red, yellow, and white, from Dahomey, and a third one, all black, from the Ivory Coast).[7] He finds his "profound feeling of humanity" hard to explain in view of the fact that he and Derain "had explored the museum of the Trocadero thoroughly and repeatedly but had never seen in the objects exhibited more than . . . ethnographic curiosities." He then confides his enthusiasm to a friend of his father who gives him "a white Congo mask and two superb statuettes from the Ivory Coast."[8] Shortly thereafter, as he is in need of money, he sells the mask to Derain:

Derain brought the mask to his atelier of the rue de Tourlaque, where Picasso and Matisse . . . were moved and disturbed when they saw it. Vollard asked Derain his permission to cast it in bronze. [This mask is] the first *pièce nègre* whence derived *l'art nègre*, and which generated cubism.[9]

Max Jacob also believes that cubism was born of African statuary. However, with him, Matisse becomes the initiator, and the discovery takes place at his home:

Matisse took a statuette in black wood from a piece of furniture and showed it to Picasso. It was the first *bois nègre*. Picasso held it all evening long. The next morning, when I arrived at his atelier, the floor was strewn with sheets of Ingres paper. On each sheet, a large drawing, nearly the same: a woman's face with one eye, a long nose which melded with the mouth, a strand of hair on the shoulder. Cubism was born. This same woman reappeared on canvases. Instead of one, there were two or three. Then came *Les Demoiselles d'Avignon*.[10]

Gertrude Stein and Fernande Olivier (Picasso's companion) both confirm Matisse's role. Picasso's version is again different: he first became acquainted with African art through his visits to the *Musée d'Ethnographie* of the Trocadero—and then only in 1908, that is, after the completion of *Les Demoiselles* (!).[11]

What is one to think of these conflicting stories? It matters little. African art was "in the air" in 1905–1906, and all must have recognized it at about the same time and for similar reasons. They viewed with a new eye artifacts which, for a number of years, had been exhibited at the *Musée d'Ethnographie*, and that one could obtain for little money in curiosity shops of the Latin Quarter. Artists and *habitués* of the avant-garde began collecting them, taking advantage of eventual trips to Marseilles to acquire more interesting pieces (this was the case with Derain, who bought for Vlaminck and himself). A number of documents (photographs, letters, articles, poems) confirm this new fad. In 1909 Apollinaire described Matisse as *le fauve*, whose collection then was the most impressive, surrounded by "objects of old and modern art, precious materials, and those sculptures in which the Negroes of Guinea, Senegal or Gabon have demonstrated with unique purity their frightened emotions."[12] The poet himself had gathered in his Auteuil apartment a Senufo mask and statuette, as well as Polynesian pieces which he evoked in *Cri*, a poem published in 1912:

> You walk towards Auteuil, you want to go home on foot
> To sleep among your fetiches from Polynesia and Guinea.[13]

Picasso also owned a few Oceanic and African pieces, one of which is recognizable in the cubist portrait of D. H. Kahnweiler, painted in the fall of 1910.

This being said, it would be wrong to conclude that the "fans" of the *bois nègres*, who were dubbed *négriers* (that is, Black slave traders), were collectors in the true sense. What counted for them was primarily the reference to visual objects detached from the Western cultural context, stigmatized by Apollinaire in *Cri* as "Greek and Roman Antiquity."[14] The quality of craftsmanship of the works was far less important than their evocative power. Certain pieces were considered less *nègres* than others, and the only existing classification was that of the "more or less moving," which can ultimately be read "more or less exotic." Function and ethnographic origin also were secondary: the mixture Polynesian-African, as we have seen, was usual, and in the twenties, Paul Guillaume suggested to include with the *sculptures nègres* the wood carvings of British Columbia (!). In fact, the avant-garde did not limit its interest to the *nègre*. Matisse, Picasso, and others gathered heterogeneous objects—Egyptian,

Arab, Hindu, Cambodian, and even European, like the *Images d'Epinal*, for instance. Paradoxically, the most traditional artifacts appeared ultra modern because they were seen out of context. In a letter addressed *à Paul Guillaume, négrier*, Cocteau could write:

Your little *fétiches nègres* protect our generation whose task it is to build on the ruins of impressionism: our youth turns towards more robust examples. It is only at this price that the world can become the pretext for a new architecture of sensibility.[15]

Regarding the initial impact of the *art nègre* on modern art, one must take into account two distinct but nevertheless related phenomena: on the one hand, an interest of artists for the laws of structure governing the artifacts, and on the other, an interest for the framework of esthetic values suggested to them by these artifacts, the totemic function of which they are generally unable to understand or unwilling to consider. This double interest conditions the nature of their borrowings: sometimes direct borrowings from tribal objects are apparent and can therefore be traced, but more often there exists only a metaphoric relationship between the tribal objects and the modern art works which they influence in various ways.

Tribal objects possess a semiotic value, their primary function being to define relational patterns within distinctive systems of reference. They embody beliefs and practices linked, in the words of Claude Levi-Strauss, "to classificatory schemes which allow the natural and social universe to be grasped as an organized whole," and consequently, they guarantee "the convertibility of ideas between different levels of reality."[16] It is ironic that such language-objects, with their well-defined cultural ascriptions, should have appeared as essentially plastic to the modern avant-garde. The reason is that the African sculptor does not try to imitate in a "realistic" way the outward appearance of beings and things (that is, as his eye *sees* them); validated by tradition, the signs that he selects are subordinated to conceptual, rather than perceptual, categories. Hence an apparent freedom exists with respect to both subject matter and spatial organization that could not but be appealing to the *fauves* and the future *cubistes* at the time of the discovery.

This enables us to understand why Matisse and Vlaminck, Picasso and Braque, although having different expressional concerns, are equally attracted by archaic art forms in general, and not just African. They find in them analogous propositions regarding such fundamental dichotomies as nature versus culture, instinct versus intellect, the individual versus society, as they apply to artistic creation. Paradoxically, archaic sculptures, because they lay outside of the evolutionary mainstream of Western art, help artists to define their position in a world now dominated by science and technology. The fact that, as observers, they do not participate in the value systems posited by these works offers them a unique opportunity for a new type of investigation, structural par excellence.

The complexity of the problems that they grapple with prevents them from being satisfied by a simple imitation of the primitive models that they have access to. African statuary is a case in point. Robert Goldwater sees in Picasso's *Dancer* (1907) "the painting most similar to its primitive prototype,"[17] a guardian figure of Gabonese origin. Picasso has preserved the oval shape of the head as well as the characteristics of the face as indicated by the African craftsman: the widely opened eyes, the triangular and salient nose, the thin and hardly noticeable mouth. However, a number of elements have been excluded: the eyelids, for instance, and the vertical band which divides the face; others have been modified: the oval contour is slightly distorted (the chin is now pointed), the eyes are asymmetric with pupils no longer rectangular, the nose is longer, and the striated surfaces are not given the same regular patterns. Furthermore, Picasso has chosen to depict a total figure, complete with arms and legs. The large headdress surrounding the face has become the raised arms, and the lozenge-like base, the irregularly bent legs (note the "plastic rhymes" selected by Picasso: the pattern of the arms reflects that of the legs).

One perceives immediately that there is no literal borrowing, but rather an interpretation of morphological traits dictated by criteria relevant to modern or, to be more precise, post-impressionist esthetics. Picasso's goal is to obtain, as Kenneth Clark states, "a totally un-Hellenized stylization of the body," and if he chooses the nude to launch his attack, it is because it symbolizes the ties between twentieth-century Western art and the Greek heritage. Kenneth Clark rightly underlines that in 1907, the nude "was a concept with many odious associations. It is difficult for us to realize how complacently the official and cultured world of 1900 accepted the standards of degraded Hellenism."[18] From the *Demoiselles d'Avignon* (spring 1907) to the *Woman with a book* (summer 1909, at the time of his departure for Horta de Ebro), Picasso undertakes a systematic de-Hellenization of the nude, and African art is instrumental in showing him the way.

In the case of the *Dancer*, the divorce from the Greek past is not total: the gesture of the raised arms constitutes an ancient *topos* possessing a complex connotative network. It was used not only with reference to the dance (compare the female figure of the Pompeian Villa dei Misteri), but also to bathing and the grooming of hair (compare Attic black-figure vase) and feminine coquetterie in general (compare *Venus putting on her necklace*). Furthermore, it allowed the artist to emphasize the gracious quality of the female body and reflects therefore a pure plastic concern. This gesture, used by Cézanne, Matisse, and others, is also found in previous works of Picasso such as the *Demoiselles d'Avignon* (central and upper right figures) and the neo-classical *Toilette* of 1905. The presence of this gesture in works of the *période nègre* can be explained in two ways: either the painter does not succeed in totally eliminating traditional *topoi*, or the incongruity of the connection of the *topos* with plastic rhythms borrowed from African statuary appears to him perfectly appropriate to his rhetorical system.

Also worth mentioning is the idea that the borrowings relative to the *Dancer*

Figure 12-6

Pablo Picasso, *Tête*, study for *Nu à la draperie*, 1907, pastel. Musée National d'Art
Moderne, Paris. Photograph by G. Aubert. The circumstances of the discovery of African
artifacts by Western artists are difficult to document. However, the tremendous impact
of Africanism on the French scene reveals a malaise about the fundamental values of the
Western world. With this *Tête* the Itumbo model (Congo) becomes instrumental. Courtesy
of the Musée National d'Art Moderne, Centre Georges Pompidou, Paris.

Figure 12-7

Henri Matisse, *Nu assis bras au dos*, 1909, bronze, 29.5 cms. Musée National d'Art Moderne, Paris. Photograph by G. Aubert. Between 1907 and 1909 Matisse's treatment of the human body often is closely related to African models. See Figure 12.2. According to Matisse, one must emphasize the articulations when representing human figures (shoulders, elbows, knees) in order to show that their primary function is to support the body. Courtesy of the Musée National d'Art Moderne, Centre Georges Pompidou, Paris.

can very well pertain to several models. Thus, the elongation of the nose, and the almond-shaped eyes and eyebrows are characteristic of a number of Congolese masks, among them the white Ogooue piece given to Vlaminck and acquired later by Derain; the long nose and comic skull (compare lower-right figure of the *Demoiselles*) are found in Itumba masks. Such borrowings can also concern art forms other than African. The long *nez en quart de brie*, which first appears in the *Portrait of Gertrude Stein* completed in the fall of 1906, is connected by critics either to the Itumba masks just mentioned, or to Iberian heads. The massive jaws and the long ears the upper part of which is shell-shaped (compare the two central figures of the *Demoiselles*) are definitely connected to ancient Iberian art (we know that Picasso owned two such heads during those years).

This analysis shows Picasso's eclecticism during the so-called *période nègre*. Moreover, the highly individualized treatment of the primitve models confirms that his aims are foreign to those of African craftsmen. In the *Demoiselles* and the *Dancer*, the figures are not presented frontally, which creates a noticeable activation of the masses, activation strengthened by the forceful pleats of a curtain (reminiscent of Baroque effects) as well as by highly decorative color schemes: blue, rose, and tan à la Cézanne in the *Demoiselles*, black, brown, and ochre in the *Dancer*. Comparing the latter to its Gabonese prototype, Robert Goldwater states, "Picasso's figure is all movement and violence. Its intensity is of an entirely different order, because instead of being self-contained, it immediately and directly engages the spectator."[19] Analyses of other works of the period, such as the *Nude* (contemporary to the *Dancer*), *Friendship* (spring 1908) and the *Head* (a self-portrait executed in the summer of 1908) would lead to similar conclusions. In fact, as we near 1909, the more elusive the borrowings become. In the *Nude* of 1907, the Senufo prototype is clearly recognizable (we know that several artists owned Senufo statuettes, among them Apollinaire). In *Friendship*, the basic shape of the Itumba masks is still present, but less so in the self-portrait. With the *Woman with a Book* mentioned earlier, there is no way of identifying a tribal model.

We see that all in all Picasso's borrowings are limited. The use of identifiable African artifacts hardly exceeds one year. What is more, these artifacts represent only a small sampling of the production of what was then *l'Afrique occidentale française*, and more particularly Gabon and the Ivory Coast. From the spring of 1908 on, Picasso's main concerns become the simplification of forms and color schemes, and the realization of a three-dimensional treatment of space without recourse to the Renaissance rules of perspective. This second phase of the *période nègre*, that Alfred Barr aptly labels proto-cubist, leads directly to the series of portraits began in Paris in late 1909 after his return from Horta de Ebro. At this point, Picasso finds at last an answer to an esthetic dilemma: how to create a totally autonomous art object, an object which is its own raison d'être without becoming abstract, that is, while retaining recognizable visual references.

If Picasso's borrowings from African artifacts are limited, those of his friends, during the four years that concern us here, are even more so. In fact, critics never speak of a *période nègre* regarding Matisse, Derain, Vlaminck, or Braque. We know nevertheless through Sarah Stein that Matisse, who, let us recall, possessed the most significant collection of artifacts, used examples from the *art nègre* in his teaching:

The articulations, wrists, elbows, knees, shoulders, must show that they support the limbs.... In the case of an attitude where the body leans on a particular limb, arm or leg, it is better to exaggerate it rather than understate it.... In a *statue nègre* where the head is large and the neck narrow, the chin is held up by the hands, giving an additional support to the head.[20]

Basing his deductions on Matisse's collection, Jean Laude has been successful in identifying the prototype to which the painter referred: a Guinean *Baga* statuette. However, such prototypes are not apparent in his works. In his nudes of 1906 (which must have influenced Picasso) it is essentially the rhythmic treatment of masses characteristic of the *art nègre* that is of interest to him. In Jean Laude's words, Matisse perfects "a system of notations" allowing him "to transcribe on one plane a dynamic emotion through genuinely synthetic forms" summing up "the different aspects of a body in space."[21]

This "system of notations" is explicit in such works as Matisse's crouching *Nude* of 1906 and the *Standing Nude* of 1907, or Braque's *Large Nude* of the same year. With respect to the latter, Henry Hope notes that the treatment of the body "is unmistakably related to the angular figures of the *Demoiselles*. The figure has the same emphasis on curves and angles.... The color is keyed low in gray, tan and pink, and the modeling is conveyed by bold parallel strokes that give the planes the illusion of tilting back and forth in space."[22] Picasso's technique is clearly marked here: there again, the activation of the masses is reinforced by the strong pleats of a Baroque curtain, the color scheme is simplified and oblique striations are selected. The leg which supports the body is exaggerated; limbs and head are at the same time oversized and shortened—all traits typical of African statuary. However, Braque does not go as far as Picasso in his rejection of Western stereotypes: the face and hairdress of the woman retain Hellenistic traits. With Matisse's *Standing Nude*, one also finds the exaggeration of the supporting limbs which he recommended to his students; but neither the pleats of the cloth nor the background are activated. The divergence between Matisse and the proto-cubists is visible: the desire for simplification will lead Matisse to the arabesque of the *Dance*, where clearly defined bodies are presented against abstract grounds, Picasso's figures becoming progressively inlaid in their environment, as the sketch of 1908 for the *Three Nudes in a Forest* shows. Matisse, like Derain and Vlaminck, will refuse "the cubist concoction," that the latter defines as "an asexual art, born of ideas divorced from nature and even from painting itself."[23]

With respect to *l'art nègre*, each of the two solutions will bring analogous results: after 1908, the relationship between tribal objects and modern art works becomes increasingly metaphoric, as confirmed by a growing interest for the still life on the part of the proto-cubists. The forms of fruit, vases, tables, and so on appear to lend themselves better to a geometrical reduction; they also have the advantage of suggesting the context of everyday life as opposed to the aloofness of the nude. In this sense, Braque's *Still-Life with Fruit-dish and Plate* (1908) and Picasso's *Fruit Dish* (1909) represent important steps in the acquisition of the cubist interpretation of space. Braque thus describes this articulative moment:

What particularly attracted me ... was the materialization of this new space that I felt to be in the offing. So I began to concentrate on still-lifes, because in the still-life you have a tactile, I might almost say a manual space.... This answered to the hankering I have always had to touch things and not merely see them.... In tactile space you measure the distance separating you from the object, whereas in visual space you measure the distance separating things from each other.[24]

In their desire to rehabilitate everyday objects, Braque and Picasso, as early as 1911, make use of additional elements such as pasted papers (fragments of newspapers, labels, and the like) and sand. This technique is not foreign to African artists. André Level notes, "Black sculptors knew how to turn to good use trade trinkets, brass nails, fragments of metal and bits of mirrors, without diminishing but rather enhancing their industrial making."[25] One may add to this the use of natural elements, such as fibers, shells, and so on and of various objects of local origin: bracelets, headdresses, belts, blades. In the case of *papiers collés*, there is no more recourse to specific prototypes, but simply appropriation of a process.

It is in the works of Picasso dated 1907 that the *bois nègres*, as our brief analysis shows, are the most recognizable. He is unquestionably the artist who went farthest in incorporating them in his paintings. It is therefore paradoxical that he should have on different occasions, both in conversation and in writing, minimized the influence of African art on his stylistic evolution. In 1935, he declared to Christian Zervos (as we mentioned earlier) that he had become acquainted with it only after having completed the *Demoiselles*, and then only by chance: one day, as he was leaving the museum of *sculpture comparée* of the Trocadero, the thought occurred to him to push the facing door which gave onto the halls of the *Musée d'Ethnographie*. In 1920, the magazine *Action* attributed the following statement to him: "*Art nègre?*... Never heard of it!"[26] (Even if this quip is not really his, the fact remains that he never attempted to deny it.)

Several reasons can explain his attitude. There is the penchant, common among artists since the nineteenth century, for *épater le bourgeois*, the philistine middle class which does not understand the *esprit moderne*. There is the necessity of originality, which incites the artist to present himself as the discoverer of a virgin terrain. There is the weariness of interviews and a disdain for people theorizing on the arts, who remain foreign to the creative experience: "Mathematics, trigonometry, chemistry, psychoanalysis, music, and whatnot," he declared in 1923, "have been related to cubism to give it an easier interpretation. All this has been pure literature, not to say nonsense, which brought bad results blinding people with theories."[27]

In 1920 Picasso is already tired of "Picassoism." The *art nègre* represents for him something else than what the general public sees in it during the wave of the *négrophilie*, namely a "fun thing" which has invaded Europe together with the jazz band, the quick step, and the short hairstyle for women. He rebels against a superficial interpretation emphasizing the exotic local color, the anecdotal—elements that he has carefully avoided in his borrowings.[28] In his view, the *bois nègres* advance a serious proposition on art, which is why he asserts to André Salmon in 1912 that "Dahomean images" are essentially "reasonable":[29] they indicate a solution for the definition of the haptic, or tactile, space referred to by Braque, and free the painter from the tyranny of an anecdotal subject matter.

The case of the *Fauves*, who refuse the cubist code, is different. They too see in African art a significant esthetic proposition, a possible answer to the problem of transcending the subject/object dichotomy inherited from Romanticism. Matisse's structural investigation of the *bois nègres* is undoubtedly as thorough as that of Picasso. If it leads him to divergent pictorial projections, it is because his expressional concerns are of another order. While Picasso, as early as 1908, wishes to go beyond emotion, Matisse seeks primarily to project as directly as possible an *émotion vécue*. Hence his use of pure, non-modulated colors, that he justifies in his *Notes of a Painter*, dated 1908:

Often when I settle down to work I begin by noting my immediate and superficial color sensations.... If at the first step and perhaps without my being conscious of it one tone has particularly pleased me, more often than not when the picture is finished I will notice that I have respected this tone.... I discover the quality of colors in a purely instinctive way.

This physical adjustment also accounts for the abandonment of the literal representation of movement:

Movement thus interpreted corresponds to nothing in nature and if we catch a motion of this kind by a snapshot, the image thus captured will remind us of nothing that we have seen. Indication of motion has meaning for us only if we do not isolate any one sensation of movement from the preceding and from the following one.[30]

Vlaminck similarly advocates a total immersion, physical and psychological, in the action of painting:

My enthusiasm allowed me to take all sorts of liberties.... I heightened all my tone values and transposed into an orchestration of pure color every single thing I felt. I was a tender barbarian, filled with violence. I translated what I saw instinctively, without any method, and conveyed truth, not so much artistically as humanely.[31]

Such a practice of releasing psychic energy, which was to become a major theme of Surrealism, helps us to understand what Matisse, and more especially Vlaminck and Derain, see—or rather choose to see—in the *art nègre*: the expression of a *cri instinctif*, an uncompromising utterance of violence and purity. Vlaminck's impassioned accounts of his first encounter with this art, as opposed to Picasso's refusal of lyricism, confirm well the existence of two distinct systems of evaluation. It is worth underlining that both Derain's and Apollinaire's descriptions of African artifacts recall those of Vlaminck: "tender barbarians," they view the *bois nègres* as essentially "frightening," and this quality (although it indicates a simplistic and patronizing conception of non-Western cultures) becomes ultimately the mark of an expressional strength lost by the industrialized Western world which they wish, like Cocteau, to rejuvenate. In this sense, Apollinaire's poem *Cri* can be read as an apology for cultures able to reconcile the natural and social universe. Apollinaire, "weary of this ancient world" buried "in Greek and Roman antiquity" in which "even cars seem superannuated," turns hopefully towards Guinean fetishes: they become "Christs of another form and of another belief" and give a new life to the *soleil cou coupé*, "the sun with a slashed throat"—an image taken up by Aimé Césaire in his *Cahier d'un retour au pays natal*.

Even if direct borrowings from actual artifacts are relatively few, the confrontation *art nègre–art moderne* in France at the beginning of our century is a momentous one. It constitutes only one manifestation of a broader confrontation, that of value systems. In a "superdiachronic" culture in which mythic structures are threatened, African artifacts acquire a new value. Their initial impact on the artistic avant-garde marks the first stage of a rehabilitation which found its logical fulfillment in the *Premier Festival Mondial des Arts Nègres* held in Dakar in April 1966. The second festival held in Lagos demonstrated the continuing vitality of African arts and artists.

NOTES

1. The first *musique nègre* was heard in Paris in 1903; cf. Jean Cocteau, *Portraits-souvenir* (Paris: Grasset, 1935), Chap. 4, "Le Cirque". Concerning the prestige of black music on the avant-garde circles, cf. Ernest Ansermet, "Sur un orchestre nègre", *Revue Romande* 10 (October 1919): 10–13.

2. Jean Laude, "La Négrophilie et al critique de l'exotisme", in *La Peinture française et l'art nègre* (Paris: Klincksieck, 1968), pp. 527 ff.

3. Blaise Cendrars, *Anthologie Nègre* (Paris: Au Sans Pareil, 1921), "Notice" (Trans. into English, where not otherwise designated, are mine.)

4. Cf. also A. Jeanneret, "Le Nègre et le jazz", *Revue Musicale* 8 (July 1927): 24–27.

5. The influence of African artifacts was felt most strongly in painting. For this

reason, modern sculpture is not treated in this short essay. As Robert Goldwater notes, "it would appear natural that primitive art, consisting largely of primitive sculpture, should have had a direct, formal influence on modern sculpture ... this in fact is not the case." Regarding the reasons for this apparent paradox, cf. his chapter "Primitivism in modern sculpture", in the revised ed. of *Primitivism in Modern Art* (New York: Vintage, 1967), pp. 225 ff.

6. Maurice de Vlaminck, *Tournant dangereux* (Paris: Stock, 1929), English tr. Michael Ross (London: Abelard-Schulman, 1955), p. 71.

7. Maurice de Vlaminck, *Portraits avant décès* (Paris: Denoël, 1943), p. 105.

8. Ibid., p. 106.

9. Letter to M. A. Leblond (April 1944), then curator of the Musée de la France d'Outremer. Quoted by Jean Laude, "La Négrophilie", p. 104 (my trans). It is noteworthy that Vollard designates as *art nègre* the works of the avant-garde influenced by African artifacts rather than these artifacts proper.

10. Max Jacob, "Naissance du cubisme," *Nouvelles Littéraires* 7 (April 1928): 9–15.

11. Christian Zervos, "Conversation avec Picasso," *Cahiers d'Art* 10 (October 1935): 173–178.

12. Guillaume Apollinaire, "Médaillon d'un peintre: un fauve," unpublished essay quoted by Alfred H. Barr, Jr., *Matisse, his Art and his Public* (New York: The Museum of Modern Art, 1955), p. 553.

13. Guillaume Apollinaire, "Cri," lines 150–151, *Les Soirées de Paris*, I, December 1912, pp. 15–22. The poem appeared the following year in the well-known collection *Alcoel* with the title "Zône."

14. Ibid., line 3.

15. Jean Cocteau, "Lettre à Paul Guillaume, négrier", *Das Querschnittbuch* 3 (March 1923): 64. For a commentary on this letter by Cocteau himself, cf. Jean Laude, "Négrophilie," p. 11.

16. Claude Levi-Strauss, *La Pensée Sauvage* (Paris: Plon, 1962), English trans. George Weidenfeld (London: Weidenfeld, 1966), pp. 135 and 76, respectively.

17. Robert Goldwater, *Primitivism in Modern Art*, p. 150.

18. Kenneth Clark, *The Nude* (New York: Doubleday, 1956), pp. 464 and 459, respectively.

19. Robert Goldwater, *Primitivism in Modern Art*, p. 150. In the *Demoiselles*, Picasso's original intention was to treat a traditional Western theme, that of *Vanitas*: at the center of the composition, there was to be a student holding a skull in his hand. The poet Max Jacob persuaded Picasso to retain only the women. The plate of fruit which replaces the skull in the final version is a well-known symbol of sensuality going back to ancient Greece. This confirms the painter's deep ties with the Mediterranean culture to which he belonged.

20. Quoted by Alfred H. Barr, Jr., *Matisse*, p. 551.

21. Jean Laude, "La Négrophilie," p. 131.

22. Henry R. Hope, *Georges Braque* (New York: The Museum of Modern Art, 1949), p. 28.

23. Maurice de Vlaminck, *Portraits*, p. 77.

24. Edwin Mullins, *The Art of Georges Braque* (London: Thames and Hudson, 1968), pp. 40–41.

25. André Level, *Picasso* (Paris: Crès, 1928), p. 37.

26. "Opinions sur l'art nègre", *Action* 1 (April 1920): 25.

27. Quoted by Alfred H. Barr, Jr., *Picasso, Fifty Years of His Art* (New York: The Museum of Modern Art, 1949), p. 74.

28. A good example of this anecdotal element is to be found in Poulenc's *Rhapsodie nègre*, mentioned at the beginning of this essay. The text which inspired Poulenc was supposed to have been written by an African from Liberia by the name of Makoko Kangourou. The first lines read: Honoloulou, poti lama/ Honoloulou, Honoloulou/ Kati moko, mosi bolou/ Ratakou sira, polama. Needless to say, the name "Kangaroo" was fictitious (and contemptuous); so was the "language." Such words as "Kangaroo" and "Honoloulou" are hardly evocative of Africa. These incongruities reveal only too well the attitude of some.

29. André Salmon, *La Jeune peinture française* (Paris: Messein, 1912), p. 42.

30. Henri Matisse, "Notes d'un peintre", *La Grande Revue* 52 (December 1908): 731–745; quoted by Alfred H. Barr, Jr., in *Matisse*, p. 120.

31. Maurice de Vlaminck, *Portraits*, p. 74.

MARIAN ASHBY JOHNSON

13

The French Impact upon African Art:
The Case of Senegalese Goldsmiths

French influence on Senegalese goldsmiths was important from the time the French arrived in 1659, but became increasingly important after the advent of colonial expositions. Colonial expositions were begun, according to some informants, in the 1830s. However, the earliest mention made relevant to Senegal in the *Archives Coloniales* in Dakar (ARS) is the *Exposition Universelle de 1855* in Paris. This tradition which affected the Senegalese goldsmith was continued until 1959, when Senegal became independent.

These expositions were important because they not only displayed jewelry from Senegal (and other places in French Africa), but in many instances allocated funds to allow the goldsmiths to participate and to make and display their work in person.[1] This gave Senegalese jewelry exposure that one would not expect during this time—at least from the mid-nineteenth century onward. The expositions were primarily organized by the French government, but many took place in other European countries, in West Africa, and even in the United States.

The expositions were often elaborate and costly to prepare for, especially when special buildings were constructed for the display of African artifacts and jewelry. The exposition of 1900 in Paris, for example, featured a copy of the mosque in Djenné, as well as other "authentic" creations. The sum of 74,000 francs was spent for the construction of the colonial pavilion, according to a list of expenditures (ARS, Fonds Séné., Expo. de 1900,2). One source called it a veritable "Palais"; significantly, in front were boutiques for jewelers and weavers where their creations could be purchased. At another Paris exposition in 1937, a copy of the Timbuktu mosque served as an exhibition hall and took a fair amount of research and work to construct (ARS, 6, Q-80 [74]).

Small huts or reed structures were constructed at the expositions to simulate the Senegalese atelier (*m'bar*). The tools and simple furnishings of the forge adorned its walls; the goldsmith worked in full view of the public. The Senegalese forge consisted of a simple hole in the ground where a charcoal fire was made. It was not unusual that ateliers were set up at the expositions, because as early as 1855, the exposition in Paris featured several goldsmiths to demonstrate jewelry making.[2]

Sometimes entire artisanal villages were reconstructed for the expositions, and an exposition in Geneva in 1896 was planned with 183 persons to be recruited from Gorée, Dakar, and other cities along the coastal railroad line in Senegal. There were twenty jewelers listed first among those craftsmen invited to attend, and the *indigène* in charge of recruiting was himself a goldsmith.

Expositions took place in the Senegalese cities of Saint-Louis and Dakar, but the goldsmiths were most anxious to attend the ones held in Europe or in other African countries such as Sierra Leone (1865).[3] There were several expositions in Paris (1855, 1878, 1900, 1906, 1910, 1931, 1937), but the most important ones for goldsmiths seem to have been those in 1900 and in 1937. There were also French expositions at Antwerp (1884-1885), Arras (1904), Le Havre (1887, 1931), Marseilles (1906,[4] 1916), Lyons (1913 or 1914), Reims (1899, 1903), Bordeaux (1932), Nancy (1909), Liège (1905), La Rochelle (1930), Vincennes (ca. 1932), Nantes (1932, 1938), Lille (1932), and Bergerac (1934).

Outside France, there were expositions at Sierra Leone (1865), Geneva (1896), Brussels (1910), Ghent (1912), Casablanca (1915), Dahomey (1916), Upper Volta, Niger, and Ivory Coast (1931), Rabat (1917), Wiesbaden (1910),[5] Edinburgh (1909), Breslau (1913), and Frankfurt (1909). There may have been Senegalese sent to expositions in Madrid in 1892 and Chicago in 1893; it is difficult to know from the correspondence. The only documentation found was letters requesting Senegalese participation (ARS, Fonds Séné., 1890-97).

The basic rationale behind these expositions was to introduce the French public to the culture of the various overseas colonies and to serve as a public relations device for the Ministry of Colonies. One Frenchman who was asked to organize the objects to be sent to an exposition was specifically encouraged to "collect things which would demonstrate local architecture, indigenous habitation, costume and adornment. . .tools, etc. . . ." and "fixerait les aspects pittoresques de la région et de la vie sénégalaise." O. Durand in 1932 gave the official rationale for the expositions: "To introduce and to popularize in France our West African possessions, so superbly brought out at the recent Exhibition in Vincennes. It also displayed, . . . 'in a dazzling fantasia of contour and color', the remarkable French effort ignored by some and unrecognized by many others to this day."

Whatever the rationale, these expositions were important to the goldsmiths and their artisans for their exposure and for the selling of their wares. They were undoubtedly of capital influence on the goldsmiths of Senegal, especially of Saint-Louis and Gorée, two of the old communes.

Proximity to the coast where trade with France and other countries of Europe had been carried on since the fifteenth century was of great influence on the Wolof. They probably had more contact with Europeans (especially the French)

Figure 13-1
Marital ceremonies of the inhabitants of Saint-Louis, Senegal.

than any other African people south and west of the Sahara. They assimilated a veneer of Western culture easily and prided themselves on a cosmopolitan reputation.[6] This helps explain their desirability for recruitment to the expositions. Yet paradoxically, the Wolof always remained very ''African,'' never abandoning their language, customs, dress, religion, or educational practices.

Other Senegalese goldsmiths besides the Wolof and those of other countries were also sent to the expositions. In an interview conducted with Al-Hajj Habitubu Sissoko (April 1972), he spoke of his grandfather Djibril Sissoko who went to the exposition in Paris in 1900 from Bondou in eastern Senegal. His father and brothers (Habitoubu, Moussa, and Sadjo Sissoko) went to later expositions (Paris exposition in 1931). There are a number of sources in the archives which mention Soudanese jewelry, and a letter from the director of *La Maison des Artisans* in Bamako discusses sending objects of ''Parure'' and ''Bijoux'' to the exposition in Paris in 1937.[7]

A letter from Paris described what the participants were expected to do: ''These *indigènes* will be employed to execute in a rustic pavilion. . .of the Senegalese exposition at the Trocadero, objects of their craftsmanship before the eyes of the public'' (ARS, Fonds Séné., Expo., de 1900, 9 April 1900). "Twenty jewelers were the first of the indigènes to be listed who would attend the exposition in Geneva (1896), then came twenty-one woodcarvers, ten weavers, eight *garçons de café*, four leatherworkers, nine tailors, one potter, sixteen members of a marabout's (Muslim holy man) family, two Fulbé families, fifty '*divers*' (probably mostly women and children), nineteen griots and musicians, and thirty-two fishermen, warriors, and house builders'' (ARS, Fonds Séné., Expo. de 1900, 9 April 1900).[8]

All the expositions had the participation of Senegalese goldsmiths and other craftsmen and their apprentices and of "village persons" including women and children. There were a number of references about women being sent to expositions for the purpose of cooking, and food was sent from Senegal to make it even more authentic (and probably cheaper). The recruitment of "local color" reveals a desire to recreate the exotic in a European setting. This helped to establish jewelry making and selling as a mainstay of all the colonial expositions.

Goldsmiths were chosen to attend these expositions in a number of ways. One was by holding competitions among the smiths. According to a letter containing notes of a meeting of the exposition committee, gold was bought and a few grams given to certain jewelers to make something to submit for possible exhibit during the exposition (ARS, Fonds Séné., Expo. de 1900, 3 Feb., 1900). Another letter mentions that 1,049 francs worth of gold was bought for this purpose by the committee. The jewelry chosen also determined, in this instance, the artists who were able to go to Paris to show their work. The French were aware of how much the exhibitors had to gain from this exposure and experience. One consideration in sending smiths was whether they had attended other expositions or not.[9]

Six jewelers and their apprentices,[10] one blacksmith,[11] two leatherworkers, and two weavers were chosen to go to the Exposition of Paris in 1900 after due consideration of their work. Five thousand francs was set aside for buying jewelry for the exhibit above and beyond the amount already spent for the contest among the jewelers or the amount that would be spent for the gold to be fashioned in Paris for the public. During one meeting of the committee it was decided to buy several bracelets totaling 856 francs (ARS, Fonds Séné., Expo de 1900, 1896-1900).

Originally jewelers were chosen to go to the expositions simply because they were known to the French administration. By 1865 correspondence from the archives in Senegal listed the items displayed and the name not only of the (usually) French collector, but also the goldsmiths who had created a number of the pieces. For example, "Exhibited by Mme. Ch. Valentin, 1 gold bracelet from Galam 150 francs, Mamadou Mame'' (ARS, Fonds Séné., 5).[12] This is unusual in the field of African art. For example, the sculptural art of West Africa was almost completely anonymous until the last fifty years and even then is not, in most cases, very well documented.

The fact that Senegalese goldsmiths were mentioned by name is indicative of the reputation the jewelers had established with the Europeans at that time. They were often the mediators or confidantes for politically sensitive issues. The jewelers spoke good French, in most cases, and had business with Lebanese, Mauritanians, and other Arabic-speaking people. As Mamé Moussa Thiam put it, (Saint-Louis, March 1972), his great-grandfather Birahim Thiam, who went to the *Exposition Universelle de Paris* in 1855, made jewelry for Europeans, mulattoes, and "tout le monde." He not only made "bijoux indigènes," but could reputedly copy anything. Senegalese smiths were mentioned in early travel sources as having the facility to produce anything from cannons to delicate jewelry.

John Ogilby described the Senegalese tools used to make both jewelry and farm tools and Jean-Baptiste Labat wrote that the smith worked both iron and gold. Golberry found that the smiths in eastern Senegal could make iron tools and delicate filigree jewelry equally well.[13]

Smiths in Senegal were known to be well informed on the political and the economic situation and were described as one of the wealthiest groups in spite of their low social status in a caste system (Camara, 1968:182).[14] They made it their business to be on good terms with all elements of society, and this increased their usefulness to the French administration. Goldsmiths were among the groups in Senegal most assimilated to French culture, and this made it all the easier to send them to the colonial expositions. The French needed artisans who were flexible and who would make easy adjustments under new circumstances. They found these qualities in the goldsmiths and their families.

Reputation had a great deal to do with whether a goldsmith was able to attend the expositions; this is made even more emphatic when one reads the correspondence in the Senegalese archives. Even before the exposition of 1900, Senegalese jewelers were making formal requests to be sent to the expositions, and several letters are preserved. A typical letter is addressed to *M. le Directeur de l'Intérieur*, Saint-Louis (the capital of Senegal at that time):

Desirous to participate at the Bordeaux Exposition, I have applied to M. le Gouverneur who has referred me to the Bordeaux (Organizing) Committee. Before getting in touch with the committee, I beg you to let me know if the St. Louis committee has met already and what arrangements it has made or plans to make on the occasion of this exhibition. In the case the St. Louis Committee would not have met, I ask you, M. le Directeur, to please summon a meeting and introduce my request.
Yours respectfully, Samba Lawbé Thiam, Bijoutier, rue de France (Saint-Louis). [ARS. Fonds Séné., Expo. de 1900, 1]

Many of the letters of this sort (despite grammatical errors) were written by professional African "letter writers" for the goldsmiths. It is interesting to note that one letter complained about the fact that the Nord (a section of Saint-Louis) "always" furnished the smiths to the expositions, while those of the Sud were never included. Three jewelers signed this letter (N'Diaga Thiam, Séga Diouf, and Makham Diaw).[15]

It is not difficult to understand the desire of these men to go to the exposition of 1900. In the archives there is a notebook of expenditures which lists the amount paid to the goldsmiths, who were paid according to their experience and expertise and, one would imagine, according to how well they bargained. For example, one Gallo Thiam, "bijoutier" was given 110 francs; Birahim Thiam, 130; Makhone, 95; Khouma Guèye, 125; Lamine Guèye, 125; Samba Lawbé Thiam, 175 (he was put in charge of the others); Séga Diouf, 82; Biram Diouf, 12; Diaga Thiam, 195 (ARS, Fonds Séné., 1899). There is no explanation as to why the difference in payment, but it can be imagined that the low salary given to Biram Diouf was probably due to the fact that he was an apprentice and undoubtedly related in some way to Séga Diouf. But an even more provocative question is why N'Diaga ("Diaga") Thiam received more than even Samba Laobé ("Lawbé") Thiam, who was given responsibility for the group. Reputation and experience must certainly have been great factors.[16]

Correspondence on the *Exposition Universelle de Paris* of 1878 mentions a jeweler by the name of M. Birabar as having made on commission a bracelet (90 francs), a cross (25 francs), and a ring (25 francs) to be sent for exhibition. This was important for several reasons. In the first place, a particular named goldsmith was chosen to make jewelry for exhibit; second, he was commissioned to make specific kinds of jewelry, which reflected the fact that certain styles were preferred by the French; and third, he was paid only for the work and not for the gold itself, an indication that the French were willing to pay well for the work done. All indications are that jewelers were as well paid for their services then as they are today.

A well-known goldsmith, Ibrahim Biram of Dakar, was put in charge of recruiting, which included signing up nine from his own family. Biram apparently procured all the materials to construct a typical Senegalese village with furnishings and went to Geneva for the exposition of 1896, but was dismissed and sent home within a few days. He was to have been paid 200 francs a month plus 0.5 percent of the profits besides what his family received as living expenses.[17]

In addition to the salary or payments given to the participants, there were numerous medals, certificates, diplomas, prizes, and gifts awarded for the work done by the Senegalese artists and artisans. Two of the goldsmiths interviewed (Mamé Moussa Thiam and Daouda M'Bow) mentioned ancestors who were invited to the 1855 exposition in Paris. One was the well-known Birahim Thiam; there are two letters in the archives stating that he received several awards for his creations, such as the *Médaille de Deuxième Classe* for jewelry.[18]

One of the letters from the *ministre de la marine et des colonies* to the governor of Senegal observed that the jewelry "*confectionnées*" by "Birahim Tiam" (Thiam) was done with "*procédés cependant fort imparfaits*" and had been

Figure 13-2
Master goldsmith of Saint-Louis, Daouda M'Bow.

Figure 13-3
Master goldsmith of Dakar, Doudou Guèye.

displayed in the second class. He went on to say that it would be a good idea to give him the means to perfect his work, which would show the government's satisfaction and would also encourage an industry which responded to the needs and the tastes of the Senegalese population. (The minister apparently did not understand the popularity of Senegalese jewelry with French women.) The minister then proposed to give a small assortment of jeweler's tools to Birahim Thiam. The letter concludes by saying that the minister would like to know if the new tools served the purpose to improve Thiam's work and that he would like some examples sent "à l'Exposition permanent des colonies" (ARS, 1B, 69 Fol. 6, 1856).[19]

The presentation of tools, which seems to have begun here, became a continuing tradition. In an interview with goldsmith Daouda M'Bow (Saint-Louis, February 1972), it was learned that he was still using the anvil his great-grandfather received at an exposition held in 1878. Medals were still given as awards, however, and in 1891 Samba Laobé Thiam received a silver medal, and Gallo Thiam, Mamadou Thiam, and Mokhor Thiam all received bronze medals.[20] In fact, the French government was still giving them out in 1959 (the final year of colonial rule) at an exposition in Saint-Louis, according to Mamé Moussa Thiam (Dakar, March 1972). The medals were of gold, silver, bronze, and copper and in one case, a bright red one was received. Sometimes inlaid boxes meant for storing jewelry were given and, of course, the tools mentioned above.

The goldsmiths invited to the expositions gained a great deal of prestige and are still remembered by people in Senegal because of this honor. In all instances, save one, informants who mentioned goldsmiths who attended expositions were corroborated by documentary evidence. There was little disagreement as to dates, names, and places, and those interviewed were aware and accurate about the facts.

Attending expositions was brought up frequently by informants in the discussion of the grands maîtres of the past, which suggests the prestige and honor attached to being invited to attend. Besides the publicity it gave Senegalese artisans, the recompense was attractive, not to mention the experience. The competition for a place in the group was severe according to the letters.

An article written in Moniteur du Sénégal (1856, p. 3) described Birahim Thiam as an "artiste indigène" in spite of his simple methods ("avec des procédés forts imparfaits"). One might expect African sculpture to be called "art" by the 1920s after the strong influence it had on so-called "Modern Art," particularly in France. However, it is significant that 1856 is very early for African goldsmiths to be seriously considered as creative artists and is indicative of the quality of work they produced.

The Exposition Universelle de Paris of 1900 had an especially large display of African jewelry from West Africa. The African jewelry occupied only four large display cases, but they were placed in the center of the exhibit hall and apparently drew special attention from the public. The author of the catalogue for the exposition singled out the jewelry cases as the most noteworthy display

Figure 13-4
Jewelry collection of Mme. Fatou N'Diaye.

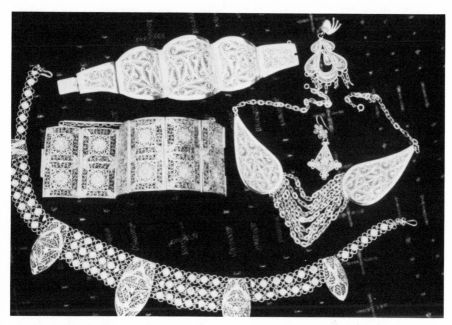

Figure 13-5
Jewelry collection of Mme. Karime Gaye.

in the entire colonial exposition. This serves as an indication of the kind of work done by the jewelers. Jewelry labeled ''Senegalese'' and that labeled ''Soudanese'' received the most attention from the critics, who compared them favorably to the jewelry displays from Dahomey, Ivory Coast, and Guinea.

The jewelry labeled ''Senegalese'' was from Saint-Louis and therefore Wolof in style. In comparison to the other African jewelry it was described as more ''*civilisées*'' and with ''*rare finesse*'' and was considered by some critics to be the finest on display. The word ''*civilisées*'' could mean many things; it is difficult to ascertain exactly what the author meant. However, we can safely assume that in this description, he meant to imply influence from Europe. The reviewer in the *Moniteur du Sénégal* observed that while Senegalese (Wolof) jewelry was of excellent quality and had a delicacy and remarkable execution in filigree, it was more inspired by European tastes than the Soudanese jewelry. He went on to say that the Senegalese goldsmiths' ability to assimilate the European models denoted "their artistic sense and dexterity."

The "Soudanese" jewelry, as it was termed in the exposition, was exhibited in two of the four large showcases in the center of the exhibit hall. All the jewelry contained in these cases came from one collection, which was taken during the siege of Ségou-Sikoro, the capital of the Toucouleur kingdom of Ahmadou after the death of his father, Al-Hajj Umar Tall, in the 1860s. The Toucouleur kingdom was located in the eastern part of what is now modern Senegal and the western part of present-day Mali. This area is considered part of the Soudan.

The collection displayed was valued at 30,000 francs at the time and was transported to Paris especially for the exposition in 1900. Unfortunately, the only trace known today of this priceless collection are copies of two of the pieces in the IFAN Museum in Dakar. This collection was not made a permanent part of the *Musée de l'Homme*, and when inquiries were made in Paris (1972) no one knew of such a collection.[21]

The Toucouleur jewelry collection was compared to the Wolof collection by the author in the *Moniteur* as being less light and refined, but distinguished by more originality and archaic qualities. This description still characterizes the differences between the two traditions to a large extent.

The expositions were also important for the development of style in Senegalese jewelry from a number of points of view. Frenchmen made up the committees who chose the jewelry to be sent and displayed. They not only chose from jewelry which had already been made, but they also commissioned much of the jewelry, especially for the expositions. There are in the archives several examples of correspondence and committee minutes which list the amount of money spent for gold to be made into jewelry for judging. The president of the exposition committee (February 3, 1900) informed the committee he had bought the gold for a competition: "It has been decided that the goldsmiths to be sent to the Exposition will be chosen by competition; each one will be given several grams of gold in order to give proof of his artistic technique." After the objects were made, they were collected for the committee to examine and judge (ARS, Fonds Séné., Expo. de 1900. 1896-1900).

Some of the jewelry was sent solely for display, but other examples were obviously sent with the expectation that they would be sold as some of the lists from the archives indicate. In either case, the lists of items sent to the expositions are frustratingly incomplete. A notation such as *"Bijoux de métaux précieux"* may be all that is mentioned among items such as *"produits de la chasse"* or *"instruments de musique"* or *"specimens de typographie,"* although they would sometimes include *"le soufflet de forgeron."* However, a number of items were commissioned by name especially for the exhibit at the *Exposition de Bordeaux* in 1864. This was particularly true for expositions after the turn of the century (ARS, Fonds Séné., Expo. de 1900, 1896-1900).[22]

The jewelry collections sent to be exhibited which were not commissioned by the organizing committees were most often those of French women living in Senegal and although they sometimes included indigenous styles, in many cases they were composed of pieces commissioned by these women to be worn in the latest fashion. According to my informants, many examples were not Senegalese in style, but rather copies of jewelry worn in Europe. In fact, most jewelers working in Dakar (the modern capital of Senegal) at present have catalogues of jewelry styles from Europe and the United States. One jeweler in Dakar took an American Peace Corps volunteer as an apprentice in order to learn more about modern styles. Unfortunately, the American student hoped to learn more of the traditional techniques and styles, and their interests were difficult to reconcile.

By 1865 European collectors' names were listed as pieces of jewelry from their personal collections were sent to the expositions of Bordeaux and of Sierra Leone. It is unfortunate that better records were not kept on what kinds of jewelry and which styles were chosen for the expositions. One might imagine that styles sent would be more indigenous in flavor, since the expositions were conceived to create interest in the culture of the colonies. For example, one item listed in a budget was, "sale of gold and handiwork for the making of jewelry 'du pays', 5,000 (francs)" (ARS. Fonds Séné., 1899). The expression "*du pays*" could refer to style, but on the other hand, the fact that the jewelers were creating for a European public and in particular a French committee, undoubtedly influenced what the African goldsmiths produced. French ideas of quality and style were what mattered. It would have been interesting to have a group of Senegalese women, for example, choose the jewelry to be sent. What differences would there have been?

The cross mentioned above which was made for the *Exposition Universelle de Paris* of 1878 was probably a filigree cross made in the traditional Christian form and not the now well-known *"Croix d'Agadès"* which is so popular with the tourists. The Christian cross had no real roots in African style, as does the one from Agadès. In this case, the techniques were more important than style, and one reporter writing about the *Exposition Universelle de Paris* in 1900 remarked how fine the filigree was (ARS, Fonds Séné., 1896-1900, *Sénégal-Soudan*, p. 61). Filigree along with the granulation technique was encouraged.

The lists of items sent included broaches made into butterflies, fish, and insects. In the first place, broaches were not used traditionally in Senegal because clothing above the waist was considered unnecessary during most of the year. The other factor is that butterflies, fish, and insects were not employed in the goldsmiths' repertoire in Senegal before colonization. Therefore, the French influenced the form and style that some jewelry took in Senegal. In fact, these forms are still popular in Senegal and can be compared to those from Portugal, India, and Italy which have been seen in contemporary collections made in those countries and bought by Americans abroad.

Some of the jewelry was lost or stolen in at least two of the expositions. Because this was a problem, in 1901 (after the 1900 exposition) a special guard was assigned to travel with a container of jewelry weighing thirteen kilos and valued at 5,000 francs. A necklace and a bracelet had already been stolen by the time it left for Senegal (ARS, Q-45, Letter, February 1901).

The influence felt from the colonial expositions made an impact on the goldsmiths from several points of view. Prosper Seck was an example of a goldsmith who profited a great deal from this exposure. He participated in at least two different expositions. In 1904 he attended the exposition in Arras where he received a bronze medal for his jewelry making and in October of 1931 was interviewed for a newspaper article as a member of the jury and *hors concours* at the *Exposition Coloniale* in Paris (*La France Coloniale*, Dakar, 8 October 1931). In the interview he was complimented on the purity of his French, to which Seck replied that he studied Arabic and French four hours each day. By 1931 he was not only a member of the exposition jury, but was a *Chevalier de la Légion d'Honneur* as well. He had gained a great deal of prestige because of his participation in the expositions and was treated with respect.

The special awards were important to the Senegalese and their families and were a proof of their abilities to compete and be appreciated. A letter from the *ministère de la marine et des colonies* pointed out that in giving tools as awards, "The Saint-Louisians could not help but see that this recompense given to an *ouvrier* who had risen above the ordinary with his own resources, was further proof of the solicitude of the administration for the least interests of the colonies" (ARS, 1B69 Fol. 72, 26 February 1856). The competition was keen, and reputations could be made or broken in some respects by the choices made by an exposition organizing committee. "The jewelry was submitted for examination by the members of the committee. It had been worked by the craftsmen who had requested to be sent to the Exposition" (ARS, Fonds Séné., Expo. de 1900, 1).

Not only was there competition to go to the expositions, but there was apparently competition to head them as well. Goldsmiths were usually chosen over all the group as "*chef*." The man chosen to head the group was expected to carry a great deal of responsibility and was apparently under pressure and became a focus of criticism. One letter expresses disagreement in the choice of one "*chef*," a Samba Laobé Thiam. It was felt by *M. le Président* of the exposition planning committee that it was better to have a different goldsmith take over this job; another member of the committee pointed out that he had seen the work of numerous other jewelers who had better qualifications than Thiam. In his estimation, Noirot, in charge of recruiting for the exposition (1900), was much too "*exclusif*" and "*personnel*" (personal) in his choice of the "*chef*." There was also disagreement about how much was proposed by Noirot to pay Thiam (ARS, Fonds Séné., Expo. de 1900, Séance du Comité, 5 March 1889). We have already discussed Ibrahim Biram (1896 exposition of Geneva) and the responsibility of recruiting 183 people for the exposition of Geneva held in 1896.

With that many people involved it was politically advantageous to be recruiting—as well as lucrative.

The expositions also afforded the better goldsmiths the opportunity to travel at the expense of the governments and educate themselves as to other styles and techniques being used, particularly those of the French. These artisans were also sent to other colonies in Africa such as the Ivory Coast. Some goldsmiths decided to stay in France, in the Ivory Coast, or in other French colonies for a season or in some instances for the rest of their lives. In other cases, they returned to the various colonies of origin. This experience apparently greatly influenced many Africans and their families. In fact, it may have been the expositions which gave the impetus to the great diffusion of Senegalese jewelers who now live and work in all the main cities of Africa.[23] To this day, one can travel to most of the major locations in West and Central Africa and find Senegalese making jewelry.

For the first time, Senegalese jewelers were exposed through the expositions to the great demand for jewelry beyond their immediate locale. They were in a position to see the possibilities of new markets at a time when their own was reaching saturation.[24] They were flexible enough to grasp the idea of what was necessary to succeed in other countries and among other peoples.

Jewelers today are perhaps the most mobile segment of Senegalese society. Many jewelers in Senegal have a history of travel and work in other African countries, France, and other European countries. This phenomenon was set in motion by the expositions and the exposure the Senegalese gained to new environments and new markets. A network of families exists in many countries where young men may do an apprenticeship and return to Senegal when they wish to settle down. Sometimes expatriate smiths were accompanied by family members, and others went alone and remained to marry and make apprentices of the indigenous people. Some goldsmiths now working in Senegal have traveled extensively, lived in several different countries (especially in West Africa), and worked as they went under the auspices of other displaced Senegalese.[25]

The expositions became a vehicle for promulgating great change in many goldsmiths' lives. They no longer harbored vague ideas of how people lived and worked in other countries; they were given the opportunity to find out first-hand. They learned new jewelry-making techniques, but they also found that their own jewelry-making techniques were, in many cases, not outmoded. They found, too, that their techniques obtained results comparable to those of the *Toubabs* (Whites). Even their tools, which were originally hand-made, were found to be comparable to those they saw Europeans using. These discoveries were a source of pride to several of the jewelers interviewed. It is not difficult to understand that they had been led to believe that the *Toubab* had superior skills and knowledge in many different sectors. In this instance, they were able to compare their tools and techniques and they were surprised to find that their methods were basically the same.

Now, of course, most ateliers in Senegal have a great many tools imported from Europe and some machines to expedite what were once painstaking tech-

Figure 13-6
A *Signara* of Saint-Louis greeting her guest. See also Figure 11-1.

niques. One such machine draws wire for filigree work which takes many hours (days) by hand. Now one can buy most sizes of drawn wire from the government-controlled office (*Service des Mines*), which was originally established by the French. Another change is the large containers of gas used in place of the oil lamp and blow-pipe in soldering. In 1972, however, the oil lamp was still being used for some purposes in almost all *m'bars* and in well over 50 percent of the ateliers for all soldering. Although most tongs, pliers, pincers, and other tools used most frequently are now imported where they were once all made by hand, tools made by great-grandfathers or other relatives are still hung with pride on the walls of the *m'bars* and in some cases used regularly. Family pride and continuity are still very important to the Senegalese goldsmith.

Senegalese women were (and are) considered by many Europeans to be the most beautiful and stylish women in Black Africa. One of the reasons for this opinion was that Senegalese women were, especially in the case of the Wolof, more easily assimilated into French culture. The well-known *Signares* (*métis* merchant women of the eighteenth century who controlled trade in Senegal for many years) are perhaps the best examples of this.[26] The jewelry they wore with their fashionable French gowns was often heavily influenced by European styles. However, the massive size (hollow in most cases), the color (more orange than the gold color preferred by French women), and the choice of form were decidedly Senegalese.

For example, a gold filigree basket of flowers called a "Kostine" or "Complet" would not have been selected by the French, especially in the flamboyant size usually chosen for this famous style. The fact that the basket is included is clearly a Senegalese stylistic preference. The French would probably have depicted only the flowers, excluding the basket. The Senegalese, on the other hand, did not put flowers in baskets for display, except in the market as a French woman might, because baskets were meant to store grain and in most cases were entirely utilitarian in use. Another touch which could be called Senegalese is the addition of a smaller pendant to hang at the nape of the neck and related in design to the central one. With this final touch the necklace is truly "Complet" or a finished costume ("Kostine") as the names for this style (taken from the French) indicate.

French influence was shown when the names of some styles were listed in the correspondence because they were often given French names or French derivatives.[27] Some of these names were helpful in tracing the styles for research. Senegalese women have always been politically active, and several jewelry styles were made popular by commemorating political movements such as the "Bloc Sénégalais" or events such as the "Loi de Lamine" (when women were given the vote after World War II in Senegal because of Lamine Guèye's support). "Tonaimar" was the name of an earring made popular because of a favorite mayor of Saint-Louis.

The jewelry styles reveal the influence of French colonial political structures and processes and much of the iconography can be traced to French influence. These particular styles must have been especially interesting to the French, and one can well understand why examples of these styles were sent to the expositions—and in many cases were commissioned especially for exhibit.

French influence was not only deeply engrained in the style, iconography, and form of Senegalese jewelry, but the techniques were influenced as well. The French wanted to demonstrate just how "*évolué*" the Senegalese jewelers were. Filigree attracted attention because it contradicted the typical notion that *les indigènes* were unable to create in techniques requiring a great deal of skill or attention to detail. This negative opinion was widely held by most Europeans during the century between the 1850s and 1950s when the expositions took place, and the committee was undoubtedly aware of this. The French, as with all representative governments, had to find ways to justify their political and economic activities—especially in foreign areas of colonization. Delicate filigree work would serve as an example of refinement making the Senegalese, in a sense, "worthy of colonization." The committee probably encouraged the making of filigree for this as well as esthetic reasons. It is not an exaggeration to speak of a *politique de l'art*.

One of the most revealing descriptions of the jewelry on display for the Paris exposition of 1900 concerned the jewelry from Saint-Louis, which "suggested an observation and gave birth to a regret. It recalled, for the most part, the models of our European jewelry, of an appearance far too civilized, by which the black goldsmiths were obviously inspired; they should have been more original in their treatment: in other words, more foreign with more local color" (ARS, Fonds Séné., 1896-1900, *Sénégal-Soudan*, p. 61). Saint-Louis was not only the first French capital of Senegal; it was for many years the capital of all French West Africa. This further illustrates why French influence would be so much in evidence in the jewelry.

The goldsmiths themselves, *à titre personnel*, were influenced no less than the jewelry; however, this comment about the colonial expositions tells much about the relations between the French and the Africans who participated. "Since the artisans did not have any way to enter into direct communication with the visitors, the knowledge of French became absolutely useless to them" (ARS, 6-Q-80 (74), Expo. de 1937, Paris, 3 March 1937). In other words, the Black artisan was completely isolated from personal contact with the public except when he was on view at the exposition. This was probably more true as the expositions went on and they became better organized; this particular exposition took place in 1937. Apparently little hospitality was shown by the French toward the African visitors. This isolation appears to have been planned, because women were transported to France especially to do the cooking and food was sent with them *from* Senegal. The Senegalese participants were also furnished with living quarters (usually close to or on the exposition grounds) where they were basically segregated.

In spite of this last observation, Senegalese goldsmiths were greatly influenced. They became a more cosmopolitan group and gained confidence in their abilities when they were able to compare their work with that of other goldsmiths. They were able to absorb new techniques and new styles and to keep abreast of developments in their field. They also were quick to seize the implications of developing markets for their creations *outside* of Senegal. Also, the French men and women who were involved in the selection of jewelry to be sent to or made for the expositions were also a major influence, but the goldsmiths themselves were probably influenced more on a personal level. It is interesting to speculate on how much more the Senegalese might have been influenced if the exposition experience had included contact with French families and opportunities for closer observation of other aspects of French life. In conclusion, both the style and creators of Senegalese gold jewelry were influenced by the French expositions during more than a century (1850-1950); the experience proved to have more impact on the Wolof than on the Toucouleur goldsmiths; and the expositions provided an international perspective for the Senegalese unique in tropical Africa.

NOTES

1. O. Durand, "Les Industries locales au Fouta," *Bulletin du Comité d'Etudes Historiques et Scientifiques de l'A.O.F.*, 15 (1932):45-46 describes the import of the expositions in regard to the jewelry from Foûta Djallon (Guinea), "Les diverses exposition coloniales ont d'ailleurs amplement affirmé ces talents et permis d'apprécier ces productions toujours empreintés d'un cachet indéniable de finesse et surtout d'originalité."

2. Daouda M'Bow, in an interview, March 1971, mentioned Guila Diagne, Tamsier Guèye, Souleymane Seye, and Birahim Thiam as the jewelers who were sent in 1855. Guila Diagne was his uncle and had been his master (*maître*). Daouda M'Bow was eighty-seven years old at the time of the interview and still active in both Dakar and Saint-Louis.

3. For this exposition, see Fonds Séné., 5 in the ARS. Lists of who sent what kinds of jewelry are among the most complete available. The lists of those who sent their collections of jewelry may provide clues to families which still possess examples of this early Senegalese jewelry. Some collectors' names which appeared in various folders in the ARS: "Mme. Bératte; Mme. Ch. Valentin (Valantin); Mlle. Catherine Blanchot; Mme. Leantier Potes; Chas. Porque; Henry Jay; Mme. Samson; Mlle. Sophie Audibert; Hamat; Théodore; M. Sarrazin; M. Bon El Mogdad; Riquetti; Dumont."

4. The documentation from this exposition is also quite good. There are a number of jewelers mentioned by name, and letters by and about them are filed.

5. The Senegalese archives have only the letters requesting them to come to the exposition, but an interview with Amadou Diop (June 1972) clarified this. He mentioned that his uncle had gone to an exposition in Wiesbaden of that year.

6. Several early travel sources mention this ability to absorb what they are exposed to. Even today the Wolof are spoken of as "more French than the French."

7. There was almost no material in the Dakar Archives (ARS, IFAN) on goldsmiths from Mali. Perhaps more material exists elsewhere.

8. In the lists of artisans sent to the expositions, goldsmiths were nearly always listed first and one master goldsmith was put in charge of all the artisans participating.

9. M. Khouma Guèye was chosen to go only after the committee checked to see if he had attended an earlier exposition (ARS, Fonds Séné., Expo. 1896-1900).

10. N'Diaga Thiam, Sega Diouf, Gallo Thiam, Birahim Thiam, Khouma Guèye, and Samba Laobe Thiam were the master jewelers while Amadou Thiam, Khone Guèye, Sulyman Thiam, N'Diaga Diaye, Amadou Guèye, and Birahim Diouf were the apprentices who were sent to Paris in 1900.

11. The distinction between goldsmiths and blacksmiths was made by the Senegalese and the French long before the twentieth century, although some men to this day practice both crafts.

12. Faidherbe, a governor of Senegal, sent a number of items, but none of them were jewelry (hippopotamus teeth, Maure rugs, silver swords, and pistols a chief had owned, and so on).

13. John Ogilby, *Africa, being an accurate description of the regions of Aegypt, Barbary, Lybia and Billedulgerid...* (London: reprinted by T. Johnson for the author, 1670), pp. 346-347; Jean-Baptiste Labat, *Nouvelle relation de l'Afrique occidentale* (Paris: G. Cavelier, 1728), II, p. 306; Sylvain-Meinrad-Xavier Golberry, *Fragments d'un voyage en Afrique* (Paris: Treuttel et Würtz, 1802), I, p. 413.

14. Camille Camara, *Saint-Louis du Sénégal, évolution d'une ville en milieu Africain* (Dakar: IFAN, 1968).

15. Other goldsmiths who wrote letters desiring to go to the expositions were Maquate Touré (Guet N'Dar, also a section of Saint-Louis); Mambaye M'Bow (Nord, Saint-Louis) "Votre Bijoutier très humble et très Deservé"; Koumu Guèye; Birahim Guèye; Amadou Guèye; Gallo Thiam, "Très devoué serviteur"; N'Diaga Thiam, Séga Diouf and Mehoné Diagne; Khouma Guèye wanted to take along two "cadets" to help him; Lamine Guèye and Samba Laobé Thiam who has the "Courage de quitter" his "foyer" and others. (ARS, Fonds Séné., Expo. de 1900, 2.)

16. The French influenced the Senegalese in another way. For the first time, in many cases, names were written down. Numerous names were written with the given name last and the family name as a first name. Some Senegalese kept their names as the French had originally written them. Others were changed. In the case of Samba Laobé Thiam, for example, he was called Samba Lawbé in some instances in the correspondence and in other instances listed as Sambé Thiam or Tiam, and still another way, Thiam Samb. N'Diaga was sometimes Diaga and Gallo was Galo. It depended on the writer, but their written names all have influence from the French.

17. No specific reasons were given for Biram's dismissal, but presumably he did not turn out to be a very good administrator or a good manager of money (ARS, Q-45). It is interesting to note, however, that his fellow *Teugue* regarded him with great esteem because he was chosen for this important responsibility.

18. There are undoubtedly more letters to be found in the archives in Marseilles or in Paris dealing with this or earlier expositions.

19. What has happened to the extensive collection which must have existed during colonial days? There are a few examples of jewelry left in the *Musée de l'Homme*, but most of them are broken. They had not been cared for or catalogued properly in 1972 when I visited. I understand the situation has improved since.

20. The name Thiam is frequent within the jewelers' caste. It is interesting to note that medals and certificates were also given to participating collectors (usually French) of jewelry, tobacco, cotton, gum arabic, and so on. The man who received more medals than the artisans themselves (which included leatherworkers, weavers, and woodworkers) was Ernest Noirot, who was the delegate of the exposition who organized the objects to be sent. He received one gold medal, ten silver, two bronze medals and six honorable mentions (ARS, Fonds Séné., Expo. 1900, 3 Séance, 20 April, 1889).

21. This collection would have been invaluable to the study of Senegalese and Soudanese jewelry. A letter in 1901 to Paris said that all objects after the *Exposition de Paris* of 1900 were to be divided between the museums in France except the "*bijoux*" which were to be sent back to Senegal. If some of the jewelry had remained in the French museums, the task of tracing the evolution of style could have been much more fruitful. There was one photo showing several people around a showcase in which jewelry appeared, but the objects were not clear enough to give an idea of the styles (ARS, Fonds., Séné., Expo. de 1900, 1).

22. However, when the popular name of a specific piece of jewelry was used, it was extremely helpful for the study of Senegalese jewelry. During some interviews some informants could sketch or describe the particular piece for which there had only been a name. In fact, this was the only way several early examples of jewelry were discovered. The "Kang" was such an example. It is no longer in fashion and was difficult to find.

23. Other factors were the world wars and simply the desire for new markets and opportunities.

24. One goldsmith (Isaac Thiam, May 1972) related that he had discouraged his son from jewelry making because of the competition with cheap imports and the fact that there were so many other goldsmiths in Dakar. Several other goldsmiths interviewed expressed their disappointment that their sons had not followed their profession, but understood their sons' concern for making enough money to support their families.

25. We met goldsmiths in Yaoundé, Cameroun; Abidjan, Ivory Coast; and Bamako, Mali who had apprenticed with Senegalese goldsmiths.

26. Early travel sources mentioned the *Signares* and their expertise in trade. They were described as being among the most beautiful women in the world.

27. Examples of this "Kourou Kourou" or "Wagne" (bracelet) (ARS, Fonds Séné., Expo. de Paris 1878, 5). "Soleil" (French for sun) is a style listed to be sent to the Sierra Leone Exposition of 1865. The "Soleil" was never found, but it is hoped that someday it might be commissioned.

VII

LITERARY CURRENTS

Traditional African society had its full measure of literary exercises and accomplishments: the oral sagas and traditions carefully preserved and related by griots in praise-songs and genealogies; the many proverbs, sayings, and tales springing from the folk; and the legends of origins and the cosmos, rich in stories of ancestors and gods. The African gift for speech and palaver was not hindered by colonial rule; rather, in the case of many West Africans, acquisition of the French tongue enhanced their ability to communicate. By World War I, newsletters and newspapers began springing up in the French colonies; the inter-war period became a time when tentative soundings in the literary world were begun by French-African writers such as Bakary Diallo in Paris in the 1920s and by Ousmane Socé Diop in Senegal in the 1930s. It became a time when a Senghor would awake in far-off France to a fuller appreciation of his homeland and people; and by the time the war was over, literary entrepreneur Alioune Diop founded his seminal *Présence Africaine* which made possible publication for hundreds of aspiring African writers and students.

Professor Hassan el Nouty speaks in his essay to the influence French literature had upon the emerging African writers during the colonial encounter, to their search for proper literary forms to convey African thoughts and ideas. The great irony of the flowering of this literature, which has won international praise and renown, is that it is still today a literature for consumption abroad. African authors have been feted and given prizes, have achieved an eminence on the French literary scene not reserved for most authors from other cultures—yet the literature of the African writers is a product of an elite for elite and Western readers. Since French is taught in schools throughout West and Equatorial Africa, one might presume that a vast reading audience might exist; theoretically it does. The reality of the situation is that most Africans cling tenaciously to their native tongue, which is the language of the foyer, and French may be used for political or economic purposes only.

Gérard Pigeon's task in assessing the other side of cultural impact is much more complicated—what impact did these French-African writers have upon the French literary establishment? We know that a Jean Paul Sartre was moved to write a preface for *Présence Africaine*; we know that André Gide was influenced by his trip through the Congo, although ironically did not acknowledge the earlier work of René Maran's *Batouala*. Would a Gide or a Sartre acknowledge their debt to African writers or sources or themes? There is no question that the literati of Paris recognize the accomplishments of a Senghor—but is it because a Senghor is in reality the most assimilated African since Blaise Diagne? Is it because he was the first *agregé* in the French language from Black Africa? Is his impact upon France solely because intellectually he is first and foremost a son of Descartes, Voltaire, and Baudelaire rather than an authentic voice from the African milieu?

We have only had space here to look at double impact in the realm of literature; but what of other intellectual endeavors, such as history, anthropology, or economics? Here and in other disciplines there are African scholars at work who openly acknowledge their debt to French university and scientific models. But here the impact of Africa can also be seen upon French social scientists, such as Delafosse. Or take for instance modern anthropologists such as Balandier and Mercier, who both were initiated into African society by research done in Senegal. Both went on to distinguished careers as teachers and researchers; but it was their experience with Africa which was a formative factor in their careers. Or take the case of a Cheikh Anta Diop, historian of Black Africa who created a furor at the Sorbonne with presentation of his thesis that held that Egypt was in reality a part of Black African civilization. While it is true that most Frenchmen lined up behind the orthodox views of a Raymond Mauny, still Diop created food for thought, brought forth theories and evidence that could not be dismissed. Perhaps in history as in literature it is too early to assess fully the African side of producing an impact upon the French.

14

The Influence of French Literature on the French-African Writers

If the influence of French literature on French-African writers means that the latter's literary production shares a number of common features with a chronologically anterior French literary production to which those writers have been exposed, that influence will certainly appear to us as tremendous. However, one may argue that this is not a valid approach to the problem of literary influences when dealing with Africa, nor, as my subsequent reasoning will demonstrate, is this a valid approach when dealing with any part of the Third World.

The African author who resorts to French is adopting the language of a literature which, on the one hand, was anciently constituted as a predominantly written literature and, as such, has no counterpart in pre-colonial Sub-Saharan Africa, and which, on the other hand, reflects in its modern manifestations a type of society again with no counterpart in Africa's pre-colonial history. Until very recently, the African society has moved to a stage characterized by the predominance of written literature and has begun to bear some similarities with the modern European society. Those similarities will multiply as the process of modernization develops in Africa. In other words the French writer was molded by a certain type of praxis[1] which the French-African writer is experiencing only now. The solutions found by the former, that is, the problem of translating that praxis into literary works, now provide the French-African writer with what can accurately be called a set of *modi operandi* so that he is able to handle this same problem. These *modi operandi* are operative in two main areas.

The first area is that of transposing to a written form a literature previously confined to oral expression. Let us take the example of Birago Diop's reproducing in (written) French the traditional African (oral) tale.[2] A simple translation would not render the same tale. The content and structure would have been duplicated, *not* the artistic value. The translation given would be but a "verbal skeleton" of the tale, the spoken narrative. The "flesh" and the "skin," to which the tale owes much of its aesthetic effect, are missing.[3] They are the non-spoken element, the storyteller's pantomime and the mental *mise en scène* in the African listener's imagination; framed, each word actively invites the listener to depict every minute detail of the African decor. How then is one to compensate for the absence of pantomime, the absence of the African imagination, since many of Diop's readers will be non-Africans?

Diop was confronted with two specific problems. The solutions were derived from two *modi operandi* found in French literature. The solution to one problem consisted of the "dramatization" of the original "verbal skeleton," that is, by inserting dialogues in it, it would retain when read some of the liveliness of the oral recitation, which, as we know, functioned as a show unto itself. The French poet, La Fontaine, was able to capture the spirit of the oral tradition when in the seventeenth century he adapted into French the fables of Aesop and Bidpay, which were in many respects akin to the African folktale.

The solution to the other problem was borrowed from the descriptive trend that prevailed in French literature during the nineteenth century and culminated in the naturalistic movement. The writer applied himself to the minute depiction of the outside reality instead of summarily designing it as had generally been the practice earlier. In some small way and by means of words, he was able to emulate the stage decorator whose artificial settings aim at creating the illusion of reality.

Diop followed the practice of the French writers who were primarily describers. Assuming the task left to his listener's imagination by the "*griot*," he rendered the African scenery and *couleur locale*. Additionally, the tales as he transposed them can be defined like La Fontaine's fables, as "*une comédie aux cent actes divers*" (a one-hundred-acts comedy). Literary historians will claim that he was "influenced" by French models, models who were either individual authors or a collective group representing a school or a genre. I submit that given his ends, he logically selected the adequate instruments to achieve them. As we shall see later, the difference between the two views cannot be reduced to a matter of wording; the difference, however, is quite essential.

The second area is that of the invention of literary forms capable of expressing the African writer's new predicament, which resembles more and more the daily, familiar predicament of the French writer. There is no African literary heritage here to transcribe. We are dealing with genres that did not exist in oral literature and whose birth and growth are intimately connected to the changes that are taking place in Africa's economic, social, and political structure.

One thinks first of the novel. The rise of the novel in Europe was a byproduct of the transition from the feudal to the bourgeois era. It could not conceivably have been transplanted to Africa before there materialized at least an embryo of an African bourgeoisie, which eventually occurred as a result of the social unrest caused by colonial aggression. As the European bourgeoisie had preceded the African bourgeoisie in the production of novels, it was foreseeable that the

French-African writer would find a series of *modi operandi* (others as we have seen spoke of models that "influenced" him) suitable to his own schemes. The novel written in the first person will channel the individualistic revolt, for example, Beti's *Mission terminée*,[4] the *roman à thèse* will evoke the grave issues debated in Africa, such as Cheikh Hamidou Kane's *Ambiguous Adventure*; the naturalistic novel will portray the Senegalese urban middle class, for example, Socé's *Karim*[5] or in Sadji's *Maimouna*.[6]

The problem of the theater is a bit more complex. This is not due to the unresolved question whether or not there was some kind of theater in pre-colonial Africa.[7] Whatever the final answer might be is of no importance to the French-African dramatists. They are disciples of Western models exclusively, models that range from the Greek tragedy to the great French classics of the seventeenth century and to Brecht's epic theater of the twentieth. Because there are some doubts that the future of the theater is the proper medium to represent changing, evolving society, the problem becomes complex. There are undisputable symptoms of its eclipse in contemporary Western societies where audience attendance is dwindling.[8] Therefore, one cannot but wonder if the theater corresponds to the profound changes taking place in the modernization of the African society. Although it can be stated, regarding the French-African *novelist*, that there was a durable historical meeting between spontaneous literary projects inspired by a changing praxis and French patterns designed for the execution of very similar projects, I am not sure that as much can be said with regard to the French-African dramatist. Perhaps the validity of that opinion will be better assessed when viewed from other perspectives.

The novel is a literary genre which is "consumed" individually. The French-African novelist can always find in the ranks of the French intelligentsia or in the French-speaking African intelligentsia a core of readers who will insure publishability (marketability) of his works. But a handful of French and French-African amateurs are not enough to insure the representability (again marketability) of the French-African dramatic repertoire. Furthermore, because of the language barrier, the French-African dramatist must relinquish all hopes to attract one day the African masses. He may envision sporadic representations on special occasions, school festivities, art festivals, special celebrations, and the like. This does not alter the fact that his plays are not primarily destined to be shown. And, if they can only be read, the whole playwriting endeavor will strike us as a gratuitous exercise warranted solely by the African author's desire to imitate a European literary genre which even in Europe seems to be fading away. This may account for the somewhat lesser quality of the French-African theater, though quantitatively it scores well.[9]

To date no explanation has been suggested for the relative proliferation of works belonging to a genre which is to be "consumed" collectively but for which there is no collective use in Africa. The phenomenon is all the more intriguing because in the French-speaking Caribbean—their cultural milieu more or less parallels the one in Africa—the contemporary writers have obviously shunned the dramatic genre (save for Césaire), which does not make the problem of the theater any easier to solve.

The French *modi operandi*, with which the African writer avails himself, should be compared to historical shortcuts that spare him an unnecessary stage of trials and errors in his race to catch up with literary production geared to a modernized society. In all fields—not only the literary one—Africa's march from an archaic state of things to modern times need not duplicate each successive phase Europe has passed through since it embarked upon the road to modernization two or three centuries ahead of the rest of the world. For example, this is illustrated by Africa's immediate use of electricity instead of the step-by-step progression which led Europe from the torch to the candle, the Argand lamp to gas lighting and finally to incandescent lighting.

There was, however, in pre-colonial African literature an area which demonstrated an inherent and yet spectacular source of power, and one which could adjust to varying circumstances. I am referring to poetry. African art, as we are aware, was functional (or utilitarian)[10] and still remains functional, not only in its popular forms which continue the traditional ones, but also in the more sophisticated forms of French-African literature. To date neither the platonic concept of art—art as Beauty—nor its present variant, formalism, have had any significant impact on the French-African writers. Eventually the door could be opened to that ''influence'' and one which would be in harmony with the ''bourgeois'' trend which has asserted itself in French-African literature since gaining independence. Returning to the subject under discussion, perhaps one can consider poetry the most conspicuously functional of all traditional African literary genres. There were poems for every important event in life, love, wedding, traveling, hunting, warring, and so on.[11] Of course, they became stereotyped because of the conservative character of most pre-colonial African societies whose structure was tailored for immutability. One could have feared that the remarkable adaptability demonstrated by African poetry at its origins might have been lost a long time ago for lack of extraordinary types of events to echo. Such fears were dissipated in 1958 when Guinea voted for independence. This event was the first of its kind. The response was swift: there was an explosion of popular songs celebrating the end of colonial rule.[12] African poetry had kept its vitality intact. Therefore, one could assume that the assistance of French *modi operandi* would become superfluous. The French-African poet could learn from his native cultural background how to appropriate his poetical production to present needs. A priori, it could even be theorized that he would be in a position to treat the French language as a purely raw material, to be fashioned at will, provided that it was not deemed impossible to produce poetry in French if one did not comply with the rigid code imposed by Malherbe in the seventeenth century.

If the African poet were to apply that code, he would be scorned by others for his literary mimicry because Malherbean aesthetics correspond to an outdated type of society. It would be amusing to indulge in some sort of guessing game, trying to figure out what the French-African poet would have done had he appeared in the nineteenth century when Malherbe's dogmas, in spite of attempted reforms, stood essentially untouched. Would he have done like his brethren in the New World, the French-Caribbean poets, slavishly copying Victor Hugo or Leconte de Lisle?[13] Or would he have displayed audacity, freeing himself from Malherbe's procrustean bed? These are rhetorical questions. By the time the French-African poets made their entry, about thirty years ago, a small anti-Malherbean revolution had triumphed in France during the last decade of the nineteenth century, thus putting an end to the poet's obligation to satisfy anything but the two *sine qua non* conditions for poetry to exist: rhythm and the music of words.

The "free verse" (*vers libre*) movement, an outgrowth of the anti-Malherbean revolution, made it possible to "Africanize" French poetry. But it was equally possible to "Arabize" it. The Algerian author, Assia Djebar, tells us that she writes in French only those verses which simultaneously appear also at her tongue's tip in Arabic.[14] As free verse is based uniquely on rhythm and the music of words, the minimal requirements for any language to be poetic, it is difficult, when limited to these two criteria, to establish who actually influenced whom.[15] To prove my point, here is an example. French-African poets who rely heavily on the use of alliteration are said to be conforming to a technique that characterizes traditional African poetry. Alliteration, which is a manner of playing with the music of words, was very much in vogue among the French poets of the "cubist" school at the turn of the century and in the wake of the free verse revolution.[16] Can it be proved or disproved which of the two models, the French cubist poets or the traditional African poets, influenced the French-African poets who cultivated alliteration? Besides, it really makes little difference! With the creation of free verse, French prosody had met the traditional African prosody on the latter's ground, no "strings" attached to poetry but for rhythm and the music of words. It is not surprising, therefore, that each will sometimes tread identical paths, on the intensive use of alliteration.

Free verse gave to the French-African poet an opportunity to sound African and the chance to achieve the best approximation of a genuine African poet, the use of a foreign language notwithstanding. Consequently, does this imply he was immune to French influence? Cases of flagrant reversion to a strictly French or European fashion (for instance, Birago Diop's sonnets in *Leurres et Lueurs*[17]) ought to be disclaimed as frivolous exhibitionism: the poet wants to show off his mastery of each form.

What can be said about the surrealist movement and its alleged influence on French-African poetry? Those who would believe in that influence[18] would have a difficult time giving evidence for it because, other than one specific technique, there is nothing with which to characterize the movement. It is marked with a diversity of ideologies which vary abruptly from poet to poet, exemplified by André Breton's occult leanings and Paul Eluard's pro-Communist sympathies. The disparities discarded, what is left to define surrealism is that it is a particular manipulation of the language which is in accord with the semiological practices of the present times.

What is peculiar to surrealism is its predilection for the unusual blending of words, *alliance de mots insolite*. The shock felt by the listener or reader is in line with the modern person's taste for what is striking, sensational, percussive. To be expressive, a publicity poster must be hard-hitting, like a fist striking a blow. This is also true of commercials, comics, pop art, rock operas, or Ionesco's *humour noir*. One can sense in all these things the same sense of calculation which strives to captivate the interest of the spectator, the auditor, the reader, and so on by force rather than by way of seduction. On that level, the so-called "influence" of surrealism appears as inevitable as the recourse to the *modi operandi* which served to render in written literature the nonverbal elements of the oral tale. Even if there had been no French model, the African poet would have inevitably sought the unusual blend of words because this directly relates to some of the processes of modernization. Europe took the lead, but had the initial role been the lot of another, in all likelihood the techniques used would have broadly duplicated the European prototype. History, as a whole, does not follow an erratic course.

Until now we have found that the alleged influences experienced by the French-African writers were, in many cases, "patterns" upon which they had to resort once Africa, to quote Alioune Diop (see the first issue of *Présence Africaine*),[19] decided to integrate the modern world and subsequently address the problem of fabricating new literary tools fitted to an emerging modern society. As France and Europe had already met and solved the problem of tool fabrication via the *modi operandi*, the French-African writers could no longer ignore that same situation. (This is analogous to the production of the internal combustion engine when it replaced the man-induced or hippomobile traction with automobile traction.) These *modi operandi* correctly solved given technical problems arising at a definite moment in human historical evolution. The laws governing literary production, like the mechanical laws or the economic laws, transcend national and cultural particularisms. Paper money has been put into circulation in modern Africa. It would be meaningless to attribute that event to European "influence." It is the corollary of the African society's entry into a capitalistic or post-capitalistic stage of development. Western colonization was the occasional cause of that entry. Nonetheless, I feel it would have occurred sooner or later.

The world "influence" should not be applied to the unavoidable crossing of like bridges on the historical road to progress. It should be reserved to designate a distinct personal choice made by the French-African writer to drink of some French source. In that restricted framework, our investigation will not bear chiefly on forms and techniques which are far too impersonal because they are the *modi operandi*. Balzac, Flaubert, Zola in France; Tolstoi, Sholokhov in Russia; Dickens, Reade in England, all are separated by wide differences if examined individually. Nevertheless, they are classified as realists because they are equally careful to restore the spatial and temporal coordinates of their characters. No other solution is possible in organizing a narrative as a world, the objective pursued by realism in literature. To label a French-African writer a realist is another way of saying that he has come to grips with that problem and has managed to overcome it. This is not a matter of "influence." Sometimes a problem is solved simultaneously by two different persons in two different places, evidenced by Leibniz and Newton, the former in Germany, the latter in England, concerning infinitesimal calculus.

It is quite another story, however, when a novelist is labeled Balzacian or Zolian. What is referred to here is not a certain form (Balzac's and Zola's realistic novels are similarly organized) but some particular theme or themes, a vision of man and society, a philosophy of life, or in short an ideology which distinguishes Balzac or Zola from other realists. To be Balzacian or Zolian amounts to giving back parts of Balzac's or Zola's ideology. This does not stem from any necessity inherent in the realistic novel. It is an attitude acquired by identifying with or having an affinity for Balzac or Zola. In my opinion, this is what "influence" really means.

It follows, then, that the proper method for elucidating the problem of French influences on French-African writers is the classification of the latter according to their ideological inclinations. Moreover, one would also know where to look for influences which may affect any particular writer.

One main factor in determining any person's ideology is his or her social background. Senghor, who was the son of a wealthy Serere merchant, could be expected to be less receptive to the influence of progressive French writers than Sembene Ousmane, who grew up in the lower stratum of the Dakar population. Indeed, the author of *Les Bouts de bois de Dieu*,[20] a novel about a railroad workers' strike in Senegal in the late 1940s, was influenced by Zola's novel, *Germinal*, in which a strike by miners furthered the cause of the working class. On the other hand, Senghor, drawing from several rightist thinkers—Gobineau, Bergson, Barrès, Teilhard de Chardin—developed his doctrine of *négritude*, which has been a precious asset to the rising and subsequent ruling African neobourgeoisie.

If one's beginnings are from the rural sectors of African society where class divisions are not as clear-cut as in the city, and if a traditional community spirit still persists, the African writer will be more sensitive to those French influences in which traces or imitations of the old popular French literature can be recognized as far back as the Middle Ages when the structure of European society was closer to that of rural Africa. What influences have been detected in the works of Mongo Beti or Ferdinand Oyono, offsprings of peasant families?[21] Critics stress the picaresque and the Rabelaisian veins in their novels.[22] These two veins constitute a modern extension of the popular comic vein which flourished in French and European medieval literature. That comic vein was the vehicle for popular discontent and protest. Humor is precisely an anti-colonial weapon in the hands of Oyono[23] and the early Beti.[24]

We believe that the mechanism of literary influences is simple enough that it can be reduced to ideological affinities. The key factor in shaping those affinities is the African writer's social status. Any change in that status will produce a change in his thinking and, consequently, in his choice of French literary models. Exceptionally though, the writer may be fortunate enough to possess an acute lucidity and a natural generosity which enable him to transcend his former narrow conditioning and accede to a more objective view of himself and the world.

That general rule and the exception to it are verified by French-African literature after Africa gained independence. Spearheaded by the "nationalists" of the *négritude* period, independence brought the African neo-bourgeoisie to power. Previously rebellious-turned-ruling class, the neo-bourgeoisie understandably desired no change. Protecting its own interests, it embraced ideologies which would eradicate any desire for change thereby reaffirming the status quo. It is no coincidence that the same kind of pessimistic feelings, anguish, despair, self-degradation, which discouraged so many in the wake of World War II and which permeated much of French literature, has also pervaded French Africa, attested by Bhêly-Quenum's *Un Piège sans fin*[25] and Malik Fall's nauseous *La Plaie*.[26]

It is possible that Bhêly-Quenum and Fall were simply motivated by the lure of commercial success, that they knew their novels would appeal to a larger market if stuffed with those ingredients which delight French and Western readers (who yet outnumber African readers). That same accusation could be directed against Iambo Ouologuem whose *Devoir de Violence*[27] abounds with themes relished in the Western world: eroticism, homosexuality, anti-Arabism. It paid off. He was awarded a French Literary prize. Certainly a clever exploitation of fool-proof, money-making recipes need not be branded as "influential" (using our definition), an influence exerted by French post–World War II absurdist literature.

We have heretofore noted that certain concessions have been made to match a vogue in the West. Whether or not that vogue falls in with the African public's expectations is not precisely known. What I suspect that unknown or uncertainty does indicate is that writers are more concerned, preoccupied, or swayed by other influences coming from the West, influences which represent a mercantile mentality chiefly motivated by profit seeking. Unfortunately, "modernization" in more than one African country brings in its train corruption, fueled by money and power. Under such circumstances one should not be astonished that some French-African writers fabricate works that flatter the fads of the larger and richer French (and Western) public and which have more and better opportunities to emerge as bestsellers. The price paid is complete subservience to French (and Western) cultural hegemony, good or bad. When such extremes have been reached, "influence" ought to be named "alienation."

As we have said, a substantial dose of natural generosity and political awareness is required for a writer *not* to succumb to the temptation of viewing himself as part of the "elite"—an attractive euphemism for oligarch—and for him *not* to espouse views which ultimately contribute to the justification and maintenance of the social order which serves to safeguard the privileged position of that elite.

Yet a few French-African writers of the post-independence generation have victoriously resisted that temptation and presented us with an unmistakably revolutionary literature. Among these writers the main figure is Zwenkou (Charles) Nokan.[28]

In order to uncover samples of genuine French revolutionary literature, one has to return to the eighteenth or nineteenth centuries. Because revolutionary struggles, like war, must be waged with the most up-to-date methods, it is doubtful that these examples can supply the contemporary revolutionary writer with really workable *modi operandi*. This is why Nokan is so original in his search for forms and techniques.[29] For lack of French precedents, he is bound to innovate, thereby serving his own purpose more efficiently. Some critics may object that this is accomplished at the expense of stylistic excellence. Are not the criteria for consummate style the judgments passed by the French elite who arrogate themselves as the arbiters of taste? Moreover, the amount of "skill" a writer possesses is commensurate with how much favor he has won from the elite. It is obvious that Nokan's revolutionary stance has upset the elite; he is thus considered a stylistic inferior to Ouologuem who has aped that elite's eccentricities. "Good style," then, belongs to a vanishing era while Nokan's "unskillful" style announces a coming age. Perhaps in relation to him (Nokan), the problem of influences should be reversed. He may well be the first of many revolutionary French-African writers, writers who will be in the domain of letters, givers instead of takers of *modi operandi*.

NOTES

1. "Praxis" is borrowed from the Marxist philosophy. It designates the action by which man transforms nature in order to make it meet his needs. He thus gets involved in a determined social structure (relations of production) by which, in turn, his "being" and his consciousness are historically determined.

2. In his *Contes d'Amadou Koumba* (Paris, 1947). In English: *Tales of Amadou Koumba*, trans. Dorothy Blair (London, 1960).

3. See, for example, the *Contes populaires d'Afrique* (Paris: Librairie orientale et américaine - Guilmoto) by the ethnologist René Basset. His simple translation of "Le veridique et le menteur" (the one who speaks the truth and the liar) can be usefully compared to Diop's artistic transposition of that same tale.

4. Paris, 1957. In English: *Mission to Kala*, trans. Peter Green (London, 1958).

5. Paris, 1935.

6. Paris, 1958.

7. An important bibliography on that subject can be found in R. Cornevin's *Le théâtre en Afrique Noire et à Madagascar* (Paris, 1970).

8. Notwithstanding the efforts that are under way to create a new theater, mainly political, geared to the people and not to the "elite." Compare René Giraudon, *Démence et mort du théâtre* (Paris, 1971) and Emile Copferman, *Vers un théâtre différent* (Paris, 1976).

9. Compare Harold A. Waters, *Black Theater in French—A Guide* (Sherbrooke, Que., 1978).

10. Compare Senghor, "L'esprit de la civilisation ou les lois de la culture négro-africaine," *Présence Africaine*, nouvelle série, n° 8-9-10 (June-November 1956).

11. Cf. Olivier de Bouveignes, *Poètes et conteurs noirs* (Anvers, 1948).

12. Cf. *Présence Africaine*, nouvelle série, n° 29 (December 1959, January 1960).

13. Cf. A Viatte, *Anthologie littéraire de l'Amérique francophone* (Quebec, 1971).

14. Assia Djebar, "Le romancier dans la Cité arabe", *Europe*, n° 474 (Oct. 1968).

15. For an opposite view see Senghor's preface to Tchicaya U'Tamsi's *Epitome* (Honfleur, 1968).

16. The poet Max Jacob (1876-1944) is a particularly striking example.

17. Paris, 1960.

18. See Jacques Chevrier, *Littérature nègre* (Paris, 1974).

19. In December 1947.

20. Paris, 1960. In English: *God's Bits of Wood*, trans. Francis Price (New York, 1962).

21. Both are Cameroonese.

22. Cf. R. Mercier and M. and S. Battestini, *Mongo Beti* (Paris, 1964). Also by the same authors: *Ferdinand Oyono* (Paris, 1964).

23. As illustrated by his three novels: *Une vie de boy* (Paris, 1956); in English: *Houseboy*, trans. John Reed (London, 1960). *Le vieux nègre et la médaille* (Paris, 1956); in English: *The Old Man and the Medal*, trans. John Reed (London, 1960), and *Chemin d'Europe* (Paris, 1960).

24. In addition to *Mission to Kala*, two other Beti novels should be mentioned: *Le pauvre Christ de Bomba* (Paris, 1956); in English: *The poor Christ of Bomba*, trans. Gerald Moore (London, 1971); *Le Roi miraculé. Chronique des Essazam* (Paris, 1958), in English: *King Lazarus*, trans. Anon. (London, 1961). Beti's later writings, *Remember Ruben* (Paris, 1974) and *Perpétue* (Paris, 1974) are more militant and of a graver tone, reflecting his own evolution from protest to revolt.

25. Paris, 1960.

26. Paris, 1967.

27. Paris, 1968. In English: *Bound to violence*. Tr: Ralph Manheim (London, 1971).

28. Because of his political stand, Nokan has been a persona non grata in his native Ivory Coast.

29. Nokan is the author of a poetical work, *Le Soleil noir point* (Paris, 1962) whose genre is difficult to define and of a novel *Violent ètait le vent* (Paris, 1966) besides a number of plays which are in line with those efforts to renew the theater that we have mentioned in note 8. Nokan is in a rather paradoxical situation: a true innovator in reference to the French theater, but with a limited audience at home because of the language barrier and the political factor.

15

The Impact of African Writers on French Literature

Before starting the difficult inquiry into the possible impact of African authors on French literature, it is necessary to attempt to define the boundaries of French-African literature. Should only the work of native-born African authors be analyzed; or should all those authors whose subject matter deals with Africa be included in this study?

It must be candidly admitted that to restrict the study solely to the works of those authors born on African soil would be too confining. Aside from some early African-Arab writers and some very late contemporary pieces of literature, very few works are available which would permit judgment about the influence of any specific African writer on one of his French counterparts.

We would, nevertheless, like to point out that it is not our intention to denigrate the African literature production in the eyes of the European and Western public; however, four centuries of harsh colonization have intensively reduced the written production of Africa.

Returning to the problem of defining the limits of African literature, again, should we only analyze indigeneous African writers or should we include their brothers of "*outre-mer*" the West Indian writers? If we take for granted the fact that Etienne Léro, Léon Damas, René Maran, and Aimé Césaire helped tremendously in raising the intellectual consciousness of Black African writers, we should logically include them in our selection of African writers; for they were an essential part of the birth and the expansion of modern French-African literature.

To continue in this vein, why should we then limit our study to the West Indies? For example, why is René Maran considered more African than Pierre Loti or André Gide? (We are aware of the enormity of such statements, but will nevertheless continue this investigation.) Yes, why should the work of René Maran, a West Indian raised in France by a French family as a true Frenchman, who was "accidentally" sent to Africa as an overseer of colonial power, be considered more "African" than that of the *Enseigne de Vaisseau*, Pierre Loti, who also had to go "accidentally" to Senegal where he wrote his novel, *Le Roman d'un Spahi*, or that of André Gide who also "accidentally" went to Africa and wrote *Le Voyage au Congo*. Only the color of their skin seems to have been the essential point of difference. Decisions made by critics ignored the divers introductions of Maran who did not see himself as a Black man, but rather as a Frenchman doing, as he said in his latest 1937 conclusion, his duty as a colorless French writer.

Il ne me reste de tout ce passé si proche que d'avoir fait mon devoir d'écrivain français et de n'avoir jamais voulu profiter de mon brusque renom pour devenir un patriote d'affaires.[1]

From that not so distant past I have only retained the feeling of having fulfilled my duty as a French writer, and that of having never profited from my sudden fame to become a greedy patriot.

To advance a step further in the study of this paradoxical literary situation, let us consider the work of the Dumas Dynasty, particularly, that of Alexandre Dumas père who was Black, considered himself Black, and was recognized as such by the French public of that time.[2] Why is it, then, that his work is not considered French-African literature, or at least Black-French literature? For even though the subject of Africa is widely neglected in his novels, the essential theme of his work seems to be the struggle of a commoner or socially destitute man who tries to reconquer his humanity, and who ultimately outwits the established, dehumanizing social order. The fate of the *Three Musketeers* is an example. They are only saved by the arrival of a commoner, D'Artagnan, who fights because he has nothing to lose: a super-hero, not noble, but with a heart and energy ready to move both mountains and kingdoms.

In another novel, *The Count of Monte-Cristo*, the destitute hero, originally a respectable man, is unjustly imprisoned for life, escapes and comes back to accomplish his revenge and regain his identity.[3] Why, after seeing the strong underlying theme of these novels, didn't the critics note the parallel that exists with the dream of the unjustly enslaved and dehumanized Black man?

As did his father and grandfather before him, Dumas tried to reawaken the French populace to the forgotten ideals of "Liberty, Equality, Fraternity."[4]

Moreover, why not attribute Dumas's outstanding storytelling capabilities to an atavistic African influence, and declare him the "griot"[5] of French literature? For this man, like a griot, was depicting history at the level of the people. Accuracy was not essential, only movement, characterization, and genealogy were important. Why, then, was such a man, using oral characteristics of traditional African literature, not taken as a Black-African writer?

Perhaps there is evidence to suggest that colonial France recognized him as a Black writer after all. For if we look at the records of history, he was clearly stripped of all his acclaim for contributions to the development of French literature, and until very recently, he was rarely mentioned in books of literary criticism or advanced literature class. Yet it is with pride that we can affirm that the very negative evaluation of his work by French critics allows us to assume that his color was indeed truly recognized; and that we can thus claim him as the first griot in exile on the French soil. Not only has he brought the teachings and techniques of African oral literature to the people of France, but he must also be given credit for the principle of the comic strip and the first romantic play, *Henry III*, performed one year before the famous *Hernani* of Victor Hugo. Moreover according to Maurois, Dumas with *Antony* cleared the way for Balzac's characters. "After the days of July (1830) it became possible to paint the morals of society frankly and without gloss. This recovered freedom gave us Balzac."[6]

So after reclaiming "en passant" Alexandre Dumas as a genuine Black writer, we nevertheless are again made aware of the extreme difficulty of defining the boundaries of literature. Should we consider the origins of the writer, his political affiliation, or his adopted language? Is Ionesco Rumanian or French? Is Joseph Conrad Polish or English? Is Henry James English or American? Is Samuel Beckett Irish or French? Is Chester Himes French or American?

Thus acting arbitrarily and for the sake of this paper, we have decided that we will consider that any Black artist who has influenced a French White writer will be labeled "African writer." We have taken this decision on the assumption that in a French and European society, a Black person will always have to answer consciously or unconsciously to the never-ending attack of prejudiced attitudes. His definition as a writer will always be challenged by the dehumanizing and abrupt reality of colonial life. As Frantz Fanon said:

> Dans le monde du blanc, l'homme de couleur rencontre des difficultés dans l'élaboration de son schéma corporel. La connaissance du corps est une activité uniquement négatrice. C'est une connaissance en troisième personne. Tout autour du corps règne une atmosphère d'incertitude certaine.[7]

In the world of the white man, the colored man encounters great difficulties concerning the development of his own image. The discovery of his body becomes an exercise of denial. It is a discovery in the third person. His body is surrounded by an atmosphere of definite uncertainty.

Until now we have only dealt with the written literature. Although we have earlier pointed out the extreme scarcity of material available, we would like to introduce an element which is one of the most neglected by Western literary critics, yet one of the most utilized, prolific, and practical forms of African literature: the oral literature.

Though this type of African literature did not leave specific names to quote, we know that the griots, masters of words, keepers of history, and guardians of oral culture, were very prominent masters of this oral art form. Aside from the technique involved, it is now certain that the oral African literature greatly influenced French written literature. Whether it is in the publication of l'Abbé Grégoire: *De La Littérature des nègres* (1808), or in the many explorer reports such as René Caillié's: *Journal d'un voyage à Tombouctou à Jénné dans l'Afrique centrale* (1830), or in the numerous works of Paul Vigné d'Octon: *Terre morte* (1892), *Journal d'un marin* (1897), or in the work of Blaise Cendrars: *Anthologie Nègre*, or Paul Morand's *Magie noire* (1928), it is impossible to deny the influence of African oral literature on these authors. They merely transcribed their superficial impressions of oral African literature in their works.

We could go a step further and say that it is mainly their misinterpretation which was the cause of the erroneous picture of African life and culture given in the early French colonial novel. The representation of the Africans as dancers, singers, men of words, buffoons with their mouths full of esoterical proverbs is derived from the misunderstanding of the deepest necessities of African oral literature. Evidently, though very often neglected, oral African literature and thus oral African performers have not only greatly influenced French writers, but have also greatly influenced the shape and spirit of the representation of Africa in French literature.

If we now focus on the written literature, the influence of Africans, though less obvious, is more clearly documented. Since France was still in its childhood when Ibn Khaldoun and Leo Africanus were writing, it is impossible to say whether they influenced any specific French writers (at least at that time), but it is obvious and well documented in many books such as *The Golden Trade of the Moors*[8] or *l'Image du Sud-Est Africain dans la Littérature européenne du XVIème*,[9] that their influence was prevalent in the early stages of the intellectual development of Europe. Aside from these early African writers who were essentially historians, political scientists, and geographers, we must await the nineteenth century to find some documented evidence of possible recognition of African writers' influence. Leaving the Dumas case, we direct our attention to the strange fate of Alexandre Privat d'Anglemont.

Born in Guadeloupe on August 21, 1815, to a wealthy colored family, Privat d'Anglemont was sent to France to pursue his studies in Paris at the *Lycée* Henry IV. There he became an intimate friend of the duke of Montpensier, son of Louis Philippe. Choosing literature as his vocation, he early abandoned his medical studies to become a full-fledged writer, playwright, essayist, and reporter. Spending more than his revenues could cover and more than the West Indian estate could support, he became destitute and had to peddle his poetry in order to survive. Finally, alcoholic, tubercular, and impoverished, he died July 18, 1859.

Strange destiny for a man who personally knew all the great authors of French literature: Hugo, Baudelaire, Musset, Murger, and others who would disappear from the literary scene without note. Strange destiny for an ardent practitioner of the dangerous Parisian night life, believed by some critics like Adolphe Lara to be the legitimate father of *Le Juif errant*[10] and the soul behind the creation of the *Mystères de Paris*[11] to find himself without a paragraph in all the main literary books and instructional manuals. Stranger still, his relationship with Baudelaire (1821-1857).

If we analyze the 1961 edition of *Les Oeuvres complètes de Baudelaire* in les Editions de la Pléïade, we are very surprised to notice in the chronology:

ler décembre 1844, *l'Artiste* insère, avec la signature de Privat d'Anglemont, un sonnet: A Madame du Barry, qui est sans doute de Baudelaire.[12]

December 1, 1884, the review *L'Artiste* publishes, with the signature of Privat D'Anglemont, a sonnet to Madame du Barry which in all certainty belongs to Baudelaire.

and a little further:

1845—Janvier-Mai-Août: Publication dans *l'Artiste* de trois sonnets, deux signés Privat d'Anglemont, le troisième laissé anonyme: A Yvonne Pen-Moore, Avril et A une Belle Dévote. Dans ses confessions, Arsène Houssaye, qui dirigeait alors cette revue, a conté la visite que lui firent les deux jeunes gens et comment Privat signa en sa présence des sonnets écrits de la main de Baudelaire et dont celui-ci ne se souciait plus.[13]

January, May, August, 1845. Publication in the review *L'Artiste* of three sonnets, two of which are signed by Privat d'Anglemont, the third one being anonymous: To Yvonne Pen Moor, April and To A Beautiful Devotee. In his confessions, Arsène Houssaye, who was at the time the managing editor of the review, recollects about the visit that both of the young men paid him and how Privat d'Anglemont, in his presence, signed a sonnet written in Baudelaire's hand and about which he did not care.

If we now look at the chapter dedicated to the "Poésies attribuées et retrouvées," we can read:

c) des poésies publiées de 1843 à 1848 sous le nom d'Ernest Prarond et d'Alexandre Privat d'Anglemont (XL-XXVII), dans lesquelles Jules Moquet (et W. T. Bally pour une pièce) a cru retrouver la manière de Baudelaire, dont la main est certe visible çà et là.[14]

These poems published from 1843 to 1848 under the name of Ernest Prarond and Alexandre Privat D'Anglemont in which Jules Moquet (and W. T. Bally for one piece) thought that he recognized Baudelaire's imprint, whose style is certainly noticeable here and there.

This is a curious literary remark that pushes the scientific mind of French critics to attribute the work of a half-breed to a full-fledged Frenchman. Why should the style be that of Baudelaire and not that of Privat d'Anglemont who was six years older? European critics seem to have deliberately credited Baudelaire with poems that were "too good" to belong to an outcast in spite of the fact that they were signed by the outcast and contained specific references to a very intimate part of West Indian folklore. We are here making allusion to the famous "Cric-crac" which is used in the introduction of tales in oral West Indian folklore.

If we continue our investigation of *Les Oeuvres complètes de Baudelaire*, we again find, just before the prologue "du salon caricatural"

Ce quatorzain fut également inséré anonymement par Privat d'Anglemont dans la *Closerie des Lilas*, avec ce commentaire: "Venez, Alexandrine,..."/Jules Moquet a recueilli avec raison ce poème parmi ses *Vers retrouvées*. On y décèle des caractères inséparables de la muse baudelairienne.[15]

This quartozain (verse) was again included anonymously by Privat D'Anglemont in *La Closerie des lilas* with the following commentary. "Come alexandrine..."/Jules Moquet has, with good reason, included this poem in his work *Vers Retrouvés* (Discovered Verses).

or in the sonnet "A Madame du Barry,"

Sonnet paru dans *l'Artiste* du ler décembre 1844 avec la signature de Privat d'Anglemont, puis repris dans *Paris inconnu* (1861), où l'on relève la variante suivante.[16]

Sonnet which appears on December 1, 1884, in the review *L'Artiste* with the signature of Privat D'Anglemont. It was then republished in *Paris Inconnu* (1861) where one can note the following variation.

or speaking of the sonnet "A une belle dame dévote":

D'abord paru (sans signature, par suite d'une chute de lettres, sans doute, qui devaient former Privat d'Anglemont) dans *l'Artiste*, le 24 Août 1845, ce sonnet ne figure pas dans *Paris inconnu*, mais doit être très certainement restitué à Baudelaire, bien qu'ayant été repris en 1850 avec la signature éronée d'Henry Vermot dans les Poëtes de l'Amour de Julien Lemer.[17]

Appearing first (without signature, caused possibly by the omission of monograph which would have undoubtedly read Privat D'Anglemont) on August 24, 1845 in the review *L'Artiste*, this sonnet never reappears in *Paris Inconnu*, but must in all certainty be given back to Baudelaire, even though it was republished in 1850 under the erroneous signature of Henry Vermot in *The Poets of Love* by Julien Lemer.

Further again regarding "Sonnet Cavalier":

Signée Cl. [sic, faute plausible pour Al.] P. d'A (il faut lire Al[exandre] P[rivat] d'A[nglemont]) dans *le Corsaire-Satan* du 19 juillet 1846, cette pièce fringante n'a pas été recueillie dans les *Vers retrouvés*, mais découverte par Jules Mouquet et réimprimée par lui, comme ayant Baudelaire pour auteur, dans le *Figaro* du 4 janvier 1930.[18]

Signed CL [sic. for Al] P d'A for Al one must read (Al)exandre P(rivat) d'A(nglemont) in le *Corsaire Satan* of June 19, 1846, that gutsy piece was not inserted in *Vers Retrouvés*.

Discovered by Jules Moquet it was republished by him and acknowledged as being the work of Baudelaire in *Le Figaro* of January 4, 1930.

As we can see, the case is less than clear on the arbitrary critical decision which appears to have been made in order to protect the memory and reputation of the French-European writer to the detriment of the probable real creator.

The only rehabilitation of Privat d'Anglemont that we have found so far is in the December 1907 edition of *Guadeloupe Littéraire*, and in the *Anthologie de la litterature Antillaise*[19] by J. Corzani.

The twentieth century marked the full-blooming of the French colonial era, a period during which the literature praised the beauty and achievements of French involvement in the colonies. Surprisingly enough very few traces of these works will be found in the overall picture of French metropolitan literature. We nevertheless feel that, regardless of the poor quality of some of these novels, their political and literary importance should at least be noted. Two works, however, are noteworthy in the otherwise dim picture: The first one, by Diagne, as an historical reminder; the second, by Maran, as an instance of the influence of a Black writer on French literature and on French writers.

It should be noted that the first creative work written by a Black African in France is not the well-known *Force Bonté* by Bakari Diallo, but rather the work of Diagne (Ahmadou Hampaté), *Les Trois Volontés de Malick*.[20] It is the work of a primary school teacher who wanted to upgrade the quality of his students' reading by adding a book relevant to the African situation. This book was published by Larousse and thus received good public exposure. We can assume that it must have triggered here and there some possible creative literary ambitions, but aside from its early date of publication, 1920, or one year before *Batouala*, we do not have any significant proof of its influence.

The second work, *Batouala*, published in 1921 and written by René Maran, was subtitled "véritable roman nègre,"[21] not because of the author's origin but due to its subject matter. With this work we can clearly see the influence of Maran on French literature. The awarding of the "Prix Goncourt" not only gave the book a royal exposure to the French public but also provoked the well-known controversy which resulted in the impoverishment and bitterness of René Maran against those he once called "his brothers," the French European writers.

Five years later, suddenly struck by an old obsession, André Gide went to Africa, visited the same locations, as in the Maran work and denounced the colonial abuses in the African plantation with the same vehemence. "Qu'allais-je donc chercher dans ce pays? J'étais tranquille. A présent je sais: Je dois parler."[22] Whatever impelled me (forced me) to go to this country? I was happy. Now I know: I must speak.

It is curious, to say the least, that André Gide should have to cry out in 1928 what Maran had shouted seven years before. What is even more astonishing is that Gide did not know, or failed or refused to acknowledge, the influence of Maran's book on his own work.

Je me suis précipité dans ce voyage comme Curtius dans le gouffre. Il me semble déjà plus que précisément je l'aie voulu encore que depuis des mois ma volonté soit tendue vers lui; mais plutôt qu'il s'est imposé à moi par une sorte de fatalité inéluctable, comme tous les évènements importants de ma vie. Et j'en viens presque è oublier que ce n'est là qu'un "projet de jeunesse réalisé dans l'âge mûr": ce voyage au Congo, je n'avais pas vingt ans que déjà je me promettais de le faire; il y a 36 ans de cela.[23]

I leapt into that journey like Curtius did into the abyss. It now more precisely appears to me that rather than wanting it and for months letting my will work toward that end; it had imposed itself to me by some kind of ineluctable fate just as did all the important events in my life. It is only now that I realize that this was only the fulfillment of a now old dream of youth. This Journey to the Congo, I was not yet 20 when I swore to journey to the Congo. It was then 36 years ago.

Must we also trust the critic Jacqueline M. Chardaune when in her work, *André Gide et l'Afriques*[24] she declares that only the reading of Joseph Conrad's *Heart of Darkness* made Gide travel to central Africa.

It seems very strange that a man as literate and as involved in literature as Gide blatantly failed to acknowledge the work of a "Prix Goncourt." It is hard to believe, but according to available documents, only Conrad and an old stale childhood dream prompted Gide "accidently" to visit the same places and the same region described by Maran. It is difficult to understand, but maybe Gide was blind and deaf and in total isolation, for during that specific time of 1921-1928, it was impossible to ignore not only a "Goncourt" but also the tremendous political turmoil that *Batouala* generated.

Firm in the conviction of his historical role, and since Gide did not seem to give him credit for his book, Maran acknowledged his own importance in his bitter 1937 addendum to the introduction of *Batouala*.

Je n'ai eu qu'en 1927 la satisfaction morale qu'on me devait. C'est cette année-là que André Gide a publié *Voyage au Congo*. Denise Moran faisait paraître *Tchad* peu après. Et les chambres étaient saisies des horreurs auxquelles donnaient lieu la construction de la voix férrée Brazzaville Océan.[25]

It was only in 1927 that I received the moral satisfaction that they owed me. That year André Gide published *Voyage au Congo* and Denise Moran, a little later, published *Tchad* and the National Assembly as well as the Senate were horrified by the news received from the Congo about the building of the railroad extending from Brazzaville to the Ocean.

God helps those who help themselves (*On n'est jamais si bien servi que par soi-même*).

If we now consider the more contemporary writers, we must then acknowledge the fact that even though more and more African writers have appeared on the literary scene, it will be less and less easy to prove their influence, for very few personal documents are available. Moreover, the pride of some European authors, will hinder the literary investigation. Consequently it will be very difficult to make any serious and objective research on that subject.

We nevertheless would like to finish with a few suppositions regarding the possible impact of some contemporary Black writers on French literature.

We think that Senghor undoubtedly influenced Jean Paul Sartre, for Senghor seems to have been the one who introduced Sartre to the new African writers. It can be assumed that without him, Sartre would never have written in 1948 the famous introduction, *Black Orpheus*.[26] Of course, in 1946 Sartre had already published *La P...respectueuse*, which was a play about racism in an American setting. With *Black Orpheus*, Sartre would have the time to theorize his views on the reconstruction of the Black ego.

If we consider Aimé Césaire, we feel that even though he was not the creator of the French surrealistic movement, his existential surrealistic experience gave to the movement the concrete reality that such a hypothetical literary innovation needed. Recognized by André Breton as the best poet of French expressionism and introduced to France by Breton himself, it is more than likely that his poetry has influenced the new generation of surrealistic poets.

We also think that J. Genet was able to carry brilliantly to the theater the systematic analysis of violence made by Frantz Fanon.

Finally, we know that the outstanding critical analysis of President Sékou Touré has greatly influenced French Marxist critics and that Bruno Mann in his novel, *Les gosses tu es comme*, clearly tries to recreate the speech pattern of Dakar.

In conclusion we can say that, far from being negligible, the possible influence of African writers on French literature is certainly a matter which needs some extra attention. New investigation will undoubtedly help to assert the extent of this influence. At least this endeavor will have the advantage of revealing to the literary critics the possibility of the existence of the other side of the mirror.

Thus the purpose of this paper was not to negate arrogantly and systematically some already unverified, erroneous, but nevertheless accepted ideas, but on the contrary, in a true spirit of justice, to render to Caesar what belongs to Caesar, and to the Black writers what belongs to them.

NOTES

1. René Maran, *Batouala* (Paris, 1933), p. 18.
2. Victor Hugo used to call him the *"Demi-nègre."* One time at the theater, after overhearing a man whispering to his neighbor: "They say that a lot of Black blood is flowing in his veins," Dumas answered: "Mais parfaitement, Monsieur, j'ai du sang noir: mon père était mulâtre, mon grand-père un nègre, et mon arrière grand-père était un singe! Vous voyez nos deux familles ont la même filiation mais pas dans le même sens." Alexandre Dumas, *Jean de Lamage, Les Géants* (Paris, 1972), p. 124.
3. This strangely anticipates *Le Père Goriot* and the well-known characters of Vautrin and Rastignac in Balzac's novel.

4. This is the cry of the French Revolution which will become the slogan of the French Republic.

5. The griot was, as we will see later, the keeper of oral tradition and history and the master of words.

6. André Maurois, *The Titans* (New York, 1957), p. 91.

7. Frantz Fanon, *Peau Noire Masques Blancs* (Paris, 1952), p. 109.

8. E.W. Bovill, *The Golden Trade of the Moors* (Oxford, 1968).

9. W.G.L. Randles, *L'Image du Sud-Est Africain dans la Littérature européenne du XVIème* (Lisboa, 1959).

10. *Le Juif Errant* is normally credited to Eugène Sue.

11. *Les Mystères de Paris* is also a work that is usually attributed to Eugène Sue.

12. C. Baudelaire, *Oeuvres Complètes* (Paris, 1961), p.xx.

13. Ibid.

14. Ibid., p. 1590.

15. Ibid., p. 1595.

16. Ibid.

17. Ibid., p. 1596.

18. Ibid., p. 1597.

19. J. Corzani, *Anthologie de la Littérature Antillaise* (Fort de France, 1974).

20. Amadou Diagne, *Les Trois Volontés de Malick* (Paris, 1920).

21. Maran, *Batouala*, title page.

22. André Gide, *Voyage au Congo* (Paris, 1954), p. 745.

23. Ibid., p. 683.

24. Jacqueline Chardoune, *André Gide et l'Afrique* (Paris, 1968), p. 135.

25. Maran, *Batouala*, p. 18.

26. Sartre wrote the famous introduction of the *Anthologie de la Nouvelle Poésie Nègre et Malgache* which was entitled "Orphée Noir."

Frequency of Publication of French Colonial Novels

Year	Number	Special events:
1920	3	
1921	1	*Batouala*, Prix Goncourt
1922	5	
1923	3	
1924	2	
1925	4	Gide goes to Black Africa
1926	2	
1927	4	Publication of *Voyage au Congo*
1928	6	
1929	3	
1930	4	
1931	5	Colonial Exposition
1932	0	

VIII

IMAGES AND RACISM

In this part we turn to a different phenomenon—that of perceptions and reactions to people of the African continent on the part of the French. France, like other European countries, had minimal contact with African Blacks before the era of sugar and slavery. African slaves were brought to France from time to time, much as they were to Britain; but the majority of Frenchmen did not really see many Blacks until the *Armée Noire* of the 1914-1918 war period. Yet as William Cohen's essay demonstrates, attitudes toward people of the Black race were being formed in France from the eighteenth century onwards. Often invoked in the name of developing scientific method, some observations were received and believed uncritically, such as the pronouncement made in the Larousse dictionary in the mid-nineteenth century that the White and Black races belonged to two different species. Much of the misinformation treated in France about African Blacks stemmed from the fact that few Frenchmen had carried out original field work there; this was remedied later in the century by the arrival of France's premier anthropologist, Maurice Delafosse, in West Africa to conduct research. Delafosse helped put together a picture of an independent culture in Black Africa that had produced earlier civilizations worthy of inclusion in world history. Cohen, who has published a study on the image of Africa in French society, concludes by relating the images of the past to those of the *négritude* movement.

With Edmund Burke III's essay on Thomas Ismail Urbain, we are not dealing with an African in French society, but a Black from the West Indies who was in essence a surrogate African who early comes into contact with the ambiguities of French culture: on the one hand, he was allowed to reach a high governmental post in Algeria, a reflection of France's attitude toward assimilation; yet on the other hand, with his defense of the Algerians, Urbain becomes an odd man out, and eventually sees this career destroyed. His book *Algérie pour les Algériens* was literally a century ahead of its time politically; he argued in favor of cultural relativism and concluded that the Algerians were equally capable of cultural evolution as the French had been, but they should not be forced into the same mold. A bold and courageous figure who transcends time and place, Urbain was an unsung hero who only now, through the efforts of scholars of North Africa such as Burke, is receiving his day in historical court.

The double impact of contact between France and Africa has only been discussed at one level here—the reactions of French intellectuals in Cohen's work, and the reactions in the world of politics to one of France's earliest men of color as a public servant. We have not touched upon African perceptions of the French; perhaps they can be most succinctly found in novels such as Cheikh Amidou Kane's *Ambiguous Adventure*, which has its African protagonist caught up in a pilgrim's progress, looking for a promised land, traveling a dangerous road between an Islam that had lost power over the inhabitants of the land to the French, and the seductions of French culture in the metropole, where Samba Diallo becomes a student. Or in the novels of Ousmane Sembene, where the perception of the French is not philosophical and obscured with cultural overtones; for Ousmane, the French are the enemy, whether in his *Les Bouts de Bois de Dieu* or in his bitter anti-colonial movie *Emitai*. Ousmane's picture is a dramatic, voluble commentary on the rotten legacy of colonialism; but there were different voices during the colonial period: men who had fought with the French in the two world wars and in Indochina. These men often had great respect for the French and were pleased to have been comrades in arms; the same was true for many employees of French government or businesses, who felt that the French represented the pinnacle of industrial society and a way of life to be emulated. It is this residue of assimilation that Kane subtly attacks in *Ambiguous Adventure* and which Ousmane bitterly contests as still prevailing in many levels of African society. At times one wonders whether such writers are not bordering upon a reverse racism; Kane's sense of irony and humor prevent him from falling in this trap, but Ousmane's intentions are not so clear. But one thing seems certain: that Ousmane's portrayal of Frenchmen coincides with secret feelings of many Africans still rankling from colonial domination.

The image of the African and the resultant racism in French society has not vanished from the scene today, as any African employed in France will testify; nor has the satirical portrayal of the French in African novels subsided. Perhaps this bitter fruit harvested from the colonial encounter will eventually disappear.

WILLIAM B. COHEN

16

French Racism and Its African Impact

The French, like other Europeans, developed certain stereotypic images of Africa in the nineteenth century. They were important in the intellectual history of France but also had an impact on Africa. After describing the nature of French perceptions of the African continent, this essay also examines the manner in which these ideas helped shape events and ideas in Africa in the last century. While attention here is solely to the formulation of ideas, it should be noted that they have meaning only as they operate in a larger social and political context.

The nineteenth century, of course, was the century in which racism developed fully, but a number of themes developed in earlier periods which contributed to the later image of Blacks. The classical view of Africa as inhabited by beastly beings was accentuated in various medieval compendia and the accounts of frustrated merchants, administrators, and missionaries who tended to ascribe their failures to the perversity of the African populations. All these views were well summarized in the *Encylopédie*, the compendium of eighteenth-century learning (which at the same time was a major publishing success), which wrote of the Africans:

These people have, so to speak, only ideas from one day to the next, their laws have no principles...no consistency other than that of lazy and blind habit. They are blamed for ferociousness, cruelty, perfidy, cowardice, laziness....This accusation is but too true.[1]

The eighteenth-century view of man was evolutionary: the record of man was the history of progress, and Europe had achieved the pinnacle of human achievement; other societies lagged behind and were inferior to Europe. But this inferiority was cultural and material due to geographic isolation and conditions of climate. Thus non-Europeans were seen as capable of evolution if they either came into contact with European influences or changed climate.

While the eighteenth century stressed environment as the explanation for cultural differences, it did not entirely eschew the notion that biology and culture were inter-related. Thus the African, Buffon claimed, if transported to Europe would not only become civilized but also turn white.[2]

Ethnocentrically, Europeans viewed Whites as the form of human perfection; Whites were either the first people from whom other races had then degenerated, or else they were the last one toward which the other races had evolved. And human physical shape and color was seen as the outer indicator of moral and cultural potential. (Ever since the classical age the belief in physionomos has played an important part in the European mind.) Thus in the eighteenth-century view, a connection between race and social and moral accomplishment was already seen. But what mitigated this racism was the belief that races were human groupings capable of transformation.

A number of intellectual trends in the nineteenth century reinforced some of the eighteenth-century racial views while discarding the environmental ones. The nineteenth century saw major breakthroughs in the field of biology, and it became increasingly common for people of that era to think in biological terms, to ascribe a large number of causes to biology. The romantic mood of the late eighteenth and early nineteenth centuries stressed not what was common among people, but what was unique and different, separating people from people and even class from class. And unlike preceding thinkers, people of the late eighteenth and early nineteenth centuries saw such differences as not being due to environment, but rather claimed innate biological qualities marking groups and separating them from each other. In France the idea that human groups were inferior or superior to each other as a result of inherited biological traits was particularly influential. At least since the seventeenth century this mode of argument had been used by different social groups vying for power in France. Made famous by Boulain-villiers, the argument held that the French aristocracy had a right to rule on the basis of its biological descendance from the German Franks who had conquered the native Gauls of France. The argument that racial descendance was a claim to political power was validated by the liberals who identified themselves as the descendants of the majority Gauls and thus claimed a right to rule also based on race.[3] Later in the nineteenth century, class perceptions were equally viewed as being biological. The poor and the criminals were perceived as endowed with certain dangerous traits biologically inherited which made them prone to be what the French bourgeois called "*les classes dangereuses.*" Thus differences in status, in political power, and in wealth were all explained in terms of biology.[4]

The differences which existed in culture and institutions of European and African societies in the nineteenth century, even more than in the previous era, were ascribed to the biological makeup of the Black. The divergences in culture and outward appearance separated Blacks in the nineteenth century view from common humanity with Whites.

The eighteenth century was monogenist believing in the unity of mankind, the descendance of all races from one common source, but the nineteenth was polygenist affirming that the different races had separate sources and indeed formed distinct species. The naturalist Bory de Saint-Vincent wrote that if four-legged animals were perceived to be as different from each other as Whites were from Blacks, they would not be included in the same species.[5] This view was institutionalized in the Paris anthropological society founded in 1859 by the medical doctor Paul Broca.

Most of the members of the *Société d'anthropologie de Paris* were, like Broca, medical doctors, and thus it came rather naturally to them to see human differentiation as having been caused biologically. Also affected by the contemporary notion that race was the fundamental cause for cultural differentiation and by the mania of the mid-century for statistics, the *société* developed physical anthropology to its further point. The society was considered as a model by anthropologists in other countries and, patterning themselves after it, societies sprung up in London, Moscow, Madrid, Florence, Berlin, Vienna, Brussels, and Washington.

To prove that Blacks and Europeans belonged to different species, Paul Broca in an extremely important work on hybridity claimed that the two races could not cross successfully. Fewer births resulted from the mating of the two races, and those who were born lived a shorter time, were weaker, and tended to die out by the fourth generation.[6] In making these arguments Broca was doing nothing more than repeating the obscene propaganda of the slavers of the eighteenth century, the writings of the Jamaican Edward Long, and the ideologists for American slavery Gliddon and Knott (the latter three he approvingly quoted by name). These ideas were not limited to the anthropological society but reflected a general assessment of the relationship of Black and White. The Larousse dictionary of 1866 proclaimed the two races to form separate species.[7] The novels of the time showed inter-racial mating as being unnatural and created by Blacks violating the laws of nature and civilization. And the novelists seemed to agree with Broca that such unions were infertile, for invariably the offspring were depicted as sickly and as dying off at an early age.[8]

By forming a separate species, Blacks were assigned to an order approaching animality. Bory de Saint-Vincent saw in the prognathism of the Black a link between the European face and the snout of animals. The *Société d'anthropologie de Paris* publicized research which was supposed to lead to similar conclusions. Measurement of the Negro's collarbone was intended to show that it was much longer than that of the White and resembled that of the primate. Paul Broca in his article demonstrating that Negroes had longer forearms than Whites, prefaced it by a quotation from Charles White in the 1790s, which had directly made out of the African the missing link between the species of Europeans and the primate. Length of thumbs and toes were also brought in as evidence to bolster up this viewpoint. If they were a link, the Africans were nevertheless sufficiently different from Whites to form a separate species, Broca and his followers argued.[9]

Not all anthropologists argued that Blacks formed a distinct species; foremost among the French members of the *Société d'anthropologie de Paris* to combat this view was Armand de Quatrefages. He upheld monogenism, claiming that all races formed a single species and seeing racial differences as being due to environmental factors. Much like Buffon, Quatrefages had an extreme faith in environment shaping not only social institutions and cultures but also human physical shape and color. He based his environmentalism in part upon the 1859 article published by Elisée Reclus in the *Revue des Deux Mondes* which had claimed that environment was so compelling that in North America, the climate which supposedly had made the native Indian red colored, was turning the Whites and the Blacks red as well. In his environmentalism Quatrefages, like his eighteenth-century predecessors, shared the basic assumptions of the polygenic racists, namely that Blacks were inferior to Whites and that their improvement could occur through a change of racial stock. This might be produced by environment or by racial mixture, but like Broca, Quatrefages was certain that there was a biological foundation of cultures.[10] So, polygenist or monogenist, by the middle of the nineteenth century French anthropologists were racists in the sense that they believed that the destiny of human groups was decided on the basis of inherited physical characteristics which were the external indicators in the case of the White race of superiority and for the Black of inferiority. While not read by the French public, Gobineau echoed the belief of his contemporaries when he announced that only the White race was capable of true progress; history, he announced, confirmed that "all civilization is due to the white race."[11]

The main concern of French anthropology—as was the case with the discipline as a whole in the mid-nineteenth century—was an overwhelming commitment to physical anthropology. Every part of the human body: flesh, bone, and hair, from the top of the head to the big toe, was measured and duly classified. The Paris anthropological society received help from sister societies in the other capitals of Europe who were equally busy pouring out data. Sometimes the published results were based on three samples, sometimes on hundreds. Orderly tables were set up and nearly all of them had Whites on the top, Asians in the middle, and Blacks at the bottom. Having a large brain was considered a virtue and thus Whites were put on the top because the table was based on descending brain weights. The possession of large toes was considered to have negative implications and thus the table was based upon ascending toe sizes. Such tables were not only intended to show racial differences but also class variations. The famous sociologist Gustave LeBon after examining about a thousand skulls established the following scale of intelligence for Frenchmen: fifth and lowest, the peasants of the Beauce; fourth level, the domestics of Paris; third, the former nobility; second, the bourgeoisie; and first level—the level LeBon belonged to— wise men and men of letters.[12] Anthropologists also found physical data which they claimed confirmed that women were inferior, their skull structure, facial angle, and collarbones seemed to reveal innate inferiority.[13]

By the 1870s a proliferation of tables had come out with physical measurements for the various races. While they were intended to build up physical anthropology, they in fact had a deleterious effect on the discipline. The methodology was not as reliable as had been thought. Soemmering gave the weight of the Negro's brain to be 1310 grammes, Tiedemann 1145 grammes, Broca 1245 grammes, and so on. Not everybody could agree on the cephalic index of different races (a measurement expressing the relationship of the length to the width of the skull); and depending upon whom you read, the Negro was longheaded, mediumheaded, or shortheaded.[14] The very mass of evidence which had been collected to confirm the tenets of physical anthropology began to cause its erosion. A number of anthropologists began to point out how unreliable the data of physical anthropology was and thus cast doubt upon the notion that physical data were the only indicators necessary to understand a people.

Trying to strike out independently, E. T. Hamy founded in the 1880s the *Revue d'Ethnographie*; its emphasis was on the culture and institutions of non-Western and pre-historic peoples. The empirical studies of the lives and customs of non-European peoples in the journal were done by naval or military officers and by colonial administrators. Throughout the eighteenth and nineteenth centuries they had, of course, contributed a travel literature which indicated something about the lives of African peoples, their marriage rites, their religion, commercial habits, manner of cultivating the land, and manufactures. Some of these accounts were highly stylized, seeing in the failure to conform to Europe a sign of inferiority; but others were relatively value-free or even full of praise of Africans and their countries. But these latter accounts made little impact on the collective image Frenchmen had of Africa and were ignored by the anthropologists.

Hamy's effort to create a new emphasis in the study of non-European peoples failed; after ten years his journal ceased publication and was amalgamated with other journals forming *L'Anthropologie*, a journal again devoted to physical anthropology.

By the beginning of the twentieth century the disciples of the sociologist Durkheim, by their stress on the environmental impact, reasserted the eighteenth-century view for the causes of human differentiation and thus eclipsed the stress on biology. One of the earliest works specifically aiming at a general discussion of non-European peoples, was Lucien Lévy-Bruhl's *Fonctions Mentales dans les Sociétés Inférieures*, published in 1910. While striking out in a new direction, Lévy-Bruhl's work in some ways confirmed the stagnation of French anthropology. First, like his predecessors Lévy-Bruhl failed to do on-the-spot research; he was an armchair anthropologist depending on the second-hand reports of observers. The very sources of the work were an indictment of French anthropology, for nearly all of them were of English, Australian, or American origin. Lévy-Bruhl evidently found few French sources of use; one of the few that he did utilize was Charlevoix, the eighteenth-century writer on the Indians of French Guiana.

Lévy-Bruhl, of course, did break with his predecessors in the sense that he no longer concerned himself with physical anthropology but rather—to use expressions borrowed from several of his book titles—"the soul," "the mentality," "the experience," "the mythology," of so-called primitive peoples.[15] His unfortunate use of the term "pre-logical" (which he himself dropped and later deplored), his notion of "inferior societies" and the whole methodology which assumed that all non-European peoples, be they Chinese, Red Indians, or Africans, had a common "primitive mentality" seemed still bound to the old racial anthropology which had established a dichotomy between Whites and non-Whites. Theoretically speaking, Lévy-Bruhl's work was not racist. Inspired by his masters Comte and Durkheim, Lévy-Bruhl claimed that he was an environmentalist believing in the relativity of cultures. Yet once he came to describe the "collective representation" of various peoples, he disregarded their milieu, the different functions which the collective representations had, and he gave an independent existence to the collective mentality of so-called primitive peoples. On Africans, Lévy-Bruhl had nothing special to say, since he lumped them together with the Aborigines of Australia, the Red Indians, and others into an amorphous group known as "primitives."

It is with Maurice Delafosse that the French anthropology of Africa reached new levels. Delafosse was reasonably well trained in the problems of studying foreign cultures by his education at the *Ecole des langues orientales vivantes*. Added to this was his long practical experience of living in Africa; he served as colonial administrator in Ivory Coast, Sudan, and Senegal. Delafosse, who went to the West Coast of Africa in the early 1890s, was one of the first French anthropologists who combined theoretical and methodological knowledge with on-the-spot research. Born from this advantageous combination came a sensitive and sympathetic understanding of African institutions and societies.

Delafosse's writings and his teachings at both the *Ecole des langues orientales* and the *Ecole Coloniale*, the training school for future colonial administrators, had an important impact in furthering the development of French anthropological work on Africa.

While Africans may be technologically behind Europeans, they were in no way intellectually or socially inferior to Europeans, Delafosse stated. They were different, their social structure was still at a tribal level while Europeans had developed larger social organizations and had also gone from collectivism to individualism. But there was no reason to assume that Africans might not develop in the same direction.

In some of Delafosse's writings, one might detect certain leftovers from racial anthropology. While clearly labeling his theories as speculations, he asserted that the development of Sudanese civilizations had been due to "considerable influence" from the Phoenician colonies of North Africa, especially Carthage. Equally, the original founders of the Ghana and Mali empires were described as White. The Fulani, whom Delafosse admired, were held to owe their civilization to Whites or perhaps a Jewish lost tribe. In justice to Delafosse, it should be noted that the *Tarikh es Sudan* and the *Tarikh el fettach* mentioned White founders for Ghana, and Delafosse based his hypothesis on these two accounts the latter of which he had collaborated in translating. Equally, Delafosse noted that whoever the founders might have been, at the height of the Ghana state, it was ruled by Blacks.[16]

Some of the racial attitudes that were reinforced by imperialism also rubbed off on Delafosse. Thus, in *Les Nègres*, published in 1927, Delafosse claimed that while Blacks did not lack foresight and the ability to plan, they rather lacked will. To accomplish great things Africans needed a strong will imposed upon them as had been done in the past by princes like Sundiata in Mali and Mamadu Touré among the Songhay and as was being done by the colonial powers.[17] These comments were mainly asides and they probably should not be allowed to detract from the main thrust of Delafosse's work, which rehabilitated the image of the African.

The accomplishments of states like Ghana and Mali, Delafosse pointed out, were of a very high degree. Such historical states and African political systems in his time, Delafosse affirmed, showed Africans capable of establishing sophisticated political organizations.

Delafosse's eminent successor at both the *Langues orientales* and the *Ecole coloniale* Henri Labouret worked on local monographs, his best-known one being *Les Tribus du Rameau Lobi* (1931). His guide to monographic studies, the *Plan de Monographie Régionale* (1934) was used by several generations of anthropologists. It was with the work of Delafosse and his successors—men like Labouret and Marcel Griaule—that French anthropology had come of age in its relationship with Africa. It should be noted that the advances made in anthropology did not have an immediate effect on the general French image of Blacks. The racist one was well ensconced in colonial novels that poured out in the interwar period, in the school textbooks, and in encyclopedias.[18] Only after World War II were the assertions of racial anthropology recognized to lack scientific underpinnings by educated French society in general. The popular image seems, however, still unaffected by trends in modern anthropology.

From the racial anthropologists through at least Lévy-Bruhl, the assertion was made that Blacks had a different destiny from Whites. These notions had an impact on colonial policy. For one, what made imperialism so acceptable was that it was universally believed that Blacks were inferior to Whites and could benefit from the tutelage of the latter. And once the colonies were conquered intellectual attitudes helped shape policies and methods of rule in Africa. First, when the French conquered Africa, they believed that assimilation would work, but their discovery that they were dealing with civilizations totally different from that of Europe made them fall back on the racist conviction that Blacks in fact were not assimilable. And thus the policy of association was instituted, which translated into a form of indirect rule. After the turn of the century the more sympathetic attitude revealed toward Africa by people like Delafosse put a different emphasis on the policy of association. Now instead, the fact that Africa had institutions and values of its own and the need to respect them was stressed. Thus both attitudes affected the policy of association.[19]

The earlier racist attitude which believed that the African was structured physically more like an animal than fellow whites translated into exploitative policies of the worst kind. Colonial administrators, who imposed heavy burdens of forced labor upon their subjects, were convinced that because of the Africans' presumably larger build and thicker nervous system, they were able to bear more than other humans. Colonel Mangin saw in the Black physique an animal-like resistance to pain and suffering and therefore pointed to the African as the ideal soldier who could be brought to Europe to fight France's wars. And thus Mangin wrote *La Force Noire*; three years after the publication of this book the European war did break out and Africans were mass conscripted and sent to France to die for *la patrie*. The Black forces were segregated from the White, and thus racism played a part in the treatment of the soldiers in France. As to their lack of proper medical care, food, and clothing, it would be hard to say that they were victims of French racism, for White French soldiers were treated with a similarly criminal negligence.[20]

In colonial policy the discovery of men like Delafosse of a separate African personality on a continent with its own institutions and history led to a greater effort of accommodation toward the African. A series of political reforms were introduced to give the African more representation in the 1920s and 1930s; economic and educational reforms were made. And at least some colonial administrators—one thinks of the liberal Robert Delavignette—began to talk about the need for France to win over overseas people by showing them that association with France would best help them express their own aspirations. Thus beginning in the 1930s at least among some, the virtue of White superiority was no longer considered an undisputed fact; instead this dominance had to be earned.[21] And French policy after World War II, the political reforms and the program of mass economic development were all animated by this changed perception of Africa. The collapse of European power and authority and rise of nationalist and protest movements of various sorts should of course not be ignored, but the changing intellectual environment helped the French accommodate to the new conditions of their rule.

The intellectual leadership behind the new consciousness of post–World War II Black Africa had been formed by currents of thought dominant in inter-war Paris. As young students in Paris a number of Africans joined and met with West Indians and Black Americans to forge together the ideas which were to become known collectively as *négritude*. The aim of the participants of the movement was to affirm a defense of the Black race against the dominance of the White, in the French case, to free Africa from its dependency upon France. But the language in which it was made and the very concepts which lay behind this proud affirmation were taken from Europe.

The young Africans found in the French surrealist critique of Western culture a welcome antidote to the positivist ideology inculcated in them in French colonial schools which had depicted European culture as the summa toward which all people strived. The surrealists in their assault on the West praised African culture, especially art, seeing it as being more closely connected to emotive human life. Young Africans in Paris read the surrealists with great interest and found in their condemnation of the West and praise of Black culture ideas upon which they could build their own identity. And from anthropology, from the writings of the German Leo Frobenius and the Frenchmen Delafosse and Labouret the Africans in Paris with pride studied the ancient African cultures in which learning and statecraft had rivaled contemporary societies in Europe. Africa's present culture, they read, while different from Europe, formed a coherent system of values and attitudes which were as worthy of study and respect as any other culture. And in Dakar at the *Ecole* William Ponty, the teacher training school, the stirrings of *négritude* were also felt. After reading the works of French anthropologists like Labouret, Diori Hamani (later president of Niger) reminisced that he and his classmates were overcome by

a feeling of joy and pride to discover that the African languages, the material civilizations of Africa...were honestly studied, exposed, explained, and recognized as realities that were essentially different, but in no ways inferior to those of the Western world. Thus, the European, this white man [Labouret] revealed us to ourselves, liberated us from a certain complex and strengthened our feeling of dignity.[22]

Within the French assimilationist system, the individual African could gain rights from the colonizer only to the extent that he abjured his own culture and moved into French modes of thought and even social life. Thus Africans who wanted to gain individual freedom had to identify closely with France. It was the experience of the young expatriates in Paris, their personal loneliness and realization of French indifference (if not at times hostility) which led them to form a group consciousness and cultivate a "counter-culture" to the official French culture. Since it was through culture that France attempted to attach the overseas Western educated young people to her, that was the field in which Senghor and his friends decided to strike and claim a separate domain for Black people. Once that had been done, then the subsequent freedom from colonialism could be achieved.

The extent to which the awareness of an African cultural heritage was awakened in these young Africans by the reading of European sources is a tragic witness of the extent to which they had been uprooted from their own cultures. The beauties and the uniqueness of African culture were discovered not by contact with the living realities of Africa, but rather by being exposed to the European image of Africa.[23]

The writings of anthropologists such as Delafosse, Labouret, or Griaule stressed the extent to which African civilizations were formed as responses to the geographic and human environment. They believed in the essential unity of people;

underlying the differences of civilizations, they believed, was a common genius for adaptation and survival of all men. But Lévy-Bruhl had been far more ambiguous, seeing in the primitive mentality an independent force which was transmitted from generation to generation among the primitives; thus a value system was formed which not only in degrees but in kind totally differed from that of the West.

In their opposition to the West and their affirmation of the singularity of the black experience and genius, the members of the *négritude* movement shunned the anthropology of Delafosse and approached the position of Lévy-Bruhl. Senghor, in an essay in 1939, juxtaposed the sterile world of Whites to the organic wholesomeness of Blacks; he spoke of a ''negro soul'' which was creative, had a sense of rhythm and poetry and was able to intuit the meaning of the cosmos. Senghor's ''Negro-African'' included all Blacks on the earth regardless of their environment or historic experience. They had, Senghor claimed, a common genius. The early Senghor thus approached the racist thought of nineteenth-century anthropology in his notion that race, like biology, is inseparable from culture. At least he paralleled Lévy-Bruhl's more subtle form of racism, in his belief of independent existing mentalities, proper to each people.[24]

In the face of the Western derision of an Africa declared devoid of rationalist philosophy and scientific inventions one could, as Senghor, uphold the supposed emotive character of the African and speak of the special gift for rhythm and near animal intuition. One could glorify this very lack of technicity as the West Indian Aimé Césaire did in his *Cahier d'un Retour au Pays Natal* where he sang the praises of:

> Ceux qui n'ont inventé ni la poudre ni la boussole
> ceux qui n'ont jamais su dompter la vapeur ni l'éléctricité
> ceux qui n'ont exploré ni les mers ni le ciel.[25]

Thus the European image of Africa was taken at face value by these members of the *négritude* movement but turned to African advantage; the very shortcomings of Africa turned into its virtues.

But there was another way of responding to the same image, and that was to take on Western values of statecraft and rationalism and to claim that in fact Africa embodied these better than Europe. That was the work of the Senegalese Cheikh Anta Diop. In *Nations Nègres et Culture* (1954)—notice the singular in ''culture''—Diop claimed that Egypt rather than the Near East was the cradle of civilization, and that this first civilization was due to a population which was Black. The first Egyptians were Black, and they gave the human race the earliest forms of organized statecraft, religion, architecture, a tradition of codified laws, and so on.

Diop described in *L'Unité Culturelle de l'Afrique Noire* the world as divided into two essential cultures: a Northern and a Southern one. The Northern one was essentially European, the Southern, African. The Northern one was tribal in nature and was only able to overcome this by borrowing ideas of statecraft and empire from Africa; it was socially plagued by individualism "moral and material solitude and disgust for existence," while Southern Culture, mainly located in Africa was healthy, cosmopolitan, had a sense of solidarity toward all members of its society and "morally believes in peace, justice and is optimistic." Thus Diop was the vengeance against Gobineau; if European racism had used history as a way of upholding the White race and denigrating the Black, Diop showed that the game could be played in an opposite direction.

Members of the *négritude* movement came to recognize that inherent in their thought was a kind of racism; at the end of the first part of *Nations Nègres* Diop warned against using his history for the purpose of creating a new racism. And speaking at Oxford in 1961, Senghor was to admit that *négritude* in its beginning in the words of Sartre had been "an anti-racist racism." Sartre had attempted to explain and write an apologia for the racism of *négritude*, to tame the movement, by pointing to its excesses as only a temporary phase in its existence.[26] He was correct at least in the case of Senghor who quickly abandoned his earliest position and since World War II affirmed that the "Negro-African" culture was but one of many, needed to create together with the other cultures of the world a universal humanism. As has been remarked by a number of commentators such a position merged conveniently with Senghor's desire for continued ties with the French intellectual milieu and between his country of Senegal and France.[27]

Négritude was an important assertion of protest, helping unite Africans in common action of protest against colonialism and leading the way toward independence. Ideas do not have an independent existence; if forms of race consciousness could be used to justify and perpetuate imperialism, they also helped rally its demise.

NOTES

1. "Afrique," *Encyclopédie* Supplement, 1 (Amsterdam, 1780), p. 194.

2. Georges Louis Leclerc Buffon, *Natural History*, trans. Barr, vol. 4 (London, 1811).

3. André Duvevyer, "Le Sang Epuré—la Naissance du Sentiment et de l'Idée de Race dans la Noblesse Française (1560-1720)," 3 vols. (Unpublished manuscript, mimeographed, Brussels, n.d. [1970]); Jacques Barzun, *The French Race* (New York, 1932).

4. Louis Chevallier, *Classes laborieuses et classes dangereuses à Paris pendant la première moitié du 19ᵉ Siècle* (Paris, 1958).

5. Bory de Saint-Vincent, *L'Homme* 1 (Paris, 1827), p. 74.

6. Paul Broca, *On the Phenomena of Hybridity in the Genus Homo* (London, 1864), pp. 27-28; Paul Broca, "Documents Rélatifs au Croisement des Races Très Différentes," *Bulletin de la Société d'Anthropologie de Paris* 1 (May 1860): 255-268 (hereafter BSAP).

7. Pierre Larousse, "Nègre," *Grand Dictionnaire Universel* (Paris, 1866), pp. 903-904.

8. See William B. Cohen, "Literature and Race: Nineteenth Century French Fiction, Blacks and Africa," *Race and Class* 16 (October 1974): 181-205.

9. Bory de Saint-Vincent, "Sur l'Anthropologie de l'Afrique Française," *Académie des Sciences* (30 June 1845): 14; Paul Broca, "Sur les Proportions Rélatifs du Bras, de l'Avant Bras et de la Clavicule Chez les Nègres et les Européens," *BSAP* (3 April 1862): 162-172; Bory de Saint-Vincent, "Polygénisme et Transformisme," *BSAP* (30 June 1869): 443.

10. Armand de Quatrefages, *Rapport sur les Progrès de l'Anthropologie* (Paris, 1867), pp. 153, 380; Armand de Quatrefages, "Histoire Naturelle de l'Homme," *Revue des Deux Mondes*, 2d ser. 8 (1 March 1857): 160; Elisée Reclus, "Le Mississippi—Etudes et Souvenirs," *Revue des Deux Mondes*, ser. 2, 5 (1 August 1859): 624.

11. Arthur de Gobineau, *Essai sur l'Inégalité des Races Humaines* (Paris, 1854; reprint ed., 1967), pp. 209, 275-279, 446-447.

12. Gustave LeBon, "Recherches Anatomiques et Mathématiques sur les Lois des Variations," *Revue d'Anthropologie*, 2d ser. 2 (1879): 103-104; Gustave LeBon, "Recherches Expérimentales sur les Variations de Volume du Cerveau et du Crâne," *BSAP* (18 July 1878): 310-315.

13. Paul Broca, "Sur le Volume et la Forme du Cerveau Suivant les Individus et Suivant les Races," *BSAP* 2 (1861): 139-207.

14. Paul Topinard, "Etude sur Pierre Camper et sur l'Angle Facial dit de Camper," *Revue de l'Anthropologie* 2 (1873): 202-212; Paul Topinard, *Eléments de l'Anthropologie* (Paris, 1885), pp. 220, 829-830.

15. Lucien Lévy-Bruhl, *L'âme Primitive* (Paris, 1927); *l'Expérience Mystique et les Symboles Chez les Primitifs* (Paris, 1938); *La Mythologie Primitive* (Paris, 1936).

16. Maurice Delafosse, *The Negroes of Africa, History and Culture*, trans. F. Fligelman. A convenient volume in English which combines *Les Noirs de l'Afrique* (Paris, 1921) and *Civilisations Négro-Africaines* (Paris, 1925) (Port Washington, N.Y., 1931; reissued 1968), pp. 32-39, 42, 69.

17. Maurice Delafosse, *Les Nègres* (Paris, 1927), pp. 56-57.

18. Ada Martinkus-Zemp, *Le Blanc et le Noir—Essai d'une Description de la Vision du Noir par le Blanc dans Littérature Française de l'Entre-Deux Guerres* (Paris, 1975); Manuela Semidei, "De l'Empire à la Décolonisation à Travers les Manuels Scolaires," *Revue Française de Science Politique* 16 (February 1966): 56-86.

19. Raymond F. Betts, *Assimilation and Association in French Colonial Theory, 1890-1914* (New York, 1961); William B. Cohen, *Rulers of Empire: The French Colonial Service in Africa* (Stanford, Calif., 1971), pp. 71-79, 114-118, 180-182.

20. Jacques Meyer, *La Vie Quotidienne des Soldats Pendant la Grande Guerre* (Paris, 1966).

21. Robert Delavignette, *Soudan-Paris-Bourgogne* (Paris, 1935); his writings are excerpted and translated in William B. Cohen, *Robert Delvignette on the French Empire* (Chicago, 1977).

22. Robert Cornevin, "Eloge de Charles Robequain et Henri Labouret, Séance du 5 Février 1965," *Comptes rendus, Académie des Sciences d'Outre-Mer* (Paris, 1965); 24-25.

23. Jacques Hymans, *Léopold Sédar Senghor—An Intellectual Biography* (Edinburgh, 1971).

24. Léopold Sédar Senghor, "Ce que l'Homme Noir Apporte," *Liberté* 1 (Paris, 1964): 22-38.

25. Lilyan Kestelroot, ed., *Aimé Césaire* (Paris, 1962), p. 105.

26. Cheikh Anta Diop, *Nations Nègres et Culture* (Paris, 1955), p. 253; Senghor in Irving Leonard Markovitz, *Léopold Sédar Senghor and the Politics of Négritude* (New York, 1969), p. 50; Jean Paul Sartre, *Black Orpheus*, trans. S. W. Allen (Paris, n.d.), p. 15.

27. Markovitz, *Senghor*; Marcien Towa, *Léopold Sédar Senghor—Négritude or Servitude* (Yaoundé, 1971).

17

Thomas Ismail Urbain (1812-1884): *Indigénophile* and Precursor of *Négritude*

In the history of French liberal opposition to the colonization of North Africa in the nineteenth century, one name stands out, today all but forgotten. It is that of Thomas Ismail Urbain. Born in Cayenne in French Guiana on December 31, 1812, Urbain was the natural son of a mulatto woman named Appoline Severin (herself the daughter of a slave) and her common-law French husband, a merchant and sometime slave dealer named Urbain Brue.[1] Throughout his youth Thomas was to be tormented by the anomaly of his origins. The society of nineteenth-century France was a difficult enough place for ambitious young men of the people. For a young mulatto of uncertain parentage how much more was this the case! But who was this singular individual, and what claim does he have on our attention today? Thomas Ismail Urbain was a man of many parts. Attracted in his youth to the doctrine of Saint-Simon, he remained devoted to the end of his days to the ideal of bringing about concord amongst the races, religions, and nations of the earth. Converted to Islam in 1835, he later married an Algerian Muslim woman and pursued a career as an interpreter and administrator in Algeria. The author of books with such contemporary sounding titles as *L'Algérie pour les Algériens* (1860) and *L'Algérie Française, Indigènes et Immigrants* (1861), he exercised considerable influence as a defender of the rights of Algerian Muslims against the greed and repressiveness of the settlers. The man who was to assume his mantle as the chief critic of native policy in Algeria, Emile Masqueray (in his day a noted ethnologist and writer) had this to say about him in 1891:

It was [Urbain] who first put before the public this formidable native question which everyone today now seems to be discovering. He studied it in all its aspects, and theoretically resolved it with the judiciousness of a man of state, the highmindedness of a philosopher, and the detachment of a monk. He died at the task, despised in Algeria, little known or carefully forgotten in France; but he lives on, even in the hearts of those who claim not to know him and who profit from his works. That is his supreme recompense.[2]

To study the life of Urbain, to explore its various facets, is to discover an extraordinary figure. It is also to encounter the spirit of the early nineteenth century in all of its romantic turbulence, its search for the exotic, and its faith in progress. Urbain was very much a child of his age, distinguished chiefly by his origins, but also his intelligence and his passionate sense of justice. In the twentieth century he would have been a leader, a Kwame Nkrumah or a Frantz Fanon. (There is indeed an uncanny parallel between his career and that of Fanon, another mulatto of passion and genius from the French Caribbean who [one hundred years later] became a champion of the Algerian people.) In the nineteenth century, with its class consciousness, racism, and social stigmata, Urbain never attained anything like due recognition of his considerable talents. Instead he served out his career as a second-rank administrator, always on the fringes of power but never holding power. Despite this, he exercised considerable influence especially in the early 1860s during the phase of liberalization of Algerian policy known to historians as the period of the "Arab empire." Toward the end of his life, Urbain's steadfast and courageous opposition to the repressive policies pursued by the settler lobby in the wake of the collapse of the empire (the infamous "*code de l'Indigénat*") sounded a call of social justice which was to make him a hero to subsequent generations of French liberal critics of *colonisation à l'outrance*.

This essay is part of a longer work on the history of French colonial sociology of North Africa, 1830-1930. In it Ismail Urbain will bulk large as one of the clearest-sighted students of Algerian society in the first generation of French dominance. Since my research on the life of Urbain is not yet complete and he left a considerable quantity of published and unpublished writings which by their range and diversity would be difficult to summarize here in any event, the best I can do here is to try to suggest something of the spirit and importance of the man. A more thorough consideration of his biography must wait until another time.

The life of Ismail Urbain seems to fall naturally into two major phases, at first glance so seemingly at odds with one another as to make one wonder if there is any connection between the tempestuous youth and the sober administrator. I will consider each in turn.

A PRECURSOR OF *NÉGRITUDE*?

We know little or nothing about the youth of Thomas (not yet Ismail) Urbain. He does not speak of it in his unpublished autobiography, which is the principal source for this period of his life.[3] We do know that he was brought to Marseilles in 1820 by his father to be educated for a career in business. Enrolled under the name of Appoline dit Urbain, and known variously as Urbain Thomas and Thomas Urbain, he soon revealed a real talent for his studies. So much so, in fact, that through the intercession of a friend of his father's, it was decided that he would prepare for a career in medicine. Unfortunately, this dream was punctured by the bankruptcy of his father in 1830. Young Thomas was put on a boat for Cayenne with several of his sisters and brothers to return to his mother.[4]

He did not long remain in Cayenne (his mother was poor, and jobs were few), but he did come into contact with his people for the first time since his childhood. What he discovered both attracted and repelled him. The existence of slavery, the domination and oppression of the White planter oligarchy, and the tenuous interstitial position of the people of mixed blood marked him for life. A poem he was to write to his brother years later says it well:

> We have in our houses,
> On our plantations,
> Black slaves.
> Perhaps a hundred?
> You know what it's all about!
> Our whole family is of mixed blood.
> Our grandmother was black.
> Men of color are not *White*.
> They are not black.
> They are not slaves.
> They are not masters.
> They are men of color.
> The blacks are very miserable.
> Lots of work,
> Few holidays.
> The whip!
> Girls of color are for the Whites,
> Black girls too.
> The plaything of their debauches.[5]

Within a year Urbain was back in Marseilles, much to the disgust of his father. There he first learned of the teachings of Saint-Simon. It was like the answer to a prayer:

Reading the Saint-Simonian works completely seduced me: to each according to his abilities, to each ability according to its achievements, what else would be needed to inspire the disinherited of society, whom the privileges of birth had stigmatized?[6]

Borrowing some money from his father, he set out for Paris with a friend. The fervor of his faith (as well as perhaps the exoticism of his origins) found him a place in the Saint-Simonian commune at Menilmontant. He took as his spiritual advisor Gustave d'Eichital. For a year Urbain lived in Paris amongst the Saint-Simonians.

The Saint-Simonian movement was at the time entering a phase of quasi-religious exaltation. The leader of the sect, Arthur Enfantin, was an intense and authoritarian individual who claimed to receive divine revelations. His young followers regarded him as a near God-like figure whose stern discipline was to be followed without question. Saint-Simonianism was a religion of love, which preached the brotherhood of all men. The communal living style and unconventional opinions and dress of its members soon made the sect a target for repression. By 1833 its notoriety had become so great that there was a public trial. Enfantin was jailed, and his followers dispersed to preach the message of concord and humanity in the French countryside. Soon the doctrine evolved in yet another direction. The cult of the Father, represented by the figure of Enfantin, was now revealed to be insufficient. What was required to balance out the Holy Family was a Mother, and given the Saint-Simonian vocation for bringing harmony amongst the peoples, it was revealed that the Mother whose discovery was devoutly to be wished was in the Near East. The conversion of oriental women, and with them of the Islamic world, to the religion of Saint-Simon could not be far behind. It was on this mystical search in 1833 that Urbain set out for Istanbul with his Saint-Simonian comrades.[7]

After various adventures (including almost being lynched for daring to preach the liberation of oriental womanhood on the streets of Istanbul) a remnant of the original Saint-Simonian band arrived in Egypt. There they were subsequently joined by Enfantin, the Father himself, and several other adepts. While the others sought to interest Muhammad Ali, then ruler of Egypt, in the importance of constructing a canal across the isthmus of Suez (a project which symbolized for the Saint-Simonians the union of East and West), Urbain found employment as a French language instructor at the artillery school at Damietta.[8]

The Egyptian experience proved to be of fundamental importance to young Thomas. Arab society, with its tolerance of other religions, absence of color consciousness, and humane treatment of slaves immediately seduced him. Not only was life in Egypt somehow more sensible, more just, but the exoticism of the Orient seemed to him extraordinarily sensual. Egyptian life-styles appealed to him, although his own living conditions were modest.

Soon he was in love with an Egyptian woman of a Christian family named Hanem. The fact that she was dark in color seemed a confirmation of his own increasing consciousness of his color. He wrote numerous poems in her honor, "the girl of Damanhour." Through his relations with Hanem, Urbain was to complete his transformation and discover his destiny. When Hanem died in an epidemic in 1835, a grief-stricken Urbain sought solace in Islam. The circumstances of his conversion are related in several letters of the period, as well as in an article published several years later in the *Journal des Débats*. There is no question that the conversion experience was a fundamental psychological event for him. By converting to Islam, he felt himself at last capable of fulfilling his mission of conciliating the different races, nations, and religions of the earth.

What I saw of the situation of the blacks in the Antilles; what instincts my maternal ancestors passed on to me; what I have suffered since my childhood because of the question of the races of color, opened before me like an irritating and painful wound,— all of that found a justification, a result, a remedy in the projected union.[9]

Soon he began to see himself as the mediator between Islam and Christianity, between East and West, and between Black and White. The Muslim name he selected for himself was to be a sign of his mission:

I took the name of Ismail, name of the prophet, a symbolic name for me in which were united almost all of the aspects of my apostolate. Ismail [the Biblical Ishmael], son of a slave, a bastard abandoned by his father. It is he, according to the tradition, who discovered a spring near Mecca and who built the Kaaba with his father Abraham. Who knows if God has not reserved for me the discovery in his deserts...of a new spring where all Muslims will come to quench their thirst.[10]

During this period in his life, Ismail Urbain wrote a great deal of poetry, which while it was never published, circulated within the Saint-Simonian community. Most of it is awful as only the poems of a sensitive and intelligent adolescent can be awful: full of high-blown rhetoric, intense romantic longings, generally in abysmal taste. The subject matter of these poems, bad as they are, nonetheless reveals his state of mind and is of some historical interest. One discovers, for example, poems which have titles such as "I am black, but I am beautiful," and "The Black." There is indeed a veritable obsession with blackness, its significance and importance. As one of the most important Frenchmen of color of his generation, it is possible to see Ismail Urbain as a precursor of the twentieth-century movement of *négritude*.

Most interesting to us in this regard is the poem, which begins, "I am black, but I am beautiful." The poem continues (it is a woman speaking):

I am black! My eyes swim in a lake white as the milk of the coconut.
They sparkle like the fire of well dried wood.

The night is black, as am I; like it I have golden stars,
For my glances sparkle when they are illuminated by voluptuousness.

I am black! And they say about my teeth: Look!
Young white lambs who return from being washed.
Only in seeing them does one find the whiteness of Indian muslins.

I am black! Look...my mouth is a banquet of amazing voluptuousness,
It is the cup from which one drinks happiness, and my lips
Are red as the delicious wine which fills it to the brim.[11]

Another poem, entitled "The Black" is less happy. Here the persona is a Black man. He begins with the burning question "Where then are those who say that blacks are the children of the devil?" The poem continues,

> I am black, and I am a son of God! They have blasphemed,
> For in truth God has not shown them all of his joy.

Further on, in this otherwise murky and passionate poem the poet, torn by the fear of rejection, proclaims:

> White man! I am your brother and if you refuse to share your life
> With me, God will chastise you for having refused [to acknowledge]
> My brotherhood.
> I am not your slave, I am your brother!

> You have loaded me down with chains to drag me into slavery.
> You have crushed me with work, drowned me in humiliation,
> But God will pull me from my abject [condition] and let me
> Share your wealth.
> And for all of the evils which you have done me, I will love you
> Because I am good.[12]

There is a suppressed rage which informs many of his poems and letters during this period. For a time Urbain seems to have been tempted by thoughts of revolt. He wishes to be the spokesman of the Black race, to preach the concord of the races in Africa or perhaps in India along the Malabar coast. The death of Hanem appears to have ended all of this. From the time of his conversion to Islam his thoughts were directed toward a still greater destiny, that of bridging the chasm between Islam and the West.[13]

In February 1836 Ismail Urbain returned to France, now confident that he could contribute something to the Saint-Simonian mission. But what could he do? Unlike most of his Saint-Simonian friends, he was not a graduate of the *Ecole Polytechnique* and was not the scion of a socially prominent family. Politics, banking, engineering, all careers accessible to his friends, were closed to him. He flirted briefly with a career on the stage, but was soon forced to recognize the obvious: he had little talent. In the meantime, to earn a living, he began to write brief accounts of his experiences in Egypt and scenes of life in the Orient. Finally, in March 1837 with the recommendation of Michel Chevallier, he managed to secure an appointment as a military interpreter, third class, in the *Armée d'Afrique* in Algeria. The second period of his life was beginning.

INDIGÉNOPHILE

From the moment that Ismail Urbain set foot on Algerian soil, he appears to have found himself at last. No longer tortured by self-doubt, he remained nonetheless convinced that his mission was to mediate between Islam and Christianity. The years from 1837 to 1841 saw him advance steadily to become the secretary of many of the French generals of the conquest: Bugeaud, Auvray, Glabois,

Valée, and Bedeau. His discretion, his knowledge of Algerian society, his talents as a writer marked him out as a man of sense. His marriage to a young Muslim woman named Jaymuna bint Mascud al-Zibari in 1840 consolidated his position in Algerian society.[14] In 1841 he served briefly in Paris at the *Direction des Affaires de L'Algérie*. He participated in the military campaigns from 1842 to 1845. By this time he had become the personal interpreter of the duke of Aumale, one of the Orleanist princes. Modest, industrious, and extremely knowledgeable, he wrote a number of reports on Algerian affairs during this period (including a brilliant *"Notice sur la Province de Constantine"*), most of which were signed by his superiors. Recalled to the Ministry of War at Paris in 1845, he remained there until 1858. He continued to write numerous articles for the French press, notably the *Journal des Débats*, *Le Crédit*, and *Revue de Paris*.[15] It is his writings which are his greatest claim to lasting fame.

At first Urbain confined himself to descriptive narratives and scenes from Algerian life. In 1847, just after the suppression of the first general insurrection in Algeria, he published an article entitled *"L'Algérie. Du Gouvernement des Tribus de l'Algérie."*[16] In it we can see in outline most of the themes that would preoccupy him in the remainder of his career. He begins by remarking that now that the fighting has died down, we should concern ourselves with the fate of the rural populations. Until now, he declares, we don't seem to have noticed that there were Arabs in Algeria until we had to fight them. Today, we are in the process of repeating the same mistake. Since land is needed for colonization, we've become aware that the land is occupied by tribal populations, and the best solution we've come up with is to dispossess them and drive them off their land. This is war by another name. In the process we have forgotten that France has a civilizing mission. He then goes on to speak on behalf of the Algerians:

What they ask of us . . . is an administrative organization which favors the development of agriculture and commerce, and organization of [matters of] religion and justice, a substantial system of public instruction and some welfare institutions.[17]

The main point of the article is that the Turkish system of rural administration can be adapted to the needs of France and will constitute a much less brutal and more efficient method of keeping order and spreading French influence than a head-on assault on the society. Islam, rightly understood, he argued, is no danger. "The inhabitants of Algeria are in general less fanatic than most of the peoples of southern Europe." If we are careful, and not in too much of a rush, then in time,

a new people, retaining its various customs, beliefs and idioms will develop under French tutelage, merging its interests, taking its inspiration from the same patriotic sentiment. This is no longer the unintelligent fusion of races, customs and religious doctrines; it is the association of labor to attain a common goal: peace and well being.[18]

The dream of a new Algeria, in which Christian and Muslim alike would live together in biracial harmony, was to obsess not only Urbain, but most of the French *indigénophiles* who followed in his footsteps. The dream was in many ways a Saint-Simonian one: the spread of civilization and progress gradually breaking down the boundaries which separated people from one another. It was predicated on the notion that societies change at different rates of speed and that there are not superior and inferior races of peoples, but only different ones. Men like Urbain believed that the laws which govern society can be understood and that it is possible to channel the forces of social change in productive directions. An enormous faith in the power of reason and education underlies the writings of Urbain and marks him off clearly from ourselves.

From 1846 to 1858 Urbain remained out of direct touch with Algerian developments, as he pursued his administrative career in the Ministry of War in Paris. During these years, Algeria underwent many important changes. These included the defeat and capture of Abd al-Qadir, the main resistance leader, the development of a system of military administration known as the Arab Bureaus, and the institution of the policy of *cantonnement* by which lands were made available for colonization. Urbain was from the outset a supporter of the Arab Bureaus, which he saw as well suited to introduce needed changes in Muslim society. But he strongly opposed the extension of colonization and the pernicious influence of the settler interests. This basic orientation was to characterize his approach to Algerian affairs to the end. His administrative career, despite the glowing reports of his superiors, was far from brilliant. Although his abilities clearly destined him for greater things, he was held back by the fact of his color and illegitimate birth, which provoked considerable hostility. Partly, however, one suspects that his liberal opinions, which were becoming known, may have helped win him enemies in high places as well. Nonetheless, he was not without allies, and in the end his obvious talents and patient and uncomplaining attitude were rewarded.

In 1860 Urbain was named to the *Conseil de Gouvernement* of Algeria, the chief administrative bureau of the colony. Returning to Constantine for the first time in a number of years, he was struck by the misery and despair of the Muslim populations. The progress of the policy of *cantonnement* had dispossessed many of their lands; many others were ruined as a result of the conquest. In November he decided to enter the fray. Under the pseudonym of Georges Voisin he published a book with the bold title of *L'Algérie pour les Algériens*.[19] His career as a political pamphleteer was launched. From this moment on until the day he died Ismail Urbain fought stubbornly, courageously against the steady advance of the settler interests. While the book received little notice in the press, it did come to the attention of Baron David, son of the famous painter and a former officer in the Arab Bureaus who had in the interim become a senator and expert on Algerian affairs. David was on intimate terms with Napoleon III and wasted no time in bringing Urbain's book to his attention. As Marcel Emerit has convincingly shown, it was his ideas, as expressed in *L'Algérie pour les Algériens*, and a subsequent book (also published under the pseudonym of Voisin) called *L'Algérie Française, Indigènes et Immigrants* (1863) which did the most to persuade the emperor of the need to intervene on behalf of his Muslim subjects.[20]

The thesis of *L'Algérie pour les Algériens* can be reduced to the notion that "there is nothing irreconcilable between the Muslim Algerians and the French." Algerians are just as capable of developing as are Frenchmen, but they cannot be forced into the same mold. Inevitably their development will take different forms. To insist on blindly making Frenchmen of them, down to the last detail, is to misunderstand the laws of progress and civilization, and to risk generating insurmountable opposition. The native would be justified to reply:

You wish to make me like you, make me renounce myself in denying my fathers, in reforming from one day to the next my beliefs, my customs, my character. No, I won't follow you in this path. I do want to resemble you, as a disciple resembles his master, but I want to remain myself, I want to retain my past and not violently alter my life.[21]

The correct policy in Algeria would be to civilize the natives, to lead them down the path to progress, but not to despoil them of their lands and their culture. In particular, this meant to allow them to retain their collectively owned lands and to not permit greedy settler interests to take advantage of their ignorance of the law to steal their lands from them. "Behind the word *colonisation* hide the most egotistical and greedy passions, as well as the most contrary to the interests of France." After vaunting the achievements of the Arab Bureaus and of the French army in Algeria in helping to modernize and defend the indigenous populations, Urbain concluded with a plea for patience and moderation.

The second book, *L'Algérie Française*, stated the argument against permitting full rein to civilian settler interests even more forcefully. "The real peasant of Algeria, the agricultural worker, the most solid and rational base of private property is the native." The Muslims must be allowed to develop the agricultural resources of the country, while Europeans should be confined to the development of commerce and industry. (This last point is a restatement of the Saint-Simonian notion that each should contribute according to his capacities.) The state should refrain from taking a role in the process of colonization and put a stop to speculation on land which profits only the few. As a whole the book is a forceful attack on the abuses which had crept into the system of government in Algeria.

The evidence of the disastrous consequences of permitting the French settlers to have their way presented by Urbain and his main allies (notably Frédéric Lacroix and Colonel Lapasset) eventually persuaded the emperor of the need to act. A phase of liberalization was begun when, on February 6, 1863, a directive was sent to the pro-settler Governor-General Pélissier informing him of the emperor's intentions to monitor closely the situation of his Arab subjects, especially with regard to the land in question. Urbain's arguments were taken up almost word for word. During a subsequent visit of Napoleon III to Algeria in 1865, Urbain accompanied him through much of his voyage and was accorded the favor of riding in the imperial carriage. By this time he had become the *bête noire* of those Frenchmen favoring outright colonization.

The hopes of the *indigénophile* group were doomed to be disappointed, however. The application of the directives of the emperor encountered systematic obstruction in Algeria from the settler interests. Even many of the military leaders were inclined to drag their heels. The new Governor-General, MacMahon, detested Urbain and did his best to retard his career. Increasingly alone, Urbain fought a rearguard action against overwhelming odds.

We are preparing a new Ireland in Algeria, together with a new Spain.... If the friends of liberty say their piece to Messieurs les landlords Algériens, if they are told that we don't want to transform Algeria into a Muslim Poland, the [government] would have more heart to resist the demands of colonial greed. But if the liberal party remains allied to the barons of colonization, the natives of Algeria whose future is tightly bound to their own will have nothing to gain if we substitute a civilian regime for a military regime. To the contrary![22]

Already he was fearful of the insurrection which would inevitably erupt if the Muslim populations were handed over to the settlers, and of the brutal repression which would follow it. By 1869, just before the outbreak of the Franco-Prussian war and the downfall of the regime, the Arab question was clearly decided. The political power of the settlers and their allies, increasingly tied to the republican currents of opposition to the empire, was now clearly established.

The last fourteen years of the life of Urbain were marked by his untiring efforts to keep the Algerian question before the French public.[23] Dismissed from his functions in the government with the coming of the Third Republic, he lived near Marseilles in semi-retirement and emerged only to fire off angry salvos against the gathering storm of settler revenge which took the form of the infamous legal measures known collectively as the *Code de l'Indigénat*. He wrote in several journals during this period, and his correspondence (which is marked by his usual acuity) shows the wearing effects of the struggle on his system. Bitterly attacked throughout this last portion of his life by his enemies in Algeria, Urbain nonetheless kept in contact with developments through his few remaining friends. To the end of his days he remained attached to his original dreams: that Algerians might still be associated with French development and be brought to progress and civilization, provided their institutions and customs were respected. He died on January 30, 1884.

The passing of Urbain did not end the struggle for Muslim rights in Algeria, of course. His example continued to inspire French opponents of settler domination—men like Emile Masqueray, Paul Leroy-Beaulieu, Albin Rozet, Victor Barraucand, and Marshal Lyautey. During the 1960s, toward the end of the national liberation struggle, the historians Charles-André Julien and Charles-Robert Ageron celebrated his legacy and looked to him as the prophet of the liberal dream of biracial harmony. By then, however, the situation had evolved far beyond such nineteenth-century utopian ideals. Thus when an indigenous Muslim civil rights movement emerged in 1914, despite the fact that they expressed their demands for equality in language which strikingly recalls that of Urbain, they had no knowledge of the man at all. With the advantages of hindsight, it is easy to criticize the latent paternalism (or worse) in Urbain. It is therefore important to remember that with all of his faults, there was no more constant foe of the regime of privilege, racism, and stiff-necked pride which was the heart of the Algerian colonial system.

NOTES

1. The correspondence of Ismail Urbain may be found in two places: in the Saint-Simonian archives conserved at the Bibliotheque de L'Arsenal (Paris) and in the Algerian ex-Government Generalcy archives in the Archives d'Outre Mer (Aix-en-Provence) Serie IX. On his life see Charles-Robert Ageron, "L'Algérie Algérienne sous Napoléon III," *Preuves* (February, 1961): 3-13; and Marcel Emerit, *Les Saint-Simoniens en Algérie* (Paris, 1941).

2. *Journal des Debats* (26 September 1891), cited in Georges Weill, *L'Ecole Saint-Simonienne* (Paris, 1896), pp. 189-190.

3. Urbain in fact left two unpublished autobiographies: France, Bibliothèque de l'Arsenal (Paris), *Saint-Simonian Archives* (hereafter cited as *Arsenal, Mss.*), "Notice chronologique sur Ismail Urbain conté par lui-meme en 1883 à ma Demande. Gustave d'Eichthal" 13744/78; and *Arsenal, Mss.*, "Ismail Urbain, Notice Autobiographique Destinée a Son Fils," 13744/76.

4. *Arsenal, Mss.*, "Notice Chronologique sur Ismail Urbain," 13744/78.

5. *Arsenal, Mss.*, 13735.

6. *Arsenal, Mss.*, "Notice autobiographique sur Ismail Urbain," 13744/78.

7. *Arsenal, Mss.*, "Notice autobiographique," 13744/78; also Emerit, *Les Saint-Simoniens*, p. 68; and Weill, *L'Ecole*, pp. 169-175.

8. [Urbain], "Une conversion a l'Islamisme," *Revue de Paris* (July 1852).

9. [Urbain], "Une conversion," p. 117.

10. Cited by Emerit, *Les Saint-Simoniens*, p. 73.

11. *Arsenal, Mss.*, 13735; the reference of the first line is to the Canticle of Canticles (translated by author). Cf. Léopold Senghor's poem "Black Girl," in *Selected Poems*, trans. J. Reed and C. Wake (London, 1969).

12. Ibid.

13. Emerit, *Les Saint-Simoniens*, pp. 70-71; just after his return to France from Egypt, Urbain cooperated with Gustave d'Eichthal in the publication of a series of letters on the race question, *Lettres sur la Race Noire et la Race Blanche* (Paris, 1839); the brochure is revealing of the muddled universalism of the Saint-Simonians, but also of the author's private obsessions.

14. The stages of Urbain's administrative career are outlined in Ageron, "L'Algérie algérienne"; his personnel file conserved in the Archives d'Outre-Mer (Aix-en-Provence) contains further details of his career, including the comments of his superiors attesting to his very considerable abilities.

15. Ageron, "Algérie algérienne."

16. *Revue de l'Orient et de l'Algérie* 1 (1847):241-259, 351-359.

17. Ibid., p. 245.

18. Ibid., p. 259.

19. *L'Algérie pour les Algériens* (Paris, 1861).

20. Emerit, *Les Saint-Simoniens*, pp. 233-287 provides a full discussion of this subject; see also Charles-André Julien, *Histoire de l'Algérie contemporaine* (Paris, 1964), pp. 422-426.

21. *L'Algérie pour les Algériens*, pp. 15-16.

22. Cited by Ageron, "Algérie algérienne," p. 10.

23. On this part of his career, see Charles-Robert Ageron, *Les Algériens Musulmans et la France, 1871-1919*, 2 vols. (Paris, 1968), 1: 401-404, as well as the article of the same author cited above.

IX

THE IMPACT OF EDUCATION

The French believed that the educational system of France was second to none in the universe; with this self-assurance and intellectual confidence, France managed to replicate in the African colonies an abbreviated version of French schools, institutes, *lycées*, normal schools, and universities. The effort cost the French taxpayer a considerable amount but was deemed worth it, even when the days of *la mission civilisatrice* rhetoric had passed. For by molding Africans' minds, France would be able to keep them within the orbit of francophone culture and hence within French designs in things political and economic. A disinterested observer, marveling at what France accomplished in Black Africa, appreciative of the sacrifices made by thousands of teachers uprooted from France to teach overseas, often most selflessly, would nevertheless be obliged to conclude that much of this was done in the domain of cultural imperialism. That phrase is not one which forms a part of the official record.

Léopold Senghor was offered the directorship of French education in West Africa in the mid-1930s; he shrewdly turned it down, since becoming that closely identified with colonial policy might be highly compromising. For just at that moment, ironically, many Africans were protesting the French-backed training schools in agriculture and mechanics; the Africans objected, arguing that they wanted access to the same curriculum that was available in France and not a pragmatic adaptation for colonial subjects. This drive for access to the means to become lawyers, doctors, and members of the liberal and academic professions culminated with the many scholarships given by the French government after World War II, when thousands of young men from West and Equatorial African countries flooded the university corridors of Paris and provincial universities.

David Gardinier, who is probably the leading American student of the history of education in francophone Africa, sketches succinctly what happened in the fourteen areas dominated by France during the colonial period. Gardinier discusses the traditional education of African societies, the Islamic schools characteristic of many areas, and the way that French schools, both Roman Catholic and secular, were implanted. He also details how the Africans sought equality with the Europeans by obtaining equality of educational opportunities and institutions.

A different approach is taken by the Guinean scholar, Aguibou Yan Yansané, himself a product of French education before taking his doctoral degree at Stanford University. Yansané is concerned with pre-French educational systems and distinguishes the goals of traditional education from Western models. He is convinced that a strong motivating factor for the French in spending freely on colonial education was national prestige and carrying out France's aims of cultural imperialism. This was the means by which Africans could be kept from attaining self-determination. Even Christianity became a tool for this cultural imperialism, since all educational institutions were ultimately under control of the French administration. And Yansané also enters the arena of elite versus mass education and argues that France kept instruction out of the reach of the people because education did not fit the economic desiderata of the imperialists. Africans were to be producers, and only a small elite was necessary to help with local administration. He is critical of the programs finally imported from universities such as Paris or Bordeaux, which were ill equipped to be responsive to particular African needs. For Yansané, France's educational policy paid off in providing assimilated civil servants and auxiliaries ready to conform to imperial policies. In conclusion, Yansané raises serious questions about Western social science and its norms in approaching the study of African society, and consequences that have followed.

There is little evidence available that France was influenced by any educational practices or substantive materials coming from Black Africa, but in order to cope with the business of exporting French education, adjustments for the colonies had to be made that did make an impact. This continuing impact is seen today in the fact that French external examiners regularly still visit and give examinations in African schools and universities.

DAVID E. GARDINIER

18

The French Impact on Education in Africa, 1817–1960

Today in the countries of the former federations of French West Africa and French Equatorial Africa and in the one-time trusteeship territories of Cameroon and Togo there exists an educational system modeled after that of France.[1] It was introduced during the period of French colonial rule, developed during the age of decolonization, and further expanded in more than two decades since independence.[2]

In this essay I should like to discuss the impact of French education in these fourteen states from the early 1800s to 1960. I touch upon the developments in education which have helped to shape contemporary African societies and nations as well as their relations with one another and with France.[3]

When the French arrived in Africa, there were two kinds of education already in existence. Traditional Islamic education was found from Senegal to Chad in the form of Koranic schools. A few communities such as Timbuktu and Abéché had advanced Islamic schools. Traditional education within kinship groups in the non-literate animist societies involved formal instruction at the time of the *rites de passage* and informal learning throughout childhood and adolescence. Though influenced by the French presence, these two systems of education would continue to exist beside Western education.

Between the establishment of French rule and the end of World War II, only a tiny percentage of the population in the colonial territories attended school. For example, in 1898 the French Congo, which included Gabon and Oubangui-Chari, had 2,654 pupils in fifty-two mission primary schools. Two years later French West Africa had only 2,500 primary pupils in seventy schools, the bulk of them in public schools. Half of the pupils within the French Congo were located in Gabon, and over half of those in French West Africa inhabited the four communes of Senegal (Saint-Louis, Gorée, Dakar, and Rufisque).[4]

As a result of greater efforts and greater state involvement in subsequent decades, in 1935 French West Africa had 62,300 pupils in primary schools and French Equatorial Africa, 15,877. Cameroon had 12,514 pupils in official programs and Togoland, 10,018 (1937). Given the populations at this time (French West Africa, 14,702,583; French Equatorial Africa, 3,386,000; Cameroon, 2,341,105; Togo, 763,420), less than 0.5 percent in the two federations were attending school. In Cameroon the figure was 0.66 percent and in Togo 1.33 percent.[5]

During the inter-war period the bulk of the pupils outside the four communes were enrolled in the first two grades. Only a very limited number arrived at the *école primaire supérieure* (the equivalent of an American junior high school), which trained primary teachers and employees for the administration and commerce. In 1934-1935 there were 930 pupils in the eight such schools of French West Africa but only ten in the one at Brazzaville, which had opened that very year. The *cours complémentaire* at Lomé, Togo, had twenty-three pupils. Between 1923 and 1937 the *école primaire supérieure* (e.p.s.) of Yaoundé produced 415 male graduates.[6] (I could not locate figures on the graduates in French Equatorial and French West Africa.)

Several post-primary institutions functioned in French West Africa during this period. Between 1906 and 1947 the William Ponty School, which prepared teachers for the upper primary grades, had 2,200 graduates. The Medical School at Dakar had 400 graduates of its four-year course between 1918 and 1937.[7] Programs in midwifery, veterinary medicine, and marine mechanics had smaller numbers of graduates.

It should be clear from these statistics that only a tiny percentage of those who attended French schools received enough instruction to be called a French-educated elite. Part IV of this book deals with elites, and therefore I shall refer but briefly to the question of who went to school during the colonial period. Access to French education helped to reinforce the privileged position of the European and *métis* groups within the four communes of Senegal vis-à-vis the African populations prior to World War I. Outside the four communes, missionaries tended to accept any children who wished to attend classes if they had sufficient resources to support them, for at this time many of their pupils were boarders who received little support from their families.

French policy during the nineteenth century in West Africa encouraged and even forced the attendance of the sons of chiefs and the children of other members of the traditional ruling classes. Faidherbe's school (1855) for them is a notable early example. It also illustrates the attempt to accommodate Islam through organization of a state school staffed by lay teachers and offering Islamic subjects.

By the early 1900s the public schools enrolled the children of new groups that had arisen as a result of the French expansion into the interior of West and Equatorial Africa. Among them were employees of the administration and commercial firms, soldiers, and *anciens combattants*. Also attending were the sons of administrative chiefs, such as the canton chiefs without traditional standing whom the French created—especially during the period between the two world wars.

The schools of the inter-war period produced most of the African politicians who sat in the territorial assemblies and the French Parliament after 1945, and who joined the first local executives organized in 1957. Among those still or recently in power are Léopold Senghor, Félix Houphouët-Boigny, Sékou Touré (deceased 1984), Ahmadou Ahidjo, and François Ngarta Tombalbaye (killed during the coup of April 1975). Touré, Ahidjo, and Tombalbaye were educated at the primary level in their home territories. Ahidjo attended the e.p.s. at Yaoundé to train as a radio operator and Tombalbaye the one at Brazzaville to prepare for teaching. Houphouët-Boigny studied at the Ponty (which offered the preparatory studies for medicine) and graduated from the Dakar Medical School. Senghor was one of the rare Africans to graduate from the *lycée* of Dakar. The *lycée* was one of the two secondary schools in Senegal offering the metropolitan curriculum and was generally reserved for the children of French settlers and *métis*. Senghor then went on scholarship to the *Lycée* Louis-le-Grand and the University of Paris, from which another prominent Senegalese, Lamine Guèye, had previously received a doctorate in jurisprudence.

Senghor's early education took place in Catholic mission schools, references to which have been made earlier in this essay. Between the arrival of the French in Africa and the anticlerical legislation in France between 1901 and 1904, which culminated in the separation of Church and state there in 1905, the government left education largely to the clergy and to mission schools. In the communes of Senegal it contracted with the *Frères de Ploërmel* to teach in the public schools. There and elsewhere throughout what became West and Equatorial Africa, it subsidized the educational efforts of religious societies and congregations in a variety of ways.[8] The officials of the July Monarchy and the Second Empire who handled colonial affairs thought that the moral basis of Christianity would help to tie the populations more closely to France. But on the whole they left the missionaries free to pursue their own goals without state control.

The chief purpose of missionary education was the formation of Christians. To achieve this goal, the mission schools sought to prepare an indigenous clergy, catechists, and schoolteachers. Because they were seeking to plant the Church in African soil, to introduce Christianity into African societies, and therefore to transform them to whatever degree and in whatever ways necessary for Christianization, they began to learn indigenous languages and to use them as the medium of instruction.

Thus in Gabon, where American Protestants and French Roman Catholics opened schools in the early 1840s, the curriculum involved instruction mainly in religion, the three R's, and the practical arts with some geography, history, music, and drawing. The missionaries taught their own national languages, either English or French, in all grades, and the best pupils in the Catholic boys' schools studied Latin. But the main instructional medium was Mpongwe in the Estuary Region and other indigenous languages elsewhere.

Increasing levels of French nationalism during the 1880s led to measures to restrict the activities of non-French missionaries and to ensure that French missionaries promoted loyalty to France through increased teaching of French language and culture. In 1883 a ministerial decree required the schools of Gabon to devote half of their time to teaching French and to use only that language in instruction. The Americans turned to the Evangelical Mission Society of Paris for teachers, and between 1892 and 1913 turned over their entire field to the French Protestants. After 1911, the mission schools of Gabon were required to follow the same curriculum as the state schools but were allowed to teach religion in addition to using indigenous languages.

Instruction in such local languages as Serere continued in rural Senegal until 1914. At that time the government of French West Africa required mission schools to teach the official programs, which were exclusively in French, but permitted the teaching of religion in African languages. Earlier during the 1880s and 1890s local French officials in Guinea and Dahomey had eliminated instruction in English and Portuguese, for which they insisted French had to be substituted. They also had barred the entrance of any more English-language missionaries. By all of these various measures the Third Republic determined that the private schools were to promote more directly the same goals as the public schools.

By the early 1880s France was ceasing to give general aid to missionaries but was directly assisting the schools and hospitals of the societies and congregations. In the wake of the French legislation forbidding members of religious congregations to teach, the government in 1903 replaced religious with lay teachers in the state schools of West Africa.[9] It cut off support to mission schools there entirely. In Equatorial Africa the government greatly diminished the level of support to mission schools while establishing the first public schools in Libreville and other towns in 1907 and after. After World War I, in both federations tiny subsidies were given on the basis of the numbers of private school teachers holding official diplomas and of pupils passing the official examinations for certificates.

In these circumstances by 1935 over 80 percent of the children in West Africa were attending public schools while in Equatorial Africa the missions continued to educate the majority of the children. In Cameroon and Togo, where missions had been very active even before and during the German colonial period, roughly half of those in official programs were enrolled in mission schools. Thus in 1935 mission schools taught 9,458 children in West Africa, 9,300 in Equatorial Africa, 6,610 in Cameroon, and 4,974 in Togo (1937).[10] Given the absence of public education beyond the sixth grade in all of French Equatorial Africa until 1935, it is not surprising that quite a number of the Fourth Republic politicians had received their secondary education in the minor seminary and that two of the four heads of government under the *loi-cadre* reforms (implemented in April 1957) were Catholic priests, Fulbert Youlou in the Congo and Barthélémy Boganda in Oubangui-Chari (today's Central African Republic).

The extent of missionary involvement in education was one of the few remaining differences between West and Equatorial Africa in the twentieth century. For as a result of the late-nineteenth-century expansion and the subsequent organization of a separate colonial ministry in 1894, greater centralization in the formulation and execution of policy was taking place. A single department within the Ministry of Colonies handled the affairs of French West Africa and French Equatorial Africa and, after 1919, the mandates of Cameroon and Togo. This organization may have reflected a desire for greater uniformity; in any case it led to consideration of all the colonies of Black Africa as a unit and of Equatorial Africa as a less advanced version of West Africa.

Thus educational models first developed for West Africa in 1903 and 1924 were subsequently extended to Equatorial Africa in 1911 and 1925, and thereafter to the mandates of Cameroon and Togo. In particular, the system of levels of schools organized in West Africa by Governor-General Ernest Roume in 1903 and reorganized by Governor-General Jules Brévié in 1924 was generalized throughout the other territories. At the base of this system were village schools with two to four grades. They were supposed to train the literate intermediaries needed by the local administrators to interpret to the masses. The regional schools, in theory one in every *région* (also called *département*, *circonscription* and *cercle* in different periods and places), had an additional two grades that led to the elementary school diploma. Their graduates could become the clerks of the administration and commerce and monitors in the village schools. When the e.p.s. (grades seven and eight and sometimes nine) were opened in the capitals of the West African territories, at Yaoundé, and at Brazzaville, they prepared the more specialized administrative employees such as printers, telegraph and radio operators, nurses, medical assistants, sanitary inspectors, and teachers for the regional schools. In Senegal were located the institutions for training the teachers of the e.p.s.'s, African doctors, veterinarians—in other words, the most highly educated subordinates of the colonial administration.

By the time of World War I French policy intended that the schools should propagate the French language and culture among as many children as possible while identifying the most gifted for training as employees of the administration and commerce. The French were anxious that the schools produce only the number of graduates that could be gainfully employed. They wished to avoid the creation of a liberally educated intelligentsia that might become the focus for anti-colonialist dissatisfaction. Thus they encouraged the missions to limit their post-primary efforts to seminaries and Bible schools and discouraged them from opening general secondary schools. The French government sought above all to prepare practically trained primary school graduates who would serve them as auxiliaries and as intermediaries with the traditionally oriented African masses.

France had to adjust this policy only slightly to meet the requirements of the two mandates acquired from Germany in the course of World War I. Articles in the mandate agreements for Cameroon and Togo gave missionaries from states who were members of the League of Nations the right to open schools; this right was to be restricted only by the requirements of maintaining public order and of good administration. France arranged for French missionaries to replace German and German-speaking ones. But it permitted the American Presbyterians, who had entered Cameroon even before the arrival of the Germans, to remain. The Presbyterians made their presence more welcome by training their personnel in the French language and by operating schools with the official programs. (They also ran catechetical schools where religion, the three R's, and often some French were taught.) The Mandatory Power continued the German policy of leaving the bulk of primary education in mission hands but gave small subsidies on the same terms as in West and Equatorial Africa for their official programs. In 1937 4.5 percent of Cameroon's budget went for education, of which 4.4 percent went to the missions (thus 0.198 percent or one-fifth of 1 percent of the total budget). In the same year missions in Togo received 8.5 percent of the education budget. In 1934 French West Africa devoted 4.03 percent of its operating budget to education (this does not include expenditures for school construction).[11] It is clear that the mission efforts in the two mandates made possible the much greater percentages in school there.

The primary schools in French West Africa employed only a handful of European instructors, so that African monitors provided most of the instruction. The level in the village schools was extremely low, for a majority of the monitors held only the elementary school diploma and had little if any pedagogical training. Many of the teachers of West Africa, Cameroon, and Togo in the regional schools had completed the e.p.s. and nearly all those in the Ponty, medical, and veterinary schools were professionally trained European educators.

The diplomas granted by all of the African schools were local ones, without standing in France, and therefore could not secure entrance to metropolitan institutions. Only the urban primary schools found in most colonies and the two secondary schools of Senegal followed the metropolitan curriculum and therefore gave access to further secondary or to higher education in France. Even then, the *brevet de capacité coloniale* awarded by the *lycées* of Dakar and Saint-Louis was treated as the equivalent of the *baccalauréat* and not as identical.

Given these circumstances under which only the teaching of the metropolitan curriculum by instructors certified according to European standards led to the diplomas which gave access to higher education and in turn led to senior positions in the civil service, is it surprising to find the African representatives to the French Parliament in 1945-1946 demanding generalization of the metropolitan curriculum overseas? They would reject any proposals for adapted curricula leading to equivalent diplomas rather than to identical ones as a possible perpetuation of their inferior and subordinate status. On the basis of their experience with the colonial educational system, equality with Europeans could come only from identical curricula and diplomas. Reflecting these pressures, statements from the Ministry of Overseas France thereafter would explain any departure from metropolitan norms as a temporary means of permitting the assimilation so much desired by the educated elite rather than of keeping Africans different and distinctive.

Faced with the decolonizing trends of World War II but unwilling to relinquish control of its African colonies at any time in the foreseeable future, France reverted to the nineteenth-century formulas of assimilation as a means of holding on to its possessions while offering them the possibility of advancement.[12] Thus the countries of French West Africa and French Equatorial Africa became overseas territories within the Fourth French Republic. Cameroon and Togo, though trusteeship territories outside the Republic, were to be treated essentially the same as the territories of the two federations.

To promote economic and social advancement of its African possessions and to show that assimilation was not just a slogan, France in 1946 undertook a Ten-Year Plan for the Modernization of the Overseas Territories, including Cameroon and Togoland. The official plan for implementing its educational goals, which was formulated two years later, contained the principles and programs for postwar educational development in Black Africa. The Education Plan called for the adaptation of instruction to the economic activity of each territory. It provided for the development of education at all levels with approximately 37 percent of the total expenditure for primary education, 28 percent for technical, 23 percent for secondary, and 12 percent for higher education. France would fund the construction and equipment of new schools, as well as contribute to operating expenses at all but the primary level, through grants and long-term, low-interest loans. African territories would be required to appropriate a minimum of 15 percent of their budgets to pay operating expenses and ultimately all costs at the primary level.[13]

The plan aimed at doubling school enrollments in five years and tripling them in ten years so that West Africa, Equatorial Africa, and Togo would have 50 percent of their children in school and Cameroon 80 percent. These goals were not completely realized, but large gains were made. (For example, in 1957-1958 West Africa had 381,753 primary pupils and 19,436 secondary and technical; Equatorial Africa had 197,109 primary and 4,529 secondary and technical; Cameroon had 293,977 primary pupils and 6,645 secondary and technical; Togo had 70,618 primary pupils and 2,033 secondary and technical.)[14] The Ten-Year Plan was implemented in two stages, which ultimately lasted twelve years. Between 1947 and 1954 the plan concentrated upon the expansion of secondary and technical education in order to train primary teachers and technicians. Expansion of teacher training in turn was to make possible the goal of mass primary education during the latter part of the 1950s. Approximately $4 million of French public funds were expended between 1949 and 1950 for education and health through the *Fonds d'Investissement pour le Développement Economique et Social des Territoires d'Outre-Mer* (FIDES). FIDES funded the construction of several thousand state primary schools and one hundred secondary schools. It paid 50 percent of the cost of constructing new mission schools. After World War II a much greater percentage of the education budgets of the Equatorial countries and Cameroon went to the private schools than previously (in Cameroon 2 percent in 1942 and 30 percent in 1951), which allowed their post-war expansion at a rate almost as great as the state schools.

The policy of assimilation led to the introduction of the metropolitan curriculum into the schools of French Africa. Consequently the language of instruction continued to be French, and at least half of the program in the primary school was devoted to the French language and culture. As before the war, some materials on African geography and French colonial history in Africa were included.

Despite considerable efforts to give new primary teachers a tenth grade education (*brevet élémentaire*), including some training in pedagogy, and to upgrade the skills of existing teachers, the level of the primary teachers remained low. Thus in 1957-1958 only 30 percent of the primary teachers in French Equatorial Africa held a tenth grade diploma, and only 7 percent had graduated from teacher training courses. The elementary classes tended to be crowded. Seventy-five pupils were not unusual. Books and teaching materials were sparse. To make matters worse, at the time of the most rapid expansion (1957-1960), which was promoted by the governments installed under the *loi-cadre* reforms, some of the best teachers left the classroom for positions in government and higher administration. Thus much of the progress achieved during the previous decade in raising the level of the teachers was wiped out.

In 1957-1958 60 percent of the primary pupils in the federation of French Equatorial Africa lived in Gabon and Congo, which had only 25 percent of the federation's population. In that year most of the pupils were found in the first three grades, and only 20,000 persons had obtained the elementary school diploma. The percentage of girls in primary schools had risen from 7 percent in 1945-1946 to 22 percent. But many obstacles to the education of women persisted.

Beginning in 1945 the French opened *lycées* in every African territory with the long courses of seven years and *collèges* with the short courses of four years. By 1957-1958 there were one hundred secondary schools. The examinations were supervised by the University of Bordeaux, and the diplomas were valid both locally and in France.

Conditions in the secondary schools were considerably better than in the primary schools, and standards were higher. Most of the teachers were French and held diplomas. The numbers of persons completing the elementary school diploma (the *certificat d'études primaires*), the tenth grade diplomas (the *brevet élémentaire*, which was a terminal diploma, and *brevet d'études du premier cycle*, which involved the study of a second European language and led to further secondary studies), and the two parts of the *baccalauréat* (the first after the twelfth grade and the second after the thirteenth or final grade) between 1950 and 1958 are as follows:

Some of these pupils were Europeans, but the numbers of Africans who earned

	C.E.P.	B.E./ B.E.P.C.	Bac I	Bac II
French West Africa	62,156	7,391	2,623	1,841
French Equatorial Africa	16,194	1,228	298	162
Cameroon	21,680	2,199	454	267
Togoland	9,723	604	154	102

secondary diplomas in France probably equalled the number of European graduates.[15]

In 1946 the French government began to grant scholarships for French universities and for secondary programs not available in Africa, but necessary for entrance to certain university programs. By the end of the Fourth Republic several hundred Africans were holding scholarships in French institutions and possibly an equal number were enrolled without such assistance.[16]

The consequences of sending Africans to France for long periods of study were not entirely foreseen. The Africans were able to enjoy the advantages of life as a student in the metropole. They could obtain an education identical to that which a European received. Grouped together in one or two residences, such as the *Maison de la France d'Outre-Mer* at the Cité Universitaire in Paris, they established contact with students from their own countries and other lands within the French Union. They acquired a new awareness of themselves as Senegalese, Cameroonians, or Congolese and as Africans, Blacks, and inhabitants of the Third World. They became part of an international francophone elite that was frequently Marxist, anti-colonialist, and critical of African politicians in their home countries.

A score of them would write novels and poems dealing with the colonial situation while students in France. They would select French literary forms to express their feelings about the colonial regime. Not many students in France became so alienated from their traditional surroundings that they did not wish to return home. But most of them experienced a cultural shock upon reentry after years of study abroad. As they adjusted, they developed a self-awareness that involved ambivalent attitudes toward both French and African culture.

Most of the first generation of graduates of French institutions, especially those who returned between self-government in April 1957 and independence in 1960, found Africans locally educated prior to 1945 holding the key positions in politics and government not occupied by Frenchmen. There would be a very real problem in assigning meaningful roles to the returning graduates in regimes that had evolved in their absence and in finding jobs for students who had not finished their programs.

In Africa itself university-level programs leading to the *licence* were introduced at Dakar in law and economics, the humanities, and the sciences in 1950 under the supervision of the Universities of Paris and Bordeaux. A university-level medical school opened in November of that year with fourteen students. These programs were transformed into the University of Dakar in 1957. At that time nearly half of the students were French, and most Africans still preferred to go to France for higher education. In 1959, despite the dissolution of the federation of French Equatorial Africa, France opened the Center for Higher Education at Brazzaville to upgrade the educational level of civil servants from the four states and to provide the first year of university courses in the same fields as at Dakar.

The French policy for promoting advancement through the extension of the metropolitan system overseas and the goals of primary education for the masses and secondary and higher education for an elite seems to have been generally accepted by the African representatives in the French Parliament and in the territorial assemblies during the late 1940s. The implementation of this policy was influenced in important ways by the Africans in the various territorial assemblies. The proceedings of Cameroon's Territorial Assembly, which I have read, show that the Cameroonians sought equality with Frenchmen by limiting the adaptation of metropolitan programs by insisting upon higher education for Cameroonian *bacheliers* in France and not in French West Africa as proposed by the French administration. They resisted the attempts of the administration to channel students into the fields most needed by the territory. They thereby contributed to the creation of too many graduates in literature and law and not enough in scientific and technical fields. The Cameroonian Assembly, like those in French Equatorial Africa, opposed the importation of French Church-state controversies that might lessen the involvement of the missions in educational expansion and thereby decrease the educational opportunities so much desired by their electors.

The expansion of enrollments in a French-derived system provided an equality of opportunity, especially in the coastal countries, that had not existed before World War II. While it offered the possibility of individual promotion to a tiny handful, it educated neither efficiently nor effectively the great mass of individuals who attended only the first one to three elementary grades in crowded classes taught by monitors. At the top of the educational pyramid, it produced an elite that could communicate effectively with elites in other francophone countries. Many of them would enter government service. The secondary level in most coastal countries produced enough graduates to staff the lower echelons of the administration.

But by the time of independence appropriate employment could no longer be found for the thousands of *brevetés* and *bacheliers*, much less for those who had failed the examinations or dropped out of their courses. The drama *Le Chômeur* (1961) by Stanislas Awona treats the plight of a talented but unemployed young Cameroonian with a secondary education that has equipped him only for further education.[17] He exemplifies the *lumpen-bourgeoisie* of many thousands of persons living in the administrative centers and hoping to secure government employment or further education which the educational expansion brought into being. These youths had their counterparts among those who attended primary school, generally away from home, and who did not want to return to their villages. This disoriented mass stayed on in the larger towns, unemployed or underemployed, often aided by kinsmen or friends who were working. Thus France in the era of decolonization failed to devise an educational policy that would create the elites needed by modern nations and yet prepare the masses for a productive life in the countryside.

At independence French Africa's leaders found an educational system that was so extensively developed it could only be modified but not basically changed. Efforts to adapt education better to the needs of independent nations seeking to promote unity and development would have to take place within the framework of the French-derived system and, as it turned out, with the aid of France.

NOTES

1. I wish to thank the Marquette University Graduate School for support of my research on education in the Equatorial states. I am grateful to Peggy Sabatier for reading the manuscript and for allowing me to read the completed portions of her dissertation on the William Ponty School and its graduates.

2. These historial periods are defined primarily in political terms, which should remind us that the development of education is best examined within the larger context of colonial rule. The brevity of this essay makes possible only occasional references to the global context in which political, strategic, and economic factors have influenced educational policy and practice.

3. My essay has not dealt with technical education or with the relationship of education to economic development because of the limitations of time. I have omitted from consideration Madagascar and French Somaliland, where French policies were similar but different enough to lengthen the essay and possibly render it even more sketchy.

4. Gouvernement-Général de L'Afrique Equatoriale Française, *Historique et Organisation générale de l'Enseignement en A.E.F.* (Paris, 1931), pp. 7-9; Lord Hailey, *An African Survey* (London, 1938), p. 1260; Denise Bouche, *L'Enseignement dans les Territoires Français de l'Afrique Occidentale de 1817 à 1920* (Paris, 1975), 1: 422-423.

5. Hailey, *African Survey*, pp. 108, 1261, 1268.

6. *Rapport annuel adressé par le gouvernement français au conseil de la Société des Nations sur l'administration sous mandat du territoire du Togo pour l'année 1938* (Paris, 1939), p. 111; Claude Marchand, "L'Enseignement au Cameroun sous le Mandat Français (1921-1939)" (Thèse de Maitrise es Arts en Histoire, Université Laval, 1970), p. 69; W. Bryant Mumford and G. St. J. Orde-Brown, *Africans Learn To Be French* (London, 1935), p. 163.

7. Figures on Ponty graduates come from the dissertation of Peggy Sabatier; Hailey, *African Survey*, p. 1185.

8. Among the Catholic groups receiving aid during the nineteenth century were the Sisters of St. Joseph of Cluny in Senegal and the Congo; the Immaculate Conception Sisters of Castres in Senegal and Gabon; the Holy Ghost Fathers in Senegal, Guinea, Gabon, and the Congo; the Society of African Missions (Pères de Lyon) in Dahomey and the Ivory Coast; and the White Fathers in the Sudan.

9. Neither the anti-clerical measures nor the separation of Church and state were actually promulgated in the African territories. But various aspects of them were nevertheless applied there, especially in French West Africa.

10. Hailey, *African Survey*, pp. 1261, 1265.

11. Marchand, "L'Enseignement," pp. 43-47; Mumford and Orde-Brown, *Africans Learn*, p. 168; Hailey, *African Survey*, p. 1265.

12. While there have always been elements of assimilation in French educational policy and practice, it was only after 1945 that France implemented such a policy on a meaningful scale. The work of Mumford and Orde-Brown, *Africans Learn To Be French* (1935), contributed to the misconception that French policy prior to 1945 was basically assimilation also. Separate studies by Timothy Weiskel and Denise Bouche on French West Africa have shown the true configurations of French policy in earlier periods.

13. The text of the Plan of 1948 in English translation is found in David G. Scanlon, ed., *Traditions of African Education* (New York, 1964), pp. 132-140.

14. Ministry of Overseas France, *Enseignement Outre-Mer*, 10 vols. (Paris, Ministry of Overseas France, 1958), vol. 10.

15. Ministry of Overseas France, *Enseignement Outre-Mer*, 10 vols. (Paris, Ministry of Overseas France, 1950-1958).

16. The French had granted small numbers of scholarships in earlier periods, especially in Senegal, but the post-1945 program extended to all territories and involved many hundreds of students.

17. Stanislas Awona, *Le Chômeur* (Yaoundé, 1968); for a critique of Cameroonian writers, see David E. Gardinier, "Playwrights and Novelists of Post-Colonial Cameroun," *Africa Report* 9 (December 1964): 13-16.

A. Y. YANSANÉ

19

The Impact of France on Education in West Africa

Education is primarily a means by which a society transmits its knowledge, values, and wisdom to young people just entering society. Ideally, education is a socialization process which fosters intellectual and emotional growth of both parents and children to perpetuate the society and its values. In the broader sense education implies all the aspects of personal development and is therefore a part and parcel of the multi-dimensional process of social change. Education so defined allows the educated subject to be versatile. He or she has self-confidence and is theoretically able to move effectively in a variety of classes and cultural environments while contributing positively and productively to the welfare of these various classes and cultures. The educated subject is autonomous, yet able to identify those aspects of social change which advance the collective welfare. Education so conceived as a social and political phenomenon as well as an intellectual and personal one is something that the French institutions of middle and higher learning did not know how to dispense to French nationals, much less to colonized people.

Today there are three distinct strands of education in West Africa: traditional, Christian, and European systems of education.

CHARACTERISTICS OF PRECOLONIAL EDUCATION

Precolonial education in West Africa was mostly based on oral tradition whereby cultural and technical knowledge was transmitted from elders and men of experience to young people.

At between ten and twenty years of age, depending upon the ethnicity, both boys and girls belonging to the same age group or professional organization take a retreat in the forest under the guidance of an old man or an old lady, somehow a person of experience and unusual technical and cultural knowledge. In this absolute solitude, which is not to be disturbed for days or weeks (varying according to groups), the elders teach the young folks how to adapt themselves to the forest mysteries, how to appreciate beauty of nature, how to gain insight into human problems; they are also introduced to the theoretical notions on reproduction, the spiritual life which animates many physical appearances; they are taught how to cultivate bravery to insure self-control; they are taught some ritual songs and a language code known only to those who have entered and finished society.

This education is initiatory. The initiates are taught also of the universal kinship relations between parents and children. Young persons learn of their living experience, of the solidarity links which hold together a family made of members serving the interest of all, and a family extended through time and space to include dead ancestors, living beings, and coming generations. Arbitration in such a family is based on collective wisdom carried through invocation or quotation of tales, proverbs, songs, and mythical accounts. This traditional education perpetuates a fundamental faith in a transcendental force upon which humankind draws its origins and a sense of vital solidarity or unity. This solidarity is evidenced by the existence of moral and social virtues such as ancestor worship, veneration of elders, sense of warm hospitality, spirit of tolerance, and a vital union between the spiritual and real forces.

Before the introduction of the formal Western educational systems, traditional educational models coexisted in some areas along with Islamic education.[1] This coexistence was due to the often easy and healthy amalgamation of many traditional African customs and mores to the Islamic Arabic structures. The new syncretic institutions which resulted did not present any peculiar threat to indigenous substructures.[2] So Islamic educational models were described by Blyden in the following terms:

We have met ulemas, or learned men, who could reproduce from memory any chapter of the Koran, with its vowels and dots, and other grammatical marks. The boys under their instruction are kept at the study of the books for years. First they are taught the letters and vowel marks, then they are taught to read the text, without receiving any insight into its meaning. When they can read fluently, they are taught the meaning of the words which they commit to memory; after which they are instructed in what they call the "Jalaleyn", a running commentary on the Koran. While learning the Jalaleyn, they have side studies assigned them in Arabic manuscripts containing the mystical traditions, the acts of Mohamed, the duties of fasting, prayer, alms, corporal purification, etc. Young men who intend to be enrolled among the ulemas take up history & chronology, on which they have some fragmentary manuscripts.[3]

The objectives of these traditional and Islamic models of education were quite different from those of the colonial model. Colonial education was intended to increase production of cheap raw materials for export to the metropole and therefore tantamount to the objectives of this education was an urgent need to improve economic, administrative, and military efficiency of the established governmental institutions and the mercantile societies. Through this educational model, a few docile and subservient civil servants, cadres, and clerks were trained to be utilized as instruments to carry to the majority of the colonized people the order and directives of the colonial machinery of control, of oppression and exploitation. Much precaution was taken to prevent the educated subjects from turning into instruments of subversion against colonialism.[4]

The encounter of the traditional African society with the Western European world through colonialism and the slave trade brought changes in Africa which sometimes turned into crises of depopulation, socio-politico-economic disturbances which led to the transformation of the traditional systems of government administration, religion, culture, and education.

The African slave trade, conquest, settlement, occupation, and exploitation on the one hand, and colonialism, the twentieth-century technological progress on the other, brought massive changes in African values and value systems. The transitions that resulted, once begun, continued until they were checked by meaningful independence, that is, that which attempted to generate an indigenous adaptation to the knowledge and the pressures of the modern world. This was the case of the former British Gold Coast becoming independent Ghana in 1957, the case of the former French Guinea becoming the independent Republic of Guinea in 1958, and also the case of UN trustee territory of Tanganyika becoming independent Tanzania in 1963. The percolation or osmosis effect of these changes is felt everywhere by people submitted to a similar colonial or quasi-colonial experience, particularly that of people of African descent living in the Black Diaspora.

COLONIALISM AND ITS EDUCATIONAL MODEL

Colonialism in Africa was motivated by national interest prestige considerations of the then-existing powerful European nations to further their commercial necessity of finding new markets for their manufactured products, discovering new sources of cheap raw materials, and finding other environments where their people could find livelihood in production, trade, and investment. In this typical colonial setting, "native" labor and wages were lower than those prevailing in the metropolitan market, and the appropriations of goods and prices were lower than those of the free-market situation because of a *dirigiste* economic situation. More specifically, colonialism was the extension of power by one country over a distant territory (colony) or people. Sometimes the colonizing country needed a new land for its people (settlers). Often the new colony had minerals and other natural resources that the colonizing country needed. Most areas that became colonies were not as highly developed as the colonizing country. The standards of living measured in modern concepts such as gross national product (GNP) were reportedly low compared to those of the colonizing country. The systems of government and administration and social, cultural, and economic institutions were taken over by the colonial administration, so that the colonized people were denied self-determination.

With increased trade and the advent of the Industrial Revolution, colonialism led to imperialism according to Hobson's theory of European underconsumption and Lenin's doctrine of Western capitalist expansion.

Empire ideally means the extended family of another country and colonial sons in remote areas under the rule of the metropolitan government. But this union seemed almost "unnatural, almost improper, like some extramarital responsibility incurred in youth," remarked Ronald Robinson and others in *Africa and the Victorians: The Climax of Imperialism*.[5] As a result of European colonialism and imperialism, a systematic ideology of dominance by Europeans over African nations was devised. Restrictions[6] were imposed directly and indirectly upon Africa and its peoples to develop their own economic, political, cultural, and educational potential. These restrictions permeated simultaneously all the aspects of colonial life to the point where it became almost impossible to conceptually separate socioeconomic, political, and military developments from educational and cultural fields because they became so interlinked.

An attempt is now made to examine the impact of France on education in the West African colonies. Colonial education was primarily given by the missionaries on behalf of the French colonial administration until the turn of the century.[7] Missionaries managed the larger schools in Saint-Louis, Dakar, and Gorée in Senegal and also in former French Soudan (today's Mali), Guinea, Ivory Coast, and Dahomey (Benin).

The number of students receiving such a missionary education was limited by the number of available qualified teachers. The teachers were often recruited on the basis of services rendered to the colonial administration instead of accredited credentials which most lacked.[8] These missionary schools were granted large subsidies by the colonial administration, yet their achievements were meager.[9] After the turn of the century missionary schools which had been semi-public became private institutions.

In 1903 new legislation limiting the activities of the missionaries, was adopted, and the colonial government of the newly created Federation of French West Africa established a public educational system which survived up to the 1960s.[10] Faidherbe introduced the rudiments of this public educational system in Saint-Louis by 1854.[11] Later reforms of this public education created the primary cycle of studies (in village, regional, and urban schools), the professional schools, the urban superior primary schools, and the normal school in Saint-Louis to train the civil servants of the Federation of French West Africa.[12]

CHRISTIANITY AND THE CHRISTIAN APPROACH TO EDUCATION IN WEST AFRICA

Christianity was related to the power of Europeans to such an extent that becoming Christian was equated to being of the high status and affluence of

Europeans. The African Christians were likely to achieve more material welfare than traditional cult believers and Muslims. Those Christian-baptized Africans were quickly recruited in missionary schools and then enjoyed the benefits of easy-to-pronounce popular Christian names.

Missionaries did make some contributions to the field of education.[13] There were many cases where colonial rulers opposed missionaries reported to be too humanitarian at the expense of colonial administration.[14] For instance, it is believed in many circles that the missionary interest in Africa developed vigorously in the eighteenth and nineteenth centuries, at first as a result of growing concern about the injustices of African slave trade.[15] This belief is very debatable. John Gunther in his popular work, *Inside Africa*, evaluated the roles of the missionaries in the following terms: "A wide furrow has been cut by Christian missionaries, the importance of whose work, particularly in education, has been incalculable."[16] In most cases, missionaries supported colonial and imperial policies at the expense of nationalism, independence, and cultural identity of the neophytes they converted. The Catholic missionaries from France, in particular, considered their church an organ for the dissemination of French culture.[17] They consciously functioned in advance of the militant colonialists to prepare or condition Africans to foreign domination, thereby suppressing the "native" culture without sufficiently acculturating the people into European systems which could have provided them with a valid set of values to insure their natural development. The missionaries did invest in the burgeoning colonial commerce, they supported the development of new industries[18] by foreign traders, and requested protection of metropolitan governments, protection which came through military occupation.[19] The colonial administrators needed to promote men and women who shared their assumptions and prejudices of assimilation. Evangelization was one method that was used. Ram Desai maintains that "missionaries arrived in Africa already despising the African and his way of life."[20] The Europeans had accepted the absurd assumption that their culture and religion were superior to those of any other region. This assumption led to a deplorably superior and condescending attitude on the part of Europeans toward the Africans, an attitude which still prompts such blatantly racist statements as John Gunther's statement, "Christianity is too complex for Africans to absorb easily."[21] A man is violated by denying him his natural culture, by converting him to one's religion through coercion and fraud. The missionary's design to subvert the culture of each African individual was an essential reinforcement for the social and economic subversion which would almost destroy the old African world and bring into existence the "native." Missionaries became perhaps the most subtle purveyors of violence.

It is at this point that a frame of reference of relative cultural comparison approach may be appropriately adopted. Only an appreciation of both cultures involved as having equally valid systems of values and goal orientations can allow one to escape the traps of European prejudices and African resentment.

Christianity was perhaps a vehicle to introduce a new and a more technically advanced, although not necessarily superior culture. While professing noble intentions, Christianity indeed was used as a tool of colonial and imperial governments. While Christian missions emerged at the turn of the century as private institutions, receiving some public funds from colonial governments to carry out some of their important activities such as education, public schools and educational institutions remained under direct control of the colonial administration.

PUBLIC EDUCATION IN FORMER TERRITORIES OF WEST AFRICA

The federal government of French West Africa (*AOF*), created in 1904, established the educational institutions which still exist today. The goals of these educational institutions were aimed at producing assistants, civil servants, interpreters, accountants, health technicians, and nurses as witnessed by the following statement:

We need interpreters to make ourselves understood by the natives; as we need intermediaries, belonging to the native milieu by their origin and to the European milieu by their education in order to have these civilizations understood and adopted by local populations whose hostility to anything foreign is beyond comprehension.[22]

Though colonial educational institutions were founded in Senegal during the nineteenth century and in other West African territories around 1896, one has to await the turn of the century for the creation of colonial educational structures. Elementary education (the first six years) was dispensed in urban and regional schools leading to the Certificate of Primary Elementary Studies. The next level up, superior primary education, was given at the superior primary school (e.p.s.) established in the capital city of each territory. This primary school extension recruited thirty to fifty of the best elementary school graduates of each of the eight territories of *AOF*. The e.p.s. lead to the diploma of superior primary education. This diploma gave access to administrative functions in the civil service. Still another school provided training for the skilled professions.

Special technical education was dispensed in the federal institutions such as *Ecole Normale de Saint-Louis* (later transferred to Gorée, Dakar, and then Sebikotane, *Ecole* William Ponty), in the Medical School of Dakar, in the Veterinary School of Bamako, and in normal schools in Katibougou, Dabou, and Rufisque. These special schools trained civil servants or functionaries, teachers, and medical and veterinary doctors.

Only two secondary institutions existed: the secondary school of Saint-Louis founded in 1847 which became *Lycée* Faidherbe in 1917, and the secondary public and private school of Dakar founded in 1917 which became *Lycée* Van Vollenhoven in 1937. These two secondary institutions granted the *Brevet de Capacité Coloniale*, equivalent to the baccalaureate, insuring admission to any French university. Here only French could be spoken and written and the curriculum taught exalted the glories of the French experience as can be seen in the following objectives of Brévié, a governor-general of *AOF*:

The colonial duty and the political and economic necessities impose to our educational program a double task: first, to form local cadres who are destined to become our auxiliary assistants in all areas, and to insure the ascension of an elite carefully selected; second, to educate masses in order to make us closer and to transform their life style.[23]

On the political level, we need to make it known to the natives our efforts and our intentions to tie them to their milieu, to the French life. On the economic level, we must prepare the producers and consumers of tomorrow.[24]

The content of our programs is not a simple pedagogic matter. The students are a means of the native policy.[25]

Governor-General Roume put emphasis on the same type of French indoctrination in articulating the goals of the 1924 education reform in *AOF*:

All the teaching of history and geography must tend to show that France is a wealthy, powerful nation capable of making herself respected but at the same time great by the nobility of her sentiments, generosity and which has never backed down in front of sacrifices of men and money to deliver peoples enslaved or to provide savage populations with peace and civilization benefits.[26]

From 1945 to 1960, elementary and secondary education in *AOF* was French-centered. Elementary education was mostly concerned with the three R's (reading, writing, and arithmetic). Though slight attempts were made to adapt the teaching of the three R's to local conditions, the most popular manuals still contained reports of colonial explorers and missionaries[27] which abounded in whimsical and prejudiced statements about Africans' primitive ancestors and the exaggerated deeds of the French civilizing missions. The story of the Africans' past was contrasted with their less developed situation in today's modern standards. This situation was tremendously influenced by French benevolence, it was believed. Colonial invasions, conquests, and settlements by what they called "representatives of white race," that is, Semites, Hamites, Moors, Berbers and Portuguese, Spanish, French, British, and Germans, and the mercantilist and commercial societies, were being thus described to arouse Africans' admiration while African heroes of national "resistance" efforts such as El Hadj Omar, Samory Touré, and Béhanzin were almost always referred to as leaders of chaos and decadence for whom one could unconsciously develop contempt. Questions on those "explorers" such as René Caillé, Faidherbe, Galliéni, Marchand, and Barthe, who subdued the African warriors of resistance, were very often asked on the examination for the certificate of primary elementary studies (sixth grade).

Secondary education at the *Lycée* Van Vollenhoven (seventh to thirteenth grade) was by far the most ethnocentric. The enrollment in this institution was mainly White European. African enrollment was minimal until 1960. The curricula in history, geography, literature, and philosophy emphasized respectively the study of French and Western heroes in French history, of French and European soils in geography, and of French and Western value systems based on Cartesianism.

Western history was extensively covered in each grade from seven to thirteen. Abundant details were given on world history, especially European prehistory, eighteenth- and nineteenth-century mercantilism, and the Industrial Revolution. African history was only rarely presented, and then it was sketched as an extension of Western conquest.

Geography of the world, of the great mountains, of France, of Europe, of the Great Powers of the Western world was substantially covered in each grade of the *lycée*. For example, a *lycée* graduate who must know the hydrography of Europe and the Great Powers did not necessarily know about the geographic features of the Senegal and Niger rivers, which drain West Africa, nor need the graduate know of the former British and Portuguese colonies of Africa.

Literature and philosophy courses covered all the classics of Western thought from Plato and Socrates to Jean Paul Sartre and the existentialists. Rationalism, Cartesianism, positivism, and behaviorism were dealt with in depth. There was no mention of African literature, African philosophical beliefs, or African humanism. The traditional West African arts and folklore, dance and music were explored only in cases where students decided to provide their own amateur theatrical sketches to campus audiences.

The colonial language was studied in all its variations from the Middle Ages to the contemporary form. All the Classical writers and poets of the past ten centuries were carefully studied. Other modern languages such as English, Spanish, German, Russian, and Arabic were taught side by side with Classical Greek and Latin. Degrees sanctioning these studies were granted through written and oral examinations mailed from the Academy of Bordeaux or Paris. Generally, only one-quarter to one-third of the candidates were successful in their twelfth grade examinations given at the *lycée*.

After World War II, the education policy was aimed at assimilating Africans in order to make them equals of the French citizens. But because of the elitist orientation of the curricula and the extremely competitive nature of the examinations, the educable or potential student population (those of school age) was still very limited. For example, 4 percent of the educable *AOF* population were attending school in 1947, 10 percent in 1957, and less than 10 percent in 1967. In 1967 out of 10,000 educable children, 970 were attending all schools, 40 in secondary schools, and 5 in liberal and technical colleges.[28]

These data reflect the poor social and economic conditions of the colonized people who live in the margin of the colonial administrative institutions and the commercial and mercantile societies. It was not in the interest of colonialism to provide mass education. The colonial economy was able to absorb only a few Africans who would become the effective instruments of colonial rule once they were provided with the necessary skills. Extreme caution was exercised in the selection procedure to screen the most zealous and diligent agents of colonialism. Yet the expanding demand for more raw materials to be exported to the metropole, for more overseas consumers of the surplus manufacture, coupled with the demand for more investment in capital, all called for an increasing number of African trainees. Also by turning the colonies into dumping grounds for European middle-class workers, the demand for semi-skilled labor and clerks was greater. By increasing the quality of education, colonial institutions ran the risk of promoting African skilled labor, who would bargain for higher wages and would soon be more and more conscious of the oppressive nature of colonialism. Therein lay the dilemma of colonial education. Though it was not in the interest of colonial exploitation to educate well many Africans, the demand for better education, technical training, and Africanization of the civil service mounted so fast before and after World War II that the colonial administration had to make concessions. Yet in the late 1950s just before constitutional independence of the West African states, education was still limited, held in control by the colonial administration, and valued by Africans as a competitive privilege, consonant with colonial elitist arrogance so that the educated subjects could be kept loyal to the colonial overlords.

Education in the French colonies of West Africa needed to be and indeed was responsive to general colonial and imperial policies. The role of French colonial education in its colonies and the assumed goals of progress, modernization, and development were closely linked with the creation of docile and usually passive civil servants, the *évolués*,[29] who were urban administrative elites committed to furthering the colonial interests. Yet this education was to be regulated. Africans endowed with French education were able to secure high-paying positions and prestige and were employed by such status institutions as public schools, missionary schools, church, commercial enterprises, government, and professional occupations. French education very soon became a major source of Western European superiority. It is easy to see (as it is argued in the latter part of this essay) why these European ideas of individual success through competition, of education, and of science and technology weakened African collective religious and cultural belief systems by affecting the individual role in the extended family context. It is also clear why traditional pre-colonial methods of education could not survive when the colonial approach, which considered the student as an instrument of the native policy, was implemented.[30] It can be understood that such an educational policy led to diverse reactions from African masses, their leaders, and the African intellectuals in terms of conflict of cultural values and social attitudes.

EFFECTS AND INCIDENCE OF FRENCH EDUCATION IN WEST AFRICA: REACTIONS OF AFRICANS

The education controlled by the colonial government was centered mostly around the acquisition of degrees and diplomas and other prerequisites linked to the needs of colonial and imperial societies. It is not surprising that the structures of these formalized educational systems imported from Bordeaux or Paris were not necessarily geared to the personnel needs of the present sovereign African nations and states. And they are even less valuable for the rural societies. The education by foreign examination and testing systems required individual competitiveness, intellectual arrogance, and general aloofness of the educated subjects from the mainstream of African societies. The belief in inequality of people became the concomitant corollary of such an elitist formation. Through this institution the personnel needs of the colonial administration were satisfied, and many educated Africans who enjoyed high status positions became the instruments of the colonial rulers. Unconsciously many of the African civil servants reacted like assimilated subjects. "Nini" of Saint-Louis (former capital of Senegal), a Black woman described in Frantz Fanon's *Black Skin and White Mask*,[31] wishes to pass for White inwardly for herself and, hopefully, outwardly in any offspring arising from an alliance with a White lover. Torn between her blackness and her intentions to "pass" for White, she is unable to reconcile herself to reality and remains in a fixed dilemma of psychological alienation. For the same reasons, Cheikh Hamidou Kane's *Ambiguous Adventure*[32] presents to us Samba Diallo the *evolué* haunted by a conflict between the spiritual inclinations of his traditional and Islamic education on one side and his Western materialistic molding on the other. The author accurately observes his hero wondering whether the gains brought by Western contact can balance the shortcomings of the new values. Similarly, Yambo Ouologuem's *Bound to Violence*[33] portrays Raymond Spartacus Kassoumi, a highly educated African, whose dilemma stems from the initial momentum of his violent origin and which overshadowed that which was imposed by his French education.[34] In all these three examples, the educated subject's spiritual return to the African values and belief systems is ambivalent, and most often there is some anguish in it.

There also existed in West Africa other personalities, real *agents provocateurs* of African freedom, who struggled ardently to resist assimilation and at the same time transcended the colonial education and Western influences dispensed by the *lycées*[35] or French institutions equivalent to American junior colleges and high schools. They used their education to reflect on the plight of their people and gain more insight on means to produce liberation. Their people have always stood against colonial police brutalities, land seizure, and the poll tax. They have always demanded fair prices for farmers' crops, better education, improved roads, technical training, medical, and maternity care. Those few educated subjects who remained in permanent contact with their people, listening to their people and learning from their people, became the grass-roots leaders. These grass-roots leaders responded to their people by forming a progressive party, the *Rassemblement Démocratique Africain*; they formed trade unions, farmers' cooperatives, and groups of youth and women for emancipation. They enlisted the support of student organizations such as *Union Générale des Etudiants d'Afrique Occidentale* and *Fédération des Etudiants d'Afrique Noire en France*. The trade unions and student unions, conjointly with the *Universités populaires*, developed in the capitals of a few territories educational workshops which spread information on the effects of colonialism and imperialism and the necessity of awakening collective consciousness for national independence.

Marxist and Leninist theories were propagated by the same conscientious militants of labor and student unions, youth councils, and vanguard political parties. They opposed oppression, dehumanization, and depersonalization of their people by any means necessary. Many who had civil service jobs were fired or sent to remote areas to reduce their effectiveness. They adopted a dignified attitude while facing intimidation and harassment by colonial administrators. Fily Dabo Sissoko, Mamadou Konaté, Félix Houphouët-Boigny, Quezzin Coulibaly, Sekou Touré, Robert Um Nyobe, Félix Moumie, and several other heroes of African independence were such grass-roots leaders. They knew the accounts of African veterans of World War I and World War II (when metropolitan France was defeated severely by Nazi Germany) and had learned of the brave deeds of the African soldiers in defense of the ruling country. Many of them realized earlier the impossibility of a French assimilation policy which would negate African national culture.

Other African intellectuals realized they were the equals of French colonizers, and that they did not have to imitate them. They were aware of their own alienation by living in an unreal world wearing Fanon's masks or the veil that W.E.B. Du Bois talks about in "Souls of Black Folk."[36] These men of culture—artists and writers—soon started questioning and sometimes challenging the omnipotence of Western values as the great masses of the people had done before them. These men of culture responded to their people's desires and aspirations by committing themselves to total independence by protesting against the colonial abuses and Western acculturative processes.

It was unfortunate that many of these cultured men utilized the sometimes racist, sometimes confusing substances and the frames of references of Froebenius,[37] Delafosse,[38] de Gobineau,[39] Lévy-Bruhl, Bergson, and Spengler. René Maran in *Batouala* questioned the importance of the civilizing mission of France on colonials; he denounced the abuses of colonialism. The authors of *négritude*, Aimé Césaire[40] and Léopold Senghor,[41] assumed that Western civilization was decadent. *Négritude* became a device to return to one's sources in order to counter the French acculturative processes. As an instrument of that cultural past, it might have borne the hopes of its founders, perhaps truly of any Black people. But today *négritude* is suffering on the horns of a dilemma—on the one hand accused of being too racist and counter-racist, on the other hand of being too surrealistic, "too French" and intellectual, and perhaps too "non-African." Despite the ambiguous and mixed stand of some of these authors on imperialism, these "early" African intellectuals contributed sufficiently to the thinking of national independence movements. They created *La Revue du Monde Noir* in Paris around 1930, *Legitime Defense, L'Etudiant Noir* around 1934, *Les Tropiques* in Martinique and *Présence Africaine* in Paris after World War II.

The second school of African men of culture included Bernard Dadié, Fodeba Keita, David Diop, Ferdinand Oyono, Mongo Beti, Camara Laye, Ousmane Sembene, Cheikh Hamidou Kane, and Frantz Fanon.[42] They more vigorously condemned Western colonialism and exploitation and their writings become a vehicle of revolt and change rather than just a conceptualized word of defense.

For example, Bernard Dadié's *Climbié* contradicts the goals of assimilation. The affluent European world of the urban resident quarters of Ivory Coast was separated from the poor and miserable world of the African village. Bernard Dadié's hero, the reformist Climbié, who has condemned war—European war intended to conquer and subjugate other peoples—has rejected halfway European jobs and education. Though he still shows some respect for the elders' advice and vision, he is faced with the daily debasement of the colonized people torn between the inclination to retain the vestiges of African culture and the ardent desire to move up academically, socially, economically, and politically. The existence of his grandfather, whom he knew, gave him vague reminiscences of his culture; yet, he compromised on several of his cultural values and social attitudes against those imposed by his education. Motivated as he was to beat the system and eradicate poverty among his people, he realized how difficult it was to succeed in the colonial world. The same ambivalences can be traced in Fodeba Keita's *Aube Africaine*, David Diop's *Coups de Pilon*, Ferdinand Oyono's *The Old Man and the Medal*, Mongo Beti's *Le Pauvre Christ de Bomba* and *Mission Terminée*, Camara Laye's *The Radiance of the King*, Ousmane Sembene's *Le Mandat*, Cheikh Amidou Kane's *Ambiguous Adventure*, and Frantz Fanon's *Black Skin and White Mask*. Bernard Dadié's hero would work for far-sighted academic and educational reforms which would discard Western academic imperialism.

EVIDENCE OF WESTERN ACADEMIC IMPERIALISM

Western social sciences have been shown to be culture-bound when preparing Africans to solve African problems.[43] They have failed to solve several problems of colonial metropolitan Europe as well as the problems of misallocation of resources all over the Western world. It would be aberrant for Africans to rely on Western interpretations, to rely on the frameworks of the social sciences in order to find solutions for the problems of reemerging Africa when there already is restoration of the collective spirit alien to the West's traditional perspective concerning development. To understand Western ethnocentrism, one need only note the following remarks in economics, political science, history, language, literature, philosophy, psychology, and sociology.

In the African ethos, the organization of social relations prevails over everything. This means that the Africans will make human relations or their relations with a spiritual force prevail first before they form relationships with things. This African humanism is not necessarily compatible with individual material aggrandizement. It is true that occasions do exist for individual gains, but the economic calculations often tend to be subject more to the sociocultural, spiritual, and religious considerations.

The claim of modern economics of the presence of the market system in every society does not seem to be totally founded for some African societies. On one hand we may agree with Firth[44] and Jones[45] that selective applicability of Western theory is possible in some African societies according to the principle of economic rationality. On the other hand, Polanyi, Arensberg, and Pearson[46] and Dalton[47] who see "man as an entity with an innate propensity to truck, barter and exchange one thing for another" suggest that traditional exchange in these societies was carried out according to the substantivist principles of reciprocity and redistribution. The reality of the African societies can be explained by both theories. The economic process should therefore depend on non-economic factors (political, cultural, religious, military, artistic) as well as conventional economic factors affecting directly production, distribution, exchange, and consumption.

The failure of modern economics here is due to the fact that the discipline of economics from mercantilism, protectionism, laissez-faire to modern Keynesian theory assumes that the individual is an individual no matter his color, creed, and national origin.[48] It opens the door to private enterprise and fierce competition. It is easy to imagine how difficult it would be for modern economic theory (science) to solve the problems of colonial societies and newly independent and quasi-independent societies of Africa which are characterized by the emergence of group identity, community life, and collective consciousness. The colonial structures which were devised for the need of capitalism to benefit mostly the former metropole and the mercantile companies remain entrusted to stimulate rapid economic and social development. Yet the correlation between the political structures and the dictates of economic development is not clearly known.[49]

Political science is not devoid of cultural bias. In the nation-building process, African nationalists found themselves heading the same colonial institutions which presided over the pattern of relationship between the haves and the have-nots. Carl Rosberg states:

African nationalism needs to be analyzed in terms of the frustrations, fears, ambitions as well as actions and stances African leaders adopt in advancing the interests of their countries and continent as they develop a new relationship with Europe and the outside world. Frustrations and fears of new forms of external control, opposition to regimes of white supremacy and residual colonialism, the continuing if not expanding gap, between developed Western economies and African ones and the economic conflicts of interests with developed industrial states, are some of the factors contributing to and conditioning this new nationalism.[50]

The nationalist appeal will depend upon the extent of deprivation and frustration that Africans have experienced in terms of educational and occupational positions. The urge for African unity means the weakening of all the powerful and often not clearly identifiable forces which have kept Africans divided. These forces can have support in the ranks of multinational corporations. Nationalization of foreign concerns in order to reduce dependency of the new societies may be seen as an act of lawlessness on behalf of the legitimacy principles of Western political science based on egalitarianism of opportunities before the law. There is in this line of thought a strong emphasis on individual rights while the urge for African unity whose realization poses many problems calls for the fulfillment of a collective potential, group interest, public welfare, and group development without the fragmentation of Western individualism and competition.

History as a discipline of study in African secondary schools as well as in institutions of higher learning misrepresented Africa's contribution to universal civilization. History books perpetuated the myths of African inferiority. These inborn biases and prejudices of colonial schools of thought caused them to ignore the important part of previous African civilizations. They perpetrated the myths that Africa's most famous institutions and monuments were designed by Semites, Hamites, and White conquerors. For example, Maurice Delafosse hypothesized that the foundations of Ghana and Mali were the work of White founders. This hypothesis of course does not account for the influence of his relatively liberal monumental work on West Africans.[51] The history books made it look as if Africa was a historical vacuum before Vasco da Gama or Mungo Park and other adventurous commercial entrepreneurs.

African history, which has moved away from European ethnocentrism, is not the story of European explorers, missionaries, merchants, and colonial administrators, whose distorted view cut Africa off from centuries of its glorious past illustrated by Africa's most famous empires of Kush, Nubia, Ethiopia, Egypt, Zimbabwe, Ghana, Mali, Songhay, to cite just a few examples.[52] Until two decades ago, Western history books failed to mention how African consciousness and cosmology had shaped African societies in a most humane form of communal living characterized by a high spirit of cooperativeness and sacrifice.

After centuries of struggle, traditional Africa seems to be discovering itself. It is in light of this cultural renaissance nationalism and internationalism that Islam and Euro-Christian influences should be treated as experiences of Africa's history.

Western languages such as French and English abound in minor connotations which stigmatize African societies. One example is the concept of "tribalism."[53] It is argued in several scholarly circles that tribalism is a major problem of new Africa. Because tribalism has connotations of primitiveness, barbarism, savagery, stagnation, no great mass consumption, no advanced technology, no rule of mathematics and logic, it is seen as a very divisive force which hinders development. Yet the tribal ideology seems to have originated in Europe! The colonial administrators devised it to divide and conquer the resident Africans. This ideology is still used to exploit the communal and cooperative feelings of Africans while exaggerating these feelings so as to make them a category for academic analysis. The phenomenon of looking down on other groups is commonly used in the approach of cultural imperialism. Nobody can readily deny the virtue and wisdom of "tribal" glory which has security, insurance, and the benefits of mass production in the absence of "civilization" of affluence, emotional outlets during rituals such as those experienced by spectators watching the conventions of American political parties. As a manifestation of strong desires or allegiances or loyalties to the "tribal" organization and culture, tribalism *is* a form of patriotism. It allows respect for the old ways and the wisdom of elders. It reflects the essence of different ethnic groups. It has seeds of cooperativeness, communalism, generosity, all of which insure against hazardous situations. It opposes the assimilation policy of Europeans by urging tribal identity. It grows into nationalism and internationalism. It is an instrument of colonial liberation and national development in many situations.

Literature and philosophy as well as psychology and sociology[54] are the outcome of a national culture and today's African values and new alternatives are not to be based only on alien values if the people are expected to be original in coping with their present problems. Many African societies which were relatively egalitarian before colonialism need their own intrinsic literature and philosophy to provide cohesion. These African societies will be self-destructive if they adhere to the alluring theory of fierce competition as developed by Aristotle: that men are not the same and do not perform the same functions in the pursuit of the common goal.[55]

France influenced Africa in a unilateral way. Yet, it is not the purpose of this paper to envision a non-linguistic, tribal, demonetized, partyless, a-governmental, stateless state. Such a model would probably not provide a capacity for change. Rather, interchange of culture may be beneficial to Africa. But up to now it has distorted African ways of life which have pushed Africans and people of African descent to self-hatred, as is witnessed in Frantz Fanon's *Black Skin and White Mask* and *Wretched of the Earth*, Cheikh Hamidou Kane's *Ambiguous Adventure*, Yambo Ouloguem's *Bound to Violence*, Bernard Dadié's *Climbié*, and many other scholarly and literary masterpieces.

Africans need at this time to put forward their own questions and answers. This does not imply necessarily that non-Africans should be excluded, because they have their contribution to make as subjective but critical analysts. But academic imperialism needs to be discarded and replaced by interdisciplinary team studies which may not necessarily be value-free but which can point the way to political, economic, cultural, and psychological independence. A certain dynamism has to be generated against multinational corporations; dubious standards and values imposed on Africa by years of colonial educational systems need to be challenged and better alternatives to be found; African culture needs to be reexamined in order to adapt old-time wisdom to the demands of modern time.

NOTES

1. This paper has benefited from critical comments by Lansiné Kaba, History Department, University of Minnesota. Any errors and misjudgments are mine.

2. J. Spencer Trimingham, *A History of Islam in West Africa* (Oxford, 1970); Edward W. Blyden, *Christianity, Islam and the Negro Race* (Edinburgh, 1967), p. 11.

3. Hollis Lynch, ed., *Black Spokesman—Selected Published Writings of Edward W. Blyden* (London, 1971).

4. Georges Hardy, *Une Conquête Morale; L'Enseignement en A.O.F.* (Paris, 1917), p. 12.

5. R. Robinson and J. Gallagher, with A. Denny, *Africa and the Victorians: The Climax of Imperialism* (Garden City, N.Y., 1968), p. 8.

6. René Maran, *Batouala* (Paris, 1938); Aimé Césaire, *Cahier d'un Retour au Pays Natal* (Paris, 1956) and *Discours sur le Colonialisme* (Paris, 1955); Léopold S. Senghor, *Poèmes* (Paris, 1964); Albert Memmi, *Portrait du Colonisé* (Utrecht, 1966); Frantz Fanon, *The Wretched of the Earth* (New York, 1968); Walter Rodney, *How Europe Underdeveloped Africa* (Dar Es Salaam, 1972).

7. Jean Surêt-Canale, *Afrique Noire L'Ere Coloniale, 1900-1945* (Paris, 1964), p. 464.

8. Camille Guy, *L'Afrique Française Bulletin du Comité de l'Afrique Française*, no. 8 (1924): 438.

9. *Territoires du Haut Sénégal–Moyen Niger, Rapport 1900-1903.*

10. "L'Enseignement dans les Territoires d'Outre Mer," *Documentation Française, Notes et Etudes Documentaires*, no. 1896 (July 1954).

11. Jean Suret-Canale, *Afrique Noire*, p. 464.

12. Governor-General Roume's statement, *Journal Officiel de l'A.O.F.*, no. 1024 (10 May 1924).

13. John Gunther, *Inside Africa* (New York, 1955), p. 12.

14. Charles W. Forman, ed., *Christianity in the Non-Western World* (Englewood Cliffs, N.J., 1967), p. 37.

15. Stephen Neill, *Colonialism and Christian Missions* (New York, 1966), p. 14.

16. Gunther, *Inside Africa*, p. 10.

17. Neill, *Colonialism and Christian Missions*, p. 350.

18. C. G. Baeta, *Christianity in Tropical Africa* (Oxford, 1968), p. 7.

19. Ram Desai, ed., *Christianity in Africa as Seen by Africans* (Denver, Colo., 1962), p. 69.

20. Ibid., p. 16.

21. Gunther, *Inside Africa*, p. 306.

22. Maurice Delafosse, *Bulletin de l'Education en AOF*, no. 33 (June 1917); Abdou Moumouni, *L'Education en Afrique* (Paris, 1967), p. 45. This second reference is the best available treatise on this topic. I am indebted to Professor Moumouni, through whose logical argument, I was able to develop new insights. Georges Hardy, "L'Enseignement aux Indigènes dans les possessions Françaises d' Afrique," *Institut Colonial International, L'Enseignement aux indigènes*, 1931.

23. Maurice Delafosse, *Bulletin de l'Education en A.O.F.*, no. 33 (Juin 1917).

24. *Bulletin de l'Education en A.O.F.*, no. 74, p. 3.

25. Circulaire No. 107E du 8 Avril 1933, *Bulletin de l'Education en A.O.F.*, no. 83 (April-June 1933).

26. Governor-General Roume, *Journal Officiel de L'A.O.F.*, no. 1024 (10 May 1924).

27. The collection *Mamadou et Bineta* and the *Contes de la Brousse et de la Forêt* are a few which come to mind.

28. Abdou Moumouni, *L'Education en Afrique*, p. 126.

29. *Evolués* referred to those educated Africans who have "evolved."

30. Circulaire no. 107E, Avril 1933, *Bulletin de l'Education en A.O.F.*, no. 83 (April-June 1933).

31. Frantz Fanon, *Black Skin and White Mask* (New York, 1967).

32. Cheikh Hamidou Kane, *The Ambiguous Adventure* (New York, 1969).

33. Yambo Ouologuem, *Bound to Violence* (San Francisco, 1971).

34. A. Y. Yansané, review of Yambo Ouologuem's *Bound to Violence* in *Black World*, 22, no. 12 (October, 1973): 51-78.

35. The *lycées* were the secondary schools created in France by Napoleon, himself a transitional product of the French Revolution and the great men of the eighteenth century who became the apostles of the "Eternal Truth and Right and the Kingdom of Reason." These great men who inspired the Revolution—Montesquieu, Voltaire, Rousseau, Diderot—influenced also their French and Western contemporaries on issues concerning equality. For them equality was based on nature and inalienable human rights. Their demand for equality was limited to political rights and the Kingdom of Reason which, they envisioned, was to lead to a barely democratic state. Their speculations concerning equality did not guarantee absolute equality (see Rousseau's *Contrat Social*). It should not be surprising, then, to see French colonial *lycées* turning out educated subjects and elites who will become instruments of assimilation.

36. W.E.B. Du Bois, "Souls of Black Folk," *Three Negro Classics* (New York, 1965).

37. Leo Froebenius, *Histoire des civilizations Africaines* (Paris, 1950).

38. Maurice Delafosse, *The Negroes of Africa: History and Culture* (Washington, D.C., 1931).

39. Joseph Arthur Gobineau, Comte de, *The Inequality of Human Races* (London, 1915).

40. Aimé Césaire, *Cahier d'un Retour au Pays Natal* and *Discours sur le Colonialisme* (Paris, 1956 and 1955).

41. Léopold Senghor, *Poèmes* (Paris, 1964); "The Spirit of Civilization or the Laws of African Negro Culture," *The 1st International Conference of Negro Writers and Artists* (Paris, 1956), pp. 51-83; "Constructive Elements of a Civilization of African Negro Inspiration," *Second Congress of Negro Writers and Artists* (Paris, 1959), pp. 262-294; *Liberté 1: Negritude and Humanism* (Paris, 1964).

42. Bernard Dadié, *Climbié* (Paris, 1956); David Diop, *Coups de Pilon* (Paris, 1965); Keita Fodeba, *Aube Africaine* (Paris, 1966); Ferdinand Oyono, *The Old Man and the Medal* (New York, 1971); Mongo Beti, *Le Pauvre Christ de Bomba* (Paris, 1955) and *Mission Terminée* (Paris, 1956); Laye Camara, *The Radiance of the King* (New York, 1971); Ousmane Sembene, *Le Mandat* (Paris, 1966); Cheikh Hamidou Kane, *Ambiguous Adventure* (New York, 1969); Frantz Fanon, *Black Skin and White Mask*.

43. David Brokensha and Michael Crowder, eds. *Africa in the Wider World* (Oxford, 1967).

44. Raymond Firth, ed., *Themes in Economic Anthropology* (Chicago, 1967).

45. William O. Jones, "Economic Man in Africa," *Food Research Institute Studies* 1, no. 2 (May 1960).

46. Karl Polanyi, C. M. Arensberg and H. W. Pearson, *Trade and Market in the Early Empires* (New York, 1957); see particularly Part III "Institutional Analysis."

47. George Dalton, ed., *Primitive, Archaic and Modern Economics* (Garden City, N.Y., 1968).

48. Kenneth Boulding, "Is Economics Culture Bound?" Paper presented at the American Economic Association annual meeting, New York, December 28, 1969.

49. David Carney, "Economics," in *Africa in the Wider World*, David Brokensha and Michael Crowder, eds. (Oxford, 1962), pp. 118-135.

50. Carl Rosberg, Jr., "Political Science and the Changing Character of African Political Problems," *Africa in the Wider World*, pp. 113-114.

51. Maurice Delafosse, *The Negroes of Africa*.

52. Yossef ben Joachannan, *Black Man of the Nile and His Family* (New York, 1972); Joseph Ki-Zerbo, *Histoire de l'Afrique Noire* (Paris, 1972); Djibril Tamsir Niane and J. Surêt-Canale, *Histoire de l'Afrique Occidentale* (Paris, 1961); Chancellor Williams, *The Destruction of Black Civilization* (Chicago, 1974).

53. The concept of tribalism is used as just one illustration of one case of aberrance of foreign language terminology on an idea which is not as backward as it may lead some to believe.

54. These themes are substantially developed in two pioneering books, Willie Abraham, *The Mind of Africa* (Chicago, 1962), p. 59; Kwame Nkrumah, *Consciencism Philosophy and Ideology for Decolonization* (New York, 1964), Chapters 2 and 3.

55. Nkrumah, *Consciencism*, pp. 44-49, 50, 84-85.

X

COMPARATIVE PERSPECTIVES

This book has inquired into the relationship between France and Africa; we have seen that double impact was the general rule in many areas. But we have also noted that the depth of African impact upon France and the French was severely limited, since few French people actually came in contact with Africans or visited Africa. The reciprocal relationship existed—in fact, it still exists today—as most Africans and French people interested in African affairs would readily admit. The rapport between France and its former colonies has surprised outside critics and perplexed other Europeans who formerly were colonial powers, and other Africans who have made a point of seeking total disengagement from a colonial past. Why then has France been successful, and why have many (but not all) of the francophone African nations sought to retain this relationship? Why would even a Sekou Touré, who suffered the ire and wrath of Charles de Gaulle, seek to end his isolation later in his career and bring about closer relations with France? The answer may just be in the fact that a two-way relationship between France and *Afrique Noire* created a special situation that has favored this continuity.

In this final chapter we turn to a brief examination of whether or not double impact and reciprocal influences played any part of colonial history in two other important European colonizing nations—Britain and Portugal.

Writing from the perspective of a historian of British imperialism and also a close student of African society, Robert Collins considers the situation in Britain during colonial times and concludes that there was little if any double impact. For one thing, Britain's dominions stretched around the world, and its interests were already concentrated in such places as India, Singapore, and South Africa, or in the dominions of Canada and Australia. Britain never became involved in educational matters with the same depth of commitment or ideology that France did; Britain left an enormous amount of the educational burden to Christian missionaries. Collins looks at economics, culture, literature, and British society and concludes that Britain really received little from the African experience.

By contrast, Professor de Sena shows how Portugal, whose policy of assimilation somewhat approximated that of France, was intimately involved with its African colonies. In fact, as most students of history know, Portugal's greatness in overseas expansion was tied closely to its colonies, and when it lost Brazil and its holdings in the East Indies and India, only a few enclaves in Africa nurtured its backward economy. Colonies became part myth, part national heritage, part national purpose. When France, Britain, and Belgium bailed out of their African holdings within several years of one another, only Portugal, weakest of the European colonialists, held firm. The reason of course was that the double impact had been total—the colonies had deeply affected the political, economic, social, and cultural life of the Portuguese nation. That is why the colonial wars of independence wrenched the ruling country so terribly, why they finally even brought down the central government. De Sena concludes by asking "What was the impact of Africa on Portugal? It shaped for more than five centuries Portuguese history and the destinies of the Portuguese people."

We have not attempted to examine Belgium and Germany, the other two powers that maintained an extensive imperial establishment in Black Africa, or Italy, which briefly held portions of northeastern Africa. It is unlikely that much double impact would be found in any of these three nations; yet, all three at one time fancied themselves as powerful colonial landlords. The German holdings were taken away by the British and French after World War I; some reciprocal influences might have started to penetrate Germany during that time. As for Belgium, which almost reluctantly took over the Congo after Leopold became embroiled in scandal, there was never widespread enthusiasm or identification with the Congo. The Congo was a faraway place one might visit to make a small fortune, or it was a place to be sent if one entered a Catholic teaching order. Belgian colonialism was never fully developed, and its superstructure in the Congo was simply a convenience for the wealthy mining and agriculture corporations that were heavily involved.

20

Africa in Britain

Although the major theme of this collection has been the impact of Africa upon France, there can be some instructive comparisons of the impact of Africa in Britain, which is the subject of this paper.

My fundamental thesis is that Africa has had little if any influence on British culture and civilization. In making such a bold and negative assertion, I am divorcing the important strategic role which Africa played in the formulation of imperial policy in the official minds of those who determined British foreign policy in the nineteenth and twentieth centuries. If one moves away from the field of foreign policy, the impact and effect of Africa on British culture, economics, and society is astoundingly small compared to the vast geographical expanse, population, and diverse cultures of the former British colonies in Africa. This is particularly striking when compared to the impact of Africa on French society and culture and is all the more astonishing when one realizes that Africa has had a greater impact on life in Britain in the post-colonial period than it did when much of Africa was a territory of the British empire.

Let us take a cursory look at the various fields in which Africa has influenced British life. Wherever one turns, the paucity of this influence appears to be the dominant factor. The literature of the nineteenth century is filled with the works of the Rough Rider's School of blood-stained fiction. Fuzzy Wuzzies, Khartoum, King Solomon's Mines, and the Zulu Wars all provide romantic themes to excite and stimulate the minds of a newly rising literary industrial proletariat thirsting for excitement after the drudgery of the mills. In our own time such themes have been supplanted by "Hawaii Five-O," "Kojak," and "Policewoman."

Yet if one examines this literature with a critical eye, one sees that the Africans are really the fall guys, playing much the role of the Last of the Mohicans. These are tales of derring-do that have no appreciation or understanding of African societies and cultures, glorifying the intrepid White man or the thin red line. They tell us little about the Africans as they really were. Even such a sensitive and perceptive author as Joseph Conrad portrays the Africans of the Congo as savages only too willing to fall into the hands of a charismatic Kurtz. One can argue that this literature created a false picture of Africa in British minds that persists to this day. The major task of Africanist scholarship has been to put right these impressions over the last generation. In this sense the impact upon the minds of the British public was profound, if erroneous, but it was always in the context of the White man representing a superior culture and with the Africans dismissed in the minds of the readers as something exotic, romantic, and not to be taken too seriously. Even Joyce Carey presents Mr. Johnson as a buffoon. When one reads the work of British novelists of Africa in comparison with the works of Achebe, Tutuola, or Soyinka, one can only conclude that the impact of Africa upon the British literary scene can be relegated to the role of Tarzan, whose author incidentally never visited Africa and yet whose works were among the greatest bestsellers of all times. Certainly, the British reader learned little about Africa from Tarzan, and what he did discover was invariably wrong. If one wishes to measure literary impact by the volume of books, then the impact of Africa was considerable. If one measures influences instead, as I believe is crucial, by the understanding and knowledge of a continent and its people, the impact has been miniscule in Britain.

If one turns to the arts, the scene is equally devoid of African themes. The dramatic, exciting, and widely praised visual and artistic creations of Africans have had virtually no impact on British artists. Influenced mainly by the impressionists on the continent and the avant-garde artists of the United States, I know of no major British painter or sculptor who has drawn inspiration from African sources. The same is true of music where the leading British composers of the twentieth century such as Benjamin Britton, Michael Tippett, Vaughn Williams, Edmund Rubbra, and Peter Fricker have not been influenced in any way by African music. Even the more popular rock groups like the Beatles appear to have ignored African rhythms and themes. This is an extraordinary and striking contrast to modern French composers, not to mention the enormous contribution of African music by American musicians, both White and Black.

If one turns to the more mundane subjects of economics and politics, one can only conclude that the impact of Africa on Britain has again been slight. Although there is still today wide disagreement on the role of markets for African commodities in the total trade of Great Britain, even a cursory glance at Britain's foreign trade will show that Africa contributes a very small percentage. I am not here concerned about the history of the slave trade and its role in the development of plantation economies in the West Indies with its direct spinoff in capital formation in Great Britain at the beginning of the Industrial Revolution. I am concerned here primarily with the nineteenth and twentieth centuries where the tropical products of Africa form an insignificant percentage of Great Britain's foreign trade. It is true that British colonies produced, even in the age of nineteenth-century free trade, preferred markets for British goods, but it is worth noting that the greatest trading partner in the nineteenth century with British African colonies was not Britain but Imperial Germany. World War I destroyed German trade with Britain's African colonies. Between the wars, the depression and the financial stringencies of each of the colonies prevented the purchase of large amounts of industrial goods for economic development. At the same time the domestic economy was not sufficiently consumer-oriented to make the colonies a significant market for British goods. This picture has changed since World War II, and Britain has experienced the paradoxical phenomenon that economic impact of Africa on Britain has increased dramatically once the colonies achieved their independence.

If one views Britain's foreign trade in its totality, the attention which scholars have given to the economic impact of Africa upon Britain has been deeply colored and distorted by Cecil Rhodes, Sir William MacKinnon, Sir George Goldie, and Trader Horn. When compared with the great British commercial firms of India and the Orient, these mercantile monarchies shrink by comparison despite the diamonds of Witswatersrand and the gold of Johannesburg. Rhodes and the imperialists had political influence in Britain, but again nothing approaching the magnitude of the Indian nabobs, the West Indian planters, or the Hong Kong merchants. In the last analysis, the arguments of Joseph Chamberlain that Africa must be painted red to employ the working class of Britain cannot be sustained.

Socially the impact of Africa on Britain has again, until post-independence times, been negligible. Although the English of the eighteenth century might have brought slave servants to Britain, they were always regarded as exotic, and although the Mansfield Decision freed Africans in Britain, very few came. A handful were sent by missionary societies or some of the trading houses of the Niger Delta or the Gold Coast, but here one must keep in perspective the fact that these numbers were infinitesimal compared to the thousands of Africans who found their homes in France. The specter of Black ghettos in the urban metropolises of Great Britain is the product of our own times and not the nineteenth and the first half of the twentieth centuries. To be sure, a handful of Africans have always studied in Britain, largely in the professions, and some, like Hastings Banda, stayed on to practice, accepted by the British public because their numbers threatened no one and their competency was appreciated. But as for having a significant influence on British institutions, there was little. The law, of course, was the favorite of most Africans attending British professional schools, but they came more for the purpose of returning immediately to Africa, ultimately to argue for their countries' independence, paradoxically drawing more Africans to Britain after independence than in colonial times.

The political impact upon Africa perhaps is more significant than that of the arts and sciences, but once again this influence must be perceived in the context of the empire. Professors Robinson and Gallagher have argued persuasively about the great shift in the nineteenth century in the pivot of empire from Constantinople to Cairo. This focused great attention upon the Nile Valley and its waters as the front line of defense for the Suez Canal—the great link to what really counted in the British Empire—India and the Orient. These policies and the decisions that arose from them were, however, the province of "the official mind"—those few men in positions of power and authority who made decisions in foreign policy and imperial strategy. They may have committed Britain to invade the Sudan in 1898 to confront the French at Fashoda, to dicker with the Germans over East Africa, to encourage but not involve the government in Cecil Rhodes's schemes for a northward course of empire, but they had little impact on the day-to-day lives of the ordinary English people, who were content to let matters of state rest in the hands of those who by breeding and education supposedly had the competency to deal with the great questions of power politics. In the administration of the colonies there were, to be sure, hosts of commissions, constitutions, and parliamentary inquiries, but again taken in the context of administering and governing a vast empire, Africa played a small role.

If one accepts the above thesis, which I believe I have overdrawn for the purpose of provocative discussion, I have avoided presenting an explanation of why the impact of Africa upon Britain was so small when compared with France or even the United States. This is a subject to which I hope the researcher will address him or herself. I would however, like to add a few of my own observations drawn from my own research and experience in Britain and Africa. In my own research I have discovered that history in colonial Africa is much the product of the attitudes and assumptions of the men who administered Britain's African colonies. To me this is the key to understanding the mind of the colonial rulers and why in the end Britain's African colonies contributed little to the shaping of modern Britain. The British who ruled in Africa were deeply racist in the belief of their own superiority and deeply imbued with the methods by which the administrator was expected to rule subject peoples. Innoculated with the values of the British public school and the squirearchy, the class from which they came, their role was to govern, not to mingle, to rule by the fewest means possible by maintaining an aloofness commensurate with their arrogance. By mingling with the "natives" or adopting their cultures and life-styles, one destroyed the aura of august authority. The idea of a Sir Reginald Wingate or Sir Frederick Lugard walking down the main street of the colonial capital as did Louis Faidherbe to register and legitimatize his African sons, boggles the imagination. These British officials were men of great courage, fortitude, and a deep commitment to the White Man's Burden. They were virtually, by the system of selection, without interest in the arts, literature, or social concerns. Their role was to dispense justice with the fairness and equity of the playing fields of Eton. Thus they would encourage a bright young African in a mission station to take up the law, but to dispense with such impractical pursuits as music, art, or literature. The British came to rule because it was their duty. They governed well and then retired to the Cotswold having maintained throughout British customs, traditions, and way of life unaffected by the peoples they served and ruled. There were, of course, a few eccentrics who went "native," but they are of no significance. The British were always in Africa, not of it. They brought little of Africa back to Britain and made little attempt to encourage Africa to come to this "sceptered isle."

These attitudes were deeply ingrained at all levels of the colonial hierarchy from the governor-general down to the lowliest clerk in the Postal Service, and they created the major obstacle which prevented Africa from becoming a major influence on British culture and civilization.

JORGE DE SENA

21

The Impact of Africa on Portugal

Certainly no other non-African country—especially a European one—has had its destiny so closely linked with Africa as Portugal. It was with the conquest of Ceuta in North Africa in 1415 that the country launched the expansion which developed into the first colonial empire of modern times, thus embarking on a course that shaped Portuguese history and opened a new era for the world. And it was because of the colonial wars in Africa, supposedly maintained to defend the last colonial empire in contemporary times, that a revolution was launched in Portugal in April of 1974, which toppled the dictatorial regime that had governed the country since 1926. The military revolution had two main aims, both directed at reversing the historical course of centuries: to recognize the independence of the colonies, and to eradicate the national structure that had been based on colonialism. Portugal underwent one of the greatest crises in its history of more than eight centuries as an independent and unified country, and this was largely because of Africa. Also we must bear in mind that, since the "discovery" in 1500 until its independence in 1822, Brazil was part of the Portuguese empire, and that the development of Brazil was largely based on contacts with Africa through the slavery that was there for centuries the source of labor (only abolished in 1888). The imperial history of Portugal had three main areas: Brazil in the Americas, Africa, and the Indian Ocean (extending its influence into the Pacific Ocean and the Far East), but in this triple process Africa played an important role, and it was, as we started by saying, the beginning and the end of an era.

At the risk of telling a learned audience what everybody knows, allow me to recall a few facts and dates, which may help us in a rapid survey of Portuguese relations with Africa and in understanding what is happening today.

The history of the relations of Portugal with Africa, during the expansion and the colonial empire, can be divided into several very distinct periods. The first includes the fifteenth century, starting with the conquest of Ceuta in 1415, followed by other conquests in North Africa. But at the same time, another policy was immediately developed: the one of discovering and exploring more or less methodically the western Coast of Africa, until the Cape of Good Hope was reached in the Bartolomeu Dias voyage of 1487-1488, which opened the way around Africa and into the Indian Ocean.

The voyage of Vasco da Gama, in 1497-1499, on its way to India, explored for the first time segments of the eastern coast of Africa. It was the beginning of the Indian empire which would dominate entirely the Portuguese policies for some decades—we could say, until the end of the sixteenth century, when, under the Dutch and English pressures, the eastern empire started to decline. Meanwhile, the discovery of Brazil and its colonization started to open a new era, which in the seventeenth and eighteenth centuries would place that country as the main focus of the empire. This period came to an end in 1822 not only with the independence of Brazil, but with the establishment in 1820 of a liberal system in Portugal. This system, after several setbacks and a civil war, triumphed in 1834. Another period starts then in which Portugal, facing the colonialist expansion of the other European powers tried to occupy and explore most of its traditional territories in Africa, remnants of outposts all along the African coast. The liberal measures of the constitutional monarchy were amplified by the republic proclaimed in 1910. A military revolution in 1926 brought the republic to an end, and a new outlook, on the imposition of the Portuguese continental structure and on the enforcement of big monopolies, based on centralized power, was consecrated by the Colonial Act of 1930, written by dictator Salazar himself. The act included the famous distinction between ''natives'' and ''assimilated people'' (the portions of the empire excepted from this distinction were only Cape Verde, the Indian possessions, and Macao). This period came to an end with the revolution of April 1974.

Now let us review as briefly as possible some events which punctuated these several periods. Portugal, which had been established as a semi-independent earldom under the suzerainty of the kingdom of Leon, became independent through a revolution in 1128, and Leon came to recognize the new kingdom in 1143. In the next one hundred years, Portugal conquered from the Moors the southern half of what is today its territory, thus becoming by 1250, the first Iberian kingdom to complete its ''reconquest.'' It is known that the Portuguese, confined between the sea and the kingdoms of Leon and Castille, very early engaged in international trade and navigation. In the twelfth century one of the daughters of the first Portuguese king became countess of Flanders, and in the thirteenth century a Portuguese prince was himself, by marriage, count of Flanders, while two Portuguese princesses were queens of Denmark.

Navigation along the coast of Africa started before the fifteenth century. Before the middle of the fourteenth century an expedition was organized in Lisbon to explore the Canary Islands. Competition for occupation and sovereignty of these islands continued between Portugal and Castille for more than one century, and it was settled in favor of Castille only in 1436, with Portugal finally accepting the settlement of 1480 which gave her a free and absolute hand in the exploration of the West Coast of Africa. But by then Portugal had established fortresses in Morocco and Mauritania, and had started in the 1420s a more or less methodical exploration of that West Coast. By 1450, the Portuguese had reached the latitude of present-day Monrovia, while they had explored the "Western Seas" and found and colonized the desert islands of Azores. The colonization of the Madeira Islands had been started in the 1420s. Around the 1450s and 1460s the islands of Cape Verde were discovered and started to be colonized. The island of São Tomé was colonized by the end of the fifteenth century and became very important in the next century as the outpost for the slave trade between the West Coast of Africa and Brazil. It was also a center for the production of sugar, like Madeira, a prosperity that lasted until the sugar in Brazil came to beat all other enterprises. Nevertheless, it has been pointed out that the system of colonization established in the Atlantic and African islands served as a kind of experiment for what was later to be the first political organization of Brazil.

We mentioned the slave trade. It was the first commercial success that the Portuguese achieved in their contacts with the western coast of Africa. The first slaves arrived in Portugal in 1441 and were sold to Castille, Aragon, Italy, and elsewhere at good profit. We have a magnificent description of the arrival of one of the first cargoes, in the *Crónica da Guiné* by G. E. de Zurara, writing in the middle of the fifteenth century. In spite of being the offical chronicler, Zurara finds the moving words of a modern humanist to describe the plight of the slaves. It was the development of Brazil a century later, which, together with the several settlements in the Atlantic, shifted the direction of the trade to Brazil.

The second success came in 1442, with the arrival of the first African gold— one of the main reasons for launching the expansion. Much has been said about the imperial justifications. The military expansion in northern Africa, which came to a disastrous end in 1578 when King Sebastian was killed with most of his army in El-Ksar Kebir when attempting an intervention in the internal affairs of Morocco, can be viewed in two ways. On one side, it prolonged the ideology of the Reconquest, which had dominated the Iberian kingdoms for centuries and served as the support for an aristocratic-military society. The other side is that Portugal was looking for the North African outlets of gold which was in great demand for new economic development in Europe. Until the 1480s the exploration of the western coast of Africa was in fact dominated by this same purpose of drawing a circle around the centers of Arab gold trade, which is symbolized by the foundation of the castle of S. Jorge da Mina, known as El Mina, in contemporary Ghana, in 1482. Yet another idea was very early mingled with that expansion: to get in touch with the legendary Prester John, the Christian sovereign of the East, whose contact would encircle the Muslim world. Prester John was a legend launched in the twelfth century in Europe and came to be identified with the emperor of Ethiopia, with whom since the 1480s the Portuguese attempted to establish close relations. At the same time that Bartolomeu Dias was rounding the Cape of Good Hope, travelers had been sent by land to India (which they visited to gather information) and to Ethiopia, where one of the travelers lived, raised a family, and died. An embassy from Ethiopia came to Portugal in 1513-1514, and several diplomatic exchanges continued in the course of the century.

By the end of the fifteenth century, it is clear that the main purpose of the Portuguese crown was to prepare everything to round Africa and reach India by sea. Africa, however, was kept very well in mind. In 1482-1486, preceding Bartolomeu Dias, Diogo Cão had explored the western coast as far as the Tropic of Capricorn, but had also navigated up the Zaire River. And in 1490, an embassy was sent to Congo, establishing with its kings a relationship that lasted well into the seventeenth century. Other travelers had tried to penetrate into Africa, visiting Timbuktu by the end of the fifteenth century, or reaching what became Rhodesia in 1514-1515.

What is now Mozambique started to be developed before what is today Angola, in spite of the explorations made inside the latter area in 1520-1530. There are several reasons, which reflect themselves in the different spheres in which Angola and Mozambique will live for a long time. The eastern coast of Africa (and in it the city-island of Mozambique, which gave the name to the country) was a base on the way to India and for the dominance of the Indian Ocean, and it was also the starting point for the attempts to reach the legendary Monomotapa with its gold and to contact Ethiopia and its Christian sovereigns. Angola really started as a monopoly of the island of São Tomé in 1550, and only in 1574 was organized as a captaincy. Luanda was founded in 1576, much later than the settlements in Mozambique, where, up the Zambezi River, the Portuguese had settled in Tete by 1531. When the colonization of Angola was started by the end of the sixteenth century, it seems that the idea was to transform it into a second Brazil. But the Brazilian interests, calling for the slave trade, got the upper hand, and at the same time the country itself and its population proved to be less easy and amenable than Brazil had proved to be. So for a long time, Angola gravitated in the Brazilian sphere, while Mozambique was part of the government of India and incorporated in the Indian empire (the establishment of a separate government in Mozambique came about only in 1752). When the Dutch had attacked Brazil and then attacked Angola (the source of manpower for the sugar plantations), they were expelled from Angola in 1648 by expeditions organized in Brazil by the big Luso-Brazilian sugar interests.

During the seventeenth and eighteenth centuries, the sugar and then the mines of Brazil dominated the empire, while by 1650-1660 the eastern part of it dwindled to some settlements which lasted to this century (Portuguese India was occupied by India in 1954-1961, Timor is still in the process of being decolonized, and Macao retains in China the ambiguous position that it has held for more than four centuries).

We may ask at this point what was the impact of Africa on Portugal during the "old" colonial empire. The new empire started in the nineteenth century in the wake of the colonization of Africa by the big European countries to compete with them.

It is very curious that, since the very beginning of the imperial expansion, the educated opinion was much divided in Portugal, in spite of all the imperial rhetoric by official chroniclers who themselves were many times very critical of the management of the empire. There were those who favored the expansion and those who feared that such ventures would deplete Portugal. One of the results of the empire, based mainly on monopolies of the crown and some grandees and other fortunate few, was to create in Portugal a double economic standard, which never allowed until very recently the creation of any powerful middle class and which consolidated a system of control of the lands in the hands of a small ruling class. Massive emigration to Africa was never implemented as it was to Brazil, whose possibilities very early attracted a stream of immigrants by the thousands and thousands which lasted until a few decades ago. At the same time, Portugal was economically placed in the vicious circle of depending on foreign capital for its imperial enterprises, while the riches were not reinvested but dissipated or served to pay the loans. On the other hand, the empire created a tradition of very centralized power around the king, which stifled almost completely the power of the urban middle classes, who as entrepreneurs had been involved in the beginning of the expansion, mainly as traders and even as organizers of naval expeditions. We must also bear in mind that the Inquisition, established in the middle of the sixteenth century (some decades after that in Spain), had as its main target the "new Christians" (or descendants of Jews forced to convert to Christianity) and so was used by the "old Christian" ruling class to keep down what was on its way to becoming a rich bourgeois class. The Inquisition which was all-powerful in Portugal itself and later became the same in India (where it wrecked the social contacts with the local population) was never entirely established in the same way either in Brazil or in Africa, where the missionary activities of the religious orders were more in the forefront. But in this respect we must stress that until the end of the eighteenth century, while Brazil was growing in European population, nothing of the sort was happening in the African territories.

As I pointed out, the loss of Brazil was a great shock for Portugal, nevertheless economically compensated by the stream of immigrants who would send money home or would return to establish themselves in the old country, exhibiting their acquired riches. By the beginning of the nineteenth century, at the same time that Portugal lost Brazil and Spain most of her American possessions, the great European countries started to launch a new drive toward Africa. Portugal, since the loss of most of its Indian empire, which had been the basis of all the imperial propaganda and pride, went through a period which lasted well into the present century, in which to dwell on the idea of decadence was prevalent among the educated classes. In the first decades of the nineteenth century, the liberal governments, once established in power, tried to counterbalance that feeling and the loss of Brazil by returning their attention to Africa in some way. On the other hand, in 1815 the Portuguese government had subscribed the treaty which ended (at least in theory) all slave trade north of the equator (which for Portugal included Portuguese Guinea and the islands of Cape Verde). The abolition of slavery south of the equator was decreed by a radical government in Lisbon in 1836, with several additional measures until 1869 that implemented the decision.

Meanwhile, many exploratory expeditions into the hinterland of Angola and Mozambique were made, since the new outlook of the European powers called for an effective exploration and occupation of the territories, as it had never been the Portuguese policy of outposts and of contacts with natives followed in the previous centuries (with the exception of Brazil). Those expeditions may be said to have started in the 1830s, culminating between the 1870s and the 1890s. The great dream was to establish a Portuguese zone going from Angola to Mozambique. The dream was shattered by the British designs, which came to a clash with Portugal in 1890 after several diplomatic and less diplomatic skirmishes when Great Britain sent an ultimatum to Lisbon. The treaties resulting from this humiliation of the Portuguese government established the actual boundaries of Angola and Mozambique. Already in 1870 the arbitration of the American President Grant had recognized the rights of Portugal to Portuguese Guinea against the pretensions of England. But the British ultimatum concerning Africa had a special political impact in Portugal. The Republicans seized the opportunity to accuse the monarchy of having betrayed the Portuguese interests and started an agitation which culminated in the downfall of the monarchy and the proclamation of the republic in 1910.

If the oldest cities in Portuguese Africa dated from the sixteenth century, there remained the need of occupying many portions inside the borders established for Guinea, Angola, and Mozambique, in which the natives resisted occupation, or, as it is known, were manipulated by Great Britain against Portugal. So intermittent ''campaigns of occupation'' were launched beginning in the 1840s, which lasted until the years of World War I. Nevertheless, with all its colonialism, the republic proclaimed in 1910 was much more progressive in its approach to the colonial problems, and tried to develop a more liberal and modern policy in the African territories. A greater autonomy was granted with the regime of high commissioners in Angola and Mozambique, a policy which lasted until 1930, when Salazar ended it. At this point, it must also be stressed that the trend of sending European settlers to Africa (mainly Angola), developed to some extent by the liberal monarchy and the republic, beginning in the middle of the nineteenth century, was also stopped by the Salazar regime. Salazar never could accept that American, African, or Asian countries should ever become, in the past or the present, independent from Europe (and he said so once when greeting most warmly none other than a president of Brazil). He was afraid of *any* kind of independence, even a White supremacist one. Portuguese Guinea and Mozambique in the nineteenth and twentieth centuries followed a different development, kept very much, as they were, like colonial "preserves" for the companies controlling large areas of the territories until quite late. The trend of allowing and encouraging European settlers (that is, Portuguese) in the African colonies was only reversed in the 1960s to answer the pressure of the colonial wars. This reversal attracted especially to Angola lots of small-scale traders and entrepreneurs, eager to enrich themselves as soon as possible. The "old" Whites despised them as much as the Blacks did.

The independence of the African colonies would come sooner or later, in one way or another. But it can be said that the conditions established by Salazar created, more than anything else, the ground on which movements toward independence, involving Blacks and Whites, would develop. The new regime established in 1926 in Portugal, for instance, signed in 1928, with South Africa and Rhodesia, a treaty for the regular export of Black labor from Mozambique to the mines of those countries. I have mentioned already the Colonial Act of 1930, which reduced the status of the territories, and as late as 1954 Salazar promulgated the Statute of the Natives to cover for a very distinctive social situation that had never, in some ways, existed before. It is curious that this was the year in which India took over some portions of the Damão enclave. The statute was abolished in response to international pressures in 1961, the year in which India occupied the old Portuguese territories there and also the year the rebellion began in Angola. The last phase had begun. In 1963, the rebellion broke out in Guinea, and in 1964 in Mozambique. It is interesting to note that the movement for these fights had, very timidly, begun in Lisbon in the 1950s, when several students from the colonies, who included most of the best known leaders of the future, met to voice a mild discontent, which was immediately crushed by Salazar's government.

To say that at first the colonial wars were popular in Portugal would be a pious lie. For centuries, with some dissenting voices, the greatness of the empire and of the old Portuguese glories had been part of Portuguese culture, and Salazar's regime had stretched that to an incredible display. At first, only the leftists and some liberals understood that the Portuguese government relied on colonial rule and the powerful interests intertwined into the system to perpetuate its dictatorial power. Only gradually did part of the population start to understand the situation, mainly with young people avoiding the draft and running away to other European countries, and thus joining the 2 million emigrants (mainly to France and West Germany) that the government allowed openly and clandestinely to leave, as the money they sent home would balance the financial situation. Even more gradually, to some extent, the colonial wars started to radicalize the armed forces themselves, who were also afraid of being saddled with a stalemate in Africa, or with full disaster.

The process started by the military revolution of April 1974 is more or less well known and included, as I have said, the decolonization. So, it is perhaps an irony of history that the militaristic expansion launched in 1415 came to an end under the direction of a government which was created and more or less run by the military themselves.

What has been the impact of Africa (and the expansion) on Portugal? It shaped for more than five centuries Portuguese history and the destinies of the Portuguese people subordinated to colonial interests. No other country in modern times had undergone quite the same effect. From Brazil to Macao in China, the Portuguese created very similar or parallel local cultures and adapted their own buildings to pioneer forms that are recognizable in all those zones as they did in Africa. Nevertheless, the impact of African usages and other cultural elements on Portugal was very small, contrary to what happened in Brazil. The slaves brought from Africa (never in any numbers comparable to the millions sent to Brazil) disappeared into the lower strata of the population. The Black people that one encounters in Portugal are newcomers from the former colonies, while in Brazil, where slavery on a larger scale lasted longer, they are the descendants of the slaves.

As a person who, from a very young age forty years ago, always opposed the dictatorial regime and colonialism, I am entitled to add something at this point. With all the evils of colonial exploitation, it must be stressed that Portugal in its dealings with the colonies, never practiced what can be described as "apartheid." The approach was authoritarian and paternalistic, and racism was always based on economic discrimination. The rare mulattoes or Blacks who, due to special protection or parentage or acquired riches, achieved a higher social status, were considered (even if not entirely) as "Whites" and not discriminated against either in Portugal or in Africa. It was perhaps a more insidious approach than more open ones, based on the idea that, by definition, the Blacks left to themselves were childlike and had to be put to work. All this is very swiftly becoming a thing of the past. It is entirely possible that the Portuguese language, as the only means of political unity, might be retained in the African ex-colonies. There, many Whites have adhered (and since the colonial wars) to the idea of independence. But whether multiracial societies with Whites as a minority are going to be developed remains to be seen.

22

Conclusion: The Legacy of French Colonial Rule and Double Impact

Twenty-five years after the French colonies in West and Equatorial Africa gained their independence, the legacy of French colonial rule discussed in this volume is still very much alive. In contrast to former British colonies, where fewer traces of colonial rule survive, or in former Portuguese colonies, where revolutionary governments hold sway, francophone Black Africa presents a picture of continuity with the last several decades of colonial rule. "The more things change, the more they stay the same" is an old French saying that is particularly apt and accurate in regard to French-speaking Africa.

It is true that leaders and intellectuals of most ex-French colonies have received merciless criticism from other Africans for their continued interest and participation in things French, even though they might deny it publicly and assume an anti-colonial stance in speeches and appearances. The evidence strongly suggests that francophone African elites have remained mesmerized by French culture and that in most instances the realities of the colonial world that were supposed to change in the magical year of independence, A.D. 1960, have in fact remained remarkably unchanged.

For example, in the mid-1980s, we find Léopold Senghor being named to the prestigious Académie Française in recognition of his talents and publications in his adopted tongue. We find Sembene Ousmane still ranked as one of the premier movie makers of the Third World and still an important novelist and social critic. We find Amadou Moktar M'Bow, former cabinet minister of Senghor, serving with notoriety as director-general of UNESCO in Paris, not fearing to take on Ronald Reagan's American government in a political controversy. We find Houphouët-Boigny at his mini-Versailles palace at Yammousoukrou still preaching "*enrichissez-vous*" to his planter and business bourgeoisie. And if one examined the politics of the two decades following independence, one would find continuity in names like Ahidjo and Touré that disappear only by 1983-1984.

These arguments suggest the utility of studying French colonial rule during the first six decades of the twentieth century as a guide to understanding the remaining decades. By looking more closely at the nine major themes of colonial life studied in this volume, we see how these indicators have remained constant or how they have changed during the twenty-five post-colonial years. There is no doubt that formal French colonial alliance and interest in overseas areas ended with the demise of *Algérie Française* in 1962, but a revamped version of *la mission civilisatrice* soon appeared. The reluctance of the French public to come to grips with the demise of the empire in the 1950s was in part related to the lack of prestige of the Fourth Republic which sought to bolster sagging fortunes by hanging on to empire. But de Gaulle gave the Fifth Republic enough self-confidence that the ultimate release of the Black African colonies in 1960 occurred quietly while most eyes were on Algeria. Ironically, during the decade of the 1960s, the new French cultural/business ventures (*mission culture-commerce*) developed especially in the new countries of Ivory Coast, Senegal, Gabon, and to a lesser extent in most ex-colonies (except left-leaning places such as Guinea, Mali, and Congo-Brazzaville). This continuing interest was buttressed by military aid and troops stationed in Senegal, Gabon, Chad, and elsewhere. The days when Georges Pompidou was in power helped to guarantee that a coup would never take place in most francophone African countries; ironically, the socialist government of François Mitterand did not abandon that policy and in fact continued to enforce it.

A main argument of this volume has been that French colonial rule developed a unique relationship between colonial ruler and the ruled. The case studies testing this hypothesis were conducted for the most part in the twentieth century during the high point of colonial rule. But if the preceding observations about the continuity of France's presence are true, then a critical review of the nine factors of double impact could be useful for understanding the continuing realities of France in Africa. We will now take a closer look at these factors for the post-1960 period.

In the sphere of economic life, France undoubtedly retreated in one basic area, that of retailing. Already the demise of retail sales by Frenchmen, often called *petits colons*, was signaled after the end of World War I. It became quite apparent that France, having lost most of its young men, was going to have difficulty in recruiting qualified men to serve as colonial officers or to staff commercial operations overseas. Albert Sarraut, perhaps France's most creative minister of colonies, worked on development plans for France's African dominions during the 1920s, but the demise of the French economy by the late 1920s and the lack of personnel and leadership caused France's colonial plans of grandeur to be shelved during the depression years. To fill this commercial gap came the Syrians and Lebanese, who had begun to emigrate to French African countries in greater numbers during World War I, since their homeland was occupied and they had no obligations for military service. By the 1930s, for example, as French railways in Senegal ran into economic difficulty, Lebanese traders taking advantage of a growing highway system concentrated in trucking and transport. Increasingly retail and small wholesalers were Lebanese.

This pattern was once again reinforced by developments during World War II. After that struggle, during the late 1940s and 1950s, there was a brief resurgence of French small businessmen during the halcyon days of French investment. The net result, however, was that by independence in 1960, most *petits colons* assessed their chances of survival as not particularly bright during the new regimes, and most of them left French Black Africa. Specialty shops, such as coiffeurs, patisseries, or boutiques, in larger areas such as Dakar and Abidjan continued to flourish during the next several decades after independence. However, as the post-colonial period advanced, it was not unusual to find Lebanese taking over French pastry shops or even French restaurants.

On the other hand, wholesale importing and trading remained largely the preserve of the French and Franco-European trading firms, such as SCOA, Peyrissac, CFAO, Maurel et Prom, and others. In fact, new firms were created to help develop Ivory Coast, where a state regulation required Ivorian participation. This created new companies for African elites to help manage and also helped spread the risk for the French, who were still anxious to invest in Black Africa but who sought protective guarantees. The dominance of French trading houses has been challenged in some areas by large Lebanese firms, English or other European firms, and now by the Japanese in automobiles. The emergence of large African-backed firms, such as Air Afrique, caused Air France to cancel many of its routes in Black Africa. Moreover, the growth of African entrepreneurs, often bankrolled by Islamic or Arab sources, has created a new dimension in economic life, since during colonial rule Africans were restricted to serving as employees in French firms or as independent traders.

The impact of French economic power therefore remains a continuing presence in Africa, despite the change in focus, with major emphasis being put upon wholesale trading and industrial development. The nature of French and African economic contact has been modified in France, however, where large numbers of Black Africans form part of an urban and floating proletariat of workers at the bottom of the French labor force. During colonial rule there was, dating from the nineteenth century, a small maritime population of Africans in France; this was augmented by veterans from World War I who chose to remain in France after demobilization and who settled in Paris and the maritime ports such as Le Havre and Marseilles. Many of them became dockers and street sweepers.

After World War II, the number of Africans living in France increased greatly due to a flood of older students; some of these Africans after finishing their studies stayed on to work in France, while others dropped out and sought employment wherever available. Their situation was made more difficult, however, by the growing number of other workers who appeared in France, especially after the advent of the Fifth Republic and the growth of the French economy under de Gaulle and his successors. Spaniards, Italians, and especially Algerians poured into France seeking work, and the Black Africans often found themselves displaced. Many of these workers sent remittances to their families in West Africa and became an important source of financial support for African populations.

These post-war developments, during the final stages of decolonization and in the post-independence period, modified French contacts and images with Africans. Perhaps the high point of Franco-African relations in the metropole occurred during and immediately after World War I, when the famous *Armée Noire* paraded down the Champs-Elysée and on the Champs de Mars before High Commissioner Blaise Diagne; this helped trigger an era of understanding typified by the success of Black singer and dancer Josephine Baker, the toast of Paris. This residue of goodwill lasted during the 1930s and among many French during the war, when the idea of possibly losing the African colonies was painfully contemplated. But by the post-war years, contacts were limited mainly to economic ones. Increasingly the world of Black Africans in France has become sharply circumscribed, and the larger French public is less aware of African problems than during the days of colonial rule.

Another basic sector examined in this volume was the military, and here we find a continuing French presence in Africa despite more than two decades of independence. Military treaties with France link many African nations, and this allows countries such as Senegal to keep French military forces stationed in time of peace on Senegalese soil. The best known symbol of French military might at the beck and call of African sovereigns was probably the relationship between Georges Pompidou and Léopold Senghor; the pleasantry went around that all Léopold had to do in case of an attempted coup was to ring up the Elysée and the paratroopers would be at his palace within minutes. As graduates of the same *lycée* in Paris, these two heads of state had much in common both in the political and cultural sphere. Such military backing may explain why certain heads of state within French Africa had a long tenure when their neighbors were suffering coups and countercoups annually.

The post-war period became terribly important for the formation of the African military, since many of the new African states drew their military commanders and leadership from the ranks of soldiers who had served in the French army. Since there was little glory connected with World War II (except serving in the resistance) and few Africans actually served in the early years of the French army before surrender in June 1940, most Africans' experience dated from wars in Indochina and Algeria. These were the conflicts which gave experience to such future leaders as General Gnassingbe Eyadema, president of Togo. His experience as a non-commissioned officer in the French army was typical of the training which made possible creation of military cadres in the new nations emerging from colonial rule in 1960. Eyadema, like Mobutu in Zaire, utilized his military experience to launch a political career which took him to the summit of power.

Many African military leaders studied in France in specialized institutes or training sessions; others participated in on-the-job instruction with French military cadres assigned to Black Africa. In this way, the French military presence, a reality in Black Africa since the days of Faidherbe in the mid-nineteenth century, was prolonged at little cost to the leaders of the Fifth Republic. In addition, French arms manufacturers continued to have a near monopoly in furnishing the young nations, although their most lucrative clients were such breakaway ex-British enclaves as Biafra during the Nigerian war.

An end of an era came in the 1970s when General Adolphe Diagne retired from the French army in France. Diagne was the eldest son of former deputy Blaise Diagne who had opted for French citizenship early in his career and had risen to be the highest-ranking Black in the French military establishment. Such careers were dramatic proof to those who continued to believe in France's assimilating mission. But Diagne's retirement symbolized the passing of a half century of Black African involvement with the French military in France itself. Senegal deputy Galandou Diouf firmly believed in 1939 that the new war would bring about a replay of what happened in 1914-1918 and that he would become the czar of Black troops during the conflict, following in the footsteps of Blaise Diagne. The armistice of June 1940 scuttled these dreams of military glory. (Diouf had been an aide to Diagne during the infamous recruiting mission of 1917-1918).

In the political arena studied in this volume, we find that France has managed through treaty, persuasion, and bullying to maintain a continuing political presence in Black Africa. On the surface, to be sure, with formal independence granted all colonies of West and Equatorial Africa by the early 1960s, France was able (under de Gaulle's direction) to prevent guerrilla and revolutionary warfare that characterized the struggle for independence of French dominions in Indochina and Algeria. Taking his cue from the British, who gave freedom to Sudan in 1956 and Ghana in 1957, de Gaulle miscalculated only in the case of Guinea, where Sekou Touré preferred to go it alone rather than to remain politically aligned in the new French *Communauté*, de Gaulle's creative answer to the British Commonwealth of Nations. The *Communauté* soon proved to be illusory as a valid political organization, and French political strategists then realized that by keeping in power the African elites they had formed and cultivated, they could guarantee continuity.

The political legacies of France are very real, despite the fact there are no further liaisons between African and French political parties as existed from the 1930s until 1960. But the training and indoctrination received by two generations of elites made a difference in the way politics was practiced, and a real predictability in African political affairs for the first decade after independence can be traced to a certain philosophical continuity. Renegades such as Congo-Brazzaville, Guinea, and Mali were nevertheless dependent upon French-inspired political and social ideas, and at an operational level, upon strategies learned from French parties and theorists. Surprising to many observers was the lack of interest in Marxist and French Communist party politics as a potential model for the new nations; those who leaned to the Left tended to develop their own models drawn from eclectic sources. Hence Sekou Touré prided himself on being his own man even in the realm of theory. Yet in the final analysis, the major impression that struck (and continues to strike) non-French observers of francophone Africa is the sense of fraternity and community that still links most of the ex-colonies. No more powerful image can be imagined to illustrate this reality than the photos taken of de Gaulle's funeral, where most of the francophone African political leaders were seated linked together in mourning in the front pews of the church.

The reality of reciprocal impact today in the political sphere is not felt by the average French person, who would be at a loss to identify the multiple Black African leaders. But this impact is a reality for the Quai d'Orsay, which has given foreign policy in former *Afrique Noire* a primacy shared by few other areas of the world. One can of course argue this was simply a shift from the Rue Oudinot (Ministry of Colonies) to the Foreign Ministry, but it is more than that—independence brought the realization that France could continue to exercise influence over its Black African possessions in a way no longer possible in Indochina or in North Africa. This gamble, taken by de Gaulle, paid off handsomely in most instances, since the French colonies south of the Sahara were spared the phase of guerrilla warfare that permanently undermined relations with Indochina and North Africa.

The implementation of French overseas action in the post-colonial period is often carried out by the *cooperant*, or agent of the cooperative accords between France and Black African countries for technical and governmental assistance. The *cooperant* provides a continuing governmental presence for the French in a way unique to Black Africa. To be sure, Israel, South Korea, Japan, Poland, the United States (AID and Peace Corps) and other countries have provided technical assistance through specialized missions or projects, but the *cooperation* accords signed between France and most of its ex-colonies have provided a continuity interpreted by some critics as the very heart of neo-colonialism. Few *cooperants*, however, stay on in *Afrique Noire* and cannot be compared to the French small business and commercial workers of the colonial era. Critics admit that many of these agents offer valuable services, especially in the technical sphere, which developing countries could never pay for on their own; on the other hand, the criticism is leveled that the *cooperants* breed a continued dependence upon things French, whether in supplies, parts, or techniques. Breaking this condition of independence would, according to the argument, go a long way in helping establish real independence.

One of the main reasons for de Gaulle's (or France's) success in managing to retain lasting influence in Black Africa has nothing to do with the French themselves, but can be attributed to the African elites. In this volume we have examined both the Senegalese elites and the William Ponty elites in order to see how France never really abandoned the doctrine of assimilation, even though, from a formal point of view, association was proclaimed as the operational policy by the turn of the century for an empire then judged to be too vast and too heterogeneous to become assimilated. Even though Blaise Diagne tried unsuccessfully in the 1910s and the 1920s to get the French Parliament to extend the possibility of French citizenship to Black Africans outside of the four communes of Senegal (which seemed like a patent rejection of assimilation to outside observers), the reality of continuing to nurture a highly educated and motivated African urban elite continued unabated. The French preoccupation with developing an elite of Black Frenchmen is often cited as the most characteristic aspect of French colonial policy. France could not claim total originality, however, since Britain nurtured elites in Lagos and Cape Coast, and Portugal based its policy on assimilation.

Perhaps the distinguishing characteristic of the French Black African elites was their belief in a partnership, in participation in governance of the empire. This is what made François Carpot, Blaise Diagne, and Galandou Diouf (all labeled collaborators by later critics) run—they were men whose faith in French institutions was born of being flattered with deference and power. When Galandou Diouf first went to Paris in 1934 after the death of Diagne, his youngest wife (he was Muslim and had multiple wives) became the toast of Paris for her elegance and style. Diouf's archrival, Lamine Guèye, who succeeded him as Senegal's deputy after World War II, was also a firm believer in the mission of empire, and only too late did he realize that his views on assimilation had not evolved as far as his younger colleague, Léopold Senghor. But it is significant that Guèye was overshadowed not by a new political militant advocating independence, but one who simply argued for more participation of peasants and other non-urban people in the process. This concern for participation was at the heart of the French assimilation policy, and the possibility of participation as equals to the French was always the glittering brass ring which many Africans sought to claim.

Even hard-headed businessmen such as Félix Houphouët-Boigny, who had attempted to gain prestige by becoming an African doctor, suggest that the desire for assimilation was not limited to intellectuals such as Guèye and Senghor or prestige seekers such as Diouf and Diagne. Houphouët-Boigny was a clear-headed realist who in 1959 single-handedly wrecked the notion of French West Africa staying together as an entity. He was absolutely correct from an economic point of view, because he could see the wealth of his own country and ways it could be manipulated to bring one of France's most backward and non-unified colonies into the ranks of the first-rate economic powers in the new Africa. By not allying himself with other states such as Niger and Upper Volta, which had little long-term potential, Houphouët-Boigny kept the potential for wealth at home and helped develop an economic elite that the French had never been able to produce during the years of colonial rule. Even though one can argue that the Ivorian elite was home grown, the very fact that no language except French is capable of unifying the Ivory Coast suggests the continuing nature of a group that could be accurately called a neo-colonial elite.

One senses a continuing presence of African elites in France, especially in the diplomatic world of Paris. Drawing an assignment as ambassador to Paris puts one at the pinnacle of diplomatic prestige; the fourteen ambassadors from former French West and Equatorial Africa and Togo and Cameroon form an elite of Third World diplomats in Paris. They are buttressed by the multiple Black African civil servants at UNESCO's headquarters in Paris, presided over by A. Moktar M'Bow, and resident intellectuals involved in publishing activities at *Présence Africaine* or *Jeune Afrique*. Such an elite community long ago found a secure niche for itself, after Jean Paul Sartre and other Fourth Republic intellectuals came to the defense of *Présence Africaine* and supported African writers at a time when the majority of French intellectuals was still supporting the idea of empire and France's civilizing and assimilating mission. As Paul Clay Sorum explains it,

Believing that the overseas peoples shared their idealization of France and its culture, they [the intellectuals] expected that these peoples would want to remain associated in some way with France. The ethnocentrism on which French colonization has been based continued, in spite of diverse attacks on it, to pervade the thinking of most intellectuals throughout the period of decolonization. It was the intellectuals, after all, whose self-esteem was most closely bound up with the idea that France's culture and language had a universal appeal.[1]

A continuing irony of this situation, which the author suggests typified the 1945-1960 period for French intellectuals, is that it continues to exist for African elites and intellectuals. The prestige of French education has made it obligatory for an African in order to be first rate to seek the coveted *doctorat d'état*. Seeking such a grueling degree makes little sense for most Third World leaders, but to the francophone African elite, it confirms a cachet of intellectual achievement that can be obtained in no other manner.

Looking at cultural factors such as architecture and art gives a somewhat different picture for the post-independence period: the advent of an international style in the 1950s, inspired by Le Corbusier and his disciples, brought to urban French Africa a nondescript style cut off from African roots. As the post-independence period advanced, functional urbanization dictated projects which had maximum show value. Hence the early centerpiece of Abidjan, the Hotel Ivoire, looked as though it could easily pass for a Hilton hotel in Hawaii. The unique character of French-built but African-inspired markets which typified colonial Dakar and Bamako disappeared. The legacy of African-inspired buildings, or French colonial structures which gave charm to old Saint-Louis or Gorée, ceased to exist as the new Abidjan—or even the new Lomé—began to rise in the 1970s and 1980s.

Whether art as a factor in the colonial world, and by extension in the post-colonial world, can be assessed is difficult to say. It is certain that African carvings and castings continue to have great currency, although one suspects now that most art winds up in the hands of tourists and fewer objects in the hands of serious collectors. In some ways, African art has become big business, with new centers of activity in New York and Los Angeles, not just Paris and Geneva as in yesteryear. One has the impression, however, that many collectors are collecting for the sake of building collections, and the older collector, who often was a colonial officer or commercial agent, has all but disappeared from the scene. Such persons were often knowledgeable about African art, society, and mores. Another dimension which has changed is the emphasis upon painting and European type of sculpture work now carried out by many European-trained artists. Painting (at least in European terms) was not a traditional African art form; but since independence, an increasing number of young Africans have studied abroad and have staked out careers in painting and other non-traditional art forms. Whether this group has made an impact in the French art market in the metropole is debatable, but the growing presence of well-trained and ambitious Africans, whether from Senegal, Cameroon, or Ivory Coast, may be of capital importance for the future of cultural expression in both France and Africa.

Literature has continued to grow in French—in fact, the greatest decade for publication of African writers was the 1960s, just after decolonization and during the flush of independence. Novelists particularly attempted to assess the colonial experience and the problems of new nationhood; French publishers continued to publish works by older writers such as Birago Diop, while putting works by newer writers such as Camara Laye and Bernard Dadié before the public. Cameroonian, Ivorian, and Senegalese writers dominated the scene; one note of change was the fact that many Africans were now published in Africa rather than in France as publishing houses grew up in Africa. At a popular level, *Bingo* magazine was found everywhere, and *Afrique Nouvelle*, affiliated with the Catholic church, crossed borders of the new countries to remain an influential and sane voice in a world of nationalistic reporting. The Daniel Sorano Theatre in Dakar has been the scene of African plays by African playwrights, a change from colonial days when Molière was often adapted for the African stage. Television now consumes the production of some writers, and a recent special on the life and times of Shaka on Togolese television demonstrates how African writers can reach a more popular audience. One can argue that the basic flaw of the older literature of social protest that characterized the 1950s and 1960s, such as *Ambiguous Adventure* of Cheikh Hamidou Kane, is that it was written for European publishers and a European audience.

Some countries, such as Senegal, are trying to cope with the legacy and primacy of French for literature by developing an African indigenous language, in this instance Wolof, as a national language of instruction and expression. But since Wolof was only effectively written down in the twentieth century, trying to build up a corpus of materials will take years. As a spoken language, Wolof and other similar lingua francas in African regions have made a comeback thanks largely to radio, since it is efficient and often politically wise to broadcast in several local languages. Mass media, such as radio and television, may offer greater opportunities to African writers than the traditional world of books, since one has the impression that most African-authored books, even in Africa, are bought by Europeans in the local bookstore.

The problem of racism continues to plague both French and African society, although in both cases there is probably a better hope for a mature understanding today than in the past. In the case of the French, despite the legacy of racism that William Cohen has discussed in this volume and elsewhere, there is today the problem of xenophobia born out of the existence of a great number of foreigners residing in France. Whether one is Spanish, Italian, Algerian, or African, one is still an *étranger* and really out of the mainstream of opportunity. Since the French have now demographically sunk to a non-replacement level in terms of births, the future would seem to include the continuance of foreigners. On the other hand, as with Polish and Italians in mines and industries at an earlier time, some of these new workers may eventually be absorbed into French life.

The image of Africa remains visible in France today, although it tends to be formed by the businessman, *cooperant*, or tourist. In fact, French interest in the tropics as a vacation land has increased, whether in Ivory Coast, Mali, or Casamance in Senegal. The success of Club Med and its imitators and the arrival of a host of chain hotels has equipped larger francophone African capitals with facilities for tourists, businessmen, and diplomats that have helped to create a mini-world of international life in even restrained capitals such as Lomé.

As for racism in African society, it continues to exist in many different forms. Still feeling the pressure of the larger society are the *métis* communities; many nations keep it difficult for people of mixed origins to participate successfully in politics. There is no question that racism exists for people of Lebanese origin, but since many Africans resent and are jealous of the solid economic successes of this minority people, it is remarkable that such a group receives as much tolerance as it does in most francophone African states. This is a subject about which much is thought but little discussed openly.

Education, intimately linked with political policy and the continued growth of African elites, continues to follow the lead of France in Africa. The language question—what to use if we don't employ French?—is a vexing dilemma that few African countries have solved. Even in countries where there is a large Muslim majority, such as the ex-British colony of the Sudan, the preferred language of instruction is English, despite the knowledge of Arabic. Such is the case in West and Equatorial Africa, and it will undoubtedly remain this way for decades to come. While intellectuals like Pathé Diagne in Senegal can argue persuasively for the use of Wolof, the gap between what is desired and what can be done is immense. The primacy of French will keep French educational forms and methods viable in *Afrique Noire* for generations; the educational politics of France, making available external examiners, resource personnel, short-term lecturers, visiting professors, and other resources means that the path out of the francophone orbit of instruction for most African countries is years away, if ever. Furthermore, one may query: what is a viable alternative? This is the exasperated reply of officials who are asked why their school and college systems pattern the French so closely.

While more Africans are studying for higher degrees in Africa now, and the universities of Dakar, Abidjan, and Yaoundé are all first-rate institutions with increasing numbers of well-trained research faculty members, the fact remains that the upper crust of the intellegentsia still seeks certification abroad. A small number of students have found alternatives in American, British, German, or Italian universities or training programs. For the masses who are in state-run schools, the books are still in French, and although primary and middle school instruction has been modernized to give African examples in textbooks, the subject matter in advanced schools still reflects the European curriculum. The prospect as of twenty-five years after independence is to remain a part of the francophone educational and intellectual community—a reality that does not really bother most African pedagogues, since most of them are still convinced of the primacy and validity of French culture. Perhaps in certain technical areas, in scientific studies, or in business management foreign degrees and training programs are seen as desirable. And one must remember that for areas such as public administration, important in developing cadres in new countries, the tendency to follow French models and forms will continue to exist as long as the legal codes and statutes are based upon French law.

It would be beyond the scope of this brief concluding section to examine in detail the fortunes of British and Portuguese African countries during the decades since 1960; the struggle for independence in Mozambique, Guinea Bissau, and Angola is well known. So too are the developments in places like Nigeria, rent by a civil war after the Biafran secession, the ups and downs of post-Nkrumah Ghana, and the vicissitudes, high ideals, and difficulty of achievement in Tanzania. One theme is clear, however, in the post-colonial experiences of both of these groups of former colonies: they have not remained (with few exceptions) close to the former colonial power. To be sure, English continues to be spoken in many colonies, but Swahili has made significant inroads in East Africa. British commerce and industry play only a limited role in the total economy of a new industrial power such as Nigeria with its oil resources. Among intellectuals there remain a respect and attachment to Britain, but not to the same degree to which one finds similar sentiments in francophone Africa. The ex-British colonies have opened their doors wide to a variety of other English-speaking nations and display a cosmopolitanism in foreign and commercial affairs rarely seen in *Afrique Noire*.

Moreover, little political continuity has characterized many of the former British colonies. There are no comparable leaders with the longevity of Senghor, Touré, Houphouët-Boigny, or Ahidjo; moreover, the military has come to play a preponderant role in many places, from Ghana to Uganda to Zambia. It is only fair to comment that colonial conditions, especially in the White settler colonies, were much more complicated than in francophone Africa, and that the resulting search for stability has been perhaps more difficult than in West or

Equatorial Africa. Having said this, a notable exception for the French areas would be the case of Chad, which by the mid-1980s seems destined to become a pawn between the Libyans and the French, largely because of its strategic value.

The reciprocal influences that characterized French colonial occupation of West and Equatorial Africa have continued in many of the sectors examined in this volume during the post-independence period. In fact, one could argue that 1960 was not really much of a turning point in the history of *Afrique Noire* and that a meaningful turning point, clearly pointing to a different direction for the ex-colonies, has not yet arrived. Perhaps the demise of Senghor, Touré, and Ahidjo, and the imminent decline of the aging but vigorous Houphouët-Boigny, will usher in a new era. This could be a plausible argument but for the fact, as we have just examined, that the areas of analysis covered here suggest a continuity with the colonial regime today rather than a break with it. Nothing short of war, cataclysmic occurrences, or a change of government in France willing to turn its back on Africa will probably provide such a turning point. Until that day arrives, it would be fair to conclude that the era of "Double Impact," characteristic of the colonial period, continues into the 1980s and may well characterize Franco-African relations for years to come.

NOTE

1. Paul Clay Sorum, *Intellectuals and Decolonization in France* (Chapel Hill, N.C., 1977), p. 241.

Selected Bibliography

Ageron, Charles-Robert. *Histoire de l'Algérie contemporaine* (Paris, 1980).
———. *L'Anticolonialisme en France, de 1871 a 1914* (Paris, 1973).
Ageron, Robert. "L'Algérie Algérienne sous Napoléon III," *Preuves* (February 1961): 3-13.
Balesi, Charles J. *From Adversaries to Comrades-in-Arms: West Africans and the French Military, 1885-1918* (Waltham, Mass.: Brandeis University, 1979).
Barr, Alfred H., Jr. *Matisse, His Art and His Public* (New York, 1955).
———. *Picasso, Fifty Years of His Art* (New York, 1949).
Betts, Raymond. *Assimilation and Association in French Colonial Theory* (New York, 1961).
———. *Europe Overseas: Phases of Imperialism* (New York, 1968).
———. *The False Dawn: Imperialism in the Nineteenth Century* (Minneapolis, 1975).
Boesiger, Willy, ed. *Le Corbusier, 1910-65* (Zurich, 1955).
Bouche, Denise. *L'Enseignement dans les Territoires Français de l'Afrique Occidentale de 1817 à 1920* (Paris, 1975).
Brunschwig, Henri. *French Colonialism, 1871-1914: Myths and Realities*, tr. William G. Brown (New York, 1966).
———. *L'avènement de l'Afrique Noire, du XIXe siècle a nos jours* (Paris, 1963).
———. *Mythes et réalités de l'impérialisme colonial français, 1871-1914* (Paris, 1960).
———. *Noirs et blancs dans l'Afrique Noire Française* (Paris, 1983).
Cendrars, Blaise. *Anthologie Nègre* (Paris, 1921).
Cohen, William B. *The French Encounter with Africans: White Response to Blacks, 1530-1880* (Bloomington & London, 1980).
———. *Rulers of Empire: The French Colonial Service in Africa* (Stanford, Calif., 1971).
Coquery-Vidrovitch, Catherine. *L'Afrique noire de 1800 á nos jours* (Paris, 1974).
——— and Alain Forest, eds., *Actes du colloque entreprises et entrepreneurs en Afrique* (Paris, 1983).

Crowder, Michael. *Colonial West Africa: Collected Essays* (London, 1978).

Crowder, Michael, and J. F. Ade Ajayi, eds., *A History of West Africa* (New York, 1972).

————. *Senegal: A Study of French Assimilation Policy*, rev. ed. (London, 1967).

————. *West African Resistance* (New York, 1971).

————. *West Africa under Colonial Rule* (Evanston, 1968).

Cruise O'Brien, Donal. *Saints and Politicians* (New York, 1975).

Delafosse, Maurice. *The Negroes of Africa, History and Culture*, trans. F. Fligelman (Washington, D.C., 1931).

Delavignette, Robert. *Freedom and Authority in French West Africa* (New York: Oxford University Press, 1950).

————. *Les Paysans noirs* (Paris, 1946).

————. *Robert Delavignette on the French Empire: Selected Writings*, ed. William B. Cohen (Chicago, 1977).

————. *Service africain* (Paris, 1946).

Deschamps, Hubert. *La Fin des empires coloniaux* (Paris, 1976).

————. *Les Institutions politiques de l'Afrique Noire* (Paris, 1976).

————. *Rois de la brousse* (Paris, 1975).

————. *The French Union* (Paris, 1956).

Diagne, Pathe. *Grammaire de wolof moderne* (Paris, 1971).

———— *Pour l'unité ouest-africaine: micro-etats et intégration économique* (Paris, 1972).

Diop, Birago. *Les Nouveaux contes d'Amadou Koumba* (Paris, 1958).

Diop, Cheikh Anta. *L'Unité culturelle de l'Afrique Noire* (Paris, 1959).

————. *Nations négres et culture* (Paris, 1979).

Domechini-Ramiaramanana, Bakoly. *L'ombre de Madagascar dans l'oeuvre de Jean Paulhan* (Paris, in press).

Dubois, Félix. *Timbuktoo the Mysterious*, trans. Diana White (London, 1897).

Duignan, Peter, and L. H. Gann. *African Proconsuls: European Governors in Africa* (New York, 1978).

————. *Colonialism in Africa, 1870-1960*, vol. 1, *The History and Politics of Colonialism, 1870-1914* (Cambridge, England, 1969).

Emerit, Marcel. *Les Saint-Simoniens en Algérie* (Paris, 1941).

Foltz, William. *From French West Africa to the Mali Federation* (New Haven, 1965).

Gann, L. H., and Peter Duignan. *Burden of Empire* (New York, 1967).

Gardinier, David E. *Cameroon: United Nations' Challenge to French Policy* (London, 1963).

————. *Historical Dictionary of Gabon* (Metuchen, New Jersey, 1981).

Gifford, Prosser, and William Roger Louis, eds. *The Transfer of Power in Africa: Decolonization, 1940-1960* (New Haven, 1982).

Gifford, Prosser, and Timothy Weiskel. "African Education in a Colonial France: French and British Styles" in Prosser Gifford, and Roger Louis, eds., *France and Britain in Africa: Imperial Rivalry and Colonial Rule* (New Haven, Conn., 1971).

Goldwater, Robert. *Primitivism in Modern Art*, 2d ed. (New York, 1967).

Griffeth, Robert, and Carol G. Thomas, eds. *The City State in Five Cultures* (Santa Barbara, 1981).

Hailey, Lord. *An African Survey* (London, 1938).

Hargreaves, John D. *France and West Africa* (London, 1969).

————. *Prelude to the Partition of West Africa* (New York, 1963).

————. *The End of Colonial Rule in West Africa* (London, 1979).

————. *West Africa: The Former French States* (Englewood Cliffs, New Jersey, 1967).

Hopkins, A. G. *Africa's Age of Improvement* (Birmingham, England, 1980).

————. *An Economic History of West Africa* (New York, 1973).

Hountondji, Paulin. "Charabia et Mauvaise Conscience: Psychologie du Langage chez les Intellectuels Colonisés," *Présence Africaine*, n.s. 61 (First Trimester 1967): 11-31.

Hymans, Jacques-Louis. *Léopold Sédar Senghor: An Intellectual Biography* (Edinburgh, 1971).

Johnson, G. Wesley. "Centenaire de Blaise Diagne," special issue of *Notes Africaines* (Dakar, IFAN, no. 135, 1972).

————. *The Emergence of Black Politics in Senegal* (Stanford, Calif., 1974).

————. "The Senegalese Urban Elite, 1900-1945" in Philip Curtin, ed., *Africa and the West: Intellectual Responses to European Culture* (Madison, Wisc., 1972).

Kanya-Forstner, A. S. *The Conquest of the Western Sudan* (London, 1969).

Kesteloot, Lilian. *Black Writers in French: A Literary History of Negritude* (Philadelphia, 1974).

Klein, Martin A. *Islam and Imperialism in Senegal* (Stanford, 1968).

Laude, Jean. "La Négrophile et la Critique de L'Exotisme," *La Peinture Française et l'Art Nègre* (Paris, 1968).

Laye, Camara. *The African Child*, trans. James Kirkup (London, 1959).

————. *The Guardian of the World*, trans. James Kirkup (New York, 1984).

Lévy-Bruhl, Lucien. *L'Ame Primitive* (Paris, 1927).

Lord Hailey. *An African Survey* (London, 1938).

Lyautey, Hubert. *Paroles d'Action* (Paris, 1927).

Mage, M. E. *Voyage dans le Soudan occidental* (Paris, 1868).

Mangin, Charles. *La Force Noire* (Paris, 1910).

Mayer, Emile. *Tres Maréchaux: Joffre, Galliéni, Foch* (Paris, 1928).

Michel, Marc. *L'Appel à l'Afrique: Contributions et réactions à l'effort de guerre en A.O.F., 1914-1919* (Paris, 1982).

————. *La Mission Marchand, 1895-1899* (Paris, 1972).

Milcent, Ernest, and Monique Sordet. *Léopold Sédar Senghor et la Naissance de l'Afrique Moderne* (Paris, 1979).

Morand, Paul. *Magic Noire* (Paris, 1928).

Moumouni, Abdou. *L'Education en Afrique* (Paris, 1967).

Mumford, W. Bryant, and G. St. J. Orde-Brown. *Africans Learn to Be French* (London: Evans Brothers, Ltd., 1936).

Obichere, Boniface. *West African States and European Expansion* (New Haven, 1971).

Paillard, Jean. *La Fin des français en Afrique Noire* (Paris, 1935).

Paulhan, Jean. *Jean Paulhan et Madagascar, 1908-1910*, Cahiers Jean Paulhan, 2 (Paris, 1982).

Pélissier, Paul. *Les Paysans du Sénégal* (Saint Yrieix, France 1966).

Sartre, Jean Paul. *Black Orpheus*, trans. S. W. Allen (Paris, n.d.).

Sarraut, Albert. *La Mise en Valeur des Colonies Françaises* (Paris, 1923).

Sembène, Ousmane. *Le Docker noir* (Paris, 1973).

————. *Les Bouts de bois de Dieu* (Paris, 1960).

Senghor, Léopold Sédar, "Dialogue sur la poésie francophone," in *Elégies majeures, suivi de . . .* (Paris, 1979).

Skinner, Elliott P. *African Urban Life: The Transformation of Ouagadougou* (Princeton, 1974).

———. *The Mossi of Upper Volta* (Stanford, 1964).

Sorum, Paul Clay. *Intellectuals and Decolonization in France* (Chapel Hill, N.C., 1977).

Surêt-Canale, Jean. *Afrique Noire, l'Ere Coloniale, 1900-1945* (Paris, 1964).

Sy, Cheikh Tidiane. *La Confrèrie sénégalaise des Mourides* (Paris, 1969).

Tharaud, Jerome, and Jean Tharaud. *The Long Walk of Samba Diouf*, trans. Willis Steell (New York, 1924).

Thiam, Iba Der. *Maba Diakhou Bâ: Almany du Rip (Senegal)* (Paris, 1977).

Wallerstein, Immanuel. *Africa: The Politics of Independence* (New York, 1971).

———. *The Road to Independence: Ghana and the Ivory Coast* (The Hague, 1964).

Waters, Harold A. *Black Theatre in French: A Guide* (Sherbrooke, Quebec, 1978).

Weinstein, Brian. *Eboué* (New York, 1972).

Willis, John Ralph. *Studies in West African Islamic History* (London, 1979).

Yansané, A. Y. *Decolonization and Dependency: Problems of Development of African Societies* (Westport, Conn., 1980).

———. *Decolonization in West African States* (Cambridge, Mass., 1984).

Zolberg, Aristide. *Creating Political Order* (Chicago, 1966).

———. *One-Party Government in the Ivory Coast* (Princeton, 1969).

Index

Abidjan, 26, 204
Adrien-Marie, 213
Africans, 314, 310, 381-82
Agriculture, 22, 23, 111, 327
Ahidjo, Ahmadou, education of, 335
Airplanes in war, 74
Alaurent, Jean, 195
Algeria: agriculture, 327; architecture of, 193, 216; army civic relationship, 64, 79; army officers, 70, 74; army tactics, 53, 54, 71, 94; army troops, 62, 93; colonialism, 54, 324-29, 328; leaders of, 58, 303, 319-20; revolts in, 59, 147, 149; settlement of Europeans in, 54
Algiers, 64, 204
Ali, Muhammad, 322
André, General, 67
Angola, 374
Angoulvant, Gabriel, 11 n.5
Anthropology, racist beginnings, 307-11, 309, 313. See also Racism
Antonetti, Raphaël, 160
Apollinaire, Guillaume, 239, 247, 256
Archinard, Louis, 102 n.4, 213
Architecture, 189-235; in Algeria, 193; architects, 195; beginning of urban planning, 193; building materials, 194-95, 198; climate considerations, 202; colonial goals, 220, 226; colonialism, 204; Dakar, 191-94, 203-5;

Djenné Mosque and Great Mosque at Mopti, 226-27; Egyptian origins, 214, 216, 220; exoticism in, 210; at expositions, 199, 215-26; Indochina, 193; literary influences, 210-14; Madagascar, 193; Morocco, 192-93; Romantic influence, 209-10; styles, Byzantine, 198; styles, International Style, 200; styles, Ionic, 198; styles, native, 197; styles, Neo-Classicism, 226; styles, Neo-Moorish, 192, 197; styles, Neo-Sudanese, 198-200, 209, 213, 220, 224, 226, 228; styles, Nigerian, 198; styles, *style AOF*, 205; Sudanese house, 217; tourism, 227; West African colonial urban planning, 191-205
Army of Africa, 51-104; Blacks as part of, 51, 84, 93, 99-100, 101, 104 n.32, 159, 162, 165, 181-82, 303, 312; civilian-military relations, 79-80, 94; in Crimean War, 62, 68, 81; education, 53-54, 60, 65, 66; effects on European warfare, 68, 70, 81-82, 84, 85, 90 n.68, 94-95, 98, 99, 382-83; leadership, officers, 51, 60-64, 69, 74, 83, 94, 98; tactics in Africa, 54-59, 67, 71, 95, 96-98, 103 nn.12, 16, 104 n.26; tactics in France, 70-77; uniforms, 77-79; weaponry, 96
ARP (Friends of the Popular Front):

About the Contributors

CHARLES BALESI is a native of France who has taught in Chicago for many years. His Ph.D. dissertation examined the nature of African participation in the French army during World War I. He has also been associated with the Newberry Library.

LELAND BARROWS took his Ph.D. at UCLA where he wrote the definitive work on General Louis Faidherbe for his doctoral thesis. Barrows held the prestigious Mellon Fellowship at Harvard for several years, has taught history in Algeria, lived in both France and Black Africa, and is currently on assignment for the Department of State in Eastern Europe.

RAYMOND F. BETTS serves as professor of history at the University of Kentucky. He took his Ph.D. at Columbia University and soon became a distinguished specialist on French imperial history, especially in regard to Black Africa. He has carried out research projects in France, North Africa, and former French West Africa.

EDMUND BURKE III is a professor at the University of California, Santa Cruz, where he specializes in the history of francophone North Africa.

WILLIAM B. COHEN studied at Stanford University for the Ph.D. and carried out original research in France and Senegal. He is currently professor of history and chair of the history department at Indiana University, Bloomington, where he teaches modern French history.

ROBERT O. COLLINS is professor of history at the University of California, Santa Barbara, where he served for many years as Dean of the

Graduate Division. Collins is a specialist on the Sudan who was trained at Yale and Oxford; he has logged many miles on research and consulting projects in Sub-Saharan Africa.

CHARLES H. CUTTER is a professor of political science at San Diego State University. He took his Ph.D. at UCLA and conducted several research trips in West Africa, especially in Mali. He later held a post-doctoral fellowship at Yale.

JORGE DE SENA was until his recent death one of the world's great authorities on Portuguese literature and civilization. A professor of Portuguese at University of California, Santa Barbara, de Sena was well known in intellectual circles for his opposition to the Salazar regime in Portugal.

HASSAN EL NOUTY serves as professor of French and North African literature at UCLA where he has taught for a number of years. He is one of the most distinguished specialists in this subject in the United States.

DAVID E. GARDINIER is professor of African History at Marquette University in Milwaukee. Gardinier has become the leading authority on education in former francophone Africa and has written many essays on history and education in Black Africa.

ROBERT GRIFFETH served for many years as a professor of African History at both UCLA and the University of Washington. Griffeth was one of the last students of Melville Herskovits at Northwestern University.

G. WESLEY JOHNSON took his Ph.D. at Columbia University and has served on the faculty of both Stanford and the University of California, Santa Barbara, as an African historian. He was visiting professor at UCLA and later chaired the colloquium on francophone Africa that led to this volume.

MARIAN ASHBY JOHNSON carried out original fieldwork for her Stanford Ph.D. dissertation in history and art history in Senegal and other parts of French-speaking Africa. She is director of the oral history program at the University of California, Santa Barbara.

GERARD LE COAT now teaches in Switzerland but formerly was a faculty member in Seattle and in Montreal. His specialty is modern art and he has investigated the impact of African art on European painters for the past few years.

PAUL E. PHEFFER took his Ph.D. at the University of Pennsylvania and later carried out original fieldwork in Senegal on the history of the railroads during the colonial period. He also did original research in colonial archives in Paris.

GERARD GEORGES PIGEON is a professor of literature and Black Studies at the University of California, Santa Barbara. Pigeon spent much of his youth in Dakar, Senegal, where he made the acquaintance of many of the writers mentioned in his chapter.

LABELLE PRUSSIN is a professor of art and architecture at the University of Washington in Seattle. Prussin has spent many years trekking over West Africa to become perhaps the nation's leading expert on African traditional architecture.

PEGGY SABATIER taught for many years at the University of California, Davis. She did original fieldwork in Senegal and other parts of francophone Africa for her dissertation on the graduates of the William Ponty School.

JANET VAILLIANT has worked for many years at Harvard, especially on projects concerning the Soviet Union. She visited France and Africa a few years ago to satisfy her curiosity about Leopold Senghor and his dual career as politician and intellectual.

AGUIBOU YAN YANSANE has taught for many years at the University of California, Berkeley. He comes from Guinea but was also educated at the French lycee in Dakar, Senegal, where he knew Gerard Pigeon. He is one of our best known specialists on economic and educational matters of former French West Africa.